LAST POST

Frederic Raphael was born in Chicago in 1931 and educated at Charterhouse and St John's College, Cambridge. His novels include *The Glittering Prizes* (1976), *A Double Life* (1993), *Coast to Coast* (1998) and *Fame and Fortune* (2007); he has also written short stories and biographies of Somerset Maugham and Byron. Frederic Raphael is a leading screenwriter, whose work includes the Academy Award-winning *Darling* (1965), *Two for the Road* (1967), *Far from the Madding Crowd* (1967), and the screenplay for Stanley Kubrick's last film, *Eyes Wide Shut* (1999). The first volume of *Personal Terms* was published by Carcanet in 2001, with subsequent volumes in 2004, 2006, 2008, 2011 and 2013.

Last Post

FREDERIC RAPHAEL

CARCANET LIVES AND LETTERS

First published in Great Britain in 2023 by
Carcanet
Alliance House, 30 Cross Street
Manchester, M2 7AQ
www.carcanet.co.uk

A CIP catalogue record for this book is
available from the British Library.

ISBN 978 1 80017 303 3

Book design by Andrew Latimer, Carcanet
Typesetting by LiteBook Prepress Services
Printed in Great Britain by SRP Ltd, Exeter, Devon

The publisher acknowledges financial
assistance from Arts Council England.

FOR BEETLE, ALWAYS.

CONTENTS

LAST POST

TO LESLIE BRICUSSE.

Dear Leslie,

You, more than any other man, changed my life. I spent my first year at Cambridge honouring my father's dated advice to wait for the world to beat a path to my door. I waited in vanity and in vain. During the long vac of 1951, my first, Beetle and I lived blissful weeks in hilltop Ramatuelle, up the coast from St Tropez. In the mornings, I typed chunks of my first novel. In the afternoons we had long, deserted Pampelonne Beach to ourselves. The Yanks had landed there seven years earlier. We ate *Thé Brun* biscuits, shared a banana for tea. Soon before we were due to return to England, it was clear that I should never finish the novel. Noël Coward had written *Hay Fever* in three days. I set out to emulate the Master. The eighty pages of *With This Ring* chattered off my Olivetti before we took our sorry way north to the tight little island.

Beetle and I had met at the Drama Group at the Liberal Jewish synagogue, where neither of us worshipped. Our friend Jackie Weiss arranged a reading of my play. It went so well that the Group voted to put it on. We rented a little theatre in Westbourne Grove for two or three nights. A quintet of my canvases, relics of Ramatuelle, dressed the sofa-and-two-armchairs set. Not to my great surprise, except when looking back, the little theatre was full each night. It didn't occur to me that the play might be reviewed, but it was, in *The Stage*, generously. The only chiding comment was that I, the producer, had at one point walked backwards on stage.

Theatricals at St John's, known (if only to themselves) as 'the Gaiety', had their camp at one end of a long table in Hall. At the first dinner of the new term, after I had read grace, a scholar's privilege so irresistibly showy as to excuse my collusive '*Per Christum Jesum dominum nostrum*', I joined Tony Becher at the far from gay end. The Gaiety swelled down the table towards us. They had seen *The Stage*. A dark horse was welcomed into their stable. A few days later, Peter Firth, President of the Young Writers' Group whose mag had published a couple of my poems, came to my rooms. The Amateur Dramatic Club was sponsoring a play competition. He had heard that I had had a play put on in London and hoped I would participate. I explained that *With This Ring* was of small sophistication. He conceded that it was not likely to win, but it would give the judges something to sit on, so to say, and they duly sat on it. The winner was Hugh Thomas's chichi fantasy about a still independent pre-war Venetian republic being wooed by Musso the Wop (as he was called in the wartime *Dandy*, unless it was *Beano*) and other caricatured suitors. Mark Boxer designed the Mondrian-style sets. Did Peter Hall direct? Some Peter or other.

I auditioned for the part of the American ambassador. My retrieved Chicago-born accent provoked no few laughs from the feet-up centurions in the stalls. An hour or two later, I met Toby Robertson, the tallest of them, outside my narrow digs in Park Street. I had been much the best of the Yanks, he told me. The selectors had gone for the experienced Tony Church, who was as American as lumpy porridge. Toby hoped I'd come to the first night. I did not. Some thirty years later, I found him a job in a radio play of mine. I can do forgive, rarely forget.

My from-day-one Johnian friend Tony Becher had joined the Footlights. I had funked the audition. I couldn't sing for toffee nuts, as they used to say. Nor could Tony, but he had a facility for witty lyrics: 'In a Graham Greenery / where God paints the scenery...' There would also be a much applauded one about Lord Montagu 'mount a few' of Beaulieu. Today it would be indictable. You recruited Tony to collaborate on

Ogden Nash-like squibs that appeared in *The Daily Sketch*. Your father was 'in distribution' for the Kemsley press. He despatched vans that delivered the papers.

At the beginning of the following year, Tony brought you to the rooms in the Wedding Cake I was sharing with a first-class soon-to-be-schoolmaster classicist. Dull as virtue, Brian Moore wore a tie-clip and disciplined his orderly hair with a triad of tortoise-shell implements. You, in double-vented, non-Harris-tweed sports jacket, camel-hair waistcoat with gold buttons, bow tie, specs more businesslike than scholarly, looked all set for something beyond Cambridge. I was never to see you dishevelled. Already secretary of the Footlights, you intended to start a musical comedy club. You had asked Firth, now President of the Footlights, who had written the best dialogue in the play competition won by Hugh Thomas's little Venetian blinder. Peter fingered me. Would I care to write the 'book' for the show you meant to put on in a few terms' time? Set on being a serious novelist, I never had the least wish to write musical comedies. I agreed at once.

Your charm had nothing to do with class or scholarship. Having spent a large part of the war in Hamilton, Ontario, you had the unrationed ambition of the new-worldly. You could even drive. You were one kind of mid-Atlantic; I quite another. You signed yourself 'Lezzers'; I was never anybody's Fredders. When I confessed that I had funked the audition for the Footlights, you said to consider myself a member forthwith. The straight theatrical A.D.C. had no attraction for you; no more did *Granta*, the smarties' mag where Mark Boxer ('Marc' when signing his minimalist cartoons), Karl Miller and Nick Tomalin determined who was in and who was out. Only in Karl's absence did Mark print a wishful story of mine about free living and loving in Chelsea. Later, I emulated Whistler's fine art of making enemies by writing a column in *Varsity* under the editorship of that shameless son-of-a-rich man Michael Winner. Bob Gottlieb, early on-the-maker and later editor of *The New Yorker*, never forgave my mocking him and a wife he later dumped by citing Joe Bain's canard that the reason they were rarely seen together was that they shared one pair of specs.

Rich and famous never occurred to me; published would do. You had no peripheral targets; success was your bull. Your surname announced you a rarity, of Belgian origin, was it? You were reading French, but the loudest volumes in your rooms in the modern Caius block, across Trinity Street, advertised your principal tutors to be Noël Coward, Cole Porter, George and Ira Gershwin. Your desk sported a framed photograph of you as a Sam Browned second-lieutenant. I cannot remember you speaking French, not even when you and I and Beetle and Tony Becher spent the following Easter vac in St Germain-des-Prés. Oh, Jonathan Miller told me years later of meeting you in the street and you said '*Tiens*'. Hard to believe, but it was reported with disdain, hence probably true. So what? We talk differently to different people, something even the best novelists rarely honour in their dialogue.

You already had songs – 'Someone, somewhere, some day' etc. – you wanted to fit into our show, no notion of a plot. You proposed that we seek oracular intelligence from Hugh Thomas. His rooms in Queen's were across the wooden bridge on Silver Street. Assembled with geometrical ingenuity, its original elements had been composed by joinery alone. Dismantled for repairs, no one could put it together again without screws. Hugh received us with curly-haired hauteur. On the early steps of a pedestal far from showbiz, he condescended to be solicited. In his lop-sided voice, he affected to improvise a plot set in Transylvania where 'youth leaders and fairies' would sing and dance in charming counterpoint.

We deferred simultaneous blurts of incredulity until back on the clever bridge. In time, having been president of the Union,

Hugh would veer left of centre and stand for parliament under Hugh Gaitskell's patronage, in an unwinnable seat. He then swung right. He wrote one novel, *The World's Game*, good title, light-fingered from a thirteenth-century Pope, before making a timely academic speciality of Cuba and becoming professorial. He married the lady daughter of an earl and was later made a peer, thanks to Mrs Thatcher. Upwards leads in all sorts of directions.

I have small memory of how *Lady at the Wheel* evolved. Its plot, about a female driver in the Monte Carlo rally, its Riviera setting, your lyrics ('Pete, y'know, / Is kinda sweet, y' know') and Robin Beaumont's and your music and my playing-for-laughs dialogue made small appeal to chic tastes. Noël Coward furnished a strip of common ground and up came *Lady at the Wheel*, at one time entitled *Zany Miss Dando*. Long live second thoughts! The sole acknowledgement that there had been a war was a comic German, played by Colin Cantlie, son of an admiral, with a feather in his Tyrolean hat. I spent much more time than a scholar should 'tickling up the book', as you put it.

You persuaded a freckled Canadian brunette called Jane Carling to bring her singing voice across the Atlantic. Pretty girls accumulated at your call, blonde and breasty Julie Hamilton in particular, daughter of screenwriter Jill Craigie ('Craggy Jill' in Bricusse-speak) and step-daughter of Michael Foot. Few A.D.C. theatricals warmed to our invitation. I enrolled its president, Gordon Gould, a Chicagoan graduate of mahogany appearance, with some funny lines and a routine he rendered hilarious in the morning-after silence that opened the second act at breakfast. The male lead was played by Dai Jenkins; his pretty, short-legged fiancée was called Norma. 'See Norma and Dai' was Tony Becher's meta-Neapolitan coinage. Dai was amused to tell us how Hermione Gingold had said, in some intimate revue, 'You can't have your kike and eat him too'. He had no idea Hermione was Jewish.

Several of *them* were sitting right in front of him, he told us. I rehearsed him with unremitting politeness.

After programmes had been printed and delivered, I saw that below the discreet directorial credits a louder one, in 14-point type, declared 'The Entire Show devised and produced by Leslie Bricusse'. When I accused you of pulling a fast one, you said 'Bloody printers!' I can't recall you using swear words on any other occasion; fuck, never. In truth, you were entitled to whatever self-advertisement you cared to append. Devise and produce were indeed what you did.

On the first night, you and I huddled at the top of the circle steps of the Arts Theatre. Waves of laughter and applause soon broke over us. A palpable hit! Nothing like a live audience. You were to have that kind of exhilaration many times. The *Granta* clique spurned our vulgarity. Nick Tomalin wrote an exposé of our venal willingness to insert a plug for drinking chocolate, requested at a café by our comic Hun. I don't know what contribution Cadbury's made to our budget, a few spoonsful probably. Few could deny that you had indeed devised and produced a hit of a kind Cambridge had never seen before. Biding my time, I delivered a *Varsity* counter-punch to Nick T., after he had invited Oswald Mosley to speak at the Union. He was nettled enough to threaten legal action. Goose and gander rarely suffer the same sauce.

Thanks to some numbers I wrote and performed in Footlights 'smokers', in the big room above the Dorothy Café, I was included in the cast for the May Week Revue of 1953. Peter Firth was an indulgent president. Would the ragbag compendium ever come together? It did, just. I remember only playing Michael Foot in a skit of mine on a weekly TV chat show. I was amazed, if not a little embarrassed when my line, delivered in Foot's best proletarian bark, 'We in the Labour Party will do everything in our power to get everything in our power' was greeted with a baying howl of laughter and sustained applause. The England of 1953 had turned blue, but I assumed that everyone under thirty remained red. Did you ever express any political opinions?

One evening, after the curtain had fallen, there was a commotion at the stage door. Word came back that someone, allegedly Hispanic, had burst in waving a knife. You went out and charmed or disarmed the intruder with well-trained subaltern cool. At the end of our two-week run, the outgoing committee distributed offices for the following year. You were, as no one ever said in those days of unadulterated English, a shoo-in for president; Peter Stephens for secretary; Dermot Hoare for some other sashed office. You promised that I was to be the Press Officer.

As you came out of the meeting, there was a raw flush on your usually calm features. Peter and Dermot had vetoed having a Jew on the Committee. I have had no experience of the horror, the horror; but the pettiness, the pettiness is not uncommon in England's not invariably pleasant land. Beetle never encountered it. How often are good-looking, long-legged females taken to be Jews? Early in the following year, P. Stephens and D. Hoare were eased off the committee. I was en-sashed as Press Officer. Thanks to your diplomacy, neither deposed dignitary appeared resentful. They were always friendly to me. Like T.S. Eliot, they had their principles.

I spent too many afternoons in your rooms, by now in Caius's first court, and picked up a lot of P-P-Penguins, your favourite chocolate biscuits. You had one of the first tape recorders. You and I and Tony Becher improvised skits on it for the 1954 Revue. At philosophy supervisions with Renford Bambrough, Tony and I donned a seriousness you would have found of no interest. What nice rhyme could you furnish for Wittgenstein? You determined to purge *Out of the Blue* of the baggy amateurishness of Peter Firth's show. I kept my Evelyn Waugh and Graham Greene number under my sole authorship: 'We were nearly subjected to rape / by the man from Jonathan Cape', etc. but Becher supplied the clincher: 'The Greene to end all Greenes / And the Waugh to end all Waughs'.

Later in the year, when it came to casting, you asked me to break the news to Tony that although invaluable as a writer... I protested, a little. He was my first friend in Cambridge. You had me believe that that was why I was the best person, etc. Tony was less distressed by the axe than I feared. He told me, and I was glad to believe him, that it was more important for him to get a good degree. He did: he was one of two Moral Scientists to get a First in Part Two; Andor Gomme (so named *intra familiam* as a sexually indeterminate embryo) the other. Served me right, Becher had done the long dull work. Our friendship survived. We later wrote scripts for Hermione Gingold's radio show.

Tony and I did not fall apart until many years down the track. Having left his wife, he promised her that she and their daughters would have the house in Weech Road, Finchley, and then claimed half. Beetle and I took Anne's side. I never much liked her. Tony remarried. After having two children, his new wife left him for another woman. She came back to care for him when he was diagnosed with Parkinson's Disease. I asked if I might visit him. He did not want anyone to see him in his last days. I remember him, young, in Putney High Street, on Boxing Night, imitating Charles Laughton's lurching hunchback of Notre Dame. A policeman, not in his eye line, watched tolerantly, until Tony bumped backwards against him, took a look and straightened up. Pure cinema: no dialogue; hold, hold; and cut!

Out Of the Blue was a palpable hit. Thanks to your manoeuvres, we were all set to transfer via Oxford to a fortnight in London's West End. We were even going to be paid, £15 a week. A few numbers were failing to get laughs in Cambridge, and you replaced them with prize pieces from previous years. You invited me to audition as band-leader in yesteryear's *Joe and the Boys*. The other contender and likely winner was Brian Marber. His slick monologue in *Out of the Blue*, a pale green anglepoise lamp his versatile prop, had proved him an agile performer.

The audition was held in the morning gloom of the Cambridge Arts Theatre. Landed with first innings, I came in from the wings in a bent-kneed rush, baton in hand, and found a Joe Loss accent in which to say 'Good evening, ladies and gentlemen, we'd like to do a little number written by one of the boys in the band... *Who's Got the Key, Got the Key to the Cupboard...* with a one and a two and a one, two, three...' That spontaneous loopiness has never come back for an encore. Brian conceded the match. All of us proved to be little more than also starring with Jonathan Miller, who did the box office a favour by becoming the Tatlered talk of London. Danny Kaye rated him the English Danny Kaye. Jonathan didn't do candy kisses. He went on to direct many operas, *un peu partout*. Was he ever heard to sing a note?

One evening late in the (extended) run at the Phoenix Theatre you beckoned me into your dressing room. In the armchair, wide snap-brimmed fedora on his head, was grey-mackintoshed Jock Jacobson, representative of M.C.A., the most powerful talent agency on both sides of the Atlantic. One-time session saxophonist, he had come to see Jonathan; your jokes and Bob Hope-style delivery proved more to his taste. You went along with his idea of promoting you as a stand-up comedian, but told him that what you really wanted was to write shows. You declared me indispensable. Jock shrugged and signed us both. It took him a month or three to get my name straight. M.C.A. had fancy offices on Piccadilly. Jock's had two white telephones on the desk. Your idea of success was three of the same, your London/Paris/New York address book next to them.

I had been awarded the Harper Wood travel studentship, a fat £350, in the gift of my college. It would last me a full peripatetic six months. Combining patience with better things to do, you wished me well and looked forward to our resumed partnership. In October, I set off for France, Spain, Morocco, then Italy, back to Paris, and Beetle. On my solitary way, I began my first novel, *Obbligato*, on a glossy block of unlined white paper. Jock 'There is such a thing as timing, fellas' Jacobson was caricatured as Franco Franks, the agents' agent.

You were taken up by Binkie Beaumont, autocrat of West End theatre, to fill Bea Lillie's breathing spaces in her one-woman show. Since you incorporated some of the material on which we had worked together, I was to receive six pounds ten a week for its use at the Globe Theatre. Abroad was a long way away in those days. Although I cribbed one or two dated numbers racked in alien streets, I did not buy an English newspaper until I reached Naples. How did I react to Ken Tynan's rave for Bea and scorn for you? He had asked us to a big party while we were a hit, but critics take pride in turned coats. 'Ruthlessly cut, Bricusse might 'scape whipping' and a paragraph more of George Kauffmanesque auditioning for *The New Yorker* job (which Ken later got) dumped you in the nettles.

Your capacity for taking it on the chin, with something like a smile, was never better proved than by your going on, rarely to a friendly reception, night after night. That Bea loved you was not an unalloyed comfort. Her large ex-U.S. marine minder, John Phillips, did not suffer displacement gladly. You took the rough smoothly. You met everyone in Bea's circle, Noël and who all else, and were assimilated into their cosmopolitan galaxy. Invited by Binkie to come and stay at his country place, known in the Biz as 'Pinching Bums', you took Julie Hamilton with you as a prophylactic.

Beetle and I came back, briefly, to London to get married. We still had enough of the Rev. Harper Wood's legacy to spend three months in two rooms in the freezing eleventh *arrondissement* while I finished my novel. By the time we returned to London, you had been hired to write a movie, *Charlie Moon*, for Max Bygraves, Jock Jacobson's star client. You cut me in for a small slice in return for beefing up the dialogue. The movie was to be directed by Guy Hamilton, later rich and famous as the director of four James Bond movies, including the first, *Doctor No*. He belonged to the reticent generation that had been to the war. Awarded a D.S.C., he never mentioned it. I remember only that he described some time-lapse idea of ours – an ashtray that, on a cut, became full of butts – as being 'page one in the book'.

Obbligato was accepted by Macmillan; advance £100. You went on tour with Bea. It gave me time to get on with *The Earlsdon Way*. One day I noticed that the regular six pounds ten was no longer being credited to me. Someone in Binkie's office told me that it had been payable only as long as *An Evening with Beatrice Lillie* was in London. I daresay my short measure was nothing to do with you. The cheapish lesson was always to read the small print. I rarely do.

For some time-shredded reason, you and I and Bea went out to Borehamwood studios where you had an appointment. You once said to me that you were better at meetings than I was. 'People like me; they don't always like you'. It was delivered without malice, like a weather report. Bea and I waited in the taxi. She turned to me quite suddenly and said, 'Do you believe in the afterlife?' I knew that she had lost her husband, Sir Robert Peel, and their only son in the war. I said, 'Oh Bea, I wish I could say I did, but honestly… I don't know'. She gave me a long look; then she said, 'Does Hannen Swaffer know?' Who he? A *News Chronicle* journalist who believed in Another World.

Who now remembers Bea herself? I shall never forget her sitting in a louche hotel and reciting 'I've come here to be insulted / And I'm not going home until I am'. Her pet idea was of a number in which the curtain rises on a majestic curved staircase down which she descends in evening dress, long gloves, mink cape, gleaming tiara. She crosses to the superbly draped window, looks out and then says, 'Still pissing down'. Another story about Bea, which I was promised (by you, was it?) was true, tells of her being in the hairdresser's while on tour in Chicago. A local Spam – tinned meat – millionaire's wife protested, loudly, at being kept waiting by the attention given to 'that actress'. Bea said 'tell the butcher's wife that Lady Peel is in no sort of hurry'.

The next thing was that you and I were asked to take over the direction of a show already on the road. *Jubilee Girl* was no more Rodgers and Hart than it sounded. If Al Kaplan had not been a millionaire, or as good as one, having married a Sieff, the piece might never have been staged. He and his amateur co-author were both doctors. Al drove me down to Plymouth (you were already there) in his sumptuous two-seated Rolls Bentley convertible, its dinky gear-change neat as a clitoris. Halfway across Salisbury plain, Al invited me to take the wheel. When I confessed that I had only just passed the driving test, he shrugged. The more expensive the car, he told me, the easier it was to drive. 'Only promise you'll never buy one of those tinny Lagondas.' I promised. The Roller was of a vintage without power brakes. Al urged me to put my foot down and overtake whatever loitered in our way. He liked close calls.

Pretty soon I saw a lorry in the middle distance coming towards us in our lane as it overtook an uncooperative colleague. I pressed one foot on the brake, then both; with small effect. Horn blaring, the oncoming lorry switched, just, into its proper lane. I glanced at Al. He was enjoying my sweat.

He and the doctor with whom he had collaborated were lovers but it escaped me at the time. Years later, he demanded to be made producer of a movie I had written of Iris Murdoch's *A Severed Head*. If I didn't agree, he would get someone to come and kill me. He was living in Italy and was said to prescribe drugs, plentifully, to the *dolce vita* set. Not long afterwards, he killed himself.

Jubilee Girl was as dated as it sounded. I was delegated to rehearse (and re-write) the chat, while you did whatever you did to the musical numbers. The girl in the piece was Lizbeth Webb. Her happiest prize, from having been in Vivien Ellis and A.P. Herbert's West End hit *Bless the Bride*, was 'me mink, me mink'. She had a lovely soprano voice and professional patience. John Cranko, short-lived fancy director of the hit revue *Cranks*, did Al the rented favour of coming to Southsea to cast an eye on what we were doing. His verdict was that we had replaced bad direction with – no, not worse – *equally bad*. Among the cast of *Cranks* was Tony Newley, who became your partner in a couple of hit shows in the Sixties. Al Kaplan watched me directing and found no loud fault. Marie Lohr, the oldest trouper, always on time, was my straight-backed supporter. Al did ask me, 'What's Leslie doing?'

We all stood on the wide green Southsea foreshore as Khruschev and Bulganin sailed out of Southampton on their way back to the USSR. Marie had been a star of the Edwardian theatre. She had stood in the same place when the Grand Fleet sailed out, in full intimidating battle order, at the outbreak of war in 1914. I asked her whether we should wave. She said we should, politely. *Jubilee Girl* foundered some time after you and I had been eased over the side.

To my surprise, if not alarm, *Lady at the Wheel* came round again. Lucienne Hill, translator of Anouilh, and her lover Andrew Broughton (aka Broughtipoo) were your partners in the resurrection. Madame undertook to revise the dialogue for West End purposes. You asked me to sign over the rights. I was damned if I did. You admitted, with small grace for once, that I had you 'over a barrel'. All the same (a tool in every fixer's kit), I was busy writing my novel, wasn't I? And you knew I hated rewrites. I settled for a half-credit. The refurbished show went on, at the Lyric, Hammersmith. Big Lulu, as you called her, with pectoral justice, had done 'the book' no marked remedial good. Beetle and I walked out halfway through. More than twenty years later, as I came out of the magistrates' court where I had been fined for nine seconds of speeding, one of the clerks came after me. He had never forgotten seeing *Lady at the Wheel* at Cambridge. He had read everything I had written since.

Thanks to you and Jock, we were offered a contract by the Rank Organisation of £115 a month, each (no small sum in 1955). You were driving a fire-engine red, four-square antique Austin. Do you remember overtaking a Jaguar, just, on the way to Pinewood Studios? The run we enjoyed in the fast lane of the Biz was steered entirely by you. The red Austin was soon replaced by a new white Ford Consul convertible. After I had recovered from a prolonged attack of glandular fever, you invited Beetle and me to spend a few days in your mother's house in Shirley, a suburb of Birmingham. I think your father must have died while I was away. You never mentioned him to me again.

It was generous and guileless of you to ask us to the little suburban house, in no fashionable quarter. Your aproned mother was a copious plain cook, forever singing pop songs as she did her chores. Her ascendant call of 'Lez... leee' summoned us to table. You treated your mother (I never knew her name) with affection, obedience even. She stood for everything you were determined to disown. During that cold week in Shirley, you taught me to drive. Your new, toothpaste-white Ford leaped and lurched as I sought to master changing gear.

You neither winced nor grew impatient. You were as generous as you were single-minded. We were going places, you promised, and you wanted me on board. I kept trying to believe they were places I wanted to go.

Without our Pinewood stipend, I should never have been able to buy Beetle's and my first car, a second-hand green Ford Anglia, personally offered to us as a bargain for £250 by Trevor (now Sir Trevor) Chinn of Lex Garages. It served us very well, even when we had to back up steep hills in Andalucia. When we part-exchanged it for our next lucky number, we were told that PLD 75 had been composed of two halves of wrecked Anglias welded together.

Never anything but generous, sometime during that year you offered us your newly acquired flat in Brighton (Brig/ton in Bricusse speak) for the weekend. It was clean and impersonal. You did have some books and folders on the shelves. Trust a novelist to be a snooper. One of the folders contained a sheaf of pages. The top one carried the legend 'The Minor Scholar, a novel by Leslie Bricusse'. The rest of the pages were virgin.

When I had finished *The Earlsdon Way*, on Pinewood's pretty penny, Alan Maclean of Macmillan's was eager to see the new book. In the hope of prompt applause, I was persuaded to hand over my sole copy (carbons kill the muse). He promised to keep it locked in his briefcase. During one lunchtime, some thief sneaked into the unguarded Macmillan offices and out again with said briefcase. My manuscript must have been the last thing he hoped to find when he jiggled the lock. Beetle broke the news when I got back from a few rubbers in the Crockford's two-shilling room. I could think of nothing better to do than get into PLD 75 and drive and drive. We got as far as Bath before Beetle suggested that the best and only thing was to rewrite the book. She bet I could remember a good deal of it, and so I did.

When you heard what had happened, you brought me the two or three Everyman volumes of Carlyle's title is The French Revolution: A history. I am still slightly surprised that you chose so pertinent a comforter. Macmillan offered £50 by way of compensation. I rewrote *The Earlsdon Way* pretty well word for word. Macmillan then turned it down. My Sinclair Lewisgunning of suburbia was not of a piece with the playfulness they had all admired in *Obbligato*. Alan Maclean told me that I should make no friends by being acid. I told him I had not become a novelist to make friends.

'Suez', as that Gallipolitan misadventure came very soon to be abbreviated, the quicker to get it over, was the great caesura in post-war England's self-esteem. The puncture of Britannia's vanity precipitated an explosion in the price of petrol all the way up to two shillings and sixpence a gallon. You acquired a ninety-to-the-gallon two-seater, front-opening bubble car. Its vroom-poppa-poppa promised your approach to Rutland Street where Beetle, soon pregnant, and I had been able to move to above-ground accommodation in a tight terrace house. Vivian Cox, a Pinewood producer, had hired you and me, soon after our old contracts lapsed, to write a film about Cambridge. He was a double blue (hockey and rugger) *bon vivant* and a very tactful supervisor.

On the day *Bachelor of Hearts* was greenlit, Vivian had us to dinner in his attic rooms in Curzon Street and opened a bottle of 1945 claret. He told the story of the Frenchman and the Englishman who shared a dugout in the Great War. They treasured a cobwebbed bottle of Château Pétrus against the day of victory. At a minute past eleven on the eleventh of November 1918, the Englishman hurried to insert his corkscrew. '*Mais non, mon cher ami, pas encore. Une telle bouteille mérite que tout d'abord on en discute.*' When the studio cast Hardy Krüger in the lead, as a German student in alien surroundings, we did ze necessary rewrites with professional promptness. In manuscript afternoons, I was writing *The Limits of Love*, about Jews in the war and after.

When M.C.A. was legally obliged by some new anti-trust legislation to cease representing clients, we said goodbye to Jock Jacobson. You found us a new, go-getting agent, suave and bearded Leslie Linder, at John Redway and Associates with flash first-floor offices in Leicester Square. You had shed Julie Hamilton and taken up with the pneumatic Yvonne ('Bonbon') Romaine. Was she related to the *patron* of the Mayfair Club in Berkeley Square, where you often played host to a round table of on-the-makers? Always drinking sparkling hock avoided fancy-pantsing with reds and whites on the wine list. Behind your back, I called it sparkling *ad hoc*. In not much later days you collected vintage wine labels and trophied them in a scrapbook.

One afternoon in 1958, as we were crossing the King's Road, north to south, you asked me to 'stand beside you' at your imminent wedding at St James's Spanish Place. It implied a promise of best-friendship. I said it was an honour I could not accept. I could not take part in a Christian ceremony. I had not hesitated to read the shielded grace in St John's College hall; now cowardice and tact sported the same gabardine.

Beetle and I came to the wedding and gave you whatever nice present we could afford. You had given us a Toledan-style paper knife. I thought it a curious, if not ill-omened choice. Beetle told me, years later, that you said you would send us a proper present when we came back to England. She said not to, and you took her at her word. Your reception was held in the John Redway and Associates' office. Was your mother there? George Baker, a middling Rank regular in English films, was. You had seen him in the street and asked him up. He had no idea what was being celebrated.

There must have been speeches. I can't remember who made them. Leslie Linder took the occasion to ask me, quietly, why I had agreed to be your writing partner. My soggy answer was that you did the choosing and I did not know how to break free. During the war, Leslie was a captain in the paratroop regiment. He advised me to pull the rip cord. 'Leslie will be fine.' Of course you were. Your songs were soon being performed all over the place; money was never to be your problem. *Goldfinger* clinched your renown. Did it win you one of those two Oscars for Best Song? I never called to congratulate you, did I? My bad, as they said for quite a while. *Doctor Doolittle* did a lot for you, despite sexy Rexy's condescension when it came to the lyrics. Harrison has been heard talking to the animals by one generation after another. Was he really a royal by-blow or was that another song he sang? I once saw him buy *The Sunday Times* at Rome's Termini station. Famous people on their own are like taxis with their FOR HIRE lights turned off.

Soon after your wedding, we went to live cheaply, and industriously, in southern Spain. You had, I am pretty sure, already found your ideal writing partner in Tony Newley. Perhaps John Cranko introduced you. I met Tony with you, by chance, in Vivian Cox's *garçonnière* in the summer of 1960. As you were leaving, Newley shook me by the hand and said, 'Good luck in whatever you chose to do in life'. When Vivian and I were alone again, I made some casual remark about 'queers'. I had had no idea, until his face changed, that Vivian was gay. Hadn't he boasted of driving his white Aston-Martin through France with sexy-voiced Joan Greenwood? I hope I never made that kind of remark again.

A year later, Beetle and I went to Paris and happened to see Michelangelo Antonioni's *L'Avventura*, twice; the first time a random choice from *La Semaine de Paris*, the second, after a hurried supper, as addicts. I returned to the movies with an enthusiasm I had never felt before. During the next forty years, I alternated fiction and other books with writing films and television of a kind that no collaboration between us could ever have produced.

You became successful and rich enough to fall for a war hero turned financial fixer, not to say finaigler, called – the name recurs oddly in your bio – Hamilton. Income tax in your fatso bracket was running at more than eighty-five percent. When the gallant (D.S.O., D.S.C.) commander installed himself in the Channel Islands and promised to secrete your surplus, you jumped at it. For legal formality's sake, the paperwork granted him fifty-one percent of the take, but you had his word, as an officer and a gentleman, that he would cheese off a mere ten. After your royalties had accumulated, you decided to buy a place in St Paul de Vence and asked him to transfer the necessary funds. There was an endless delay. You deputised Richard Gregson and the pair of you went to Jersey to confront the heroic swindler. He took you to lunch at a good restaurant and was as nice as could be.

Yes, he said, when the time came for cards on the table, you were friends, but between absentee friendship and four hundred grand... What could you do? Nothing legal. For once you lost your cool. Did you truly, as the story goes, hire a hit-man to go and take care of the stranded submariner? The rubberised rubber-out is said to have landed from an inflatable and scaled the cliff below the commander's address. He eased his way inside, but stopped when he saw that the startled owner had an unmistakable face nothing like his target's. It belonged to 'hullo, good evening' Tom Wicker, a nasal TV regular of the day and many, many nights. The gallant commander had taken you (and your money) seriously enough to decamp. You were wise enough not to pursue him. There was indeed plenty more, and more, where that came from. Living better and better was the wisest revenge.

I don't remember seeing or speaking to you again until April 1966 when the phone rang in our house in north Essex and woke us up at seven in the morning to break the news that I had won the Oscar for writing *Darling*. Evie, as she was now known, came next, then Joan Collins and her then man, Tony Newley, *encore lui*. You sounded genuinely delighted. You had had enough success to fill your cornucopia. Was *Stop the World I Want To Get Off* already a hit? The following year, Stanley Donen wanted you to write the title song for *Two for the Road*. Looking back, prosaic Orpheus, I was small-minded and, worse, uncommercial, in not wanting your name in the credits. Then again… if you'd won an Oscar for the song, it would probably have become better known than my movie. So? Blame Broughtipoo, why don't we?

For the next twenty years and more, Beetle and I flew, first-class of course, countless times to L.A. When we borrowed Yvette Mimieux's house up at Oak Pass Drive, we passed your house, down in the valley, at least twice a day. There was a white sculpture on the watered front lawn. We never thought to call in. You had become rich and successful. I had not the least feeling of envy. We were two of very different kinds, that was all. If it had not been for you, I might have found my way into the movies but you gave me the bounce that had me believe that cinema was '*no gran cosa*', as Marcello Mastroianni once said at dinner with Beetle and me and Faye Dunaway. The comedy is that, whatever our contemporaries thought, or think, we were the only members of our Cambridge generation to win an Oscar; two, in your case.

The next time we met was at an Oscar dinner at Hampton Court, in the early nineties, I think. We were again as easy with each other as we had been when chomping P-P-Penguins in your rooms. Two of a kind, but never the same kind. Remember Ben Kingsley crossing his eyes as Dickie Attenborough delivered his prolonged, tearful allocution? Poor Dickie would later have genuine tears to shed after the Tsunami swept away his daughter and grandchild. The Oscar brought us together again, you and me, at St James's Palace a few years later. Glasses in hand, we exchanged pleasantries with Camilla before standing side by side, antiques in no privileged location in the cheesy group photograph. You had achieved just about everything that you hoped for back in the days when Tony Becher brought you to my rooms.

Not long after that St James's Palace parade Beetle was stricken, all of a sudden, with the swingeing stroke that has stranded her in a wheelchair ever since, bright and beautiful though she still is. We learned abruptly that misfortune leads to cancellation from the good address books of no few of those you took for friends. You and Evie must have heard what happened. On your way through London, you brought dinner and some very good wine (no Hock) to Stanhope Gardens. We had a very enjoyable what turned out to be last supper. We even talked of collaborating on a culminating musical comedy based on *The Prisoner of Zenda*. You were uncreased and all but unchanged. Your goldfingered songs are on the air all the time. You have your starred tile in the hall of popular fame. You gave a lot of people a good time, Lezzers. You and your credits were you. Nice work if you can get it, and you did.

Love, Freddie.

TO TOM MASCHLER.

Dear Tom,

I should never have met you but for the old school tie; yours, I mean, the one you never wore. In London in the late 1950s, I played occasional bridge – low stakes (6d. a hundred), highish standard – in a dusk-till-dawn school which included Donald Simmonds. He had been with you at Leyton Park, the Quaker school. Fair-skinned, freckled, with the dry, curly, cornflake hair that never lasts, neither boy nor adult, arty but no artist, Don lived in a Chelsea basement. At any hour, he might just have emerged from a lonely bed with change-me sheets. Playing at grown-ups, we lunched a few times at the *Ox On The Roof* at the lower end of the King's Road. I never knew what he did other than play bridge, rather well, with a tendency to 'psychic' (bluff) bids. Since he had no job, there may have been money in the family. I took him to Crockford's a few times for duplicate partnership evenings. He proved a sharp observer of my mistakes. Told I was a writer, he introduced me to you, his publisher friend, at a Dutch lunch – each of us paid three and sixpence for three courses – at Schmidt's in Charlotte Street, your choice; it was near where you worked.

Two years my junior, you were already an editor at MacGibbon and Kee. You had been offered a place at Oxford, you told me, but preferred to go into the world. It made you older. Your thrust contrasted with Simmonds's languor. You were dark, handsome, seemingly sun-tanned in the way that Nancy Mitford and Alan Ross had recently declared 'continental': U-term for bronzed persons, not as scathing as 'a touch of the tarbrush', all but synonymous with 'swarthy' in good old England. In those days, City businessmen still wore bowler hats and carried tightly rolled, silk-sleeved black brollies (colours were reserved for being conspicuous on the golf course). Enthusiasm made you audible, very, in a *sotto voce* world. When I used you as the maquette for a character in *Lindmann* called Milstein, his dialogue often MAJUSCULE, his English banged on like a loud knock at closed doors. I cadged 'Milstein' from the great violinist whose performance of the Beethoven violin concerto was the second L.P. Beetle and I owned (Amália Rodrigues the first). Donald Simmonds became Loomis in the same novel.

You were the editor of *Declaration*, a compendium of essays piquing current complacencies. Contributors composed a home legion of 'Angry Young Men', a term derived from John Osborne's *Look Back in Anger*. There was also Doris Lessing. Your foreword announced you the coach of a discordant team. Colin Wilson and John Hopkins (soon to be filed under 'Who he?') played on the right, John Osborne, Lindsay Anderson and Ken Tynan on the left, John Wain in the centre. There must have been others; they did not include Kingsley Amis. Riding high on *Lucky Jim*, reprinting again, and again, soon-to-be Kingers felt no call to share his single-occupancy spotlight. It had already faded on John Wain, once Kingsley's Oxford oppo. I remember W.W. Robson saying at dinner, in Lincoln College, in 1958, 'One thing you can say for Amis and Wain, they do have a good sense of humour, except for Wain'.

Your father had been a publisher of children's books in Berlin; your mother a racy lady; literally, on skis, and off. They brought you to England in 1938, just in time, and then parted. Was your aversion from female make-up kindled by her flash? At one of our lunches, *sans* Simmonds, you remarked how shameful it was that C.P. Snow's 'Mr L.' (based on Victor Gollancz?) was the only pronouncedly Jewish character in current English fiction. Before the war, in popular fiction and posh poetry, Jews were sinister or ridiculous, or both (see John Buchan, Graham Greene, Uncle Tom Eliot and all). During the war, it was a commonplace to presume them at the heart of the Black Market. The police caught the people it was easy to convict or, in unpublished cases, easier to shake down. Choosy editor of *Horizon* (he nixed a contribution on detective stories by Willie Maugham), Cyril Connolly was the first to give Arthur Koestler rationed space to tell England about the on-going extermination of Europe's Jews.

Foreign Office toffs dismissed the evidence as typical of 'whining' Jews. In April 1945, Dachau made savage truth undeniable, then unspeakable; a shame-filled reticence set in. Belsen was the one camp – by no means the worst – that stood for all. On newsreels, Richard Dimbleby delivered a hushed obituary which doubled for the cover story that the British had liberated, if not saved, the Jews to whom they had closed their ears and their doors. That victorious summer, I took the Winchester scholarship exam. The college's canonical headmaster asked what I felt about going to chapel. I was guileless enough to say that it didn't bother me. I came fourth when all the scholarship marks had been added up. After 'weight for age', distributed at the reverend H.M.'s discretion, a squad of those a few weeks younger than me were declared better scholarly prospects. Thirteenth and out, I was hived off to Charterhouse where, in my first term, Oration Quarter 1945, a skinny boy (Maxwell, C.J.M., later a philanthropic medico) was nicknamed 'Belsen'. The lethal factories of Auschwitz-Birkenau, Sobibor and the others harboured such reeking horrors that it was as if their victims had contributed to the obscenity which it became unseemly to mention.

Years later, John Peter, *ci-devant* Hungarian, *Sunday Times* tiro, invited us to dinner with a TV writer, Alfred Shaughnessy, who had been in action throughout the war; he claimed that it was fought to save the Jews. Who was I to contradict a decorated veteran, just because he was full of shit? The Wimpole Street dining room we ate in had sit-at-attention chairs with upright backs, each spiky shoulder capped with a red witch's cap, made out of paper, by our obsessive hostess, once famous for her breasts. John Peter later wrote a book of drama criticism that George Steiner declared 'almost major'. George took pleasure in catching John out on a (literal) point of recherché detail. Discussing the old, old story, J.P. had failed to know that each of the nails used to crucify Jesus had a specific name. Imagine! Shaughnessy scripted many episodes of *Upstairs Downstairs*.

After 1945, if Jews were hardly less Other than before, fewer people said so out loud. Two great public schools, Eton and St Paul's (where my father had been taught by the legendary Elam) took the hit-them-when-they're-down opportunity to reduce Jewish admissions, until shamed by righteous old boys, Ayer and Berlin respectively. As Britannic crocodiles dried their tears, the sainted Attlee government shipped refujews back to the same camps they had been sprung from, in order to appease the Arabs, who had supported Hitler. Zionists who fought to get what was left of European Jewry into Palestine were denounced as devious and ungrateful. A Ukrainian S.S. regiment received a ready welcome in the English coalmines. Trust the guilty to put uncomplaining shoulders to required wheels.

The British Foreign Secretary, Ernie Bevin (exalted as the dockers' Q.C.) met no criticism when he said that he wasn't "avin' the Jews push to the front of the queue'. Despite an absence of aitches, he was highly regarded by the old-school-tied in the Foreign Office. During a Labour party conference, he once chased the young Shirley Catlin (later Williams) round her hotel bedroom and, she told me, into the street. Anthony Eden had shared Bevin's view of the Chosen. Ignoring Churchill's orders, not a single R.A.F. bomb was ever dropped, deliberately, on any of hundreds of concentration camps. '*A quoi bon, monsieur?*' as the girl said in *Le Grand Meaulnes*.

Until the Eichmann trial, in Jerusalem in 1962, the Final Solution was more an embarrassment than a charge worth pressing against a now key component of the Free World. The West needed Adenauer's scarcely purged Germany more than any Jew, man, woman or child merited justice. My old Charterhouse headmaster, Robert 'Bags' (they were under his eyes) Birley, had been sent to Germany in 1946 with what amounted to a bucket of whitewash. It served to absolve useful Nazis from justice; the more agreeably accented their English, the better the chances of long-grassing their crimes. 'Bags' returned to his reward: the headmastership of Eton and the 'sir' already attributed him by a sarcastic Charterhouse beak called H.C. 'Harry' Iredale, rarely seen outdoors without his 'grid', Carthusian slang for bicycle. Harry taught French, Alphonse Daudet's *Lettres de mon moulin* his play-safe text, without the smallest Gallic aptitude beyond grammatical accuracy.

In 1956, *The Scourge of the Swastika*, by Lord Russell of Liverpool, a Nuremberg prosecutor, ruptured the diplomatic mummery. Whatever nice indignation the text aroused, crumbled crumpet photographs of naked women, pubic hair and all, being herded to their deaths added uncountable numbers to its sales. Germans had been keen with Leicas. Their snaps of the last crusade were damning mementos. Voyeurism and Holocaust denial began their counterpoint. Can Marcel Proust, master of the sequence of tenses, perfectionist with the past subjunctive, corrector of his housekeeper ('*Tu t'oublies, Françoise*') when she put fingers inside the glasses she was collecting, have been the same man who took pleasure in watching rats being skewered with hat-pins? Can he not? Was he, in secret, revisiting Dreyfus and, against his public stance, sharing his persecutors' glee? Duplicity is essential to a novelist's heart, dialogue its beat.

The success of *Declaration* won you a new job at Penguin books; Allen Lane, once an innovating bounder, now recently knighted, brought you in to rejuvenate the list. I gave you a proof of my second novel, *The Earlsdon Way*. After reading the first, *Obbligato*, Macmillan's chief reader, Jack Squire, renowned 1930s bookman (and flannelled fool on summer weekends), had urged them to hang onto me 'with both hands'. Owing more to *Main Street* than to any English model, *The Earlsdon Way* seemed knowledgeably sarcastic about the north London suburbia I never lived in. Its bumptious hero was scornful enough of true blue humbug for Macmillan to dust their hands of me, nicely. Over lunch at Simpson's in the Strand, Alan Maclean, the Moscow-bound Donald's brother, reshuffled from the Foreign Office, and his colleague 'Auntie' Marj warned me that I should not make any friends if I went on writing rebarbative books. I told them that I had not become a writer to make friends and went to Cassell. Soon after reading *The Earlsdon Way*, you sent me a telegram announcing that I was going to be a Penguin. You became my luck.

In the post-Suez 1950s, Ken Tynan set the style by falling in love, on paper, with John Osborne's nihilist Jimmy Porter. At the same time Ken was moonlighting with Princess Margaret and any in-group likely to yield kudos and kicks upstairs. In his bastard case, the clenched fist and the limp handshake were fellow travellers. You, Tom, were immune from fear of seeming pushy; push was you. Scarcely interested in Judaism, undeniable Jews, both of us were haunted by what you had tasted at cruel first hand and I, as a schoolboy, only in waspish, insular form. Your rage was sublimated by campaigning for Nuclear Disarmament. The aggressive annual march on Aldermaston publicised its pacifism. Led by Canon Collins, the Michael Foot-soldiers of the new Salvation Army combined blistered idealism with good chances of pulling birds. A joke of the day had a girl say that she had tried using the pill, only it kept falling out.

Exalted by *Declaration*, your next idea was a rejuvenated version of the wartime Home Service, Sunday afternoon *Brains Trust*. In 1958, commercial television was on its way in. Under Sidney Bernstein's patronage, you gathered a panel of young on-the-makers in a big room with a long, polished, oblong table in Soho Square. There was unbuttoned talk about fucking. A Granada executive sat silent. I heard myself speaking up for marriage. I was just finishing *The Limits of Love*, in which, for all their variety of social attitudes, three couples stayed together. Doris Lessing, hair in a bun, long parted from an East German communist husband, wore her 'Mrs' like a veteran of foreign wars. Combining *noli me tangere* with come-and-get-it, she smiled at my defence of matrimony, a touched-up Mona Lisa.

Thanks to Leslie Bricusse, his ambition as resourceful as yours, he and I had been put under contract by the Rank Organisation. I was not proud of *Bachelor of Hearts*, directed by Wolf Rilla, but there it was, my name on the credits. Did it alert you to how useful I might be? You told me about your boyhood as a refugee in unwelcoming 1940 England. Might there be a movie in it? I was keen to prove, if only to myself, that I could do better than I had when co-writing a confection in which the star part was allotted to Hardy Krüger, as handsome a fair-haired ex-fourteen-year-old member of the Hitler Youth as market research could enlist. I was either too supercilious or had too keen an eye on the main chance (yes, yes, or both) to take exception to the casting of *Bachelor of Hearts*.

Your friend Tom Wiseman was then film critic and showbiz columnist on the *Evening Standard*. For both of you, common decency went up the chimney at Auschwitz; for the lucky few, insulated from the horror, it seemed to have survived. Wiseman *père*, a gambler who thought that he could roll profitable, if loaded, dice with the Nazis, had stayed in Vienna. Having made deals to save Jews with the means to buy blind Nazi eyes, he gambled too long and was murdered before he could cross the border with his takings. One of my mother's uncles suffered a similar fate after a winning poker night with Kansas City mobsters.

When Wiseman went to do an *Evening Standard* interview with Hardy Krüger, he was in no forgiving or forgetting mood. After a long talk, however, it seemed that the two men had reached some kind of understanding. As they went to the door, Hardy's wife called out, 'Mr Viseman, vy do we not agree zat as far as the Jews and ze Germans were concerned, zere ver mistakes on both sides?' *Tableau*, as they used to say. Ruptured childhoods, lost language incited both you Toms to what-the-hell pursuit of women and success in a new tongue: one of your New York contacts addressed you as 'Tomcat'. Giving pleasure can be a form of revenge; withholding it too.

Wiseman became the scourge of Pinewood studios; insolent copy pleased Lord Beaverbrook's readers, hence the Beaver too; every threat of libel action procured a bonus. Your eye for talent boosted your employers' lists, enriched lucky authors; both sides owed you. I had presumed fiction an art; *Lucky Jim* proved it an artefact. Kingsley would become one of your proudest authors. When do cash-cows fail to find lush pasture? Your unsung virtue was that Cape subsidised writers such as Rudi Nassauer, author of *The Hooligan*. I still have several cases of the Château Latour 1964 he sold me (and to John Schlesinger) just before his wine business collapsed in bankruptcy, his own cubic volume shortly after, due to a deflating heart attack. To keep the wine, which had been in bond, we had to pay for it all over again. It still drinks well, as the trade has it.

You recalled your arrival in England with such clarity that I saw cinematic possibilities. Like many other once ladylike immigrants, your mother had had to become a skivvy, first cousin to a charlady. Virginia Woolf, paragon of feminism, disdained such sorry articles, their buckets, their mops, the water on their overworked knees. I imagined your mother employed as a domestic in a prep school like the one I attended, Copthorne, relocated to Lee Bay, North Devon. 'You' and 'I' were cast as uneasy fellow-pupils. Having recently shed my American accent, 'I' typified the assimilated Anglo: more embarrassed than touched by cousinship with a refujew.

Writing the screenplay, I was reminded of a Copthorne boy called Joseph who informed us that females had some sort of covert apparatus 'down there'. He took his roundhead equipment in one hand and hauled it upwards, leaving a vertical seam to stand for that mysterious object of desire. Only son, puzzled and somewhat enlightened, I had never seen a naked human female. I never knew that women had pubic hair until my mother took me to the Picasso show at the Tate in 1946. Joseph notched my memory on just that one occasion before vanishing from the scoreboard.

The script grew quickly and easily. I believed myself to be compiling something worth saying, in cinematic dialect. My 'I' played an ignominious role when he fails to speak up for his secret 'brother'. 'I' am more relieved than outraged when 'you' disappear after your mother is disgraced for a reason 'I' know to be false. You thought well enough of the script to show it to Karel Reisz. Czech fugitive, his book *The Art of Film Editing* established him as an authority. My script had, he informed you, 'the wrong values'. Forty years later, the first episode of *After the War* was a not very revised version of that early script. It played well, whatever the want of ideological propriety. Karel's son Matthew became editor of the *Jewish Quarterly*.

Born in England, his inflections hint at a childhood among expat Europeans, with the right values.

You primed something in me that might never have been there had you not. I was trying, with diligent difficulty, to make a living. In the morning, I ghosted his memoirs for Colonel Maurice Buckmaster, who had been in command of the French section of S.O.E. When I was puzzled as to what had happened to this or that *réseau* when people were betrayed to the Gestapo, Buck invited me, with his Old Etonian smile, to make up something plausible. I was shocked, but complied. The only occasion on which I saw someone reading *They Fought Alone* (it did not sport my name) was on a bus in Guatemala in the 1970s, on the way to Chichicastenango. The reader's name, it emerged, was Dr Raphael. He ran a top-to-toe clinic in San Diego, California, and would be glad, he said, to give me a rate if I happened to be in town and needed an overhaul.

In the afternoons, in the late 1950s, I worked at the Oxford and Cambridge club on the long manuscript which became *The Limits of Love*, until there was a quorum for tea-time bridge. Clem Attlee once said good afternoon to me. He had declined to have too many Jews in his government (Glaswegian Manny Shinwell was enough) and deposed an African chief, Seretse Khama, after he had vexed the apartheid lobby by marrying a white woman, Ruth Williams. In time, Seretse Khama became the first President of Botswana. Attlee is the latest totem to be resurrected as a model socialist.

Beetle, year-old Paul and I were living in a ground floor flat, giving onto a green and rosy garden, in an unpaved road in Highgate. One night you came and baby-sat for us. As you walked into the living room, I was locking my current Joseph Gibert notebook in my Heals desk drawer. 'What's the matter', you said, 'think I'd go through your personal papers?' 'What's the matter', I said, 'aren't you interested?'

You had an idea for making us both a few bob: a sophisticated tribute to Dale Carnegie's *How To Win Friends and Influence People*. You would give me a few pages of notes on how to make it in the marketplace. I could then fatten them into a book. We would split the proceeds fifty-fifty. I wrote ninety percent of *The S-Man*; I should never have done any such book unless you had primed it, nor sold it without you to busy bidders. Your notes were smarter than I expected. Once prompted, tricks I should never dream of attempting occurred to me in shameless clusters. *The S-Man, a Grammar of Success* parodied Wittgenstein's *Tractatus*. It began: 'Roughly speaking, money and success are synonymous'. One of your more durable observations was 'No good idea looks good on paper'. I had a good time standing proxy for a shit for all seasons. *The S-Man*'s aptness would be confirmed when Harold Macmillan went to the country, in 1959, on the slogan 'You never had it so good' and won in a canter. Weary of being penurious and stiff-upper-lippy, the British lowered their colours, then their pants: Carnaby Street Y-fronts flaunted the Union Jacksie.

Beetle and I had sunk our (mostly her) meagre capital in buying the stub of a lease only after our nice grey landlady, Miss Pearce, gave her word that she would renew it later that year. When I went, blithe flowers in hand, to confirm the arrangement, she told me that she was sorry, her sister had been widowed; we would have to vacate the flat. Family was family. She was sure I understood. I certainly did: trust is a form of laziness. We had small hope of finding another place to live in London without 'key money', the then routine, illicit, means of procuring a lease. You had an immediate idea: why not go and live in Spain? One of your clutch of ex-mistresses, a hyphenated lady, who wore gloves and hats, owned a seaside cottage in a small fishing village called Fuengirola, not far from Malaga. She would let us have it for the winter for three pounds a week. Miss Pearce tripped us into a European way of life on which we should never otherwise have embarked. Sojourn in the Caudillo's Spain proved our salvation. Passing rich on twenty pounds a week, I finished one novel on a Friday and began another on the Monday. The Muse said 'What kept you?'

I also supplied well-paid dialogue for a movie starring Dickie Todd. War hero and ladies' man, he relished my decorous *double-entendres*. Jean-Luc Godard – the one genuine innovator in the *Nouvelle Vague*, unless Alain Resnais was another – was right to call his film about a Parisian prostitute *Vivre sa vie*: you owe nobody anything when you do things solely for the money. You found a prompt publisher for *The S-Man*. Hutchinson's Ian Hamilton – not *the* Ian Hamilton, editor, poet etc – accused you of bargaining 'like an Armenian', a not wholly flattering instance of displacement sideways. I never scrutinised any paperwork, though I must have signed something somewhere. Our pen name, Mark Caine, was of your devising; did I add the 'e'?

Beetle and I had a good time in Fuengirola. We had to leave after rents escalated for the tourist season. When I won the Lippincott Prize for *The Limits of Love*, we could afford to return to England, at least for a while. Film work of a kind was available. Cassell was publishing my novels and keen for more. You had saved our bacon. *The S-Man* had a *succès de scandale*. My friend Peter Green, with no notion of my involvement, was at that time a leading *Daily Telegraph* critic. His outraged denunciation of Mark Caine's recipes for making it did sales no harm. Elizabeth Jane Howard compared our little number to Laclos's *Les Liaisons Dangereuses*.

I was never shown how many hardback copies it sold, but you had no difficulty in getting Penguin to pay a £750 advance for the paperback. You proposed another shameless handbook, about seducing, and satisfying females. The pill that had supposedly liberated the sex sanctioned men to make free with them. You cited the female navel as an underrated erogenous zone. I did not feel the vocation. Once you were included in *Who's Who*, you listed *The S-Man* among your publications. *Moi non plus*.

Beetle and I went to live in rural East Bergholt. Sarah was born, in August 1960, in The Old Mill House, a cottage that once belonged to John Constable's father. You drove down from London for the weekend several times, each with a different female. When *The Limits of Love* was published, Peter Forster's *Daily Express* review filled the best part of a full page. It declared that I had entered 'the big league'.

Stella Richman had already enrolled me to write plays for Associated Television. They took a week to write and were promptly in production. One day a youngish actor approached me, during a coffee break in the rehearsal room opposite Finsbury Park, and asked whether I thought the hydrogen bomb would put an end to the world. I gave an educated 'on the one hand, on the other hand' response. He thanked me and wandered off. Carmen Silveira came up to me and said, 'Freddie, may I tell you something? When an actor asks you a question about the future of mankind, the first and only thing he wants to hear is "I think you're giving a marvellous performance"'.

Wolf Mankowitz, once an undergraduate Leavisite reviewer (predictable thumbs down for Dylan Thomas in *Scrutiny*), by then a mini-tycoon, with Piccadilly Arcade offices, had denied me a job writing a screenplay for Peter Sellers on the grounds that I was too piss-elegant. His own Cambridge diligence and accent had been camouflaged by a reversion to East End tones and vocabulary. His revised persona was symbolised by an outsize matchbox of rubber-banded five-pound notes on his desk, beside his scholarly study of Wedgwood china. He liked to have things three ways. Was he ever any kind of a Soviet agent, as MI5 suspected?

After Peter Forster's rave review of *The Limits of Love*, Wolf changed tack and hired me. By the time I had written a draft of *Memoirs of a Cross-Eyed Man*, Peter Sellers had been warned off the subject by his clairvoyant, whose brightest eye was for the main chance. He divined stellar sanction for his credulous client to do only whatever was lined with the most gold in the way of a backhander. When Peter met Sophia Loren, he willed himself handsome. BBC radio producer Roy Speer had once told me that radio was God's gift to actors like Sellers. The Goon Show's Bluebottle willed and coiffed himself irresistible, with custom-made specs. A few years later, Wolf sold my £1,500 script to Paramount for a hundred times that price. He had had it retyped, of course. What do we remember of Wolf's work? The title *A Kid for Two Farthings* and the line 'Do me a favour, Fender', pronounced 'Fend-air'.

Beetle and I went back to Fuengirola in 1961. You came to visit us, when we were living in a *casita* with just enough room for us, Paul and Sarah. The *Costa del Sol* bulged with foreign visitors. You found somewhere to stay (no doubt on expenses) but spent most of your time, when you were not with us, or me, among the expat writers, of varying quality. As a publisher, you were not short of invitations to lunch, despite the poverty of most of those who entertained you. You were impressed by a novella by Charlie Reiter about a black call-girl. Her white client found her such delightful company at dinner that he told her that he would feel better if he didn't take her to bed. She said, 'And how about me? How will I feel?' Daring topic for those days, a woman with the hots. Barney Rosset's Grove Press printed the book. Did Charlie ever publish anything else? Dark and East Coast smart, married to a beautiful blonde opera singer called Anna, he drove a black VW. The marriage did not last, nor did his looks. He put on weight editing a Teamsters' newspaper on the West Coast and died young.

At the end of your week in Fuengirola, you asked our friends Harry and Charlotte Gordon whether you might borrow their cook, Pepa, and their rented town house, on the Avenida José Antonio, in order to repay *d'un seul coup* all the local hospitality you had received. Pepa delivered a fine and ample meal. At the end of it, as we were sipping *Fundador*, you finished your second helping of *flan*, sat back and said, 'First time I've had enough to eat since I got here'. I walked out of the house and paced the shameful streets for a long while, before going back for Beetle. Did you have any idea that I had been mortified by what you said to our friends? On your lips, more often than you knew, a joke was not a joke. A routine mistake: implicit acceptance of radical distinction between Jews and Aryans when both are German-speakers. What krauts German Jews can be! How perfect their English, how often with a hole in the heel!

It was not a good season for me. All the money I had earned in TV was gone. I had finished a neat new novel, *The Graduate Wife*, but Selwyn Lloyd's squeeze was draining my meagre freelance reservoir. When Beetle's father died, an Israeli friend of Charlie Reiter lent us money for tickets to fly home. I can't remember how I repaid him, but I know I did. We left Fuengirola in September and drove in divorced humour to Sainte-Maxime. I had no idea where we were going to live or how.

Stella Richman, my benefactor since the moment we met back in 1960, greeted us with the news – no surprise to her, relief to me – that she wanted to renew, and fatten, my contract to write plays for Atv. Then a phone call told me that David Deutsch was offering to buy the movie rights of a play of mine that had just been on TV and have me write the screenplay. Wallet all set to bulge, we headed back to England, signed contracts with David, the nicest film producer one could imagine, exchanged our grey Ensign for a new Standard Vanguard station wagon, and drove to Rome, via Germany.

Our one-night stay outside red-cliffed Heidelberg was interrupted by loutish shouting: French soldiers on the town. Once in Rome, we rented a modern basement flat at 7948, Monte Mario. I do not remember thinking about you during those days. Modest affluence confirmed Karl Marx's view that economic circumstances determine, certainly inflect, so-called consciousness. Roughly speaking, success and money…

In the spring, we crossed to Greece, landing at Igoumenitsa, close to Janina, where Byron was entertained by the tyrant Mohammed Ali. He loved British sailors. At the city gate, Byron rode by a human arm hanging from a gallows, all that was left by local birds and dogs of some rebellious Epirot. One of my friends at Cambridge remembered that his parents had dined in pre-war somewhere with Hermann Göring; they liked him. After taking oracular advice, from Thalia Taga, in Athens, we sailed from Piraeus to the Cycladic island of Ios (pop. 200 and dwindling). Under a spring sky, I finished *Lindmann* in a ten-hour session of 8,000 words. My marathon clatter was observed by a Turkish-trousered peasant who called me *effendi*. He had never before seen a typewriter. On our last day on Ios, we bought a hillside shack above three shelves of cactus, olive and fig trees, and a trapezoid plot of beachside land, all for three hundred pounds, my happiest investment ever.

You had sent a telegram suggesting that we meet up in Mykonos, not yet fashionable, but a renowned *rendezvous de tantes*. The best hotel would cost only a couple of quid a night. Your new woman, Martha Crewe, gourmet Quentin's ex, would be coming with you. Just before we left Ios, a telegram arrived from my mother saying that the London press, the *Observer's* Jack Davenport *en tête*, had raved over *The Graduate Wife*. As we were going ashore on Mykonos, I noticed that the lady in front of us had that newspaper in her open straw bag. Vanity impelled me to ask if I might have a look at it, because… etc.

She said, 'Sure, of course, a good review's never out of season'. The charming low voice belonged to Elaine, third and last wife of John Steinbeck. Recent recipient of the Nobel Prize, he looked at me (and pretty well everyone else) with a basilisk eye. Vilified by Robert Lowell and *la* Sontag for his obsolete, patriotic attitude to the Vietnam war, he knew where paths of glory led. Jack Davenport was a witty contemporary of Cyril Connolly's. Everyone at Oxford with him had predicted that Jack would be *aut Caesar aut nihil* in the literary world.

Martha was beautiful, dark and aloof, with a musician's composed fingers. She had come to Mykonos to be with you, not with us. You moved from the smart, if cheap, hotel to cheaper rooms in the village. Did we ever have a meal together? Did you or she say one word to our children? Beetle had cotton pants tailored to measure, within twenty-four hours, by the Mykonos *roi de pantalons;* did Martha? We did all go to Delos in the same *caique.* Martha pronounced the e short, just as she called the Peloponnese the Peloponessos. You and she walked away from us between the couchant lions.

Four years later, I was awarded the Oscar. Martha asked us to dinner in her handsome house in Gibson Square. You reported that she found me very attractive. *Toute réussite a son propre parfum*, as someone must have said. Beetle and I saw Martha one more time: in a Festival Hall box, still beautiful, and alone, she was setting those fine fingers together for Rosalyn Tureck, who had a characteristic vertical wave for the audience. Tureck had had a love affair with James MacGibbon, whom we got to know later. He and Robert Kee, a meteor with no lasting blaze, were no durable duo.

Meanwhile, your career was careering: success at Penguin led to your becoming the still very young managing director, or something of that order, at prestigious, once stuffy Jonathan Cape. You were eager that I join your stable. *Lindmann* had been received with enthusiasm by Desmond Flower, M.C., at

Cassell. In a canvass of publishers printed in the *Sunday Times*, it was his sole selection from his list for the coming season. Jack Lambert gave *Lindmann* my first solus review, by David Hughes; it was both effusive and uneasy. I had, he implied got something off my chest. My assault on the Foreign Office as accessory to the drowning of a rusted, overloaded ship full of European Jews smacked of ingratitude; to whom, for what? Not long before he died, I thanked David (recently fired from the *S. T.*) for what he had said about *Lindmann*. He had no memory of it.

Lindmann (it included a full-length screenplay by Milstein) differed, by its pointed scorn, from the work of insular quasi-tragedians such as David Storey whom you so much admired. His diamonds were as rough as Rugby League, topic of his first novel, *This Sporting Life*. The subsequent film, with Richard Harris, made it clear that, among other things, Lindsay Anderson fancied a bit of rough. After fifty years of being a prizewinning writer, Storey still wrote 'with you and I' in his overblown last long novel, *A Serious Man*. Much it matters? It has to matter a little.

I am tempted to blame you for my betrayal of Desmond Flower's faith. Had it not been for your solicitation, I should never have moved to Jonathan Cape, but the opportunism was mine. Impersonating Mark Caine, Julien Sorel *de nos jours*, I imagined myself to be exercising my wits; your example had proved infectious. There was something of you in Jimmy Brewster, the on-the-make anti-hero of *Nothing But the Best*. Although Tom Wiseman gave it a rave, the movie was no hit. It did roll on to fortune: Jo Janni and John Schlesinger culled me to write what turned into *Darling*; it also brought me to the attention of Stanley Donen.

When we bought that dilapidated cottage on Ios, it emptied my pockets. Four years later, thanks to *Darling*, already with a house in rural East Anglia, we had the means to begin its renovation. Beetle and I had our siesta in a big bed in the only room on the top terrace. Paul and Sarah slept in a tent below. One hot afternoon, Paul knocked on our door and announced a wet stranger, complete with snorkel and flippers. Enter Milstein Maschler. You had swum ashore from a yacht riding at anchor in Milopota bay. You, Kingsley and Jane Howard just happened to be passing.

We took you to dinner that evening, after drinks on our terrace, to Drakos at the far end of the bay. On the way, Jane lifted her skirts and pissed, standing proud, on our beachside field. Kingsley was dyspeptic, not to say hungover. He ate *poly ligo* of a small omelette. I cannot remember what he drank or said, apart from thanking me for my polite review of *The Anti-Death League*, his one attempt to play the nice guy. My frail command of Greek elected me host. I remember the evening mainly because Sarah, aged six, fell asleep towards the end of the meal and I carried her the long, heavy, sand-soft way, back up to our *spiti*; the last time I ever did that.

You and the others talked of taking us to a meal the next day; you sailed away instead. Kingsley wrote a prompt, vivid article, for some colour supplement, about the *piata kykladika* he had eaten in a beachside *taverna*. On another occasion, no doubt. He had already written a skimpy novel entitled *I Like It Here*, meaning the good old UK. Did he ever like it anywhere, or anyone, very much except perhaps Philip Larkin, who did not quite return his compliments? Success filled and refilled Kingsley's glass with more and more emptiness. Alcoholics end up living in pickle jars.

Beetle worked for you, one serious day a week, as a reader, alongside the old Cape hand Daniel George (author of a book entitled *Solitary Pleasures*, by which he meant books, but was taken, mischievously, to be referring to Onan). Jane Miller and Claire Tomalin her colleagues, Beetle's recommendations were so intelligent, so wittily expressed, that the chairman,

Wren Howard, suggested that you raise her salary. You called her in and said that you now intended to give her six pounds a day. Beetle said, 'That's what I'm getting as it is'. 'Oh, well', you said, 'in that case... (Pinteresque pause)... keep up the good work'.

Is it unkind to mention how I came to Cape one midday and you suggested we go to the *Alpino*, in Tottenham Court road, for coffee? I had noticed that you had installed a coffee machine in the hall. Why go to the *Alpino*? 'That machine only makes weak coffee.' 'Put more coffee in it.' 'Too expensive. The staff use it all the time.' The *Alpino* bill for two *cappuccini*, in transparent plastic cups, was twenty pee. You started patting your pockets. I had seen the routine before. When you said, 'Got 'ny money?' I said, 'I'll pay for the bloody coffee but you owe me ten pee and I shan't forget it'. You reached into the depth of your trouser pocket and produced a green 2p piece, which you slipped under your plastic saucer. 'Now I owe you nine.'

In those days, I thought you too cool to be hurt, but I was wrong, wasn't I? I was told by one of your lovers that you (and she) had times when you sat and wept together. I was surprised and then, quickly, not. In those days, public male tears were always unBritish. Your ambition was striped with desire for revenge; anger and some kind of remorse, or shame, went together. I used not to understand why anyone should feel guilt for having survived the Nazis, by whatever turn of good fortune, and now... now, as antisemitism is again *à la mode*, the shame returns, shame at counting oneself lucky. Those tears I never saw might have changed what I felt about you; then again... I needed you to be my tough guy.

I used to play bridge at the Savile Club with a not very likeable engineer who had fled Vienna and, in time, became a colonel in the British army while still being an alien. Having spent post-war time in India, Herbert Samek always called a spade an 'eshpade', and always explained why. One evening, while having a drink, he told me how, in 1938, he had seduced a woman in the Danish embassy and so gained passage to safety. He left his mother and sister in Vienna. He could not imagine that they would be in mortal danger, even from the Nazis. Both were murdered. As he told me the story, Herbert took the cigar from his lips and began to weep. How could he have done what he did? He apologised again and again for being so weak. It was the only occasion on which I felt affection for him.

You always wanted to get into the movies and hoped that I could smooth, if not pave, your way to gold. When Beetle and I went to spend a couple of winter months in Jamaica, you sent me the manuscript of John Fowles's *The French Lieutenant's Woman* in the hope that, having just won the Oscar, I could enhance its movie chances. Why not? I thought it over-written, the forked ending pretentious; otherwise fine. Verbosity did not stop it becoming a bestseller. Back in England, I had a meeting with you and Dick Lester (director of *A Hard Day's Night*) and suggested how the twin-track narrative could find an equivalent in alternating black and white sequences, of rehearsal in today's world, with the colourful past. Lester backed away; Karel Reisz came in; then Harold Pinter. My two-tone idea – guess who told them – was adopted. I doubt whether you named whose it had been. It didn't work all that well. When Harry Saltzman asked me to write the next James Bond movie, I said I had better things to do. 'Who can I get?' he said. I said, 'Harold Pinter?' Harry said: 'What's he done?'

As Jack Lambert had warned, success in the movies blighted my literary standing. The first novel of mine that you published, with no lack of enthusiasm, was *Orchestra and Beginners*. It received a few polite reviews but was scorned by a Cantab contemporary – who else? – in – where else? – the *Observer*. He accused me of an excess of *marivaudage*. I had to go and look it up, but the charge had some justice. I had been reading too much O'Hara. Thanks to you, the American rights were bought by Viking.

Impressed by *The Golden Notebook*, I wrote to Doris Lessing: was she interested in making it into a film? I suggested lunch. She wrote back to say that I sounded like a typical film producer. Umpteen years later, I was co-opted into a Manchester audience to which Doris read, for a BBC broadcast, one of her own unshortened stories. 'He said' and 'she said' came, as in Elizabeth Bowen, in all the wrong places and much too often. The lady had no ear and no humour; as Antonia Byatt has proved, this combination can pass, frequently, for being Serious. Straight faces are a plumed element of the will to hegemony. Picasso painted Picassos; Pinter typed Pinters. Did solemn Doris get her Nobel Prize as a reward for that set of who-can-possibly-have-wanted-to-read-them Sufi sci-fi novels? Such books have didactic dialogue in common: cut-out characters exchange slogans on stilts. Doris was taken to be important because she never smiled. Laughs? You're kidding. She wrote one good, short novel: *The Grass Is Singing. Martha Quest*? I trudged through several volumes; sieved no treasure.

You always received my novels with enthusiastic telegrams, but I never delivered a manifest hit. You published me handsomely, but Hollywood rewarded me so well, even in slump years, that you were the victim of my artistic conscience: I was keener to write clever than successful books; they proved that I had not emigrated permanently to Capua. The reference is, of course, to Hannibal; today how many people will know that? See what I mean? All the same, fair never being all that fair, I blamed you, a little, for my not becoming a bestseller. My work was not included in that famous, some say notorious, Book Bang that you mounted in Bedford Square. It was nixed less out of malice, I am sure, than fear that the stacks would not descend quickly enough to confirm your Midas touch.

Asked for the novelists whose work you thought would last, you named Storey, Sillitoe and Shaw (Robert); a slew of sibilants among whom Sillitoe alone remains of period interest. You did your best for me, Tom; I never doubted it, although we had no climactic moment when sales give publisher and writer cause for sincere, reciprocal embraces. Sillitoe dumped the Left and became a supporter of Israel after he heard a comrade gloating over the murder of a kibbutz child by a peerless Palestinian. He also took to wearing improbable waistcoats, without ever losing his working-class carriage.

Back in 1968, you set yourself to create an annual fiction award for British writers that might have something of the prestige of the Prix Goncourt. That the Booker was sponsored by a sugar company proved both apposite and, when awarded to John Berger for his tricky little novelty *G.*, offered an opportunity for conspicuous ingratitude. Berger was the very instance of the man who would not have it except both ways. Presided over by unliterary celebrities, the Booker Prize has descended into being an award to enhance sales, rarely to promote excellence.

Cape was so manifestly the best house in London that Kingsley migrated to your company. Roald Dahl consented to be enriched by a Jew. On Wren Howard's retirement, you could have settled for being the dignified chairman of a thriving, if not quite affluent company. Your marriage with Fay, *née* Coventry, was quite a literary occasion. Beetle and I drove to your Welsh cottage in our red Mercedes 280SL. Arnold Wesker and others supplied the eulogies, yours not Fay's; in those days she was no celebrity, more a little lamb, albeit a pregnant one. Pale bride, she wore scant make-up and paraded small radiance.

Arnold Wesker, the socialist, thanked you for uttering a cry of 'Hold it!', cash in hand, to a local estate agent after someone had already put down a deposit on a cottage that Arnold later acquired; a nice instance of so-socialism. Salting your flatterers' tales, Doris Lessing took it on herself to say that you could be a bit of a bastard. It sounded like the nicest thing she could think of. Doris considered herself a great person; like many dullards she took verbosity for seriousness. Fearing that her famous name, not its quality, sold her books, she sought, on one occasion, to make a new career by throwing herself under a pseudonym.

Another renowned guest, John Fowles had the Jamesian *embonpoint* and fame which your salesmanship had procured. He played the great writer with no hint of complacency; it was written all over him. Odd that he never got a knighthood; or did he refuse one? On the matter of honours, it seems to me disgraceful, never unexpected, that your long service as the Diaghilev of post-war British fiction remained unrewarded by even so little as a knighthood. The story was that some malevolent person on *Private Eye*, affecting to be a Home Office official, telephoned to ask whether you were amenable to being named a knight in the forthcoming honours. Having intimated your willingness, you were warned to tell no one at all of your imminent dignity. The mean assumption, duly honoured, was that you would never keep the news to yourself. Once your credulity was made public, by whatever friend, you were promptly poked in *The Eye*. Its wrinkle-nosed editor has a way of proving his impartiality by not fearing to attack Jews; Larry Adler a recurrent target. Taking malice for flattery, his own wincing smile for sportsmanship, Larry kept coming back for more, as if he needed it.

You had a tendency to misread situations. Another old schoolfriend of yours, Bob Gavron, told us how you had been one of a party that went skiing together at Klosters, I think it was. It was agreed at the outset to have a communal account at the bar. At the end of the two weeks, Bob discovered that the bill was bigger, much, than you might expect. Recent millionaire, he immediately paid his share and yours. When you proposed to settle, Bob told you that he had already taken care of it and that your share was x, where x was something like a third of the actual sum. You said, 'I'd like to see the bills'.

The impression was that you feared you were being swindled. Bob's response was that you were welcome to see them. He never again wanted to have anything to do with you. You scanned the bills, realised what you should have had the wit to guess. You then sent Bob a handwritten letter in which you regretted your gaucherie. He was so touched by your abject tone that, with a smiling sigh, he had to retract the divorce. He told us how, when he made his first million, he bought himself a Rolls Royce. Within a short time, he realised that it gave him no pleasure and disposed of it. He became a copious patron of the National Gallery and of the Folio Society.

Bob was again your trusted friend by the time you and Grahame Greene were offered the chance of buying Jonathan Cape from the Howards. Grahame, from the same East Anglian brewing family as his quasi-namesake, was rich; you could scarcely cover the needed half million. For all its eminent back list and present bestsellers Cape was barely profitable. Bob could not see how you would ever recover your capital. Having asked his advice, you were daring enough not to take it. A couple of years later, American corporate marauders offered you and Grahame eleven million pounds for the company. Gavron was quick to draw the moral: when gambling, never take advice from people whom you assume to know more than you do. After Anthony Cheetham sold Orion to Hachette for fifteen million pounds, you asked him how much he had distributed to the staff. Cheetham said 'None of it; I took the risk and I took the winnings. How much did you give the Cape people?' You are said to have said, 'I only got five and a half million'.

Riches made you rich, scarcely happy. At that Welsh wedding, Fay had seemed a pale likeness of Ben Jonson's *Epicene, or the Silent Woman*. Her dependence on you, once she was delivered of Hannah, your first daughter, irked her. With proper ambition, she entered a competition to be restaurant critic on the *Evening Standard* for three months. Her bright and chatty copy secured her the job which she held for almost fifty years, brightly and chattily. Success made her name; although she still carries yours, she became disenchanted with matrimony. You told me that she suspected that you had rigged the competition in order to make her happy. The untrue charge did not long tarnish the prize that made you superfluous. For renouncing amorous adventures, your reward was the modern Epicene's much chatted about affairs. You were a better man than the newspapers made you out to be. When old and suffering from a distorted back which left you walking at a right angle, you twice took a bus load of books to Africa, Uganda, I think, for distribution to children who might otherwise never have had a chance to read. Almost anyone else, I suspect, would have received some due honour.

In society, you became maladroit in areas where, previously, you had been the smoothest of S-Men. When you wrote to say that you were going to be staying with Robert Littell, quite near Lagardelle and asked whether you might come and see us, I replied that, of course, but it would be best if you came late in the week (after I had done what is often called my 'stint', never by me) and also in good time for Beetle to prepare a suitable lunch. Please to give us ample notice. Only someone who did not know you would fail to guess that you turned up, with the just teen-age Hannah and little Ben, at a quarter to one on a Monday. Hasty omelettes served you right. Hannah signalled her own unhappiness by calling our eight-year-old son Stephen 'four-eyes'. You told me she called you 'Big Nose'. When you asked to stay overnight, we were sorry: other people were coming: the Wisemans, in undeclared truth.

When I think about you, one phrase of yours comes to mind more than any other: 'Mind if I help myself?' You never waited to be invited. I made a character based, affectionately, gratefully even, on you say that if he had waited for invitations he would never have got anywhere. Waiting for you to prove yourself, yet again, in character was part of the comedy of life. However exasperating it was to watch you slice large pieces of fillet of beef from the joint I had only just finished carving, I saw the innocence of the liberated victim in your shamelessness. I all but loved you for it.

It is now more than thirty years since I went up to Bedford Square and told you that I was going to another publisher. He had offered a £100,000 advance for my new novel. You tried, with moist eyes, to get me to stay. Somehow, a grudge had built up in me which you had done little to deserve. When you realised that I was not going to change my mind, you kissed me on the lips. But I was the Judas.

I did see you again, at your invitation, in that big flat in Oakwood Court, the same block in which my great-aunt Minnie, the Christian, had us served a proper English tea (hot scones in a double-decker dish) when we first came to England. Leaning on a stick, you were bent at right angles by your painful back but made little fuss about it. You were hoping to re-issue *The S-Man*, half a century after its recipes for success had become common practice. When you took it to an agent who was said to be the new Tom Maschler, he thought it too naïve for today's hustlers. You told me that you were planning again to fill an old London bus with good books and take them to Uganda to back that sorry state's educational programme. You went and went again, I think. However hard you tried to be the essiest-man around, a good person inside you was always struggling to get out (and in, of course).

Love, Freddie.

Dear John,

I knew of you, before I met you or, more precisely, before you swivelled a glance at me, in medium long shot. Beetle and I had been asked to dinner by Clare and David Deutsch. You had just finished shooting *Billy Liar*. David was producing *Nothing But the Best*, the first movie I wrote *da solo* (in a small flat on Rome's Monte Mario), for Anglo-Amalgamated, aka Nat Cohen and Stuart Levy. The same company had sponsored your two North Country movies. You and Jo Janni had had enough and then some of the grandest hotel in sooty Bradford and wanted to do something metropolitan, in the rich traces of Federico Fellini's *La Dolce Vita*. Nat and Stu seldom interfered in shooting or the choice of subject. Success renewed your licence. Their principal passion was racehorses: one of theirs won the Grand National, didn't it?

Alan Bates was slated to play Jimmy Brewster in my script. He had starred in your first hit, *A Kind of Loving*. Small worlds can be very cosy once you've ducked to get in. Your award-winning documentary *Terminus* first drew you to Jo Janni's attention. *Terminus* had none of Tony Richardson and Lindsay Anderson's political commitment. In what they flagged as 'Free Cinema', they advertised their socialism by reddening the black and white wake of the wartime Crown Film Unit. Lacking what Patrick Sergeant called 'scratch', the jaggedness of their cuts was excused by the ardour with which they accused the bourgeoisie, their common cradle, for ill-using Smithfield porters and other no-days-off toilers. Sincerity is always low-budget; audition pieces likewise. The three of you had been together at Oxford, but you – a BBC off-the-rank series director for most seasons – were little regarded by the other two, though you all belonged, in different registers, to the same fraternity. When *A Kind of Loving*, more pastoral than *engagé*, was an undeniable hit, the radicals deemed it lacking in revolutionary rectitude; it was too candid about the dreariness of provincial working-class life. How June Ritchie pronounced 'we mussn't' – when pressed to go the whole way by Alan Bates – remained a code word between you and Jo.

David Deutsch offered me a generous introduction to quality movie-making. At Pinewood, in the mid-1950s, I had learned little, apart from how to present a script with professional punctuation, avoiding radio's 'cross-fade' in favour of 'dissolve' and 'cut to', and never venturing a witty line. Wit divides an audience; some get it, others not; knockabout, tits and violence, unite. I retreated to print; fiction promised autonomy, and a frugal life.

The advent of commercial television, in 1960, offered the fun and funds that came of writing play after play for Atv and Stella Richman; forty-five pages, each completed in one week, before being shot on the Dalek-like cameras of the day. Trailing cables were liable to snag unless the operator was an adroit steersman. Long dialogue scenes were favoured because static and easy to shoot. Walking-and-talking was not yet in favour. Take Two was acceptable only in case of a technical snafu.

You had done your time in the army. Peter Nichols told me, years later, how he had been posted to an entertainment detail in Singapore. When you met him on arrival, something impelled him to say that he had heard that the whole outfit was 'riddled with queers'. Was it true? Your smile was a promise. Almost as nice as he seemed, Nichols profited from his far eastern experience, however far it went, by writing *Her Privates We*, a title as subtle, as my mother would have said, as a hit in the head; and a hit it was.

One of my forty-eight minute plays for Lew Grade's Associated TV, plumped to an hour with ads, attracted David Deutsch's attention. He commissioned a movie version of *The Best of Everything*, unlimited by ITV's implacable shears. Nat Cohen supplied what he thought a catchier title. David also paved a bridge to Jo Janni, for whom I had done a little repair work when he was a Rank producer at Pinewood.

I first met Clare Deutsch when she was Mrs Raymond Stross. In 1955, Leslie Bricusse and I had gone to see Raymond in the hope of convincing him to produce a movie of Gavin Maxwell's *God Protect Me From My Friends*. Just back from a first trip to Sicily, Beetle and I had been in time to see Palermo's baroque waterfront mansions before *Cosa Nostra* had the municipality rip them down and replace them with jaundiced tower blocks. The *mafia* invoiced the town council for more bricks and labour than went to make Babel. Maxwell's book was all but a love letter to Salvatore Giuliano, the Sicilian bandit who, soon after the war, glamorised himself by his Robin Hood exploits, before being betrayed by, yes, his best friend (poisoned in his turn, in jail, before he could puncture the official story).

At the same time, Danilo Dolci was striving to spring Sicily's peasants from the trap in which Giuliano came to be ensnared, due to the usual collusion between politicians, *mafiosi* and police. Dolci was so saintly (and so sure to fail) that the Mafia chose not to get a bad name by harming him. Suso Cecchi d'Amico, one of Jo Janni's Roman friends, later wrote the screenplay for Francesco Rosi's film about Giuliano. Rarely in close-up, he said almost nothing; that white coat made him emblematic. The last shot was of a riderless white horse running free and upbeat on a Sicilian hillside. The mafia was hired to take care of security as the movie was being made.

Cut to: the beautiful Clare Stross-as-she-was leaning close to me, while passing a plate of biscuits as hostess for the not notably responsive Stross, and telling me, as if promising an assignation, how much she had admired my send-up of Graham Greene in the Footlights. Her *sotto voce* tone promised a convent education. It had appealed to Raymond, she told us later, to rig his innocent bride as a black-laced whore. As soon as she had slipped away, he married Anne Heywood, the latest film star in the English style: annual, rarely perennial. At the time of the Six Day War, he asked me to come and see him (he was in a many-pillowed bed, for some valetudinarian reason). You and Julie Christie had just won me the Oscar. He had been a bad Jew, he said, and wanted to make amends. I wished him luck as I did not kiss him goodbye.

Cut back to that night in Farley Court. *A proposito*, do you not agree that an almost immediate flashback indicates, much more often than not, that a movie or a book has started in the wrong place? When a card has to be inserted with SIX MONTHS EARLIER on it, we may be sure that the director (and the writer, unless he has been overruled) lacks dexterity when it comes to the management of time, key element of cinematic artfulness. Your work at the BBC, under the head-monitorship of Huw Wheldon, disposed you to down-the-middle, fact-backed narration. You always craved a documentary warrant for fictional fancy. When you were directing a version of his memoirs, Field Marshal Montgomery wanted to know your exact responsibilities. After you had explained, he concluded (as you mimicked perfectly) that you were 'commander-in-chief of the whole opewation'. My father arrived at St Paul's as Monty was leaving, to no one's marked regret. When did a nice man last win a decisive battle? And what victory is not at least in part against people on one's own side? I once had dinner in the company of Monty's Viscount son, a genial public relations officer, no doubt much nicer than his father, but for whom no one could care to go over the top.

As Beetle and I were presenting Clare with a suitable bouquet, I was alert to your turning your head, over by the bookshelves at the far corner of the L-shaped room in Farley Court: surreptitious recce. I have no notion of what had been said to you about me; you were always wary of arranged liaisons. The privilege of autocracy is what every film director craves; Final Cut most of all. Who was it you were huddling with in that corner, close to the snacks? Peter Sellers was one of the guests at Clare's sumptuous table. He was kind enough to be amused when I was put on, as Classics masters used to say, to entertain the company. The Deutsches pressed me, like a button, to tell the story of my millionaire uncle Frederick Jessel Benson and how he took my father to the Brighton races in his chauffeur-driven Roller and, without malice, left him there.

After a detour to the paddock to pat his horse, Jessel was driven back to the Connaught where important businessmen were waiting. Thanks to his last florin, my father finally got back to London, on a charabanc. When he burst into Jessel's suite, in righteous rage, Jessel looked up from the conference table and said, 'Good Lord, Cedric, I knew I'd forgotten something'. Nowadays, I should flinch from being lured into a monologue in front of P. Sellers, but I sang well enough for my supper to amuse the company. Nothing beats getting a laugh, dear, does it, especially when the pros are in?

You had a bunched weightiness; tightly packed. I had seen the back of your shaven, rumpled neck, bulging over a field-grey collar in a Pinewood movie or two, in which you played a *jawohl* extra in the S.S. You often Teutonised your own name as Schlay-zinger. Self-mockery added a pickle to your vanity; another way of getting there first. As I approached you, David at hand, I affected deference. Your films had been competent; you were no Antonioni. The mention of his name, or that of any continental director, excited no keen response from you, ever. But then did anyone ever hear Billy Wilder speak well of any other director, except for Lubitsch, whose most famous film, *Ninotchka*, Billy himself had scripted? Stanley Donen was a rarity: he never failed to praise other people, when they deserved it, Billy not least.

By putting you and me together, David Deutsch was aiming to do us and our common employers, Anglo-Amalgamated, a service. His father, Oscar, had been the Mancunian founder of the Odeon cinema chain; David was what the Cambridge University Appointments Board, had he passed through its scathing sieve, might have called 'a Jew but the refined kind'. Towards the end of the war, he had spent a year in Cambridge, attending some institution adjacent to the university. I remember his generosity but only one particular story. He had been waiting for a girl to come to bed. As she approached, naked, she was dabbing cotton wool on 'a place' on her shoulder. 'My little lifetime's companion', she called it. 'It went down like a lift', David told me.

You were not the first John Schlesinger I had met. At the beginning of September 1939, my parents took me to stay with Teddy and Gladys Schlesinger, no relations of yours so far as I know, in their double-gated country house in Sussex. Their double-breasted, blue-suited, eleven-year-old son, another John, had an electric Rolls Royce, an eighth of the size of the real thing. Neither friendly nor unfriendly, he steered along the pebbled paths that enclosed the grass tennis court and rode on into the arboretum while I followed on foot. Teddy was a surgeon who, before he was successful, or deserved to be, volunteered to remove a kidney stone, the first of several, that agonised my father. The novice overreached himself, severed Cedric's urethra. The resulting stricture pained and humiliated him for the rest of his long, shortened life. Today, keyhole surgeons crush kidney stones to passable powder.

Your father, Bernard, was a paediatrician. He and Winifred, your sociable mother, took in several Jewish refugees in 1939 and cared for them with generous attention. An old-style Freudian might wonder whether your homosexuality had a source, at least a primer, in the enduring, unconcealed passion of your parents. You told me how you had surprised them *in medias res* (as you would never say) when they were well advanced in years. Your father, being 'medical', was not embarrassed. Were you? Why did you mention it? Did the primal scene spur you to being a lensed voyeur? I rarely saw my parents kiss, never heard the creak of their Macy's bed through the thin wall that separated their Key Flat bedroom from mine.

You and I had talked easily enough that night for us to meet again in familiar humour. Jo Janni led the way to Godfrey Winn's white and blonde apartment; his own colour scheme, face and corrected hair. Meanwhile, you had seen your Oxford friend Bob Robinson (he in an open car, you on foot) and told him that there was a project you might be doing with me. Bob said, so you said, 'You've got pure gold there!' I came to know Bob for many years when he was the Question Master of all kinds of nice quizzes and allied distractions on the radio. Long connection with the BBC sealed him to minor eminence. Middlebrow, middle-aged, middle-of-the-road, never bumbling beadle, he settled easily into one easy chair after another.

Tenured corporation men often parade some token of contrariness: Jim Cellan-Jones wore socks and sandals in all weathers; cameraman John Hooper dispensed with socks and favoured khaki shorts. I remember him giving a late-night foot massage to a girl in a café in the Piazza San Marco after a day shooting my drama-doc about Lord Byron. Contrary by staying in line, Bob Robinson wore clean shirt and tie, with anchoring slide, waistcoat and regular jacket in a time of open shirts (gold necklets optional) and Left-Bank *blousons*. Was he a shade too proper to be the gentleman he took such trouble to resemble?

Godfrey Winn had typed eighteen pages of an outline for the movie he hoped you had in mind. *Woman on Her Way* was as decorous as what Lizbeth Webb, star of the first stage show I ever saw, *Bless the Bride*, called 'a faiwy fwock', the one time I happened to work with her. That you and Jo considered Winn's screed worth discussing lowered the hurdles. Seated at his shiny table, I was as insolent as may be, a posture warranted, so I imagined, by my recent recruitment as a regular *Sunday Times* fiction reviewer (thirty pounds a week and all the buckshee books, many from Victor Gollancz, I could re-sell at half price). I took being Cyril Connolly's colleague to resemble being a pipped subaltern in a smart regiment, complete with swagger *shtik*.

With his faired hair, Winn was a woman's journalist with a weekly – or was it bi-weekly? – page in the *Daily Express*. His fluted columns comforted dismayed ladies with the sympathy of one who might well have been in their place. Did any kind of current pass between you and him? I think not; nor did I think about it. What was clear, after not many minutes, was that he had no contribution to make to any smart send-up of the early 1960s in-world where TV celebrities, pretty girls, property sharks and dodgy peers, ermine and mini-skirts wallowed, or were shed, in a common pool.

I floated the idea of a modern girl – Jo had an italicised way of pronouncing 'modern' that made it 'mod urn' – kept in a luxurious flat, Mayfair or Belgravia, by a consortium of five men, of various types. They take advantage of the current lazy legislation by forming a limited company to own the flat and sustain its luxury and salaried hostess, at their permanent disposal, off tax. I had heard from Wolf Mankowitz's accountant, Cyril V., that such arrangements were actually current; wasn't that nice Max Bygraves one of the shareholders? The same accountant told me that he enjoyed the weekly favours of an amiable tart who preferred him to fuck her from behind. Why? Did she get more pleasure that way? 'I do actually', she said, 'long as you're not too quick about it. I can lean on my elbows, smoke a cigarette and flick through a magazine, at the same time.'

When I proposed a scene in which, for the annual general meeting of the company, a full-scale nude model of our girl, with caviar pubes, otherwise made out of ice cream, oh those raspberry nipples!, was wheeled in for dessert, Godfrey Winn said, 'This young man frightens me'. I was tall, talkative and I had a lot of black hair. I doubt that I frightened you and Jo. I wished, as too often, even when I want to get out of something, to prove myself indispensable. Shocking the decorous Mr Winn, I proved that I was capable of putting cream on his tart. If you ever considered *Woman on Her Way* a good basis for a movie, you needed me more than I needed you.

By the time we left Mr Winn, with vain promises to come and see him again, you and Jo were hooked on my improvised wickedness. I can't remember what Winn's lay-figure was called; was it Diana, as our eventual heroine was labelled? If so, it was his sole contribution to *Darling*. The story was current, when I was working in old Fleet Street, that now and again G.W. felt a surge of desire. He would then mantle himself in a long black overcoat, large-brimmed black hat, scarf across his face, and head for Kensington Gardens. Guardsmen were on plain-clothed parade, all set to augment their petty stipend for a bob or two in return for a few minutes availability in the bushes. On one such occasion, my source promised, the guardsman pocketed his recompense and, as Winn buttoned and turned to go, said 'You're that Beverley Nichols, aren't you?'

Not many years later, I went to Sotheby's for the auction of a number of effects from Willie Maugham's Villa Mauresque.

The wide mahogany desk at which he had worked while his guests enjoyed themselves, on the far side of the window he had had shuttered to avoid his being distracted by the view, was knocked down to Godfrey Winn, I think it was, for five hundred pounds. Or was it Beverley Nichols?

In pre-Wolfenden days, and nights, few male homosexuals did not fear being nabbed by what you and your friends called 'Mavis' (short for 'Mavis Polizei') and humiliated in the courts, as Peter Wildeblood and Lord Montagu had been, a few years before. As you did not at all deny, fear sharpened the thrill; the illicit doubled as appetiser. 'Sent 'er up!' was a common camp boast. Reminds me: I used to play sixpenny bridge at the Oxford and Cambridge club in the early 1950s. Many of the indifferent players were lawyers of one stripe or several, Cyril Salmon, later a Lord Justice of Appeal, the rarest. One told the story, a chestnut maybe, about a youngish man recently elevated to the bench. At tea one afternoon, he approached an experienced judge and asked, 'What do you give them for buggery?' Choosing a biscuit, his senior said, 'Oh eighteen pence or whatever you happen to have on you'.

Cyril was not the judge in question. I played backgammon with him when we were waiting for a fourth. At some point, after rolling unsuitable dice, he said, 'Oh well, I shall have to open my legs'. I asked if he ever went in fear of those he had sent to jail. No; thanks to the wig and the rig, they seldom recognised him as their judge. One had, on a train, and told him that his trial had been fair and he had no complaints. Cyril delivered a masterly three-hour-long judgment, without notes, back in 1968, in the case of the Notting Hill assailants of black men. Eminently modest, he went into Alzheimer decline in old age. Fortune turns Lear into his own fool.

You and your friends relished being outrageous in the confines of The Biz. In the theatre it was a positive advantage, I was told, to be queer: 'Binkie' Beaumont, the tyrant of

H.M. Tennant, thane of Shaftesbury Avenue, was reported to have turned on a young actor and said: 'You're no good on the stage, you're no good in bed and you're no bloody good to us'. I remember the pleasure you took in sharing ownership with Geoffrey can't-remember-his-name of a Kent Oast House called 'Strawberry Hole'. You couldn't make it up; and if I had you would never have bought it. Oh! Sharpe, was it he was called? You once had an all but rupturous quarrel about who had emptied the fridge and failed to re-stock it with ten quid's worth of provisions.

It was generally assumed, Bryan Forbes told me, that most theatricals 'swung both ways'. I don't think Bryan batted for both sides, but he had played sailor boys, in white ducks, in Pinewood's steady-as-you-go Rule Britannia repertory. He was approached in a theatre interval by a bull on the prowl who was indignant when rebuffed. Bryan was a rarity: he became nicer after his career foundered. Writing speeches for Madame Thatcher gained him no knighthood.

You told me early on in our association that I should never regret not being queer. No one yet said 'gay', although Ivor Novello had a long-running musical called *Gay's the Word* at the Hippodrome. Homo-sex had, and has, in truth, no temptations for me. Should we analyse that? I like, and sentimentalise, women not least because I never went to school with any of them. You had no shortage of bedfellows but you were always fearful, less of the law than of being ditched by the next charmer who lured you into caring about him. Age was the dreaded stalker; money an unreliable alleviant.

You told me, in the Eighties, how you used to go to a gay 'Bath House' (in New York, was it?) where you'd take a room, undress and wait for a tap on the door. One time a very handsome young fellow knocked, was admitted and then saw your domed, ample, not young person on the bed and, with polite apologies, begged to be excused. Rumour had it that you had at least one affair with a female. Did you indeed say that it was quite enjoyable, but nothing like the real thing? And did some adhesive partner of yours not say to a handsome rival, camp Penelope to Calypso, 'You were his true love, but I'm getting the real estate'? I'll bet he did.

You, Jo and I had meeting after meeting, and then more. Much time was spent disinterring contentious moments while you were making *Billy Liar*. You reminded him of the axed C.U. which would have boosted Julie Christie to the stardom which Jo insisted she had already, for God's sake, achieved. He had signed her to a contract which we now had to honour with a script that was sufficiently – here it came again – *modern* to justify his investment. Bickering bonded your *association*, as you regularly called it, not least when saying 'This association is coming to an end', which it never did, except perforce, when Jo was stricken. The banter extended, when fully alight, to your calling Jo a 'war criminal'. '*Ma*, John!', he would say. He never abused you in any reciprocal way, though you and Alan Bates had discomfited him, on that protracted location in Bradford, by your conspiratorial closeness. You gave Jo an alibi when Stella grew suspicious; he promised to know what to do, whom to call, if the pre-Wolfenden Polizei made trouble. I was the third in a double act, there to prove that we had had productive meetings. To claim that I was paid a pittance would be overdoing it.

In search of background, we went to Bentley's oyster bar in the City to have lunch with 'de Bess Rogan'. Beth was Diana Scott's comely prototype. Known to Jo for several years, she was a one-time Rank starlet, plucked from Pinewood's array of beauties by millionaire Tony Samuel. She volunteered to be our source for the wicked and wanton ways of the jet-setters whom we proposed to pulverise. Your belief in research remained incurable. Could it ever procure anything to match, for 1960 instance, that image of Marcello Mastroianni with the helicoptered statue of Jesus which began *La Dolce Vita* with celestial clatter? As we leaned towards her on our tall bar stools, Beth told us nothing wicked enough to scandalise Godfrey Winn.

As if in a play by Ionesco (not yet trendy in translation), it turned out that I had been in the same house at Charterhouse as your cousin Chrissy Raeburn, whose name, I had never guessed, had been changed from Regensberg, your mother's maiden name. Chrissy had been a memorable Dauphin when G.B. Shaw's *Saint Joan* was the C'house school play. I can still hear him saying 'Another lecture, *thank you*'. I never imagined that he was a Jew; nor did he, I think. Your Jewishness resembled mine, 'liberal', inescapable, undenied, otherwise all but irrelevant, we imagined. June 1967 was a few years ahead. Assimilation the ambition of all our tribe, our families were long enough established in England to license insolence. Every Yorick relies on the applause of the court he teases. What Carthusians of my day called 'being festive' draws its rewards and its daggers.

You and I had several Jo-less, never joyless, meetings in the neat little terrace house in Peel Street that you referred to as 'an upper and a downer'. You showed me your present cupboard: all through the year you picked up bargains which might later be wrapped for appropriate occasions. Foresight is not my thing. You hated your neighbours, you told me. At the weekend, you were liable to throw open your street window and scream obscenities, loud evidence of frustrations which they had done little to excite. We talked around what we wanted to satirise. Your mimicry was my cabaret. You took pleasure in entertaining and had the grace to be entertained. If exasperated by your caution, when it came to anything new, I never looked at my watch, except to see if I could squeeze in a rubber of bridge at Crockford's before my cheap day return ticket to Colchester lapsed.

In overdue time, I proposed that I go away and do a month or two's hard work on a draft script before I showed you and Jo anything more. Then you (meaning he) could either pay me some proper(ish) money or we would go our ways. Some nice man who lived in Grosvenor House rented Beetle and me his cottage in Le Rouret, a few miles north of Cagnes-sur-Mer; five pounds a week in the very cold English winter of early 1963. It was sometimes warm enough in the *arrière-pays* for us to take deck chairs onto the long grassy slope common to all four cottages in our enclave. One afternoon, as I was re-reading my morning's pages, I was startled by the silent proximity of a man with a curious smile. He might have been a spy; as indeed he had been. Peter Churchill was no relation of Winston; the coincidental surname saved his life when he was captured by the Gestapo while serving in SOE. At the time of his arrest, he was actually serving Odette, in a hotel bed. The look-out whom they had posted had either done a bunk or made an insufficient whistle to unlatch the lovers.

Lacking grand connections, Odette was treated much more cruelly by her captors than Winston's namesake. She and Peter C. married after the war. She was awarded the George Cross, he something less meritorious. There is a subject no one has broached, even after the deaths of both of them: the uneasiness between two heroes who could not quite forgive or forget the perhaps unmentioned imbalance between them. Had Churchill not escaped being brutalised, would the marriage have lasted? Ambiguities have had little place in film, British film anyway. What did P.C. say to me? No more than a sudden good afternoon; any excuse to see if he could reproduce wartime slipperiness. All the world is stagier than I ever quite accept.

After I had compiled a hundred pages or so, I sent word to you and you flew down to Nice. Cut to you sitting on the bench under the lee of the outdoor steps to the cottage door. In pink, cuff-linked shirtsleeves, wearing glasses with pale blue plastic frames, marginally camp in those days, you sat slantwise as you conned my unique pages. I never could compose with carbon paper in the machine. Affecting to be reading some new novel for the *S. T.*, I tried to draw omens from your expression, the speed or thoughtfulness with which you turned a page. What writer is free of submissive apprehension once his work is in another's hands? I still wait for ticks in my margin.

To be totally honest wiz you, as Jo would say, often, I cannot recover from memory's cluttered floor what your verdict was. That you were not wholeheartedly enthusiastic I can guarantee; that would have sprung me from your power. At the same time, to judge from the geniality that marked your stay with us, you were not a little impressed. 'How do we do it, dear?' took precedence over enthusiasm. Had I been more experienced, I should have recognised apprehension lest anyone else be credited for whatever appeared on the screen. You were torn between embracing my ideas and dreading that not all of them might pass for yours; so did Mr Kubrick wince at wit.

I was innocent (and vulgar) enough to look for nothing but fun and money in making movies. Fiction was what mattered. My new novel, *Lindmann*, published later that year, contained a full-length screenplay that made sport with the distortions that ambitious conceit can work on sombre facts. One night you took us to the Hôtel de Paris at Monte Carlo for a Michelin-starred meal. During the *riz de veau*, the roof slid open and framed the stars as they switched on their nightly twinkle. We laughed a lot.

Back in Harold Macmillan's twilight, I cannot count, even in dozens, how many times I took the train from Colchester (thirteen and sixpence for a day return) and up to Liverpool Street, and thence to the 36, Bruton Street office where you and I and Jo rehashed sequences which, at very long last,

I took away to the country, and pasted and polished into a first draft recognisable as *Darling* in embryo. I always work better and faster on my own; I don't have to explain to myself why Arthur and Martha say Hullo, not Hi! (English people rarely did till twenty years ago; similarly 'bored of').

You came down, with a present of smoked eel, and stayed with us during the week that Macmillan announced that, after the then usual cryptic conclave within the Tory party, Alec Douglas-Home was to be foisted on the country as the next Prime Minister. Your imitation of the earl's prognathous false modesty hit the mark, what there was of it. We did a lot of laughing, not least at and with Jo. I was innocent enough to imagine the three of us equal partners. Since Jo was a client, as you and I were, of Richard Gregson's agency, I trusted everyone to be, as the squaddies used to say, pissing in the same pot. The nearer we got to a script that you didn't wince at and Jo didn't say was '*nyein nyein*' (pronounced *à la française*, meaning cheesy), the more unworthy I thought it to concede inferiority by rattling my empty can.

I am not sure when precisely in 1963 your sister Susan killed herself, not long after her lover, the playwright John Whiting, died of testicular cancer, as had my Cambridge friend David Gore-Lloyd ten years earlier. Photographs prove how much Susan resembled Julie Christie. She and Whiting's wife alternated at his bedside. You blamed your mother for honouring a dinner date on the night Susan killed herself. Who knows what, if anything, your mother could have done? What did you? Susan had tried before; she would almost certainly have tried again. Saving other people can be a form of vanity, Jesus knows. 'Better save yourself', Shelley said, to Byron, in a storm on Lake Leman, not foolishly. That script I wrote about Lord B. was never made. You went off 'period' after *Far from the Madding Crowd* bombed in the US. I derived a short biography from my research for the dumped script.

Metro's London lawyer, whose name was something like Oscar Buselink, managed to chisel $50,000 off my fee by asking to see my bibliography. A wiser man would have denied having such a thing. O.B. then claimed that I had acted illicitly by reading standard works on his Lordship.

When I'd written what you and Jo agreed was a final screenplay of *Darling*, it seemed to take forever to find the funds and complete the cast to start shooting. As soon as Stanley Donen commissioned a screenplay of *Two for the Road*, Beetle and I and the children went for a holiday in our little *spiti* on Ios. If you want anything to happen in the world, turn your back on it. It may not be nice, but it'll be something. That September, after our spell on the Aegean, Beetle and I went on to Rome (and stayed at the Hotel Byron). I went to American Express in the Piazza di Spagna and collected a handwritten letter from you at the *poste restante*. In elegant script, you let me know that shooting was beginning and that you and Jo had enrolled Edna O'Brien to do some bits and pieces on the script. The credit would, of course, still be mine. It was an apology and a relegation, typical of directors as soon as that green light shines. Sydney Pollack and Bob Redford did much the same thing to Bill Goldman. I hope I was wise enough not to reply to your letter. There is durable merit in Louis B. Mayer's advice when crossed, 'Turn the other cheek; turn the other cheek… and bide your time'.

Beetle and I found a large, bright first floor flat in Vigna Clara, out towards the Via Cassia, and I settled down to write my script for Stanley Donen. When the *Darling* unit came to Rome to shoot a few scenes, you stayed at Caesar's Palace, I think it was called, in the Villa Borghese gardens. Things were already going so well that you had grown markedly grander, and rounder. Green lights do that to people. Fed by whoever was doing publicity, the trade press had already carried several stories of how well it was all going. My name was seldom mentioned.

When a press conference was scheduled in Rome, you asked me to come in with you. Your Italian was not as good as mine, you said. I said I was tired of playing the elephant to your Hannibal.

The ease with which *Two for the Road* came to me dispelled any notion that you and Jo were my sole passport to the movies. Hurt gave me strength, as Nietzsche promised (but did not exemplify). I wrote the first draft in a few delicious weeks and mailed it to London. Stanley called, very promptly, to say it was going to be the best thing he ever did. Did you ever bring yourself to say anything like that to anyone? We drove back to London, at Stanley's invitation, to go over a couple of things. I said to Beetle, 'Nice he didn't ask Edna O'Brien'. Beetle had edited Edna's *August Is a Wicked Month* and saved it from not a few ineptitudes, as Edna herself was good enough to say. While we were staying with Stanley, I made an excursion to Pinewood, your base for shooting some early scenes with Dirk and Julie. There had been a problem with Julie's cozzies. The first designer you hired made her look, in Jo's unfoolish opinion, just like a boy, for God's sake. Julie Harris rushed out and bought a smart choice of ready-mades for whose design (and sprinting delivery) she would receive an Oscar.

Every summer for many years, when we were in Lagardelle, I expected, and received, a telephone call from the then offshore *Île de Ré* where Jim Clark's wife Laurence had a house. Talking French gave our conversation a borrowed intimacy, confirmed by the second person singular. Jim was often not there with her; usually he was in the States, being very well paid for giving a second or third operation on some movie in the cutting room. I enjoyed talking to Laurence because of the freedom a second language supplies, the flow of genuine imposture. Jim and Laurence drove down from the *Île de Ré* at least a couple of times to have a meal with us at Lagardelle, never following any urgent invitation. Jim seemed relaxed and often amused, and amusing. After *The Glittering Prizes* was on BBC2, he took the trouble to make a cut of his recording with the sections in which you and Jo were veiled, just and justly, as the fictional director and producer of the movie that Adam Morris won his Oscar for after they had not considered taking him with them to Los Angeles. I imagined at the time that Jim was being slightly salty in sitting you down to be nicely ridiculed, Jo more than you: the director, Mike Clode, was a stitched-up version of you and Peter Hall. It did not then occur to me that there was an element of malice in Jim's making sure that you had clear sight of how I had caricatured the two of you. With made-in-England sportsmanship, you showed no symptom of resentment.

When Beetle and I were staying in Yvette Mimieux/ Donen's house on Oak Pass, Beverly Hills, Jim and Laurence came up to have tea with us. Back in London, we had them to dinner a couple of times, once to meet Will and Susan Boyd because I thought that Jim might direct a movie that Will was writing. Laurence talked of asking us to dinner so often that it sounded more like an excuse for not doing so than preliminary to setting a date. We were not offended; our social schedule was full enough. Then, whenever it was, in the 1980s it must have been, Laurence asked us to dinner on a specific night and we said we were looking forward to it. On the morning of the set date, Jim called to say that, owing to a personal matter, the dinner was cancelled.

I was guileless enough to ask if there was anything I could do to help. Jim said brusquely that there was nothing and rang off. I never spoke to him again, though I should like to think that I wrote a note of congratulation when he won his Oscar (for *The Killing Fields*), as I did to you, when you did. Soon before he died, Jim wrote a privately printed autobiography. Will Boyd, who was mentioned with admiration, sent me a copy. Laurence had edited a short movie of his, *The Trench* I think it was called. When I checked the index, as Cyril

Connolly would, I found that I was mentioned only in a brief hostile sentence or two, accusing me of making an undue fuss about antisemitism.

Laurence had told me that throughout the war she had lived in the so-called *Zone Libre*, where – although French citizens – her family had had to register, under the Vichy law, as Jews. When, in 1943, the Germans invaded the region, they had access, of course, to local police records. Every day, Laurence's parents expected the Milice or the Gestapo to arrive and arrest them all. The day never came; the allies did. Laurence told me, during one of our Saturday chats, that she had taught Jim all about sex. Speaking French gave such instruction a matter of fact aspect. Jim remains an enigma. I never said an unkind word about him to anyone. Not a few of the people who have proved most spiteful during my life have been those to whom I rendered some signal service. Clare Boothe Luce posted the warning: 'I don't know why he says nasty things about me. I never did him a good turn.'

You sent me a three-page telegram from New York after *Darling* opened. There were lines around the block. Coining a hit mended whatever needed darning between you and me and Jo. The studios couldn't wait for our next picture. The prospect of fat fees and percentages confirmed our solidarity. If we had kept our cool, we might have, and should have, thought of something more wicked and *mod-urn* than Woodrow Wyatt's idea of Julie as Bathsheba Everdene in Hardy's *Far from the Madding Crowd*. It appealed to Metro because it could be in production as soon as I had written the script. You and Jo and I conferred only to celebrate. At the same time, the Woolf brothers commissioned me, for $75,000, to adapt and you to direct Iris Murdoch's *A Severed Head*. Jack Priestley had already made a play of it. When was there ever a shortage of money for old rope? How many people have done for themselves with it!

Your elegant rendering of Hardy's verbose masterpiece is now something of a classic, especially in the dim light of a recent re-make. My heart was never in it; my head was all it needed. Looking back is always likely to cause a crick in the aging neck. It now seems a big shame that you and I and Jo did not take a deep breath in the time success had bought and come up with something bolder and braver. You could not have done '*Far*', as we soon abbreviated it, better than you did, but it was bound to be reproduction furniture. You backed out of *A Severed Head* when Jimmy Woolf tried to force Dirk on you as the leading man. As *Darling* still proves, Dirk was always better than one thought. He would have been close to perfect for the weak charmer in Murdoch's tribute to Rudi Nassauer. You had bolder and braver ideas. The result was *Sunday, Bloody Sunday*. You came up to me after the first night and I managed only tepid congratulations. We had sat in the dress circle with Clive Donner and Roman Polanski. The topic was bolder than the treatment: that kiss between Peter Finch and whatever the swinging boy's name was came as a shock, never a thrill; appetiser with no main course. Roman made a wanking gesture. Gareth Wigan said to Beetle, when she failed to enthuse, 'It does say that half a cake is better than no cake at all. That's worth thinking about.' 'Yes', she said, 'it is, for roughly thirty seconds.' Gareth's cake was Georgia Brown; he would have done better to settle for a biscuit.

I remember Glenda in *Sunday Bloody Sunday* making Nescaff in a hurry with water from the hot tap; not a lot else. How much does one ever remember from a movie? Usually, it's a line not an image: Edward G.: 'Is this the end of Rico?'; Clint: 'Make my day'; Bogart: 'This'll put you in solid with your boss'; Zero Mostel: 'If you've got it, flaunt it'; Monica: '*Diec'otto anni e molti, molti mesi*'; Landru: '*Ça, c'est mon petit baggage*'. But then there is that last-instant look back at the sneezing occupant of the room he has just left by Walter Matthau in *The Taking of Pelham 123*.

I went with Jo to collect the latest script of *Sunday, Bloody Sunday*, from Penelope Gilliatt's apartment on Central Park West. She was an adept climber on all available ladders, journalism her way of covering ambitious tracks with suitable salt. I remember having dinner with her at the Hilary Rubinsteins when she had just returned to London, in horizontal form, thanks to whatever she had taken her to arm her for the flight. Her flash situation at the *New Yorker* had been short-circuited when it was discovered that one of her caustic columns had been cribbed from some other source. My mother would say that she had outsmarted herself. It was said that she was a great wit. Did her applauded script show any signs of it? Did she ever write another? I think she spent herself on *Sunday, etc.*, not that one word remains. Oh, I lie: a twitch on the hoist from the memory well has just come up with: 'Here come those tired old tits again!' An unfunny-for-your-money provocation without credibility. Or do some people say things like that? Is there anything some people don't say? Penelope told us that her recent electricity bill had been for $150,000. The consumption for the entire block had been wired to her meter. It took some time and litigation to convince the electric company that she had not left too many lights on.

The Wolfenden report liberated you to good effect. You asked me to read Herlihy's *Midnight Cowboy*. I wished I thought I had anything to contribute, other than second-hand cabbage. The homoerotic world, and its deviations, kindled no secret appetite. After the movie was a big, big hit, and won you the Oscar you didn't get for *Darling*, Jo Janni came to regret that he too had 'passed', but agreed we had had nothing to contribute. The word is that Doctor Clark and his scissors, not to mention very good music and lyrics, gave the final cut its compelling urgency. I remember Jon Voigt thrusting a white (was it?) telephone into the mouth of a john who had assumed that he was the kind of cowboy he could ride. Otherwise: Dustin's urgent limp. The Oscar gave you a shot at pretty well anything you chose. Quite rightly, you went for something classy, Nathanael West's *The Day of the Locust*: no nibble quite as tasty as the hand that feeds you. I knew and admired the book, but you went with your lucky writer, Waldo Salt and why not, until he lost his savour? I never saw the movie; it came and went, as did others, quickly.

You had long abandoned the Peel Street upper-and-downer for a big house in the Hollywood Hills. When Julie dumped Warren (his tactful way of saying that he dumped her?), she came and stayed in the hideaway at the top of a retractable ladder to your loft. You showed it to me the night I came to dinner with Christopher Isherwood and other now candid friends. I was alone in L.A. for whatever buck-ballasted reason. Isherwood is the only person I can remember asking me whether I was, as the liberated jargon had it, 'gay'. When I confessed that I was not, I felt out of things, but not sorry.

You were said to have relished the sexual *gourmandises* available on Hollywood Boulevard with conspicuous appetite. Is it true that you particularly fancied a bed full of Japanese boys? Should I not say so? Was there anything wrong with such succulent fodder? You gorged yourself while you could. What your movie projects were, I fail to recall. I do remember coinciding in L.A. with you and Jo. As we walked down Hollywood Boulevard, John Calley slowed down in his big convertible. For a moment you assumed, I could tell, that he wanted to talk to you. In fact, he confirmed a meeting I had with him the next day and off he went. The three of us went to *Hamburger Heaven* and supped on, I wish, unaffected hamburgers. Mine made me sick all night; I never bought junk food again. What did we talk about, sudden Old Pros? Old prosing: nothing that anything came of.

The next day, I went to my meeting with John Calley in whichever studio had persuaded him to drop anchor. His real passion was for sailing; his yacht sprang to three masts, I was told. As too often, I was being well paid for a script which was admired but eventually came to nothing. Calley had a cottage office on whichever lot it was. He told me how, when he was brought in to beef up the current projects, he had been quick to axe a starless movie that was being shot in Spain and had gone grossly over budget. The rushes were junk. The director, Sam Fuller, was highly rated by *Les Cahiers du Cinéma* but had no golden record. Next case. A few weeks later, Calley's secretary in the outer office buzzed him to say that there was someone demanding to see him and he had a gun. There was no back door to the cottage, so Calley had to say to let him in. Fuller was playing the Lone Ranger. He said, 'Are you the goddam sonofabitch who cancelled my movie?' Calley figured a dead man might as well tell the truth: 'Yes, I damned well did and I'll tell you why. You're a lousy director and that silly gun doesn't make you a better one. Worst rushes I ever saw in my life.' Fuller's tough guy expression puckered into tears. He said, 'I know, you're right', or so Calley told me. I once saw a Fuller movie entitled *Dead Pigeon on Beethoven Street*. Did anyone else?

You did some good work over the years but you learned, as I and no shortage of others did, that the Oscar was at once sceptre and hoodoo. Bob Evans claimed that *Marathon Man* redeemed your commercial reputation, but it did little to enhance your reputation for daring. I was working with a friend of Bob's, on a second re-make of *A Night to Remember*. I can't even remember the poor guy's name. I recall only that he wore an expensive fur jacket on a hot California afternoon. He was dying, never complaining, of AIDS. Bob Evans gave him access to his Beverly Hills house and, sportingly indeed, gave him the joke reel that you and Dustin and that other guy made while shooting *Marathon Man*. Each of you took it in turns to send up Bob; you and, yes, Roy Scheider did well, but Dustin was king of the hill, reproducing Bob's jerks and jitters, realistic dildo for prop.

Bob was happy to say that *Marathon Man* restored your reputation for success and so it did, for a while, at the price of having no credible content. Dustin did a literal re-run of what he had done for Mike Nichols in *The Graduate* and Larry Olivier did you a laconic favour as the Nazi dentist with not too much to say because he had difficulty remembering his lines. Even in a manifest concoction, Dustin insisted on going through his Method routine. When he wanted to precede a scene with Olivier, which took place, supposedly, after Dustin's character had been running, by doing a lap or two around the lot, in order to be realistically out of breath, Larry is alleged to have said, 'You could always try acting'. Dustin was a movie star; Olivier starred in movies.

Bob Evans helped you back onto some kind of a pedestal, in commercial terms, but a few years later you fell more heavily than any number of king's men could ever repair. You alone knew what led you to make *Honkytonk Freeway*. You told me that you and Jimmy Clark, who failed to come to your rescue this time around, had no idea that your 'off-the-wall-comedy' was anything but hilarious. It was not so much a flop as a catastrophe. It lost Thorn EMI over $20,000,000 and you your retrieved kudos. Plenty of excellent directors have had dips in their fortunes; your fall left you permanently lamed in executive eyes. They had tolerated your sneers at Hollywood – *The Day of the Locust* not the least – because you had had a big hit and the Oscar and because stars liked working with you. All of a sudden you were a pariah – much like our friend and sometime agent Richard Gregson after he had been caught by Natalie Wood making love to her secretary on the living room carpet. Richard was as good as run out of town. Did you know he was nominated, back in 1960, for an Oscar for his share in writing *The Angry Silence?* You stayed in California after *Honkytonk Freeway* and kept your friends, but you were forever off the A-list.

To your credit, you took it on the chin, as Paul Theroux was advised by V.S. Naipaul (one England's golden treasures I never reckoned twenty-one carat), and boxed on. Literally, in the case of the little movies you did for television about Guy Burgess and Anthony Blunt. Both advertised and gloried in your contradictions. Both main characters were traitors by conventional standards, Blunt almost certainly the nastier. Their outrageousness, overt and covert, appealed to you and to Alan Bennett. The two sparklers could scarcely have been better mounted. Who but a spoilsport could fail to be amused by your two-faced coinage of their mythical instances? Were there gay Nazis, I wonder, whose duplicity might have been equally naughty? If *Zelig* came close, it lacked insolence. That's the key element in your whole *oeuvre*, once *Darling* billed you as some kind of satirist. You flourished no political axe, but you did grind one, with no shortage of sparks, when you had a chance to shock the straights and, for a capper, garner their prizes, large and small. I once asked you why you had never been given one of the knighthoods lavished on theatricals and athletes. The CBE was as far as you got in initialled distinction. Once your parents were dead, you told me, you had no appetite for straight honours. You ventured only so close to the wind but you did love to feel it in your sales.

You had enjoyed Hollywood but you returned, never retired, to London with a certain sense of relief. The house in Victoria Road was a foursquare statement of bourgeois homecoming. When Dirk came back from the South of France to live near Harrods, you gave a gay party in his honour. With a contrariness that he never failed to parade, he arrived early, when you were still in the kitchen. Did he bring you a present? He looked at the house and said, 'John, this is a rich man's house! And you've had nothing but flops!' Did he never forgive you for not going ahead with *A Severed Head*? Trust Jimmy Woolf to tell him the details. Dirk was never quite honest about sex, as you were; perhaps he thought your invitation pinned an unwanted label on him. Or did he behave differently in private, when he said, 'They dropped off years ago, dear'? Dirk combined charm with testiness. He wished he had been accepted for what he never was.

You returned to California, for a while, some time in the late Eighties. Was it *Pacific Heights* that baited the hook? Melanie Griffith and I've forgotten his name (oh, Michael Keaton) were apt casting, plus A.N. Other, but there was no concealing that it was no more than a decent B movie. I recall asking you about the key moment in the plot, when the young couple find that the Keaton character has cleared out his apartment and disappeared and then discover a scrap of paper lodged in the floorboards, wasn't it?, with an address on it, thanks to which the plot could move on. I asked you whether the address had been left there on purpose by the villain of the piece, to lure the nice young couple into a devilish trap. You sighed and confessed that you and the screenwriter had not been up to saying 'But wait!'

That a single scrap with an address on it should have been left in a scoured apartment *by mistake* promised that you had not but-waited for the twist that might have dignified the movie. Suppose that the Keaton character had become so fascinated by the innocence of the young couple that he could not resist leaving them a clue. Now you have the story you never told, of a villain who cannot quite bear to disappear without trace. Yes, the movie would then have to move into dark territory, but it just might have had something of the devil to be found in Billy Wilder's *Double Indemnity*. Billy's pic was scarcely credible, but nobody left before the end.

You had the courage and the connections to go on working; never again for a big studio. You must have sold the Victoria Road house before that brief return to L.A. When you came back to London you bought a handsome duplex flat not far from us in SW7. You and Michael Childers had stayed with us in Lagardelle and did some fancy cooking. Did we talk about a movie? I think you had some kind of a treatment about a man who dies and is so grievously missed by his lady that he comes back from the Other Side to comfort her or encourage her to find someone else or something. *Blithe Spirit* it wasn't; nor, on recent second viewing, was *Blithe Spirit*. You and I never failed to be at ease with each other but we knew that we had had our chance to cap *Darling*, if we could, and had been hustled out of it; our bad, as the kids were saying in the Nineties.

Marty Scorsese had passed some allegedly promising script to you. I had just been enrolled by Stanley Kubrick on what became, after a long pregnancy, *Eyes Wide Shut*, but I had a few sessions with you, playing at being serious over something that excited little enthusiasm from you, none from me. You never asked what I was working on. It amused me to make no mention of Mr K. I was too busy with Kubrick even to notice that you once again absconded from England in order to do that last Hollywood movie, *The Next Best Thing*, with Madonna and Rupert Everett who had enhanced his notoriety by publishing his history as a sexual hireling. You were no longer a director with whom it was a privilege to work. You worked for them and they had you know it.

There's a nasty, twisted *donnée* in the mastering of a one-time master by two quasi-stars who take their pleasure in the knowledge that he has a job only because they chose him. Billy Wilder might have had some fun with that one. Before you had a third or fourth chance to come back to Blighty, you were struck down, while trying to draw fresh breath in

Palm Springs. The story was that Sinatra offered to fly you to London in his private jet. Perhaps you were in too bad a state for that. Perhaps, the offer was more show than businesslike. I called you in Palm Springs. Our conversation was brief, if fond. You found it difficult to speak. I said I'd call again. We knew I wouldn't. Not many laughs there. Fuck 'em all, dear, you used to say; God knows you did your best.

Love, Freddie.

Dear Ken,

How many people, other than touts, ever addressed you as
'Dear Kenneth'? Few; Kenny none, I imagine. Having others
call you 'Ken' sanctioned you to have, as they used to say, one
hand up. As for Tynan, no common name, to whom did it
ever attract attention save to yourself? Your first advertised
persona was as an Oxford aesthete: purple corduroy jacket and
trousers; whatever shoes – buckled not laced? – were chic and
rare in the couponed Nineteen Forties. Did anyone ever see
you wearing a tie? Old School, never. If Greek, they might
call you *Hapax*, Mister One-Off. I do recall you rigged in a
bullfighter's double-string toggled noose. Whatever became
you, you became, almost. You needed no stage to be stagey;
small art to be arty. The Player King was your sole part in a West
End theatre before flipping that magisterial seat in the stalls.
Did you play the king as if someone had just played the ace?
That verdict (not on you) belongs to George S. Kaufmann, a
classy 1930s New York bridge player renowned for lancing wit,
co-authored stage plays, charge account with a fancy madam.

Was it Edmund or Edgar who said 'God stand up for
bastards'? You steered by your bar sinister, your *morgue* the
merrier from being a provincial baronet's by-blow. Did you
ever run for President of the Oxford Union? No shortage
of celebrities first lorded it with that presidential tinkle; you
topped them, from below, by making the office of 'Librarian'
a rare distinction; never before, or after, did it distinguish
anyone. What did you read at Oxford, apart from the
New Yorker? Your taste crossed the Atlantic before you did.
Did you get a First? Did you as much as stay for Finals?
You were a sudden London Name in the late 1940s.

After the publication of *Childe Harold*, Byron woke to find himself famous; you woke others by the force of your knocking. You had swarmed aboard the *Evening Standard* and challenged the sitting drama critic, Sir Beverley Baxter M.P., to a scribblers' duel on the no-quarter deck. It ended with Max Beaverbrook awarding you both ears and B.B.'s tile. Did you defend some maligned *avant-gardiste* or plant a *pic* in a sacred cow? What you were hot for above all was your own celebrity.

After you had long-jumped from Isis idol to metropolitan *enfant terrible*, Terence Rattigan caught a packet, in dialogue form between you and his nice Aunt Edna, for wanting to have things both ways – in *The Deep Blue Sea*, wasn't it? – in case he lost his matinée audiences: hence daring themes, reticent treatment. 'Before you could say *naif*', there's a vintage piece of Tynan smart-assery worthy of George Jean Nathan. What editor, however high his falute, would print it today? 'Before you could say knife' itself no longer figures in the platitude kit that supplies televised tongues with 'decade', 'inappropriate', 'amazing', 'iconic', 'issues' and 'spiralling out of control'. Representing no political or aesthetic school, you stood very tall, nothing if not striking, never handsome, gauntly blanched, colourfully caparisoned in a time of grey flannel bags, leather-patched elbows and admirers of C.P. Snow, that swollen, now melted, flake of the *neiges d'antan*. Translated to the *Observer*, you were Shaftesbury Avenue's shaftiest dandy, married to Dundy, Elaine, smart booty from the raid on N.Y.C. that left you a perennial postulant for stateside fame and, less easily acquired, fortune.

When Peter Wildeblood and Lord Montagu of Beaulieu were arrested, in early 1954, you had the instant *m'as-tu vu?* courage to stand loud bail for them. Their offence was not only, as the law used to say, sodomy but also – hardly less heinous – sharing their favours with Other Ranks; aircraftsmen, weren't they? After our two should-have-known-betters were sentenced to some months in prison, a Cambridge friend of mine wrote a wicked number for the next Footlights 'Smoker'. I remember only 'Lord Mount-a-few of Beaulieu', but there was much more where that came from. Renowned for camp, the all-male audience upstairs in the Dorothy Café uttered not a murmur of displeasure. Was Tony Becher fuelled by personal animus? Absolutely not: he was playing for laughs. Opportunism, like perversity, has no heart, would you not agree?

That Wildeblood's name recalled Oscar was fortune's bitchy *repêchage*. Beaulieu rode his bad luck with such a good seat (prison, he said, was nothing like as punitive as being a Mons officer cadet) that he incurred only admiration and, I imagine, lost no friends he cared to keep. The affair did more to accelerate the abolition of a vindictive law than to chasten anyone who batted for the other side. The common assumption was that you swung both ways, though none of your many recorded sexual scores indicate as much. Nice that the son of the chairman of the 1957 Wolfenden Report, which recommended rescinding the cruel law, soon came out in his true colours. Any old irony, as you might say. As for Oscar, what he went to jail for a year or two in turn-of-the century London – sex with under-age boys culled from the street – would have him sent down for ten times as long today and with a larger chaser of obloquy.

In the summer of 1954, after the Cambridge Footlights' sell-out success, thanks not least to your review, at the Phoenix Theatre in the West End, you invited Jonathan Miller, Bricusse and me to a party in a big London house I took to be yours and Elaine's. I suspect it was on a short lease, like the marriage, during which she produced a daughter called Tracy, a name soon as naff in U-England as it may once have sounded Philadelphia story-like in the US. Amiable as you could be, your slithery handshake codded no lasting contract.

When you introduced me to Frankie Howerd, a comedian as popular as he was outrageous, and told him how brilliant I was, he looked at me, two, three, and then said, 'I hate talent'. Your pool was all deep end. Many years later (that ever-widening bracket of time), my friend Ken McLeish was invited to go and see Howerd about some project to which I was not privy. F.H. was in the bathtub when his door was opened to Ken, whose appearance made no sort of louche promise. Before proceeding to business, F. asked Ken to lend him a helping hand. Ken told me no more, except that, whenever the time came, Howerd did not warm to whatever idea Ken had in his other hand.

Soon after *Out of the Blue* closed, I went, thanks to a Cambridge studentship, on my solo travels to France, Spain, Algiers, Morocco, Naples, where I heard of and tasted pizza for the first time. I spotted a racked, dated copy of the *Observer* and, scanning it with touristic shamelessness, happened on your review of *An Evening with Beatrice Lillie*. You must have said choice things about Bea, but I recall only that you contrasted her rare quality with the mereness of Leslie Bricusse, your *quondam* guest, my *entrée* into the Biz. 'Drastically cut', you said of Leslie, 'he might 'scape whipping'. Was I sorry for Leslie? The Duc de la Rochefoucauld has the answer. As for ''scape whipping', there was a crack for some biographer to plumb while tallying your pleasures. I was getting six pounds ten shillings a week as co-author of some of the material that you recommended, probably rightly, for scissoring. Did I feel punctured? Not even pricked. In my unduly heavy luggage (a never-worn pinstripe suit was folded in my kit), I had a fat wad of pages of what I knew would be my first published novel.

Leslie was wise and tough enough to take your kick in the pants as a help on the way to success. Thanks to Bea, he played the salmon thrusting upwards in the A-stream. Your diaries tell of how a few nights after you had panned Noël Coward's musical *Look After Lulu!*, adapted from a Feydeau farce, you walked into whatever restaurant was chic of the week, and saw Coward sitting, alone, at his expected best table. Did you slink haughtily to your corner? And then were you just a little alarmed to see Noël heading across in your direction? Whatever you expected, it cannot have been: 'You're a cunt, Mr T. Now come and have some dinner with me.' The ace of trumps was trumped.

Beetle and I gave a party, in our roach-ridden flat on, not to say under, Chelsea Embankment, to celebrate the publication of *Obbligato*. You brought Elizabeth Jane Howard, a beauty in her late twenties already well-known for *After Julius*, a novel which paraded her affair with Arthur Koestler. Was your marriage to Elaine already not enough for you? Michael Ayrton told me, over a quarter of a century later, that Jane had a penchant for pleasures of a kind that chimed with yours. Elaine later announced that she dumped you because she was not turned on by being whipped until she bled. You claimed that she lied: you drew the line at drawing blood. Weals within weals was another matter. Elaine's waspish novel *The Dud Avocado* owes its title to you, does it not? Don Quickshot, that was you in your prime.

Our party was loud with young and postulant on-the-makers. Julian Jebb went up to Peter Green, the best literary friend I ever had, and asked what he had to do to become a fiction reviewer, as Peter now was, fortnightly, for *The Daily Telegraph*. Peter said, 'It helps if you get a double first and win the Craven scholarship'. Did you and I say more than hullo to each other? Your presence was compliment enough.

That party was the last we gave before Suez. Larry Durrell's *Alexandrian Quartet* soon supplied a requiem for imperial *ton perdu*. Did you admire it? Looking back – that now addictive, rueful, reliably revenue-raising British exercise – I wonder if you were ever much of a reader. Did anyone ever catch you wearing specs? Did you care about music or painting? You despised ballet as bourgeois decadence, didn't you? Opera? Did you ever watch a football match?

Suez was less red-lettered in your register of turning points than the opening of Harold Pinter's *The Caretaker*. It might have all but coincided with its closing had you not grabbed the chance to deride Harold Hobson's dismissal, in *The Sunday Times*, of his quasi-namesake's first fullish-piece. Did Pinter's play advertise any rare artistic or political revolution? What he had to say was freighted with what he did not. Where was he more eloquent than in polysyllabic pauses? *The Caretaker*'s asyndeton owed more to Beckett and *avant-garde* Parisian theatre (Adamov as well as Ionesco) than you chose – or was it knew? – to notice. More Francophile than you, Hobson was made to look an insular fogey. Later you said of Ionesco's plays, 'when you've seen them all, you've seen one'. Would Oscar Wilde have wished he had said that?

If *The Caretaker* had been generally applauded and Dorothy Parker hadn't beaten you to 'There's less in this piece than meets the eye', might you have piped another tune? These things do too happen. Clive James told our daughter Sarah that he had had to come out of a different hole on the Sunday after the daily press gushed over *The Glittering Prizes*. 'A dull start' was the best low blow he could contrive. Thanks to Sarah, Clive and I lunched together several times before he died, of leukaemia, on the way to meet a deadline. He sent me his last, fat, book of poems affectionately dedicated. He always spoke of composing poems; were reviews cobbled?

When it came to John Osborne's *Look Back in Anger*, you went full frontal in declaring that you could never love anyone who did not love the Royal Court production. Your influence at its peak, you had to be the principal reason why Larry Olivier switched out of old-style theatre and invested himself in Osborne's next number, *The Entertainer*. Archie Rice's warning to the audience not to applaud too loudly 'because we're in a very old building' derided that other old stand-up performer, Harold Macmillan, who was twice wounded in the Great War and made less parade of it that you did of your cowardice. What old ham ever matched his brilliant slowness on cue when challenged in the UN by the shoe-banging Nikita Khruschev?

Ken Haigh had his single long slice of luck as unlucky Jimmy Porter. I knew him only when were fellow-members of the Savile Club. That nice Nigel Stock told me of sitting in all but deserted Lord's, smoking his pipe and conning his lines between overs, when Ken came and sat close to him and, after a silent reception, asked Nigel why he thought it was that people didn't like him. Nigel waited for last ball of the over and then said, 'Probably because you're such a cunt, Ken.'

The next time you and I talked was after I had been commissioned by BBC radio to do a set of radio interviews with trendy figures. I was licensed to warm you up over lunch at Overton's in St James's before we went to some quiet place and I turned on the cumbrous, just portable khaki army surplus W.T. set to record whatever you had to s-say. Your stammer was less impediment than emphatic, as in the f-famous case when you took the opportunity to be the first person to say 'f-fuck' on primetime television. 'Jejune is busting out all over' should have been you, but I b-beat you to it.

When you ordered steak *tartare*, I asked for the same, ignorant that it consisted of raw minced beef with a raw egg on top. Did some atavistic revulsion declare itself in the effort needed to swallow what Mosaic law deplored? Not at all. In hamburger form, superficially scorched, I should have downed it with pleasure. One of the silly things we shall never discover: did you yourself know what you were ordering? Dirk Bogarde recalled, rather loudly, that he once asked Harold Pinter why his supposedly sophisticated characters were always said to be eating Lobster Thermidor. Harold said, 'What else do the rich eat?' Antonia Fraser was to supply a fuller menu.

Of the interview which followed our lunch, a shred dangling in my memory is your answer to my deliberately, I hope, callow question: by what standards did you judge a play? You said that you had no such measure; either the piece turned the key in your lock or it did not. Oh, another thing: I suggested that your bold parade of irremediable physical cowardice would not survive a call to arms to defend, oh all right, civilisation. I still wore some vestige of the J.T.C. keenness which led to my Under Officerdom at Charterhouse. You declined to fall in. There were more chips than pips on your shoulders. Was it your form of thank you to tell me that what was wrong with London life was its lack of Jews? You meant *American* Jews, I think.

A year or so later, I sent you a play written on a typewriter with a half-and-half ribbon; dialogue in black, stage-directions in red. With luck, no archaeological scrounger will ever find a copy of my attempt to be daring by writing about two prostitutes and whatever happened to them. Your reply was more generous than I thought at the time. You hinted that I had been as bold as unwise in seeking to emulate 'Tenn Williams' and let it go at that. You signed off with 'Luv, Ken'.

When Bertolt Brecht brought his Berliner Ensemble to London, it triggered a new enthusiastic spasm. The company depended on the East German regime for premises and funding, while producing work that was both agitprop and, *disait-on*, seditious. Duly empressed, Beetle and I went to one of the productions. Should I be ashamed not to recall which it was? Your assumption of the Brechtian role of *Dramaturg* at the National Theatre lent you another distinction not unlike Librarian. No one else sported the title – more grey than eminent – once you renounced it. Larry Olivier proved an old-style theatrical actor-manager. If he never called you 'laddie', he had small appetite for a neo-Marxist supervisor. You had become impatient enough with old England to read Mao-Tse-Tung's China as a happy example of 100 percent employment. What coward doesn't wish he was a killer? Was it you who said 'Every heel has his Achilles'?

Your passion for bullfights merits unpacking. Ceremonial cruelty and killing stood for everything you might be expected to deplore. Tauromachy's ritualised sadism served to glamorise the Caudillo's brazen reign. You deplored fascism, of course; that was its charm, *no es verdad*? In your dreams, were you the bull or the fighter? Your Edmund was excited by what disgusted your Edgar. I heard that you met Ernest Hemingway, a no less passionate *afficionado*, during the 1959 season when you and he covered the series of *corridas* featuring precocious Antonio Ordoñez and old master Luis Dominguín, *beaux-frères-ennemis*. Was Hemingway's passion for danger a mixture of virile conceit and desire to be mastered?

It excited you more than what you could never imagine doing, a *pas de deux* with a baited beast, surrogate of actors who never stooped to charge you head-on. Paired with Hemingway during that commissioned truce with Franco, you dared to observe, as a result of whatever exchange, 'Three inches can make a big difference in some marriages'. Rumours of Hemingway's wilting virility were probably spread by his next-to-last wife Martha Gellhorn (a name on-the-button enough to be a fiction). You and he, each of you, doubled the bull and the baiter, braving what you feared. Sadie and Maisie, what you had in common set you at odds.

In the sexy Sixties, you concentrated trendy attention on the theatre long enough for the National to become London's tourist attraction, if scarcely the politico-artistic *avant-garde* post (you its captain) that you had in mind back whenever. The Royal Court usurped that role. Bad luck that the South Bank's design was left to the innovatory, instantly dated,

Denys Lasdun. He inspired a decked concrete complex that might have doubled for the carpark he failed to make allowance for. The stage had been the prime public art when you made your prodigious play for attention. Who now has heard of that prototypical egotist James Agate? For young writers, independent TV became where the action was. *Play for Today* delivered a weekly kitchen-sink to every drawing room. I went from regular exercise on the box into big-screenwriting. You moved at much the same time from the theatre to writing about the now trendy movies. Of all the things you wrote, the most adhesive in my memory is something you said about the one-time Tennants' favourite playwright, N.C. Hunter. You chose to mock his quasi-Chekhovian line 'We waited all winter for the daffodils to bloom and now they are all gone'. I think of it every spring.

Beetle and I were living in Rome while *Darling* was being shot and I was writing *Two for the Road*. We were still habit-ridden enough to buy the English Sunday papers. So was Rex Harrison; Beetle and I all but bumped into him one morning, a switched-off star, at the newsstand in Termini station. One of your *Observer* pieces on cinema struck me as, oh all right, *naïf*. I wrote to you explaining what the economico-aesthetic realities of The Biz really were and was rewarded by your using most of what I had to say in a subsequent column, crediting it to 'an anonymous Marxist', the sole occasion I've been tagged with that distinction.

By the time we were back in London, *Darling* had finished shooting. There were rumours of strong American interest. I had delivered the script of *Two for the Road* to Stanley Donen, who promised it was going to be the best thing he ever did. Audrey Hepburn agreed to play the lead. Willie Maugham said that nothing was so easy to get used to as success. I was no longer a callow suppliant when you invited me to your Mount Street pad. The reception room had no books, little furniture, no nice photographs. The north wall was covered with a black and white mural of Hieronymus Bosch's *Garden of Earthly Delights*. It looked oddly cut-priced. We had a drink of some kind (I'll bet I accepted something I didn't really want) before you told me of a movie that Albert Finney was about do, a brilliant script in which various stages of a marriage were intercut during a journey from London to the Riviera.

I sipped in deferential silence as you proceeded until, with something adjacent to a blush, you caught my small smile, stopped and said, 'You r-wrote it, d-didn't you?' I smiled a gotcha smile. Can it be that a flush of embarrassment showed on those gaunt cheekbones? As if on cue, a spotlight went on at the back of the room where a set of steps up to a ramp gave access to other rooms. The beautiful Kathleen Halton, gleaming in a white dress, made what may have been a scheduled entrance, stage left.

If not yet married, you were certainly joined at the hype. You told me how you had been to see Oscar Buselinck about Kathleen's divorce from whoever it was. He said, 'What have you two been up to then?' He was prompt with a money-saving ruse. Kathleen was a shining prize. Jo Janni said to me, after we had interviewed her for an aborted movie job, 'I must tell you, Fred, she is just my type'. I said, 'I must tell you, Jo, she is just everybody's type'. The kicker, as some callous Yank might have said, turned out to be that she was everybody's type but yours.

Showpiece certainly, innocent never, Kathleen gave me a certain smile when she saw that I had been allotted dress room 69 before she interviewed me on BBC2. *Quand même*, she proved no more turned on, or over, by the sexual activities that dominated your reveries than Elaine had been. There was something at once insolent and callow in your presumption that spanking was a *meum-tuum* turn more sophisticated than plain f-fucking. Your appetite was neither rare nor wicked, if shared with others with congruent taste. When Kathleen declined to be cast, you advertised for fellow-feelers and had little trouble in recruiting Nicole (was that the semi-pro's name?) and then culled an eager amatrice called Sarah.

Whose business was it but yours what you got up or down to? That you advertised, in your published diaries, the occasion on which, with those two willing accessories, you used a variety of implements to spank the females, and have one spank the other, suggests, loudly, that what you did one detailed evening, before Sarah hurried home to hubby with a hot behind, was fulfilled only after your rave notice for the performers. Your pleasures were primed by potted amateur dramatics, in which you played the master of the house, Nicole the lady, Sarah the naughty maid. The dated scenarios you chose to enact seemed necessary preludes to the punishment, one after the other, of the thieving ladies. Tynan, the admirer of Brecht and Mao, could come up, so to say, with nothing wittier than quasi-Victorian, peep-show reprises of Sade's *Justine*.

You were true to your scorpion self when you came to review *Darling*. It had already opened to round-the-block success in New York before you were called upon to pass judgment. Julie Christie's princess Diana was labelled 'Identikit Girl', which sounded nastier than it was true. If you ever reviewed *Two for the Road*, I have not retained a vestige of what you said. Your writing about the theatre had blown the dust off the West End and supplied a fair wind for innovation. You may have thought that cinema was, in essence, two-dimensional theatricals, but you brought to it little more than misconceived condescension. You had loved the theatre; you made a living, of a kind, out of writing about movies. You were more your old swank self doing prolix profiles for *The New Yorker*. When it came to framing full-length portraits of celebrities, you were more gossip columnist than any kind of Saint-Beuve, a much better biographer than Proust cared to allow: cf. Sherwood Anderson and Ernest Hemingway, Hemingway and Scott. Throughout the arts, pats on the back double with stabs in the same quarter. In your case, the recklessness of youth yielded to a wish to please the money. Dorothy Parker's line, that the two sweetest words in the English language were 'cheque enclosed', subtitled your increasingly anxious ambitions.

The scene that led you to realise how parlous your physical condition was is more cinema than theatre. Someone at a candle-lit party, overhearing your laborious intake of breath, asked if you suffered from emphysema. You had no idea. He brought a candle towards you and asked you to blow it out. With or without a frown, you made to do so. The flame fluttered and stayed alight as it passed your death sentence. Note, a callous didact might say, how little dialogue was needed and how such a scene would never play on the stage as it would on the screen, silence the last word.

Was Kathleen disillusioned when she discovered what you meant, very specifically, by making love? Your name gave her a lift in the Biz and access to the modest fortune that went with writing a commercial screenplay, not to mention the beauty that added a nought or two to her price. Armed with the nerve and the cash, as well as the beauty, to defy as well as deny you, she could afford to profit from the marriage and find comfort elsewhere. You contrived, in your diary, to play, if not to be, the wounded party. Shades of Byron's 'no one is more put upon than poor dear me'.

Nothing in your wilfully candid (some read 'candied') diaries is more revealing than your confession of feeling driven by your own overpowered, overpowering Jaguar. It was as if you dreamed of contriving your own disaster, one way or another, or both. Your sexual obsessions mastered you even while you played the master. Oh yes, you hoped also to profit from them while posing, a little nuttily, as a sexual liberator. The title of your first erotic revue, *Oh! Calcutta!* did at least harbour a clever pun, *quel cul tu as!* Is it any kind of confession to say that I went as far as booking tickets, but no further? We were warned off by someone who had seen it. As for the sequel, *Carte Blanche*, it became more of a share-a-bang attraction than any kind of latter-day *Hernani*. My niece Natasha Morgan was in the cast and remembers you as a joyless presence. Might be that you were just slightly embarrassed by asking her and others to do, or mime, what you yourself were never persuaded to do in public? The inspiration came, didn't it, from a porno show you visited, when much younger, in Hamburg? Am I taking it all too seriously when it occurs to me that the S.S. and their confederates' stripping and humiliating of their victims, before murdering them, was a mass preview of the S.M. thrills you commercialised and the buses brought the punters to gasp at? There is a difference? A big one; and a similarity.

Truth to tell (an activity that rarely makes friends), your desire to promote story-lined flagellation into some kind of delicious art blighted your reputation without furnishing reliably cushioned *je m'en foutisme*. You had had a keen eye and ear for absurdity in wilting Britain and the vanities of the many Nelsons who clapped the wrong ends of their telescopes to their silly eyes, but you were sunk by the duplicity that Heraclitus of Ephesus mapped so brilliantly when, without being commissioned, he coined the phrase 'the road up and the road down are the same road'.

The last time I saw you was in George and Joan Axelrods' house in Beverly Hills. Even when they had gone down in the world they lived well above the no-dough line. You came in alone and, despite notoriety's bright shadow (the Greeks had a word for that), seemed close to being not at all one of us. When I shook that old limp Dover-sole-of-the-party hand, I was close to being kind, the last thing your appetite craved.

With an edge of flattering malice, you said, 'Ah, the novelist'. If this letter reads as some kind of riposte, that was never my intention. You played the kind of dodo every chancer might wish to be. Your last oxygenated breath disdained the sentimental sympathy your children were kind enough, perhaps honest enough, to leave you with. Like Oscar, Mr T., you were one-off all the way, merely unforgettable, you bastard.

Luv, Freddie.

Dear George,

I met you first in 1965. You had just given a lecture at the Royal Society of Literature's then mandarin premises, in Hyde Park Gardens. At a time when it seemed to mean something, I had recently been made a Fellow, thanks to the advocacy of Peter Green, whom I encountered in Cambridge in summer 1951, while seeking a fourth for bridge. My friend ever since, I have no idea whether he plays or ever did. Squash is the only game I ever played with him, in Iowa City. He won; but one zinger left that rare scholar with a bruise plumb on his right buttock. I said 'Sorry'. He said, 'Your point'.

After I had signed in with Byron's pen, the then Home Secretary Roy Jenkins in the chair, you waged fortissimo in declaring the merits of reticence. Ardent for cool, you insisted that, when writing about sex, the explicit – licensed by the recent verdict in the Lady Chatterley trial – was the enemy of art. Never mind Sir Robert Walpole's 'Let us talk bawdy, then all may join in', you had it that imagery and metaphor primed the reader's senses without bruising his sensibility: obscenity one thing, literature another. The naming of parts belonged in the kind of book that Jean-Jacques Rousseau held was designed to be read with one hand. You commended the artful image of Dorothea, in *Middlemarch*, attempting to re-ignite the embers in the fireplace of the conjugal home she shares with the burned-out scholar Casaubon; her frustration, his impotence encapsulated in domestic detail; Thomas and Jane Carlyle sullen shadows in the room.

As your audience spilled, with applause-ripened hands, onto the pavement a few doors up from where Stanley Donen then lived, you were escorted by Tom Maschler and Ed Victor.

When Tom introduced us, you said that you guessed – or hoped, was it? – that I did not share your views. Your Quixotic sense of mission required that others be windmills. For all its accusative delivery, your principal point had little relevance to my own fiction. You seemed eager for further conversation, not there, not then.

Your name resonated in a manner you are unlikely to have known. In Federico Fellini's *La Dolce Vita*, Marcello (Mastroianni) walks into a room and sees his old professor. One word, softly delivered, 'Steiner' conveys that Marcello loves the man and fears that he has betrayed him, and himself, by becoming a handsome hack. Such is the art of film, occasionally, that we know, in a second, that 'Stein/air' carries a freight of memories that others may be able to shuck and Marcello, doomed and blessed (false cousin to *blessé*), cannot. Like Primo Levi, twenty-five years later, he is never alone: what he escaped forever is forever with him.

Annotators came to refer to you as a 'Holocaust survivor', quite as if you had been in one of the camps. Yes, in those days you bore fervent witness to the murderous Nazi dominion over most of Europe, but you had no more been in danger – having moved with your parents to New York – than I was in London during the Blitz; less in fact. Our fortunes had been shaded by events to which, as children, we were marginal. In Paris in 1939, your banker father insisted that you not hide your ten-year-old eyes while *fascisants* marchers tramped down your street in the sixteenth *arrondissement*. You were to stand on the terrace with him and observe History and malevolence march in step. Hegel, you remember, watched Napoleon, impersonating destiny, temporarily, prance on his high horse on the way to Moscow and disaster (and excision from Beethoven's fourth symphonic title). In 1940, you were off to New York, not long after my parents and I had left it. Like Maschler, you were an ousted European; unlike him, you travelled first-class. I, Chicago-born, may tread as delicately as any Agag, but I have no debt to honour for having been admitted to pre-war England. My father was a British subject; so then was I. We saw the enemy as Germans, you, Nazis.

Mastery of despoiled languages and cultures paraded your European provenance. Great books, even (especially?) by malign authors, were your gospel: you preached Heidegger, the antisemite, whom the Vienna Circle – Wittgenstein a tangent to it – read only for laughs. I remember an antinomian word or more in praise of Lucien Rebatet's *Les deux étendards*. I proved to be the first person to have taken it out of the London Library in twenty-five years. As with Céline and Paul Morand, Rebatet's antisemitic riffs primed a jazz of louche Gallic secretions. Post-war, Céline became a pariah, Morand an *Académicien*. I suspect you envied both. That strident Naziphile Robert Brasillach was never of equal interest to you, was he? He was executed, after de Gaulle's decision not to reprieve him, despite Mauriac's earnest imprecation, on the grounds as much of intellectual iniquity as of the treason with which he was charged. De Gaulle found it easier to spare the second-rate; excellence merited mercilessness. He could not reprieve Joseph Darnand either, head of the Vichy Milice during the occupation, holder of the *Médaille Militaire* in the Great War. De Gaulle signed Darnand's death warrant but promised to oversee the education of his children. Do you remember Brasillach's last words? '*Vive la France, quand même!*' And yours? Did you ever compose them? Pity '*Je est un autre*' is already tied to Rimbaud! '*Quelques autres*' might cover your multiplicity, if never displace the poet. You might have been any number of things; you ended by being not quite enough of too many.

I recall that, while I was writing a piece, for the *TLS*, about *ces années-là*, you reminded me of the scholarly qualities displayed in Brasillach's precocious study of Racine. I was guileless – meiotic term for unscholarly – enough not to verify your professorial reference. A reader's letter corrected me politely: the subject of Brasillach's monograph was Corneille. Did it amuse you to land me in it or were you yourself mistaken? Duplicities – the dupe, in this case, being me – linger in the petty crux. The novel, whatever its alleged bourgeois datedness, is an irreplaceable arena for human ambiguities. For all your erudition, you were seldom immune to silly mistakes.

Insolence and deference were folded together ahead of your *parachutage* into post-war Cambridge. Impersonating a Trilingual Loeb edition, you were bent on caulking and reconciling cultures scored and scarred by greed and vandalism. Hermann Göring, thief and connoisseur, had played Nazism's bulging Trimalchio. Did you know that his brother Arthur helped Jews escape into Switzerland? What did you not know? Marshal Pétain said of someone, '*Il connaît tout, et rien d'autre*'. I'm sure you could identify the target.

Bostonian contagion fashioned you into a deutero-Henry James of whom T.S. Eliot said that he wrote with magisterial authority in a European language of no specific location. Someone might well have said 'So look who's talking', but Uncle Tom had a censor's clamp on English letters until, decorously as may be, you indicted his antisemitism in *In Bluebeard's Castle* (1970). Robert Graves, M.C., had biffed Pound, draft-dodger and howler-prone translator, but no one had pounded Eliot. Uncle Tom had buttoned up his Yankee doodle and became England's laureate in striped trousers. Clerically-cut, royalist centurion, he said to some 'go', to others 'stay'. As *miglior* Faber, he was neither bailiff to cross nor buffer to hit. His royalism had more to do with Charles Maurras than with the Windsors. The spirit of St Louis (his thirteenth-century sainthood conferred for burning Jews and Jewish sacred texts) fuelled both Mr. Eliot and Charles Lindberg when they crossed the Atlantic.

On an occasion which may have preceded your *réquisitoire*, Eliot had been at a poetry reading by Danny Abse. One of Abse's poems made sour allusion to 'the jew is underneath the lot'. That nice Stephen Spender took it upon himself to stand as tall as a toady well could (six feet four) and call out 'Tom is not an antisemite'. Head in temporary hands, Eliot motioned him to sit down, saying 'Let him go on. It's a good poem'. The fate of actual Jews counted less, in literary circles, than what was well or badly said about 'the jew', to whom Eliot eventually conceded a capital J. His cleverest trick was to style himself Old Possum, his *Book of Cats* a purr-verse treasury.

One-man double act, you combined Mario and the Magician in an economic re-make of Thomas Mann's novella of a Hitlerian spellbinder. Revelling in egotistic duplicity, you read Eliot's lines *re* rats beneath the piles, you-know-who underneath the lot, as a sullen confession that Christian civilisation was founded on Jewish premises. Hegel all but conceded their priority and damned the Jews at the same time. You once told me that when stuck for a pertinent obscurity, you would attribute some knotty *fausse trouvaille* to Hegel. His works were too voluminous for any bookish Javert to have time for the *triage* to prove your *citation* spurious. In the same who-can-prove-me-wrong spirit, you told the story of the aristocrat in a tumbril on the way to the guillotine ignoring the howls of the crowd as he read a book. When the tumbril reached the *Place de la Concorde* and he was called to ascend the scaffold, he folded the corner of the page, as if he expected to resume reading in due course. The interface of the historical and the fanciful was your private lode.

You had the wit to see, the nerve to say, that European antisemitism was not so much about the murder and spoliation of hounded and confounded actual Jews as a convulsive reaction against the inoperable inner Jew wished on Gentiles by Christianity. Catholic ardour was fuelled by resentment that dared not speak its name. Nietzsche was the first to observe that Judaism, spliced with Socratic self-consciousness, had blighted beery Teutonic spontaneity. In temporal truth, the Elders of Zion were not, as malign myth had it, huddled in gabardine in some furry Siberian bunker; they traipsed with pots and pans from door to door. As Michael Gold reminded Theodore Dreiser, 'the Jews' of pre-Great War America were more often penniless tenement-dwellers than Rothschilds. Once the Jewish faith had been traduced, its abusers could sit ensconced, in gilded, cross-patched drag, in the Vatican, free to peddle perfidious libels to cover their virtuous larceny.

Nietzsche's *also-sprach* mouth, out from under that burning bushy moustache, foretold the coming of the *Übermensch*. He would by no means necessarily be German; nor was it promised that he would be booted, spurred, arm-banded and goose-stepping. Whatever his vision of enhanced virility, thrice rejected by Lou Salomé, Zarathustra's spokesman burst into tears and necked a Torinese cab-horse. Sister Winifred delivered him to be Nazified, posthumously, by Adolf. Who today, other than you, remembers that *der treue* Friedrich compared Germans unfavourably with the *Juden*? Germanic disunity had issued in great music, literature, scholarship. When all together, the master race could do little better than take the *Horst Wessel Lied* for its anthem.

You spoke, early in your career as *arbiter literarum*, of the decline and imminent fall of The Novel. How keen you were that whatever was beyond you be outmoded! All your books were glosses, were they not, a layman's Talmud, one hundred percent Hebraic, as Wittgenstein said, belatedly, if ruefully, of his own work? See under the apple and where it pitches. Only in much later years did you murmur that you had lacked the nerve to be an original artist. Meantime, playing Lord High Executioner, you exulted in the apprehension that possessors of vital functions are billed to excite.

The *New Yorker* paid very well for sophisticated by-the-wordiness. You combined polyglot condescension with hireling anxiety: any change at the top might bring some keen new blade – like that of the swift Chinese headsman who said 'Kindly nod' – to sever you from prestigious gold. As for art, you recall Kafka's character, sitting at that half-open door, waiting for a summons to make his pitch. In the evening, a flunkey comes out of the office and says that the door has been left ajar, all day, available for K. to come in. The flunkey said that he was now going to close what you might call the portal. The careerist, however stellar, abides a summons; artists presume.

As the *New Yorker*'s bookman-in-chief, you worked in the wide wake of Edmund Wilson. *Classics and Commercials*, with its many declarations of independence, was so much a part of my literary mulch that I could hardly believe it when you told me that Bunny, never cuddly, had often sought a professorial chair and was flopsy every time. Sabre-toothed personality and porcine alcoholism were handicaps enough; in addition, hard-boiled egghead, he lacked a speciality. The only other literary Bunny I knew of was Garnett, D. who had little else in common with Wilson, E. I once described Garnett, with whom I spent a day in the Lot, as being 'bisexual and sometimes buy-sexual'; a squeamish editor blue-pencilled it.

As you came to prove, a generalist, however special, seldom meets open arms in academic circles, except as distinguished orator for high days and holidays. When Volodya Nabokov applied for a professorship in the English school at Princeton, someone said that, despite his paucity of scholarly publications (unless you included those on lepidoptery), surely no one could dispute the merits of his fictions. Roman Jakobson said that that might be so; were elephants therefore eligible to be professors of zoology? Jakobson was known to be fluent in several languages, all of which, on his lips, wore ze same accent.

You, *par contre*, addressed intellectual senates like a tricephalic native. Eloquent Cerberus, you spoke, if not barked, ancillary languages with fluent assurance. You boasted that, when in Rome, someone credited you with a perfect Milanese accent. I chose not to mention that, when addressed in Russian, it amused Vladimir Nabokov to congratulate an alien interlocutor on his Muscovite accent. Courtly old Russians prided themselves on St Petersburg tones, never the Stratford-atte-Bowe equivalent to be heard in Muscovy.

In the all-but-a-decade between your addressing the R.S.L. and our meeting again, at lunch *chez* Michael and Elisabeth Ayrton, you had shaken off the fenland dust and were installed in your Genevan professorship. Zara, now a tenured historian and Fellow of New Hall, stayed alone in 36, Barrow Road, the finest house in Cambridge, so you claimed, with artless complacency. Safely lodged *chez* Calvin, honorarily degreed *un peu partout*, smiling contrarian, you had the nerve to utter a perverse word for the Soviet Union, where *intellos* were taken, you said, with enviable seriousness. Censorship evoked subtlety; dissidence donned artful mufti. When anything goes, you implied, it rarely gets anywhere very subtle. Marcuse's often misunderstood 'repressive tolerance' ticked your margin: today's English-speaking world is gagged by dread of giving offence to *qui que ce soit*.

If on the spot, what would you have said that the evasive Pasternak dared not, when telephoned by Stalin, after Mandelstam had called him a black beetle? Asked, when in range of the NKVD, your opinion of Osip's verses, what kind of truth would you have told that Pasternak funked? When the latter distanced himself from his fellow-poet and so gained time to write *Doctor Zhivago*, that quondam poet Joseph Dugashvili said, 'Is that the best you can do for your friend?' Did you ever say that Pasternak's Nobel-winning novel proved that even in secret one can write like an equivocator?

Let's say you did; *mots* are more impressive when attributed to another. Compared with Piotr Rawicz's *Blood from the Sky*, *Doctor Zhivago* is self-puff pastry. Your body, distorted at birth, made it look as if you had been tortured. Symbol of craving for domination and for calvary, provided it was on the high ground, that crabbed claw gave you mastery over those unsure quite how to shake it. I called you 'shorty' once or twice; lefty, never.

In the course of later meetings, you told me how, precocious *parvenu*, you were recruited to a Fellowship of recently established Churchill College, Cambridge. Before the premises were ready for occupation, you were given dining rights in King's and the run of Cambridge's lecture rooms. Your arrival coincided with the ferment of the *soixante-huit* 'psycho-drama', as the unseduced, soon isolated, Raymond Aron called it. As usual, nothing would ever be the same again, until it was, almost. Spinoza was no less sceptical of Sabbatai Zevi three hundred years earlier. In 1968, the students said that they would sooner be wrong with Sartre than right with Aron. *La trahison des élèves* succeeded the treason of the clerks; and has yet to go away.

Your challenging charisma and *à la mode* continental accents conjured Cambridge student audiences so numerous that bigger and bigger lecture rooms had to be devoted to their reception. However large, no amplifier was ever called for. Speaking your mind in bold, you reminded the *jeunesse plus ou moins dorée* how much more there was to read than Mao's Little Red Book. You preached in counterpoint to Daniel Cohn-Bendit. Pied pipers both, you triggered insolent, distinct uprisings among the young. Ass and ox yoked in common, discordant traction (you take the allusion, *physiká*, to Odysseus' attempted evasion, pretending to be mad, when conscripted by Palamedes to go to Troy), you promoted neo-Platonism, cultural not political, while C.-B.'s opportunism prompted

Parisian students, *Marxistes tendance* Groucho, to make '*Nous sommes tous des Juifs allemands*' their meta-Marseillaise.

Alain Finkielkraut broke step: parading parodists did not amuse him, Pierre Vidal-Naquet *non plus*. Their fathers had been murdered by the Nazis. How many brave Gentiles chanted in Jewish drag when it mattered? However many years ago, Beetle and I were in a late train from Liverpool Street with some bemedalled veterans on the way home from a reunion. One told of an occasion in a Stalag when he and others British POWs were paraded and an S.S. officer ordered that all Jews take one step forward. There was a moment's pause and, he promised, everyone of the Brits took one step forward. The same man said that what the Germans needed were 'white officers for two generations'. That was then.

Something in you rated martyrdom above justice; 'Here I am, take me', your unspoken shout. Yet, like old, once bold, Ibsen you craved decorated entitlement. *Le bon* Dany was at the same time representing red-hot youth against institutional prudery and taking revenge on the French, *tendance Vichy*, for their collaboration. It included setting up, and filling, several hundred concentration camps within the *métropole*. Ken Tynan, of all chic-by-jowlers, chided Cohn-Bendit for lack of a serious political prospectus. Camp ideology likes to invite adherents to lethal fancy-dress parties.

Ken was never sure whether he wanted to play Stanislavski or a pantomime dame; camp/analogist beating out that rhythm on a bum his bedroom jazz. Are you ashamed of me? Silly-clever, Tynan saw Mao's China as an example *à suivre* of full employment. Shunning terrestrial panaceas, Zionism in particular, you chose to wander on, one-man bandsman, never quite in step with yourself. You had the brazen heterodoxy to be what the Cambridge University Appointments Board marginalised as an 'unapologetic Jew'. Beetle had access to the files when she worked for the amiable chief secretary Jack Davies, during my last year in St John's. At Lord's cricket ground, he once bowled Don Bradman for a duck, if you know what that means. To be tolerated in 1950s Butskellite England, four-by-twos were advised not to sport loud ties or radical opinions and not to embarrass themselves and others by seeking membership of golf clubs with 'royal' on their escutcheons. What better sums up urbane malice than the entrance forms' dotted line for 'Name of father, if changed'?

When we were on TV together, in the week Ian Smith declared Southern Rhodesia independent, I asked Tony Lambton, after he had mentioned him several times, what his father's name was. He said, 'Durham'. A few years later, accused of smoking dope and daytime dalliance with tarts, which he considered nobody's business but his own, Lambton followed Byron and quit Albion. In his castle in Italy, self-indulgence was no crime. When his father died, his name became Durham, briefly.

Skid (né Skidelsky) Simon used to say that the worst mistakes as declarer, when playing bridge, are liable to be committed at 'trick one'. The remaining twelve tricks are often punctuated by 'trancing' in the hope of rectifying some first, hasty misjudgement. How could you have known that the sponsorship of Charles Snow could never, alone, guarantee you favour in the Cambridge English faculty? Some well-intentioned marker of your card must have assured you that, with 'Charles' on your side, you were forty percent there. What your adviser did not tell you was that, with that particular sponsor, forty was as high a percentage as you were ever likely to attain. In the squared Cambridge circles on which your ambition was set, Snow – atomic scientist and New Man in 'the corridors of power' – was so cordially *mal vu* that the Fellows of Christ's College, the manifest, if unspecified, location of his best novel, *The Masters*, pinned meteorological clippings on the notice board: SNOW FALLS HEAVILY IN SCOTLAND, etc. Charlie, if you get my drift, was not everyone's darling. My philosophical godfather, Renford Bambrough, came to be a real life Jago, Snow's fictional runner-up in *The Masters*, unfavoured favourite for the top job.

After vociferous lingering, you had to accept that, whatever embarrassed consolation Churchill College might confer, faculty enrolment was never in prospect. The undergraduate audiences you attracted in those early years more alarmed the old Eng. Lit. guard than disposed it to present alms. Dr Leavis, ostracised pundit who kept slamming doors but failed to leave the premises, was troublemaker enough in the English school. Your abstruse references, in accents at once harsh and seductive, mocked the tradition which, before the arrival of the Beatles, made understatement the Anglo-Saxon trademark. Just because you spoke with tongues did not make it Pentecost. Until Wittgenstein set the example of using his hands for periodic parentheses, what educated Briton did not scorn manual gesticulation?

Many lecturers in Cambridge found that their small audiences grew smaller as the year went by. Cosmopolitan polymath, you were a drawcard; an ace of trumpery, of the pale blue pack never. A continental spellbinder was the last thing the curricular flag officers wanted on the quarter deck. Readers of Ross and Mitford's *U and Non-U* will recall, from the dusty distance, that 'continental' was, *à l'époque*, synonymous with untrustworthy. The young who crowded your cornucopious lectures had small leverage in university politics. You taught well, listened badly, especially to what was not said, *chez les rosbifs*. Despite and because of your boundary-crossing agility, you became the most brilliant of those shelved under the fell rubric '*prox. acc.*'

Cut back, as you would never say, to the Ayrtons' house. Michael led Beetle and me into the big sitting room where you and Zara were already being entertained. Elisabeth had the rusty allure of a woman with a bulky past. As everyone knew, she had been married to the popular novelist Nigel Balchin. His wartime books had the unadorned syntax of utility furniture. They were a little better than one expected, unless the one happened to be you. Like Snow, Balchin was a plainsong herald of the New Man.

Before lunch, we had several drinks. Michael, a whisky man, was against going to table sooner than he had to. Beetle and I sipped prudent wine. Zara had the lively conversation of a New Yorker who could never rely on her looks. She did not claim attention; she offered it. You sat warily, at first, allowing Michael primacy in his spacious, unremarkable house. In the knock-up, you spared us vigorous volleys. Did I talk too much? The outsider dresses his novitiate with a flash of bright answers. You preferred to rehearse cadenzas for the Great Evaluation.

At what prandial point was it that you asked, to be overheard, why I talked so much more intelligently than anyone in my latest novel? *April, June and November* opened with over a hundred pages of the dialogue of scarcely disguised Gloucester Crescent regulars *dans ses oeuvres*. The reader had to imagine what the company looked and sounded like by lending his wit and recollections to their accumulated chatter. My *bravura sostenuta* amused some reviewers, maddened others; Julian – *ci-devant* Alphonse – Symons, in what I imagined to be my own paper, the nastiest. I answered your I-must-be-honest query by saying that it had to be that that day's company was more stimulating than any to be found in NW1. Beetle looked at you.

Not long afterwards, your hungry cuff knocked over your wine glass. A spreading red badge bloomed on her white sleeve. Sudden old wife, you spooned therapeutic salt onto the soiled linen. Beetle made nothing of it, though she had scant trust in your homeopathy. Perhaps in apology, you entertained us with a story of your early weeks in the Cambridge from which you had now all but severed yourself, apart from 36, Barrow Road. Remaining an 'extraordinary' fellow of Churchill, a walking *hapax legomenon*, you had consoled yourself with a professorship in Geneva (Swiss passport a feature of your emoluments) and a call-sheet of visiting punditries.

You told us how, back in the 1960s, at your first dinner in King's, you had taken a modest seat one place from the end of high table. Your neighbour, an old professor of mathematics, did not return your vespertine greeting. You and he sat with your backs to the serving table, from which college servants brought charged salvers to the Fellows and their guests. At dessert, a heaped silver platter of the first strawberries of spring was carried first to the Provost and then along the far side of high table. You watched the towering treat being sapped by more or less voracious dons. Eventually, the platter came to your elbow, the penultimate diner. Twelve strawberries remained.

'The question that I posed to myself', you told us, 'and which I now put to the company is, in view of the fact that the senior wrangler on my left was the only Fellow to be served after me, how many strawberries should I, a guest of the college, be advised, *en bon débutant*, to take?'

Playing up, I made the stooge's choice of six; so, I believe, did the others, except for Beetle, who said, 'Five?'

You looked at her quickly and then said, 'Five is precisely the number, after brief reflection, that I myself chose, with due deference to my professorial neighbour'.

'And?'

'Indeed. As the waiter switched the salver and its diminished cargo to the one remaining, so to speak, candidate, the old professor looked at me for the first time, eyes brimming with contempt. "You bloody fool", he said.'

You replied, you told us, with obsolete courtesy, 'I beg your pardon?'

'You bloody fool', he repeated.

You said, *en bon* H.J., 'Might you do me the honour of explaining your sanguine choice of courtesies?'

The old mathematician swivelled round to point at the serving table behind your back. Another wide salver, freighted with glistening strawberries was even then being removed, unbroached, to the kitchen. 'Had you but had the elementary wit to take *all* the few remaining berries', your neighbour said, 'I should have been free to help myself as copiously as I had looked forward to doing'.

A confident guest of the college might have smiled and said, 'Aren't I indeed a bloody fool?', trumping the trump. A sense of humour sometimes cuts a key to society. You did not have one on your ring. You had returned to Europe with a mission to minister to the breached and bruised culture of which Erasmus was the emblematic precursor. Laureled precociousness advertised availability to repair broken bridges and spring dependable new ones. If the antisemitism you had witnessed on that privileged Parisian balcony left you with few illusions about the European basement, America had admitted you to a high haven at Harvard, despite its principled reluctance to welcome any but exceptional Jews; that was its charm for the chosen Chosen: the king's Jews recycled as the Republic's penthouse élite, at once privileged and patronised.

At Princeton you fell under the wing and the spell of J.R. Oppenheimer. Under his leadership, the Manhattan Project had provided infernal means of victory over Japan. Oppy's cloistered praise led you to hope that repairs and reparations were in prospect when you came again, in academic glory, to the *vieux continent*. Less pilgrim than redeemer, you were booked to play a remounted Galahad. You told me you had worshipped Oppy until the day when he reported how, in Paris, he had seen a play about his fall from the role of national hero. The mastermind behind the A-bomb watched himself cut down to sighs as an untrustworthy all-but-Red, excluded from further access to the project he had inspired. Edward Teller stepped in to play the silvered Judas. The web of vanity and self-pity in which J.R.O. mooned over his own Calvary broke the spell he had woven for you. You discovered why Harry Truman, the old Prendergast gangster then in the White House, called him a cry-baby.

I wish you had had occasion to meet Heidegger, as Celan did, and been no less disillusioned by the venomous bravura of that other Master of yours, the metaphysician as quack. How often the Jewish genius imagines himself the exception who will make the beast his Beau! Allen Ginsberg went to Denmark to shame Pound and to charm him. Self-endearing Ole Ez (cf. Hemingway as 'papa') had the spineless nerve to claim that his antisemitism, venomous outcrop all through the *Cantos*, was a suburban prejudice contracted, so to say, from sneezing golf-clubbers, never aped from toxic storm troopers. I confess to a *faible* for Schopenhauer. Was he, like Gilbert Ryle, a lifelong virgin? In 1936, the aristocratic captain of the German bridge team had been so captivated by the sportsmanship and humour of 'Skid' Simon, star of the English team, that in the concluding courtesies he said that he wished he could take Skid to meet the Führer. Adolf would realise at once the absurdity of his antisemitic folly. *Vous croyez?*

I cannot recall through what worthy topics you conducted us on that *journée fatidique* with the Ayrtons. The brittle chickens we had for lunch suffered from third-degree burns, despite Elisabeth being a voluminous cookery expert. Might it be that she was nervous? I once went to tea with a then married ex-girlfriend who forgot to put tea in the pot and fell invitingly backwards, as Freud would predict, on the sofa. I had my chance and did not take it, wisely. When you and

Zara departed importantly for Cambridge, you left your reputations behind you, as Byron put it as he quit Holland House. I had enjoyed Zara's gravelly levity. You made more effort to impress than to charm, unless being impressive was the only charm you knew.

I remember having tea with you at 36, Barrow Road on one occasion when, as I was looking at my watch, you suggested that I stay for dinner. Arthur Koestler was coming. Some other guest must have cried off. I had never met Koestler, though I did correspond with him, briefly, when I edited a little anthology to raise money for Brigid Brophy's campaign for authors' lending rights. He told me that writing in English was still an onerous undertaking. You would never confess to difficulties of that kind, whatever the tongue. I relished the idea of an evening with the author of *Darkness at Noon*, but I had promised Beetle that I would be home for dinner. 'You are uxorious, sir', you said. So I was, and am. Off I went. Fool?

Was it on that occasion that Christopher Logue was also your guest? After Koestler had been encouraged into telling, not for the first or second time, we may guess, of his harrowing days in one of Franco's many condemned cells during the Spanish Civil War, from which he was sprung by having international turnkey connections, Logue trumped him by boasting of some fourteen months (was it?) in a British army glass-house on account of some signal misdemeanour. Oddly enough, in view of your bruited Protean ability when it came to languages, you were an advertised admirer of Logue's *Iliad*, of which Richard Bentley might well have said, as he did of Pope's version, 'It is a pretty poem, Mr Pope, but you must not call it Homer'.

Logue implied, loudly, that learning Greek would come between him and the poetry. You enjoyed the rough-n-tough insolence from which, by nature and nurture, you were barred. You championed Heidegger, and all but flirted with Hitler, not least, I suspect, because Zelig-like versatility was a trapezoid display of your polly-lingual versatility. Yes, yes, there's a clove or two of envy in there. 'How not'?, as Sybille Bedford would say. Who she? So it goes. The last time I saw Logue he was toting a not too comely Rothschild female on his arm like a soiled trophy.

Michael died of a stroke that November. Did you weep? I cannot quite imagine it. Did I? Tears come not uncommonly to me, but one need not be La Rochefoucauld to have a sense of escape, if not exhilaration, when others fall. Be that as it probably was, I missed Michael not least in his chatty absence, during which we exchanged irregular letters, his in saleable calligraphy (three pounds a letter, he said, the likely return). Michael dead, the *facteur*'s call, '*Un peu de lecture*', was abruptly less promising.

I wrote to you, assuming shared dismay, and explained, with callow candour, what pleasure my correspondence with M. had given me, and suggesting that you and I exchange letters. You were never more generous, perhaps never more genuine, than when you accepted the proposal. Can it have been that, ensconced in your *garçonnière*, you received fewer personal letters than you did academic solicitations or scriveners' petitions? No matter: you were unconditionally and – it seemed – wholeheartedly willing to come in, as you would never say, or understand, as Michael would, at first wicket down.

Our correspondence, yours and mine, stretched into all but two decades. You were always a busy man, but your letters came regularly. I never gave them to Beetle to read, perhaps (again!) because you never made any reference or sent any message to her. That casual spillage at the Ayrtons' lunch stood, in your version of George Eliotesque understatement, for sanguinary assault. Your letters were often a typed rehearsal of the many convocations you received to address this or that learned body, *ici et là*, rarely in stuffy Great Britain, in return for yet another bloom in your buttonhole. You resembled, just slightly, the brand of champagne touted by Felix Krull, flash with medals from rare sources, the fancier the flash, the poorer the vintage.

I tried hard to trump the wit you rarely displayed. Strange that the expression 'knocking up' applies both to the preparatory rallying of tennis players and, in barrack-room parlance, to the inadvertent impregnating of females! I have no idea whether you kept my letters. I certainly kept yours (seldom more than one single-spaced typed sheet), though I am not sure where. One conveyed the quasi-Proustian, gladiatorial pun '*Mort, Iturri te salue, tante*'; not a gag to try out at the Palladium.

You told me, with a typical mixture of seeming affront and practical pride, that all your correspondence – including carbons of your own compositions – had been promised by Charles Snow, your unsolicited sponsor, to the archives of the University of Texas. Did my letters go in with the rest of the laundry? I suspect, with a faint hope that my suspicions are masochistic, that you have junked my party turns. The dead letter office, there's a phrase to mortify the man who lacks initialled credentials to garnish academic filing cabinets! I tried, often at length, to entertain you; if I succeeded, was I despatched *à la poubelle*, as undersized Henry de Montherlant used to say, when reading correspondence which, however worthy, contained *fautes de grammaire*? Does every exception long to set the rule? *Tante* he may have been, *le bon* Henry; *elle savait écrire, lui, con même.*

Soon after you so generously took up the relay from Michael, BBC TV broadcast *The Glittering Prizes*. The producer phoned me to say that the reviews were 'all raves'. While I enjoyed a Warhol patch of fifteen-minute fame, you had to draw my attention to the one adverse notice in the national press, by Clive James in the *Observer*. I responded quite sharply: Clive was your idea of a good critic because he said nothing agreeable about anyone. You backed off, all but *solidaire*: how could I imagine that Clive's catchpenny stuff had your imprimatur? Did success make my friendship a trophy worth retaining? Not a little of Clive's criticism fell into the *m'as-tu-vu?* category, Maileresque advertisements for himself and what he had failed to do.

I may also have hinted that your own practice was not above the brand of stiltedness in which what looked like a plinth doubled for falsework. Criticism may wreck creative work; it never trumps it. Ken Tynan was always about to write a play, Jonathan Miller that novel novel. The closest Ken came was to supervise an erotic anthology of theatrical sketches, by other limp hands, that failed to make him rich and poxed his intellectual complexion. Jonathan never wrote anything; even the pseudo-textbooks published under his name were dictated, so I was told by Someone Who Knew, and made printable by some discreet Jonathan Cape female *amanuensis*.

Clive happened to become friendly, never more, but not for want of trying, with Sarah. She enjoyed his company but demanded an explanation of why he had said the things he did about *The Glittering Prizes*. He was shamelessly up-front: since his review would not appear till the Sunday after all the daily papers had done three-cheering, the only way to make it new was to yawn in print. Endearing and unforgivable, such candour placed him, beyond appeal, among the opportunists. You had quoted him with glee and then filed him under mere journalist. You were seldom reluctant to answer an editor's call, but never admitted to being mere. *Feuilletoniste*? Why not? Under that convenient flag, who was there to fear but the late Karl Kraus? Master Levin?

After Babel was the big book your admirers were waiting for, if not around the block. It had the garrulous versatility of the man whose intellectual baggage required towering accommodation. Who matched your competence in the three-dimensional chess (your only game, I think) that moved from one language to another, none the master? Translation was a boundary-skipping exercise that advertised intellectual libertinism: you had a language in every port. *After Babel* proclaimed that any side of a triangle may be called the base; as Bogey never said, here's looking at Euclid.

As for what went on in your Genevan *garçonnière* (cosy term that seemed to intimate one-on-one extra-curricular activities), who shall ever know what's true, what's false, not always in that order? Did female pupils take your attention for flattery and join you in a *pourquoi pas de deux*? '*Beh, le donne!*' said the lame maestro whose fame has lapsed since the days when *La Romana* led white-breasted Fenella Fielding (bet you never heard of her!) to sing 'Nothing is more calculated to deprave ya / Than the novels of Alberto Moravia' at that little theatre, the New Lindsey, in Notting Hill Gate. How many females, I wonder, figure in the index of *After Babel*? Marguerite Yourcenar perhaps, whose Cavafy rides easily in the master's traces. Sappho? Arendt? My copy is not, as they used to say, to hand.

I consented to be baffled by your play with the *épaulage* of *traduttore/traditore*, but is that similarity not a *recyclage* of Derrida's *différence/différance*? The polyglot may boast rare frustration in hooting traffic between linguistic *frères-ennemis*, but Alexandrian taxi-drivers, for instance, juggled three or four languages all their lives without *états d'âme*. You linked the plurality of languages with the revenge of the Almighty at the sight of altogether-boys humanity essaying *campanilismo*.

What you never broached, unless I am wrong, is the recurrent oddity that the polyglot, however Sweeney-swift, is as often lackey as prodigy. The Jew has not uncommonly served in that role and been more often suspected of duplicity than *comblé* with gratitude. English gentlemen prided themselves on being monoglot men of their word; narrow-mindedness and integrity wore the same striped ties. Cavafy warned Morgan Forster that if they ever lost their money, the British would discover how much respect other people really had for them. Willie Maugham had said the same thing. No Cassandra like a *prox.acc.*

You did not admit to the ambition, implicit in your erudite elegy, to lead another force, of however many languages, in the attempt to heap Ossa on Pelion and storm the heavenly heights. That the singular language of the original Babel builders was Hebrew, before they were cleft by a plethora of tongues, was no small element in your recursion to the myth. Jewish selection by JHVH (in some accounts, a fusion of two divinities, one mountain, one desert; one male, the other possibly female) was privilege and burden. All other languages were chatty rivals, nagging Hebrew's back-to-frontness, but never able to dislodge, if likely to bemoan, its primacy. The writing on the wall might threaten whomever it did, but it was also, inescapably, a tribute to language as the vessel of awful warnings. Did Plato not promise that whatever is said can never be other than an approximation to the incommunicable ideal? Would you go as far as the shut-your-Trappists? Not in practice, certainly. Did the Browning version, 'Ah, but man's reach should exceed his grasp / Or what's a heaven for?' figure among your epigraphs?

I was innocent enough to take your linguistic prosopography to be indisputably scholarly. Only recently did I hear what may be a very old story, not necessarily true for that reason, that the great Oxford professor of Semitic languages, Edward Ullendorff, posted, whether publicly or in a private letter, a list of, they say, some five hundred Homeric nods in *After Babel*, with the counsel that they be corrected before any reprint. Unflattered by his attentions, you did not alter a syllable, did you? Odd! Hence you remain the pundit who wrote that Greek choruses were in iambics, the one metre in which they were never composed. Who but you could have corrected John Peter, when he said, for some reason, that the nails in the crucifixion were never written about, by quoting whatever arcane source gave each hammered head a distinct moniker? Can one of them have been Estragon? Do I not remember (the generalist's elderly lament) that you found some link with Samuel Beckett's tramps in *En attendant Godot*? Nevertheless, you declared that J.P.'s book about Beckett was 'almost major'; faint praise to crown its shoulder.

I wonder how you would have reacted had your correspondent's name been not Ullendorff but Ohlendorf. Imagine a return address in Patagonia. Visualise yourself slitting the envelope, thrilled one way and another by alternating currents of pride and prejudice, wondering what the ex-head of Reich security, S.S. general and commander of *Einsatzgruppe* D with its mass murderous credentials, might have to say to you. Would you not just slightly be hoping that he had read your book with admiration and a sense of having no alternative but to topple his king and concede your mastery? You will certainly recall, and probably envy, that Carl Schmitt, the all but respectable academic Nazi philosopher, confessed that Leo Strauss, one of a not that small number of doctoral and humourless Jews, had made a point against him to which there was no properly philosophical response. This was with regard to the arbitrary selection of the Jews as the enemies of Aryan civilisation.

Blonde beastliness was never so self-revealingly inadequate as in its dread of what it affected to despise. In the condemned cell, Julius Streicher, always termed 'the Jew-baiter' (thus loading much of the odium on his loutish person), sought to convert to Judaism. Since the Jews had won the war, he was ready to concede them the mastery. Blaise Pascal would have seen his point, *nicht war*? Streicher was condemned to death more because he was not a gentleman, as Speer persuaded the court that he himself was, and thus deserved the fate of *Jud Süß* as a counter-jumper (a term I last heard used by Guy Ramsey) than because he called for genocide. Speer's own deputy was hanged for crimes to which the handsome Albert had conscripted him but from which he had the sophisticated gall to distance himself.

You and Zara came to stay with us at Lagardelle in the early 1980s. You were exemplary guests, bringing a handsome decanter in your BMW saloon, taking tactful excursions to spare Beetle from cooking more than one very good meal a day, and pulling rank only by asking Paul, then in his early twenties, not to play his barbarous music when your ears (one crumpled) were nearby. You wore a dated continental white peaked cap while in the swimming pool where we never joined you. On the second or third day, you became suddenly suppliant. You had brought a manuscript on which you craved my advice, not so much concerning the style as whether or not it would be – what? – dangerous to publish it. You were happy to be provocative in discussion, but *The Portage of A.H. to San Cristobal* sought, it soon appeared to me, to claim a place alongside *Darkness at Noon* and *1984* (then an imminent date) as, first, a *texte provocateur*, then as an undeniable classic of contrariness, a meta-novel.

'Portage' – at once superior and a little soupy, next in line to *potage* – promised a gourmet dish. I need scarcely rehearse its recipe; the key ingredient was announced in that unmistakable abbreviation. The star turn, the only eloquent voice among a montage of lay figures, was delayed, as any showman would wish, to the latter pages. The attendant characters were culled from stock. None of the porters, I think, was British or American. Until the toted and touted A.H. was sprung from his silence, parody ruled, as in Peter Ustinov's play *The Love of Four Colonels*.

The dangerous essence of what you were proudly anxious for me to read lay in A.H.'s own defence: had he not done what he did, the state of Israel would not exist. You came alive in Hitler as in no one else; he the magician, you Mario. If you had hoped that, like Captain Queeg in *The Caine Mutiny*, he would condemn himself with his own hectic apologia, you were too hot for your own schema. A.H., in your impersonation, became the deliverer of the people he had set out to exterminate. Israel was his creation; without him, the Jews would never have been suffered to be at home.

By the end, I could see that you had less fear about what Hitler's open or covert supporters might say or do than whether you had added a cubit to your literary stature. Your anxiety for acclaim dressed the text as an exercise in literary experiment. It ended without a full stop, as if the complete version had been torn apart by the thought police. It allowed for the possibility that you had more to say and just might be driven to further glosses. You were the virtuoso waiting for cries of '*bis*'.

As it happened (title of Clement Attlee's flatfooted memoirs), the storm that greeted *The Portage* was generated by Christopher Hampton's theatrical version. As *maître charcutier*, he gave A.H. the last word, a *bombe surprise* that infuriated Martin Gilbert. In typically flat prose, Martin denounced the whole project. He and others are said to have aborted the production's run. I am cynical enough to think that, had it been a hit, Bernard Miles and the Mermaid management would have greeted the furore as money in the bank. Did you know that Martin, industrious archivist, his lack of prosaic lustre in marked contrast to your euphuism, married *en troisièmes noces*, one Esther Goldberg, whose family name had also been Martin's, until his father decided on a tactful makeover?

The Portage trumpeted your genius and whispered its limitations; an essay in fictional fig, in a language without roots in the vernacular, drew the accusation levelled by Céline against Proust. I found it *littérature* except for that *tour de force* which, no doubt, it had been conceived to elevate. As I took my time to be magisterial, I enjoyed your suppliant expression, Zara's detached maturity: you her concern. Michael was wrong: she was by no means the least attractive woman in the world, provided she remained dressed. I played the easy notes: the thing was done, it was not for anyone else to decide or forecast its fate. If published, however, what you had had the nerve to say could never be unsaid. I was flatterer enough to compare your invented Führer with Dostoyevsky's Grand Inquisitor. You had already announced that there could be no national, territorial cure for the Jewish condition. To have Hitler proclaim himself the objective founder of the state of Israel flaunted some loopy truth.

Had the *Shoah*, as we have come to call it, thanks to Claude Lanzmann, never taken place, would the powers ever have ceded the Palestinian littoral to Zion? Benign malice was never so inadvertently manifest as in the previous British suggestion that 'the Jews' make their home in Kenya, a poisonous gift if ever one was offered. Imagine if that had happened. How could anyone, in due time, have defended the appropriation of African soil to make a gimcrack reserve for a doomed species? What better confirmed your clever suspicion that what my father always called 'the Christians' had been saddled with a faith in which they were locked without the prospect of parole and for which the Jews deserved the blame, doubled after they themselves failed to be gulled by it? The ghetto and the Inquisition stood for the resentment that never ceases to be visited on the Chosen for passing the parcel.

Freud's Oedipus was Jesus in clever drag; he killed and supplanted the Father and became the favourite of a mother never seen or imagined to have anything personal to do with the Almighty. Translation becomes pernicious, unless one is very careful, its abiding lure, is that Babel's coded coda?

Are you all but smiling with those thin moist lips, in the hope that I am getting myself into silly trouble? Yes, George Steiner, you are Goethe's countryman, double-dyed if never of his blood, Faust your role, damnation your prize. No torrent of honours could sate your appetite for martyrdom, the knock on the door that would prove the Christian world as fatal as Fellini's Steiner promised. We fabricated a friendship, you and I, contrived proximity without intimacy, candour without revelation, secrecy without a secret.

The fault perhaps was mine. I should, I am still sure, have been a fool to declare myself unreservedly to you, even if I had had contraband to disclose. My comedy was that I came to shuffle your letters out of sight, lest Beetle be irritated by the persistence of our exchanges. You did your generous best to introduce us to the best Cambridge company. I remember a dinner party to which you convoked the vice-chancellor and other office holders whom you introduced by their titles. One had the nice nerve to say, 'George, for goodness' sake when did I stop being Harold?'

It is now over a quarter of a century since we last spoke to each other. I have often been sorry, never very. Can it be that it gave you a certain pleasure to put me in the bind you did? Must I remind you? In 1994, Sarah did several paintings for my book of revisited Greek myths, *Of Gods and Men*, published by the Folio Society. That we had dedicated the volume to you made it all the more stinging that, in a letter of lemony gratitude, you said that my daughter's subtleties were 'dire'. Cleverly, but not very, you wished that Michael Ayrton had been alive to provide images worthy of the text.

I predicted that you would defend yourself by reference to the dark root of the Latin word *dirus*, full of dread; and so you did: oil and vinegar your typical dressing. In my letter of adieu, I said that hurting and being hurt seemed warp and whoof – as in express trains – of your vanity. To ignore your malice would have conceded that I held your friendship so dear that I was willing to have you abuse our beautiful and brilliant daughter. Fat chance. Your envy had shown itself many years before. At Sarah's degree show, in 1980, you had found nothing better to say to Beetle than ask why all the paintings were 'so dark'. Was dire already loaded in your magazine? She turned away, taller than you.

I implied just now that I have not missed you. Have I not proved the opposite? Just as your mistakes contrived to be proof of your erudition, your gaucheries of your grand ambitions, your vanity of your self-doubt, I have protested too much to be beyond suspicion. And yet, given similar circumstances, I should again cut loose without hesitation, remain so without regret. All the same, there was something rare and almost lovable about you: your faith in high culture paired with your doubt concerning its honour, your craving for eminence, your knowledge that it guaranteed nothing, that at any moment you might dangle, like Veit Harlan's *Jud Süß*, in a Christian cage, *pauvre petit juif*, booked to have the bottom fall out. I made a telephone call, when I knew you were unwell, but the carer lady said that you were asleep; so was Zara.

Adieu once more, Freddie. *De tout coeur quand même.*

TO STANLEY KUBRICK.

Dear Stanley,

Did I ever hear you laugh or see you smile? I may have amused you from time to time; laughter was scarce among your responses. A pause stood for applause. During the many months we worked together you were often friendly, always sombre. You never hinted why. That rebarbative frown hinged shutters on your secret self. Private anguish was nobody else's business; work its narcotic. Might it be that, throughout your life, success was as much revenge as pleasure? I remember you referring to 'those people', meaning the unfathomable Gentiles who – so you said – always know when you-know-whos are around. At the same time you said that you weren't a Jew; you just happened to have two Jewish parents. The paranoid's paranoid, you didn't do a whole lot of forgiving or forgetting. Hence your diagnosis that amnesia was the one complaint Jews never suffer from? Michael Ayrton once told me of an artist who boasted 'I hoard my turds'. Those deep cartons of papers filed in the vast spartan bastion in which you chose to be boxed promised that nothing was lost on its blue-jeaned Bluebeard. You might have been assembling some kind of a case, defence and accusation confounded, to be delivered before whatever judge or clown proves the assessor of humanity's inhumanities. As for clown make-up, you sure started something with *The Killing*. Enough already? I think so.

You seemed as much lonesome as autocrat; mark of the still photographer you first were; and the kid before that? As far as our script was concerned, you apologised, often, for not being able to specify what you wanted. You could promise only to recognise it when you saw it. Tell you something though: when you said you were 'absolutely thrilled' by those first forty or fifty pages of mine, it beat all the awards I was ever given. Later, you became anxious lest what followed was not as good. You even suggested that maybe we should make the first part of the script worse, to avoid an anti-climax. I said, 'Come on, Stanley'. On we went, and on. Again and again you asked me to re-do a scene or a sequence. Sisyphus, the Holy Roller, tried to stay happy. Si-si-fuss? Yes, yes indeed: working for you became a proud peonage. Remember what the streetwalker said was her prize satisfaction: 'He chose me'. I can hear you saying: (Pause) 'What's your point?'

The closer we got, slowly, to a shooting script, the more the burden of decision shifted onto you. Director and producer, you became *solus rex* with his board before him, pawns gone; your move. Reminds me: did you ever play chess with Vladimir Nabokov when you were doing your *Lolita?* He specialised in *solus rex* situations. He called you an artist, in my presence, not a garland he looped around a whole lot of necks. If you did play him, and you won, I can be pretty sure that that was the first and last time he proposed facing you. I have it from Jeremy Bernstein that you were never the grandmaster overstatement proclaims. Nor yet was V.N.: beaten, twice, in a quick row, by Max Black, the Baku-born Cornell Wittgensteinian, he retreated to devising devious problems to which he alone held the key.

Like Heidegger in that at least, in interviews Nabokov would not answer questions that had not been submitted in writing ahead of time. He was a premeditating, solitary craftsman; for all your industry, you were not above allowing others (and chance) to make a contribution. V.N. caught, pinned, catalogued butterflies. Never lepidopterous, you let butterflies work for you: planning and happenstance fluttered together: '*Mein Führer*, I can walk!' Unscripted Peter Sellers came up with Dr Strangelove on his crooked feet. Even the ranks of Tuscany could scarce forbear to smirk: the other actors, seen-it-all George C. Scott included, were all but corpsed. You had no cover, the wit not to worry about it: print that one! Chaplin said that no movie was ever better for being technically perfect.

Bernstein told me you used to call him up for a game of chess at all sorts of times and you'd send a taxi to bring him to the house. He won a few games; maybe you won more. Would Botwinnik have paused to watch either of you? Jeremy presumed that you were buddies of a kind. One day he called, you asked if he'd seen *A Clockwork Orange*. When he said he had, you said, 'Enjoy it?' Jeremy said, '*Enjoy* it?' He never heard from you again.

Reminds me how, one time, you told me a New York doctor friend had supplied some useful information. A while later, you asked me how much you thought our hero would make as a GP. I guessed around two hundred grand a year, but suggested you call your doctor friend. You said, 'We don't talk any more'. Here's a creative writing exercise: what scene on a transatlantic line ends with S.K. and Dr Quilibet never wanting to speak to each other again? I hear you: 'Quilibet? I never knew any doctor Quilibet.' Let it go, OK? Nabokov would get it though, Moses Hadas too, in sleep. Young Kubrick, the outsider, gatecrashed Hadas's classical lectures at Columbia, didn't you say? *You* were Spartacus. I know: you didn't like that scene; Dalton Trumbo (recently re-upholstered as Hollywood's victim-hero) was never your sweetheart.

Might it be that what was wrong with your *Lolita* was that you honoured V.N.'s words too piously? It was your one verbose film. You also fudged what you were trading on: the scandal of Lolita being a brat with those shining, 'lightly flossed' pre-pubescent shins. Jazzing her up as teenage ready-when-you-are jailbait killed the perverse appetite that Nabokov wished on Humbert Humbert. Lo's false innocence was calculated to lure the reader (never this one) into inadmissible complicity.

Has any learned on-the-maker compared H.H. stalking Lo with V.N. netting lepidoptera? They will, Stanley, they will.

As a movie, they said *Lolita* couldn't be done, and it couldn't; not and be licensed above ground. Did you ever look at a book called *Nabokov's Dark Cinema* by Alfred Appel (never of Volodya's eye)? It argues Nabokov's work was conceived in his intra-cranial projection room. He told me that, when composing, he visualised the letters of the alphabet in technicolor. Lurid *Lolita* was first published, in 1955, in Paris, by Maurice Girodias's Olympia Press, famed for supplying English visitors with texts such as *White Thighs* and *Thongs* which could keep them up at night. Once *Lolita* had been hailed as a masterpiece by Graham Greene, V.N. woke to find himself famous, in more than literary and scholastic circles. He then affected to be shocked to discover what low company was keeping him. Think so? He was too *rusé* to play a convincing dupe. He now wished he had sold the rights for more than a mess of pottage.

G. Greene liked making waves as much as reputations. As a pre-war London film critic, he had created a scandal by accusing Hollywood of picturing Shirley Temple as a 'Hullo, sailor' tartlet on the good ship Lollipop. If *Lolita* had been published by a mainline publisher, would G.G. ever have named it a *Sunday Times* Book of the Year? Back in the 1980s, Anthony Burgess complained, a lot, that you had paid only something like £500 for the film rights of *A Clockwork Orange*. I'll bet it was a bargain he was happy to make, until he wasn't. The movie generated huge sales of his book.

You discussed making a quality blue movie with Terry Southern, when he was working with you, in the early 1960s, on *Doctor Strangelove*. On the screen, *Lolita* turned out nothing like as salty as its source. Hence the abiding wish, next time you had a chance, to concoct something too exquisite not to be art, blue perhaps but ultramarine. Dick Zanuck sent me Southern's (and Mason Hoffenberg's)

Candy back in Rome in 1965, in the flattering, unwarranted expectation that I would know how to package it as popporn. I passed in sleep, as bridge players used to say. Did you ever see the movie they made of Philip Roth's *Portnoy's Complaint?* If so, you and who else? Blue movies depend on participants granting peepers furtive anonymity. Who wants to see anyone he recognises engaged in the old double act or to be seen watching them?

Settled in England, you seemed too remote, if not too fine, to have anything to do with the Hollywood system. Yet you always had an appetite for stars, especially male; their casting alone could promise the funds you needed. When I did my first outline of that last big scene (which you resisted, for a long time, because there was nothing equivalent in 'Arthur'), you said it was great; unfortunately you couldn't get Bogart and Greenstreet. Would I do it again? Were you totally satisfied with the version shown to the public? The play between power and its gulls deserved what archaeologists call 'another squeeze', smarter scissors, some nice, inappropriate music over (from *High Society?*). In your best days, even perfection was apt for improvement.

The few actors you believed in you trusted completely; P. Sellers especially, a mimic whose real life originals, Alec Guinness not least, seemed ever afterwards to be imitating him; but also Jack Nicholson, James Mason, Sterling Hayden, Leonard Rossiter. Tom Cruise was never on that list. Since *Eyes Wide Shut*, he has spent a lot of time running for his living, winning fixed fights or hurtling into space. Nothing like a helmet for heading off dialogue.

For the big bad Doctor Ziegler, played by Sydney Pollack, your first choice among the living had been Harvey Keitel. He flew to London, foist cless of course, and was billeted in a waterfront suite at the Savoy. When I had tea with him, he had been in storage for a month or three. Eventually summoned to the set, he is said to have said – or was it done? – something unforgivable to *la* Kidman and was sent home under sealed cover. Miss K., they say, could be quite fastidious when roused; or was it, as rumour suggests, when Harvey was? Always was a street kind of a guy. Kidman has been a star for many years for many people; can you think of a single movie of hers you wanted to see again? She flashed a neat ass though, early on, in something set in the Bermuda triangle. You were in no hurry to have Cruise and Kidman know that I had anything to do with the script. Remember Naboth's vineyard?

Did you ever read a lot of what was said about you and your movies? You just might have smiled, or not, at the claim of some academic thruster who divined, not long ago, how deeply you delved for Jewish antecedents in your work that you named our Ziegler in memory of some thirteenth-century Hasid. In fact, that dull trader, you could confirm that the name was my choice for a character whose part in the piece supplied a pay-off that you, and Arthur, had no time for, until you did. I named him for a garrulous agent I had, for a short time (too short for me to get to call him Ziggy). He represented Roman Polanski at the time when Sharon Tate was murdered and told me all, all about it. I'd sooner he'd found me some worthwhile work.

Reasons are often obscure when actors get dumped or sidetracked: sometimes they are too good, like Alan Rickman, as the sheriff of Nottingham, in the nth remake of Robin Hood. Kevin Kostner was costlier and had the last word. Our son Paul didn't get as far as the cutting room floor. When a tall and handsome eighteen-year-old, he was going to be an extra in Ridley Scott's first movie *The Duellists*. Rigged in grenadier's uniform and bearskin, he was paraded right next to Harvey, who exercised a star's right to deny an extra the chance to outshine him. Tall Paul was promptly demobbed. Joe Losey's less glamorous son, Joshua, stayed on parade.

Joe was the only other director whose call for my services gave me the sense of election that yours did. Not least because he was a fugitive from Senator McCarthy, Losey was a *chouchou* of *Cahiers du Cinéma* in the days when it played pitch and toss with reputations (Vincente Minnelli went out with the empties). Losey's *The Servant* was pretty damn good; *The Go-Between* won the Golden Lion at Cannes. I went to see him in his Chelsea house, Royal Avenue, already. Horizontal on a *chaise longue*, like a cross-dressed *poule de luxe*, he played hard to get and I didn't that much want to get him. We parted civilly. Later he put it about that I was a pretentious phoney. Takes one to know one, did you say? I doubt if you'd bother. Later still, he sent me a book he wanted me to script: Roger Vaillant's *La Truite* (featuring another innocent young morsel). I said I didn't think there was enough stuff in it. After he made the flop he admitted I'd been right. Big deal. Waning directors are liable to find merit in whatever there's money available for them to make. Not a charge anyone could bring against you.

Years later again, Joe called me in France seeking advice on how to persuade his son Joshua to find an honest job. I said, 'Can there be an honest job in a capitalist society?' 'Come on, Freddie, what do I do?' I didn't say 'get another writer'. Another funny thing about directors: when they have had a big, big hit, studios often asked them what they'd really, really like to do next. Nine times out of eleven they pick a loser: remember *Malice in Wonderland?* Poor Joe, his last movie was *Ladies Night in a Turkish Bath.*

For all his apparent contrariness, Losey was a main-chancer, not unlike many Fifth Amendment martyrs. Ideology is a regular cloak, left and right, to upgrade second-raters. Billy Wilder made one of his typical remarks about the Hollywood Ten unfriendly witnesses: 'Two were talented, the others were just unfriendly'. Being nominated a martyr was Joe's big break.

Only Dirk Bogarde had the nerve to accuse him of selling out when the Burtons pressed his button. As Dirk proved, often, grievance and truth are old accomplices. Marxism did for Joe what Catholicism did for Graham Greene: franked the merchandise with a moral watermark. Did anyone ever pin an ideology on you? For you, fear fused with future. Happy endings? Try down the street.

Has anyone yet composed that scholarly essay on females in Mr Kubrick's *opera omnia*? Is there a single scene in which a woman has the last word or anything much to say at all? Physicians and movie directors are often shy, without their shingles, when it comes to women. Each category authorises, by degree or status, demands – get 'em off, among others – which its tenant would never dare utter *in propria persona*. On location in Tuscany, John Schlesinger lumbered me with persuading Julie Christie to shed her clothes during a long tracking shot in *Darling*. I dished her the usual sincere bullshit about motivation. Our Princess Diana was throwing off, so I told her, what made her what she was not etc. She said, 'I know, I know, but I just don't have the figure for prolonged attention from behind'. She did the shot though, bravely. Motivation? Nuts. Tell them anything, ain't it the truth? How beautiful and how true David Lean made Julie in his otherwise cardboard *Doctor Zhivago*! Tom Courtenay as some kind of Trotsky? Get out of here.

Back in the Sixties, I made bold, in the introduction to the script of *Two for the Road*, to deplore the squareness of Lean's movies. It never occurred to me that he would ever see, or give a damn about what I said. He did not make another movie for ten years. We often underrate how prone invulnerable people are to be wounded, don't I? A decade or more later, Lean got in touch with me, while we were both in L.A., and asked me to come and see him, in his *cabana* in the Hotel Bel Air, about writing a pirate movie for him. Can it be that Marlon

Brando was going to be Sir Henry Morgan? Lean looked and acted more than a little like Field Marshal Alexander. By way of apology for what was never mentioned, I affected more enthusiasm for skulls and crossbones than I actually felt. Working with him would require a year of my life. I did my best to play honoured, but felt no urgent vocation for 'avast there' and similar of by-the-yard dialogue.

Perhaps because our script offered her brave lines, Nicole Kidman did do a little prattling in *E.W.S.*, rigged in an unattractive slip that gave imagination no naughty work to do. In the long scene after she and Cruise return from that fancy Park Avenue party, nothing came out that might dent Cruise's conceited carapace. That's the danger when stars are incited pretty much to re-enact themselves. François Truffaut thought it was unwise to give a character the first name of the actor who played him; he would never be sure whether he was being himself or the other.

Whatever drove you to cast Cruise (hence Nicole), it was never admiration for his versatility, was it? From all accounts, you gave him slow hell for Warner Brothers' money. You slave-drove him for what he cost and he took it like a man. What do you suppose he ever told the Scientology brass that locked him in hock to them? Imagine someone who confesses what isn't true in order to deserve his sour medicine. Does every tyrant miss a master, the one luxury he can't hire? I read somewhere about a successful businessman who paid a specialist lady to whip him every time he made a lucrative deal. Darryl Zanuck, they say, demeaned himself in pursuit of a Lesbian mistress. Having everything he wants can leave a man wanting only what will never want him, the one thing he doesn't have is all he needs.

Was there something just a touch naïve in your idea that casting a married couple as a marred couple would enable you to put 'the truth' on the screen? One thing you can be pretty sure of: whatever any conjugal duo may disclose in public about their relationship, they rarely let any crucial cat out of their bag. Did you honestly suppose Cruise and Kidman were bound in genuine passion, rather than embraced in a careerist merger? It's tempting, very, to guess at something two-edged in your screened deconstruction of a famous pair.

Then again, if *Eyes Wide Shut* had got them Oscars, it might have Burtoned them together again. Calculation too has its passions. You told me how, when they first dropped in at your hermetic compound in an unassuming helicopter, just like any other sweet unspoiled couple, they sat side by side on the sofa, holding hands already, while you made the demanding pitch you could be pretty sure they would fall for. Who comes in a chopper to say no? How about all three of you were star-struck with each other? You were genuinely touched, it seemed, by the way that Cruise would say, 'What do you think, Nic?' Did you ever say anything like that, concerning your career, to any of your wives? It sounds to me like high-class audition talk, but you read the pair for down home sweethearts. Might it be that the innocence was yours, not theirs? Who is ever quite as grown-up as he likes to suppose? You looked at life, other people's lives, through a glass, darkly. You did possession; did you ever do love?

Jack Priestley, the English novelist whom you are unlikely to have read, or heard of, told me, on the one occasion we met, that he had always felt as if he was pressing his nose against the plate glass that separated him from the lives of others (title of a good German movie). During the war, Priestley was promoted as 'jolly Jack'; miserable Tyke that he was. I had dinner with him at the Cheltenham Festival in 1963. He presided, resentfully, over a table of his juniors. Asked about wine, the provincial waiter made the offer of red or white. Denied a chance for vinous punditry, Priestley behaved as condescendingly as Randolph Churchill might have, and often did. Who he? Let it go, OK?

You talked, in an early one of our extended conversations, of casting Alec Baldwin and his then wife Kim Basinger, a far more delectable lady than *la* Kidman, dishy enough to play the seductive masochist in Adrian Lyne's *Nine and a Half Weeks*. I was offered a lotta lotta money to put some salt on that particular tale, but I knew better, just, than accept a job that would never be over until the producer said so. There is something, isn't there, about female beauty – its seeming self-sufficiency, perhaps – that excites a wish to punish it? And have her like it is the kicker. Not a few early directors paraded on set dressed like lioness-tamers, *mit* boots and riding crop. In his declining years, Otto Preminger was propped in a chair in his living room. His wife, who seems to have bided her time, disclosed him to visitors as 'the terror of the floor'.

Women and the devil go way back. Beauty can enrage the male it so often makes ridiculous or – worse – superfluous. Pretty well the only beautiful woman in any of your movies was Marisa Berenson (her rich name part of her cachet, was it not?). You had Ryan O'Neal blow smoke in her face right after their wedding. That was the story? That was your story. I once congratulated you on the brilliant silent scene, on some Baroque terrace, in which Barry wooed the then still married diva. Having neither of them say anything, I said, was better than any imaginable dialogue. This prompted you to say that there had been dialogue in the script but you cut it. 'Did you ever hear her voice?' You mimicked scratchy prattle. I was accused, by the usual tribunal, of treachery to you or cruelty to her by recounting what you'd told me. Whatever indiscreet stories people tell writers might as well be pasted on the wall; everyone knows that. Isn't that why they tell them? Beats writing on water when it comes to immortal hopes. 'When you no longer care to hurt me, I shall know you don't love me any more'. Am I quoting Strindberg correctly? Said by a male or by a female? George Steiner would know.

In Greek iconography, only females are regularly depicted looking in a mirror. Narcissus proved himself a narsissy by falling in love with his reflection in the water that eventually drowned him. How pretty was he by any standard but his own? Some smart ass described him as 'that plain boy'. The ancient warrior sought and redeemed his reputation, and identity, in battle; the goddess and the beauty settled for reflecting on themselves. I remember a Christmas Eve party on Zuma beach when Natalie Wood spent the time lying on a towel looking at herself in her make-up mirror, as if keeping an eye on herself would save her from age. Someone asked her, casually, what she wanted for Christmas. She said, 'Yesterday'.

Male envy of female self-sufficiency has something to do with desire for the sex's subjection. Think of the way, in *The Shining*, you had Nicholson – axe in hand – say, 'Here's Johnny!' to Shelley Duval, seen only through a terrified crack in the wooden door, as if already split in two. The story goes that Jack came to you the night before that scene was due to be shot and warned you, with no sort of aggression, that he might not be able to do it with full force more than two or three times. You said you understood very well. The next morning, Nicholson did his stuff brilliantly. After the third take, you kept your word, promised you were very happy and wrapped the scene.

You never showed rushes to the actors. Nicholson looked at you inquiringly the following morning. You indicated how excellent he had been, how pleased you were, stuff like that. As the day proceeded, he read you for somehow discontent. You told him again how good he had been. He was not deceived. 'Come on, Stanley; is there something I didn't do you were looking for?' 'I told you', you said, 'you couldn't have been better.' 'But what?' 'Her face. Did you see her face?' 'What was wrong with it?' I'm told you caricatured Shelly Duval's expression. 'And I don't have any cover, because you…' Nicholson said, 'So what are we going to do?' You said, 'Would you mind doing it again?' Know something? I've never had the nerve, unless it's the patience, to watch *The Shining* to the end.

The usual people are eager to pad your *solus rex* myth by insisting that you and I never got along. They insist how negligible my contribution was to *E.W.S.* (to the dwindling members of my wartime generation, those initials stand irrevocably for 'Emergency Water Supply', as available for dealing with incendiaries during the London Blitz). As if it mattered, one fact stands: after the William Morris office was crass enough to forward my first draft to you in one of their folders, you were enraged, not least when I responded to your reproaches by calling your obsession with secrecy a 'foible'. You had an unquestionable opportunity not to exercise your option on my further services. You huffed and puffed. 'Regards' replaced 'Best regards' at the end of your faxes. I was upset that you were upset, but I was too proud, unless it was too old, to grovel. Your indignation waned, slowly; then suddenly it was gone. No one could accuse you of being soft-hearted. You fired a lot of people, Bertrand Tavernier among them (at three in the morning, he told me), when he was a young publicist. The last time I saw him was at a packed screening of his 2013 movie, *Quai d'Orsay*, in the small French village of Le Buisson in the Perigordine countryside. When Bertrand went out of his way, during his introductory speech, to mention that I, the writer of *Eyes Wide Shut*, was *présent en salle*, the entire rural audience rose to its feet and applauded in sustained tribute, to you.

You renewed my contract because you depended on me; until you didn't. On we went, walrus and carpenter, with our congenial flyting. The pages, written and rewritten, mounted. I have five deep boxes full (the rest I threw out). I have never once looked at them again after that 'shit load of work' became all yours. How shall we ever know whether you truly rated

Eyes Wide Shut your clinching masterpiece? That's what eulogists claim; possibly for your sake, certainly for their own; no admirers like leeches with profits to suck. One such gospeller claimed to have tried several times to get in touch with me before composing his libellous quasi-truths. In fact, he never made any effort whatever and he must know it. All kinds of professors and fixers want to play cardinal roles in your elevation into a free-standing demi-god who could have walked on water, had he had time or inclination. Remember Peter Sellers in *Being There?* Monotheism underlies the presumption that there can only be one creator when it comes to the movies. *Passons outre*, as you would never say. You told me that one phrase in French was enough for you to get along with. It sounded to me like 'cat oo dee'; turned out it was '*Qu'as tu-dis?*'

One of your amateur fans let it be known the other day that she had had to see *E.W.S.* literally a hundred times before she could decrypt what it really meant. Every fan likes to play Alan Turing. Others jump to quicker conclusions: a nice professor in some minor college sent me his solemn interpretation of *The Shining* as a denunciation of the Holocaust and found kabbalist proof in the numbering of the hotel rooms. Another claims that you always and everywhere avoided overt allusion to Jews, the better to lard everything you did with sly Semitic significance. You can't see them, but he can prove they're there. Remember the old story about how to recognise members of a Jewish firing squad? They stand in a circle.

I can still hear you on the telephone, saying 'Freddie? (Beat) Can you talk?' A moment of diffidence, as if I might have had more pressing things in hand. When Beetle answered the phone, all you ever said to her was 'Freddie there?' Might it be that you lacked the vanity to be charming except for an ulterior reason? You gave no indication of what you were enduring after your daughter Vivian suddenly lit out and went to California. It has to have happened around the time you first called me. I heard only very much later that you sent her a twenty-nine-page, handwritten letter, pleading with her to come home. She failed to respond with a single word. Maybe that's how torn she was; maybe. Might it be that your favouritism dispossessed her of herself? How about she was an Elizabeth Barrett who ran away with herself while she still had her legs? What do I know? Only that you endured something close to bereavement by making yourself seem single-mindedly set on business in hand. One obsession effaced another. They say life's the thing; you preferred movies. As if it mattered, Vivian is one of those names, along with Leslie/Lesley and Robin, which seem to create uncertainty, if not ambivalence, in those labelled with them. Oscar Wilde called his son Vyvyan.

For all the drudgery of rewriting scenes – I sometimes felt more than a little like Jack Nicholson doing those stacks of lines in *The Shining* – working for/with you was grim fun. We talked on the telephone for many hours, very easily, about all sorts of things, on and off the subject of Arthur Schnitzler and the New York translation of his Viennese nightmare, never about your own work, except once: when you pretty much disowned everything before *The Killing*. My admiration – especially for *Paths of Glory*, *Dr Strangelove* and *Barry Lyndon*, that unlikely, un-American masterpiece – all but embarrassed you. You did tell me one story about the making of *Paths of Glory*. There was a big set piece sequence in which the French infantry advance across no-man's land. The attack disintegrates under machine-gun fire from the German lines. You were shooting in southern Germany and all the supposedly French soldiers were, in fact, German. You had five or six cameras in various positions to catch the evolving fiasco. When you called 'Action!' Kirk blew his whistle and his troops surged out of the trenches, advanced in rapid order on the enemy lines and had all but captured them before you could call 'Cut!' You then explained to the German assistant director that the whole point of the scene was that the attack faltered and fell apart. Would he please explain that the attack had to be a failure? The A.D. turned to the assembled German extras and, keeping it simple, told them that they had to advance, when the whistle blew, 'like Frenchmen'. They laughed and nodded. You asked if he was sure that they had really got the point. *Jawohl:* when the whistle blew, they advanced in ragged disorder and faltered or took shelter as the machine guns started rapping.

Resting on your laurels was not your style. You were always out to cut new ones, whatever trespasses you might commit to crop them. Breaking bounds is the outsider's favourite walk; parody – admiration as malice – his tribute. For instance? When you had Malcolm McDowell mimic Gene Kelly in Stanley Donen's *Singin' in the Rain.* The musical was one style of movie you never did; you had delicate white hands, never neat feet. The first and only time I met you before you solicited my services was at dinner in Donen's house in Montpelier Square in the early 1970s. You must have been less of a recluse in those days. Christiane was with you. S.D. had bought one of her paintings and sat her under it. He did nice as you never did. Your expensive Christmas presents were delivered as if you were paying an annual subscription. You seemed like a man who wished he could feel something he never did, or did no more.

The only other guest at S.D.'s table that I can remember was Lord Goodman, an obese lawyer who had been ennobled for acting as Prime Minister Harold Wilson's fixer at a time – now all but idyllic – when, it seemed, there was plenty to fix in the political machinery. After supper – instead of what might have been an interesting, not to say worthy, conversation – we played that silly game where everyone has so many matchsticks and each in turn declares something he or she has never done.

If another player had done it, one of his matchsticks went into the pool. Goodman said, in his Hitchcockian voice, 'I've never taken legal advice'. We all pitched in. Stanley Donen said that he'd never travelled on the London underground. I said I'd never slept with a movie star. Stanley D. paid up, big time. 'In our youth', the old Hollywood line goes, 'we lie on the sand and look at the stars; later, we lie on the stars and look at the sand.' Never my story, nor your idea of a joke; then what was? You said that you had never had an item of clothing made to measure. I paid up: in the Swinging Sixties, Douggie Hayward had done his tight stuff for Peter Sellers and for me and many others. I split a pair of his pants bending down to pick up a bag in Miami airport. He allowed less than the minimum of material for his hems. I never had anything tailor-made for me again.

After that dinner, I sent you a copy of Henry Treece's *Electra*, with the suggestion that it might make a mould-breaking movie. You never responded. Another correspondent of yours, Patrick McGoohan, author of old-time TV's *The Prisoner*, complained to your assistant that you had failed to reply to his heartfelt expression of fellow-feeling. Tony Frewin asked him, 'Did you enclose a stamp?' Willie Maugham deplored, back in 1954, that those requesting autographs rarely included a stamped addressed envelope. I didn't when I wrote to him, but he still answered, promptly, 'in his own claw', as Winston Churchill did in personal matters. Maugham invited me to tea at the Villa Mauresque.

Those we take for great are often lonely. I once spent five hours with Barbra Streisand. Every time I got up tactfully to go, she found reason to detain me. You must have heard how she was at some Academy lunch and had Billy Wilder placed next to her. She had recently directed *Prince of Tides*, starring Nick Nolte, one of those busy actors whose name on the bill always prompted the question 'Who couldn't they get?' At some point Barbra said, 'Billy, I hear you were like that…', she paddled her hand, 'about my movie'. Billy said, 'No, Barbra, I wasn't like that…' He repeated her paddle, 'about your movie. I hated it.'

When I met Stanley Donen in Westwood in 1975, after *Barry Lyndon* had taken a pasting from the US critics, he was wearing a lapel badge declaring your movie a masterpiece. He had no envy. He liked liking things; but when he didn't, he sure didn't: I remember coming out of a movie with him in Century City and seeing a long line below us at the box office. Stanley called out, 'Save your pennies'. When I included any small sign or word of amusement or affection between the main characters in our script, you said you didn't want them to sound like something out of Stanley Donen; sneer as tribute was as close as you came to admitting having seen *Two for the Road*. Stanley once told me how he was called up by some studio head who was worried about a movie a famous director had just made. If they sent a quiet car, would he come and take a look and say what he thought? It had to be done very discreetly, because… So: a car came late one evening, took him to a projection room on the back lot. The movie was screened, in silence. The lights went up. Worried executives looked at Stanley. He said, 'I liked it'.

You seldom mentioned other directors, rarely with admiration: Kieslowski's *Decalogue* the only exception I recall. Oh, and you did recommend I see Christopher Hampton's *Carrington*. I did; and reported how much we had enjoyed it. 'Did you see the whole thing?' 'Of course.' 'When we last spoke', you said, 'I'd seen the first twenty minutes. Might as well as have not seen any more. It was the same twenty minutes over and over.' You weren't wrong, but… nor did you mention that Emma Thompson, never my favourite lady, gave a remarkable performance as Dora. In your own work, your urge was again and again to trump what had gone before, following the principle of what Catullus called *variatio*. Meaning? Avoid butter on butter, Liv Ullmann's expression, maybe cadged from Ingmar the heavyweight champ.

During one of our many long, long telephone conversations, you told me that you'd been looking at *Gone with the Wind*. 'Vivien Leigh, you ever see a worse performance?' I remembered watching her having her stays tightened, her breasts promoted, before the ball. Fifteen years old, I never thought about her performance. You were a hard room for ladies to play. Did you get as far in *Carrington* as the moment when Dora (Emma T.) is in bed with Lytton Strachey (Jonathan Price) and reaches down, chin up, under the covers, with squeamish generosity, to grope him? Exemplary! The same Emma T. wrote in a magazine article that Audrey Hepburn couldn't act. Yes, she could (Audrey offered me five different ways of saying 'Hullo'); then again, did she need to? Any hullo of hers was a hullo of mine.

'Make it new' was your watchword, never spoken, always honoured, from *The Killing* onwards. For proof of your determination to axe the obvious, can any cinephile find just one scene, in all your films, where a conversation takes place in a car or iridescent waves break on some shore; was any kiss in your whole *oeuvre* just a kiss? The kiss of death was your preferred form of embrace. You never did love but you knew what Sadie and Maisie knew.

Avoiding the obvious is the artist's route to originality. Looking again is the only clever way to look; 'But wait...' the best advice. You rarely made a movie not based on some previous text; your imagination craved a skeleton to hang on. Still photography as you practised it in your solitary youth was a way of picking unsuspicious pockets, *en passant* like any unremarkable pawn. Geddit? The camera concealed in that cumbrous peep-holed bag of your teenage self when plodding and plotting around the New York streets resembled the third eye that used, some say, to be sited in the centre of the human forehead (you'd as soon have had yours in the back of your neck, am I right?). When I compared you to the snake in the fable – one of Aesop's, was it? – that hitches a ride across the river from the frog, promising he won't hurt him, and then stings him to death as soon as he's home and dry on the far side, you said (Beat) 'What's your point?'

There is just one thing I considered out of character in all your work as a young photographer, and that was the snap of the vendor in a newspaper kiosk on the day of F.D.R.'s death. It looks like a fresh-off-the-street the Great Weegee-style image of a grief-stricken, normally hard-assed New Yorker. In fact, you are said to have admitted you asked the guy to assume that end-of-the-world expression. How much more like the against-the-stream Kubrick it would have been if he'd had been grinning, not necessarily at the news, perhaps for some uncharted personal reason! Why, that once at least, did you solicit the obvious? Someone – it just might have been your adolescent buddy Paul Mazursky, who directed my *Coast to Coast* – gave me the worldly answer: no editor of any magazine would ever have bought anything that seemed to make light of F.D.R.'s death. Any practitioner of the public arts, however wishfully provocative, is wasting his time if he doesn't give at least one market what it wants. That's the difference between a tradesman and an artist. No wrinkled dugs, but I've been both. Who makes a good living in Arcadia? Not *ego*. A few not too abstruse allusions do a text no harm.

Mazursky remembered you as an ambitious, if contrary teenager. He was Irwin Mazursky, in those days. Back then, when they went West, actors whose original names sounded as if they came from eastern Europe were well advised to change them to something more native and sunny: Kirk Douglas and John Garfield and Edward G. Robinson were reborn occidental examples. One of your crowd (not a big one, I think) told Irwin where to go and what to do to

Anglo-Saxonise himself. When he came back, he said he'd done what you all suggested. 'So what do we call you from now on?' '*Paul* Mazursky'. Tableau, the old stage directions used to say. You never thought of dropping the Kubrick, did you? Was there originally a -ski attached? I can't remember, or care, if you were that kind of a kike. In *Our Crowd*, Stephen Birmingham claims that Manhattan's mainly German Jewish establishment was the first to label as 'kikes' the impoverished east European *Juden* who packed into the Lower East Side in the early 1900s and made it a ---ski resort. There have always been Jews and Jews, right?

Your career can be read as a succession of exercises in savoury sadism, especially when it came to women. 'Hup Debby, hup, Debby!', remember Gloria Grahame in *The Big Heat*? The only sequence in *Clockwork Orange* that lacked your unhurrying brilliance was the speeded-up sex scene with Malcolm McDowell and a couple of naked girls. It was as if you were getting it over as fast as you could. The same applied to the ineptly improvised 'love' scene in *Eyes Wide Shut*, in the back of a station wagon between Nicole and that dreamboat naval officer. You were rarely so uneasy as when doing genuine feeling.

John Malkovich once told me that the one scene in a script I wrote that he could never do was one that had his character declaring what he really felt. When did art and sincerity go hand in hand? Your spicy three-star dishes both delighted the consumers and slid them a dose of the medicine they deserved. Fusion of the cryptic with the blatant, the unsaid with the trumpeted, procured you the fun of making a fortune from successes that candied no kisses. I doubt you ever loved yourself very much. You kept having to prove how exceptional you were; what good was anything nice?

Fame was a spur that scored your own flank while needling you to excel yourself, and others. Steven Spielberg won all the awards, plaudits and power that should have proved to him that he was your superior, yet so mortified was he to read that you regarded *Schindler's List* as a movie about success, not about the Holocaust, that he insisted that I had made the story up. I like Steven and would not ever have thought to invent anything to hurt him. Truth is hurt enough. You know you said that and I know you did. Why in hell would I make it up, or any of the other things which I am accused, without a shred of truth, of having fabricated? I don't do fabricate; I do watch and listen. It was a consummation of a kind to be asked to work with you; it was of small importance to me as an artist. I made fiction out of something like you in a radio piece about a director called Jake Liebowitz; legitimate poaching and scrambling. Here's an extract for your coterie to deny sounds a little like you:

> JAKE: Do you ever want to see another tilt up to a skyscraper, sunlight on the office windows? Need any more wide shots of traffic on a clover leaf with a time lapse already? Speeded up always slows things down. No silhouettes against the sunset on the horizon. No full moon coming from behind clouds. No washing of hands and face in cold water, blinking and feeling better. No running hand-in-hand, with or without dogs, on the deserted sandy beach. No breaking waves on rocks. No driving without looking at the traffic. No cars pulling up and slotting neatly into shot and the headlights get turned off. No subjective camera looking up at trees with or without the sun shining through spring foliage. No nice-seeming families living in lakeside properties. No top shots as seen from where no one could possibly be. No stairwells with people coming up or going down. No racing the elevator to the top storey. No arriving and

finding an apartment door unlocked and the dead guy or girl in the last room we go into. No panning shots of family albums and photographs followed by a zoom in on Mr or Mrs Gotcha. No discovery of anything in a shoe box high up in a fitted closet. No side by side pissing and buttoning in the men's room. No scary scene followed by the guy sitting up with a start in bed and whaddya know: it was a dream! Dreams have no frames, which is why movies can't do dreams, unless they are dreams. What else? Please don't open a drawer and there's a gun in it. And how about dull dialogue doesn't turn to gold because you get the actors, whether they're doctors or not, to walk, talk and go downstairs at the same time? What else else? No titled British actor with a mouth full of dialogue showing the people what acting really is. No macho scientologist running after speeding cars and almost catching up. No girl with her back to camera, the guy's in front of her and she discloses her full eye-popping potential to him, but not to us. No girls who clearly never played before potting black, in a pool hall. Nobody sitting at a bar looking into his drink. Finally and absolutely: no sun-flowers. Now you've been to film school.

I recall your remarking, a tad plaintively, 'You don't think I'm an artist, do you?' I said, 'Oh, Stanley, what does it matter? All I know is, in order to do my work all I need is a pencil and a piece of paper and you need fifty million bucks, movie stars, a unit, cameras, lights, locations and who knows what all else.' You said, 'You sure know how to hurt a guy'. And I said, 'Depend upon it', or old English words to that effect. The truth, which your hierophants cannot abide, so busy are they confecting your messianic gospel, is that our relationship depended on the need you had to feel challenged, engaged in a competitive game. '*Competere*', in the Latin you never learnt, has the basic meaning of 'seeking together'. Nothing like it for dividing people; see under Gold Rush.

Screenwriter and director are often involved in a protracted exercise of capping each other's ideas, if they possibly can: having the last word is the prize and both of them know who is going to get it. And yet... Billy Wilder – never, for all his qualities, the sort of dialogue-laden director you'd ever bother to put down – worked with Izzy Diamond on all his later movies. He told us that Izzy would acknowledge that Billy had had a good idea by saying just two words: 'Why not?' Billy's first regular co-screenwriter was Charlie Brackett. Always an admirer, he lost patience with Billy's incorrigible egotism. The only director he was ever heard to admire was Lubitsch, especially *Ninotchka*, which Billy himself had written. When he set out to do an autobiography, he chose to dictate it, not write it down. He needed an audience to trigger him to be himself, or was it the self he wanted to be? Bill Goldman told of a producer he was working with who had a phone call from a senior executive, covered the receiver and called out, quietly and urgently, 'Bill, which lie did I tell him?' Which lie do we tell ourselves is a darker question.

No big surprise that partnership and antagonism often go together. Think of Rosalind Franklin and/versus Watson and Crick racing to uncover the structure of DNA. Did the winners have the grace or decency to give her credit? Did they fuck, as I never heard you say. Back to you and me: your hagiographers imagine that, by insisting that we were never buddies, they are showing how small my contribution was. A little wit – rare among third-rate academics (and not all that common among first-rate) – would have helped them to see that the friction between us freshened the sparks necessary to your forge. Deference seldom has a lot to do with creative partnership. For quite a while, you mocked my penchant for shapeliness. I was bold and old enough – was I ever? – to persist without seeking to make myself any kind of adhesive liegeman. I had books to write. I wanted to be brilliant for you, not to traipse into a twilight career, full of has-beans. A masterpiece would do for a capper, even if it was bound to be yours, not mine. Sadie and Maisie were always in there with us. Finally, to my surprise, you went along, a little sulkily, with my ideas about the end of the movie.

Under every long relationship worth a damn there are unaccountable wrinkles and fissures, which is why the search for 'motivation' is something no artist should ever waste a minute on. You remember Hitchcock's answer to the actor who wanted to know her motivation for walking to the window: 'Your salary'. You and I got along pretty damn well is the deposit of all this, because there was so much we didn't have in common. Michael Herr was very keen to show how buddy-buddy you and he were, but what did he contribute, aside from meat and potatoes, to what became *Full Metal Jacket*? Two movies in one, the first the one worth seeing; due more to you than to Herr is my guess. You needed him to tell you of what you avoided all your life: the crash and bang and blood of actual, not re-enacted, horror: war and its savage preliminaries. He was indispensable; apart from that you could have done without him. Terry Southern was something else, and you ended up not forgiving him for it. Like the man said, correct me if I'm right.

What's sad, for the specialist, is that Spielberg's hit with *Schindler's List* took away your confidence in *The Aryan Papers* project. The novel was full of dark hints about the Jewish character: even when denying being a Jew saved a character's life it served also to rob him of his integrity. Survival came with its own version of hell. Who better than you to explore that tarnished salvation? I remember your saying to me 'I'm not really a Jew. I just happen to have two Jewish parents.' I didn't laugh, but I did smile. I kinda know the feeling, but my mother was too beautiful to be read for Jewish, even by herself. I have never been called a liar by anyone as I have been by the Harlan clan and by Tom Cruise, egocentric control freak to whom I have never spoken. He did offer me a job though, soon after you finished shooting; the better to have me on a leash, no doubt. In his turn, he too seems to need the control he finds in Scientology, a cult which became a religion as a tax refuge for the fat tithes its officers could then exact from the credulous. That's a story that merits telling, just the kind you'd never get into, even if your daughter had not become what she did. What pleasure could she have taken in so brutal an apostasy, had she not guessed your loneliness to be as incurable as your appetite for punishment?

Here's a true story that no one will ever be able to verify. While I was still hot from writing *Eyes Wide Shut*, I had a meeting with Jerry Weintraub (who shared a last name with my second cousin, Irving, a U.S.A.A.F glider pilot murdered by the S.S. at Arnhem in 1944). Jerry was making *The Avengers* on a Pinewood stage adjacent to where you were shooting 'our' movie (self-deprecating inverted commas OK with you?). One day, he told me, he got to the studio, found his cameraman close to tears. 'Whassamatter?' 'I had a call from Stanley Kubrick. He says my lights are affecting his shooting.' Jerry told me that the accusation was not only nasty but impossible. There was no way that light could pass from one studio through three feet of brick into the next. Weintraub was not the kind of Jew to be intimidated. 'When I called him up', he told me, 'Kubrick's people said he was busy and couldn't come to the phone. I said, "Then get a pencil and take this down and give it to your boss: If you ever so much as speak to my cameraman again, I will come round and do you bodily harm. Signed Jerry Weintraub." A few minutes later, Kubrick called me back and explained that he had not meant to upset anyone and it was all a misunderstanding, stuff like that.' Would Weintraub make up a story like that? I doubt it, very much. He was what Rich Cohen called a 'tough Jew': buddy of Sinatra's, he made a fortune fixing venues for concerts. You don't do that without having to mix it, nicely as may be, with a bunch of mobsters. While I found Weintraub charming, he was no sweetheart: he beat up his wives and bullied his assistant. He also paid me a lot of money to write a screenplay about the guy who murdered Versace. He said it was the best first draft he ever read. It never got made: seems in those days no one cared to make a movie about a gay serial killer. Imagine! Shoulda been a musical? Just your kind of thing, if it was.

You made several masterpieces, won few awards; the greater your fame, the greater your isolation. You never deigned to canvass for votes; not getting them is the masochist's form of election. To judge from the earliest images I have seen, you were never a sweetie-pie. You made little attempt to charm anyone, including yourself. You may have looked young once, youthful never. Carefree? Forget it. You should have been smart, in the American sense, but something no biographer has even suggested seems to have led you to secrete your rareness behind an undistinguished school career. You didn't have the grades to get into college, especially since Columbia, where you ghosted in on Moses Hadas's lectures, was crammed with returning G.I.s. Was all the reading you did later an apology to the scholar in yourself that something led you to frustrate? You could be accused of seeking out your academic betters the better to better them: Arthur C. Clarke, Jeremy Bernstein, the Napoleonic pundits and who all else.

If I had the chance, there is one masterpiece I would do my best to get you to make into a movie: *Blood from the Sky* by Piotr Rawicz, a true Shoah story like no other. It trumps *The Aryan Papers*, if that matters, by having its leading character Boris (based on Rawicz), a fair-haired Jew, look so convincingly Gentile that he passes for one in the company of Ukrainian antisemites. The paradox is that only a Jew can enjoy the pleasure of passing successfully for being a Gentile. The genuine article has none of the fun, however dangerous, of being a passable fake. Boris's appearance of being unexceptional gives him the rare satisfaction of tricking his interrogator (much as Adolf Eichmann trumped Hannah Arendt's banality). Rawicz himself was a master of several languages, including the French, the sixth, in which his book was composed. No wonder the interpreter is a regularly mistrusted (often Jewish) figure! Language too is a kind of make-up, as Sellers proved. My novel *Lindmann* featured a reverse version of Rawicz: an English civil servant, humped with guilt for his bureaucratic part in the drowning of many Jews from the occupied Balkans, takes on the characteristics of a Jewish refugee.

You seemed to have regular parents, your father a doctor, but they scarcely figure in your resumé or in your biographers' spiel. Something was broken in you very early; the fracture made you whole, and alone. Am I right? Does it matter? The camera licenses a kind of larceny; you got your own back by taking other people's. Sure you know what I mean. The spy, like Genet's thief, knows exactly what he is: seeming to be what he really isn't obliges him to persistent, if inverted, dandyism. He dresses like a rumpled Brummell, taking care to look like a *schlump*. Behind whatever street guy you made yourself are those middle-class parents, the buddies you never quite trusted. You concealed being a Jew by looking like a nobody. Disguise yourself as what you really are, there's a singular form of duplicity. Try that for size; when it doesn't quite fit, that's you, which brings us back to the movie you never made of *Aryan Papers*.

Jean-Paul Sartre's *Genet, comédien et martyr*, belongs in some adjacent file, wouldn't you say? Of course you wouldn't. It does though: how we read other people is the usual way we get them wrong. Genet boasted of being a thief, because that was the label they franked on him (not without justice, that form of miscarriage). Being called a saint and a martyr, by Jean-Paul Sartre, brought out the honest man in him: he refused the halo. Yes, I do think all this has something to do with you; imprecision is a form of accuracy. As soon as you think you've nailed someone, you can be pretty sure you haven't got him or her right. Sartre preached political virtue, a common decency, but his work saps any durable belief in a society without blood for shadows: it is full of treacheries, quite as if the ideal was to be created for the greater pleasure of being its devil. Sartre aped the brave resistance man, but he didn't deceive himself: the counterfeit mounted a high horse to destroy Albert Camus, the genuine article.

Tony Frewin was the only one of your entourage whom I ever met on my visits to whatever your place was, near St Alban's. I was never quite sure why he called me now and again. Now we have become friends (and quasi-outcasts) of a kind. He was generous enough to break the Harlans' ranks and tell me that he had never seen you so happy as when you were reading that opening set of pages I sent you, unless it was when you saw the first instalment – some five million dollars – of profits from *2001*. You best proved your genius to yourself by making no sociable concessions, no deliveries of modesty, no affectations of devotion, especially when it came to executives. You did make an exception in the case of my friend David Brown, who went out on a limb in praise of *A Clockwork Orange*, I think it was, when all the others at the screening stayed silent. David, along with Dick Zanuck, backed *Two for the Road* when others flinched from its seemingly disorderly scheme. Did accurate gush ever have a more genial dispenser? Thanks to David, I got to direct a little film from

Mary McCarthy's *The Man in the Brooks Brothers Shirt*. You were kind enough to say 'You're a pretty good director, know that?' As the little American boy I once was, I might have answered 'Aw shucks!' You said: 'That's why you're never coming on my set'. You couldn't resist the vinegar. But you did once say that if I ever did want to come to Pinewood, I should make it on one of the days that Nicole had agreed to take her clothes off (for some scene that never made the final cut). I always think it's a little sneaky to take that kind of advantage. I do remember Barbara Kellerman though, when she was some beauty, posing like the Rokeby Venus in a scene in *The Glittering Prizes*.

I just happened to have David Lean's cameraman on my little movie, as well as a first A.D. called Derek who had worked regularly with you. One day, the story goes (and once they go, they never come back), when you were stressed, he asked you some routine question and you said, 'Fuck off, Derek'. A little later, crisis over, you wanted him to do something. Someone told you, 'He went home'. 'Home? Why?' 'You told him to fuck off .' 'And he went *home*? Get him back here. He knows I need him. All I said was fuck off.'

Life is a game of joining up the dots. Shooting *The Man in the Brooks Brothers Shirt* coincided with the great storms of 1989, which literally tore up trees in our garden. We were shooting in a studio with some kind of corrugated iron roof. When the wind gave it a loud shaking, Derek played the old hand and called 'cut'. It was not in the least presumptuous, but I remembered what Rydell told me and said, politely, 'Derek, I know you meant well, but if you call cut, any minute now the sound man will do the same thing and then who knows who. I have a two-word part in this production. It consists of calling "action" and calling "cut". Please leave me with it.' He said, 'My mistake'. A few years later, he might have said, 'My bad'. So it goes.

I suspect (with no shortage of clues), you feared that displays of genuine affection offered hostages to fortune. Stick to hard ball and you never owe anybody anything. Alexander Walker, long-time critic of the London *Evening Standard*, had the two-facedness of his profession, and a bouffant grey hair-do that caused him to hate *Strictly Ballroom* with enough passion to make him hate anyone who liked it. He truly believed that you and he had a genuine friendship. The notion that you admired him held him in perpetual fee. Your idea of amusement, was that?

There has been an incessant campaign, led by the Harlans, whom I never met during the two or three years of addressing myself exclusively to you, to deny that I had anything much to do with the final version of *Eyes Wide Shut*. Until the Writers Guild intervened, they tried to eliminate me from the credits in your travelling show. The guy who got me reinstated told me specifically that he would do anything for the man who wrote *Two for the Road*.

The Harlans and Master Cruise have managed to insert some derogatory stuff in my Wikipedia entry. There must be some way of excising the libel, but I lack the modern skill or the dreary energy to pursue the matter. Their sullen purpose is to establish your grand-masterliness and install you as *solus rex*. They ignore the fact that expertise often requires an opponent who is, in some regards, a collaborator. General Montgomery had a picture of Marshal Rommel on the wall of his caravan. Your boosters deny you subtlety by wishing that you found me superfluous; aesthetic Stalinists, they have sought to write me out of your history. I'm their Trotsky, George Orwell's Emmanuel Goldstein. You will believe me when I say that, proud as I was to be working with you, I knew very well that you were always bound to make what began as 'our' movie entirely your own. The *Cahiers du Cinéma* crowd's 'discovery' that directors, especially those in their *bund*, were 'authors' advanced the presumption that all creative contribution to a film came from one source only. The downgrading of the writer and of the stars was part of a heist that left one person alone entitled to credit; a self-serving bourgeois theory for a clique and claque of radical iconoclasts.

How often does a director need no creative input but his own? Chaplin and Orson could claim as much, but it was contested even then. I can't remember whether Pauline Kael made Herman Manckiewicz superfluous to *Citizen Kane* and Orson's apostle Peter Bogdanovich rated H.M. part-author or vice versa. They were probably both right. Screenwriting, especially the adaptation of an existing story, is a form of catering, however many stars may get pinned on the chef. All the same, I remember Diaghilev's remark, after Jean Cocteau asked him what kind of designs he wanted for whatever ballet was being prepared: '*Etonne-moi!*' It was a licence to surpass expectation. You set me a puzzle, but you dreaded inventiveness going too far, didn't you? I can't count how many times you urged me to observe Schnitzler's 'beats'.

After any number of pages had been written, you paid me what I took to be the compliment of saying, 'You look quite a bit like Arthur, know that?' I didn't and I don't. I suspect it was more reassurance to yourself than tribute to me. The compliment eclipsed its recipient. Assimilating my appearance to Schnitzler's elided me with the dead. Deceit was an ingredient of your activities – a form of liberty, was it? The photographer who looks innocent, as you did in your adolescent rambles, is the one who snaps or snaffles the truth as the pickpocket his mark's wallet.

Remember the story about Mel Brooks on the way to lunch with a naïve young conscript to Sid Caesars' now legendary writers' consortium)? Brooks turned off down a side alley, saying it was a shortcut to the usual deli.

Once alone among the trash cans, Mel asked if his companion had twenty bucks. Did he even produce a gun? I forget. Anyway, the young guy handed over the money. When the bill came after lunch, Mel was asked to give back the twenty so that… Mel said, 'I mugged you fair and square, kid'. I'd like to think that the episode was a lesson, not a heist. Both? 'Why not?' Izzy Diamond would say.

You rejoiced in what you never declared. Your power – as manipulator, not as director – depended, in part, on what you withheld. When you sent me Schnitzler's little number, with the author's name carefully excised, I was innocent and vain enough – the two go easily together – to believe that it was a new project of yours. It had the quality of being good, not great, that promises the adaptor that he can make a clinching contribution. It was not until I was well into the case that I discovered that any number of other writers had sought to crack it. Among the predecessors of whom I knew nothing was a clever, over six-foot female writer called Candia McWilliam, who later wrote to me. Her father, Colin, was the head monitor of Lockites when I first went to Charterhouse School. Have I lost you? I'll bet. But the silly coincidence stands. As for other failed entrants in your twenty-year stretch of examinations, they remain nameless to me. You mentioned no one and, as far as I know, advanced none of their ideas. But then they had, I am sure, signed away their entitlement.

You were smart enough to let chance make its contributions to your recipes. We're promised that *The Blue Danube* flowed around the opening sequence of *2001* because it happened to be playing on a turntable in the studio where you were dubbing the music. I believe it. Might something similar have happened, had you had the time and the luck when editing *E.W.S.*? I wonder who had the idea of the plastic furniture in the form of crouched naked white females in the café at the beginning of *A Clockwork Orange*. You?

I suspect you said yes to something trendy that hasn't kept as well as using *Singing in the Rain* over the rape scene. *Homage* to the other Stanley was also, indistinguishably, a form of deferential disparagement. That was Kubrick, whoever else it was. The droogs' costumes and bowlers were right on the money. The movie director, however individual his mark, had better be a good picker. Writers and others serve him with ideas. What he most wishes he had thought of becomes his; *droit de seigneur*. 'You will, Oscar, you will', was Whistler's shrewdest crack.

There was something almost comic – the comedy was the proximity – in your unblushing willingness to appropriate any credit that was going. *Auteur* and *hauteur* were all but identical. Nothing very unusual in that, in my experience with directors, except in the case of Stanley Donen, but why should a man so frequently badged with genius choose to deny other people their petty due? Terry Southern was another example in your case. You said, again and again, that you wished you could tell me what you wanted. You would recognise it when it was served, even though you could offer no recipe. Odd though how often first drafts turn out to be the best after many a summer's revisions. Remember Noël Coward going back to the theatre during the run of one of his plays? He called a meeting for the following day in order to delete the improvements. Sure you get it. He is also supposed to have said, *re* the actor in *2001*, 'Keir Dullea and gone tomorrow'. Say it aloud, in Cowardly tones. Now do you get it?

You did some brilliant casting (Leonard Rossiter, in *Barry Lyndon* not least) and some quite strange: what was Bill Sylvester doing in your space piece? He was a nice man who underacted as much in your piece as he overdid it in an early TV piece of mine (playing a Jew does bring out the hand-signals in some people). It was as if you sometimes chose actors because they lacked individual character. You could be sure they would not add unwanted flavour to the piece. But then again… Sellers, Hayden, James Mason and, whether you liked him or not, Ryan O'Neal. In Ryan's case, you had the idea, I've been told (and believe), that he was making illicit advances to that favourite daughter of yours, then in her lo-teens. It is likelier, much, that she had a crush on him and that you resented the charm he exerted. Your original idea was that O'Neal should read the commentary which fashioned the singularity of your picaresque story, but I gather (no shortage of fruit from under the old gossip tree) that you were so displeased that you took that honour away from him and gave it to Michael Hordern, whose inimitable (often imitated) tones gave the movie an ironic dignity that no first-person narrator could supply. However spiteful your motive, having those butterflies work for you gave the piece a lift it might otherwise never have had. Even paranoia can furnish a touch of genius.

Your myth promised that hard ball was always your game. There might be no greater tribute in the game than to be selected as your back-stop, but there was also resentment on your part for confessing the need of him. Even dentists sometimes have to call the dentist. Listen, nothing in the cinematic department of my life ever beat the pleasure of hearing you say – on Christmas Eve 1995, wasn't it? – that you were 'absolute thrilled' by the first stack of some fifty pages that I had sent you, with the usual confident apprehension. The scholarship boy never quite loses that blend of insolence and dread which came with handing in his pages.

I was as much relieved as flattered by your praise. Ouf! It seemed that I could jiggle my way into your confidence ('jiggling' is what policemen do when they use a master-key to feel out and finally turn an alien lock). I had the honest whore's feeling of having given value for money. The screenwriter had better learn to be amused by those whose claim never to have needed him is conclusive proof of how well he has served them. Bill Goldman told me how he came into Sydney Pollack's office to find him typing out the script he had delivered a few days earlier. Quizzed, Sydney said, with no sign either of embarrassment or humour, that he was 'making it his own'. You did exactly the same thing, pretty well, if very late in the day, when you asked me, with a trace of anxiety, to read through and comment on the version of *Eyes Wide Shut* which you had pretty well decided to shoot and had certainly, in many ways (my old friend Jo Janni's regular phrase), made your own.

I thought you had made several unwise decisions; never foolish, not necessarily wrong, just… unworthy. For instance (no, I don't think it *matters*, especially not now) in having the long, 'frank' after-the-ball-was-over discussion between Cruise and Kidman – what fun Freud could have unpacking that coupling! – primed not by their several experiences in the rich man's house but by smoking pot on their return home. Schnitzler, whose 'beats' you incited, if not instructed, me to honour, knew better than you, it seemed, that the events of the evening itself supplied stimulus enough for their unbuttoning. If they needed to be primed with pot to turn on the flow of their witless improvisation, the party itself was as good as superfluous. Oh, the naked girl in the upstairs room had her unguarded pubic naughtiness, but the Austro-Hungarian count who flirted with the tipsy Nicole hardly did or said anything much to turn her on; hence the pot, no doubt, lubricant for the witless.

I recognised your rare brilliance that afternoon in 1958 when I went to that King's Road double-header of *The Killing* and *Paths of Glory*; lunch and dinner for the price of breakfast. I had never heard of you (Kirk Douglas hauled me into that King's Road theatre), but I came out stunned by those callous masterpieces. Was Kirk the man you wished you had been? The story is that, after propagating his kind, he had a vasectomy to counter accusations of extra-marital reproduction. Kirk changed his name, but he wore no other sort of camouflage. Clean shaven, undisguisedly a *mensch*, he played white, you black.

It's said, and I believe it, that Kirk had a sidekick to whom he would indicate which of the females in a conducted tour of the studios appealed to him. The chosen lady would be approached and told that Mr Douglas was about to take a break in his Winnebago while they changed the set-up. Would she care to come and have a coke with him? Once the door was locked behind Kirk and his dish-of-the-day, there was no loutish presumption. Kirk offered the promised drink and then, it's said, admitted that he found the lady very attractive and, if it would please her, etc. Nine times out of ten he pleased her plenty and gave her a secret to treasure as long she chose. Yes, similar stories are told about a lot of stars, from Cary Grant to Warren Beatty, to name but the cocks of the walk. Not all the *macho* men matched their reputations. Joan Axelrod asked Hope Lange what Frank Sinatra had been like in the sack. Hopey said, 'Oh, you know, push and squirt'. Asked what had impelled her to divorce Alan Pakula, she said, 'I kept falling asleep all the time'. Not an easy room to play, the lady.

There is, as you can guess, a flourishing, voluminous Kubrick industry, with every commercial reason for portraying you as a single, if not singular, genius meriting unceasing flows of incense and myrrh, never mirth, from which gold can be culled for your epigoni. Their loud indignation has been aroused by the little book, as close as may be to hagiographical, that I wrote after 'our' movie opened. Never before had anyone written of the experience of working with you, not because of lack of appetite but because the contract they had signed stipulated that they renounce the right to do so. I had insisted, before I signed, that an adjacent clause be deleted, in which you arrogated to yourself to decide who had written any part of the script and hence who, if anyone, apart from yourself, should receive credit. I told you that I felt privileged to be invited to work with you, but pride had not entirely banished my wits. The Writers' Guild, to which I paid regular dues, had a recognised procedure for attributing credit and members were expected to make use of it. First you seemed surprised that I should raise the matter at all. Did I not trust you? I ducked that one by saying that there was no way I should sign myself into anyone else's hands, however illustrious. Quite abruptly, you then said how about if we just delete that whole clause in the contract.

I got the impression that you maybe expected me to wince at the wording you tried to slip past me, not necessarily out of malice or greed, more probably just to test whether I was proud enough to dump the prize of working with Kubrick when I saw that I was being, as my mother and perhaps yours (she gets very little press) would say, tutsi-frutsied. The whole clause you told your lawyer to cut out of the contract contained another item, denying me the right to publish any account of our working together. You conceded more than you realised, unless a Freudian error allowed one writer the chance to publish the truth. I remain innocent enough to hope that you just might be amused, a couple of times, by what I have had to say about you. No one quite like you, Kubrick, OK? As you must have been tempted to say to that paper-seller you snapped the day F.D.R. died, 'Smile, please'.

Best regards, Freddie.

Dear Guy,

I was a Charterhouse schoolboy when I first met you, my father's old friend from your days as lounge-lizards in the 1920s. You and Celia appeared to take pleasure in treating a callow adolescent as if he were your contemporary. Young in the 1940s was immeasurably younger than it is today (female noses also needed regular powdering). Unlike most adults of the time faced with an adolescent, you did not vary your tone, your instructive range of allusion, your pleasure in the mildly salacious. Scanning my jejune stories with a sub-editor's instructive impatience, you took my ambitions seriously, never sparing the blue pencil. 'Cut, cut, cut' was Celia's curt, curt, curt advice when it came to what a tiro imagined was fine writing and was more often cliché.

Her first novel, *The Least of These*, had been saluted on a full page by James Agate, the *Daily Express*'s top critic, who addressed her, in the headline, as 'Celia, dear!' She happened to be secretary to the then editor, Arthur 'Chris' (to some) Christiansen, a rigorous boss capable of standing up to the dreaded 'call from the country', meaning that the Beaver was on the line, with insurgent hackles. Others were instantly servile. You told me how George Malcolm Thompson had taken a call for the Beaver and informed whoever it was that 'the Lord is walking in the park'. 'On the water, I presume', said the other. Thompson told someone that when working with Beaverbrook, he felt 'like Marshal Ney with Napoleon'. 'Surely you mean Marshal Yea', said his friend.

Celia loved you without needing you to prove or improve who she was. No one could call her a beauty; few denied her wit. She spoke of her own shiny son, with unblinking accuracy, as 'looking like the bacon-slicer at the Co-Op'. You lived in a book-ridden, high-ceilinged flat in an Edwardian house in arty, cosmopolitan NW3, a borough my parents had avoided. Wartime bus conductors were said to have called out, 'Anyone for British North-West Three?'

You were outspokenly pro-Semitic, due not least to your devotion to 'Skid', S.J. Simon, the great bridge player and comic author who died in 1948. His glossary survived on your tongue: 'Give tube' for 'Do you have a cigarette?'; 'Couldn't A with you M' (for 'couldn't agree with you more'); 'The late J. Christ, esquire'. Was it Skid who first said, when someone let something fall on the floor, 'Slight case of dropsy?' You made it your own if so. You too 'circulated the pasteboards' when other merely dealt the cards. Has Skid's *Why You Lose at Bridge* ever been bettered as an introduction to the lifelong addiction which you and I have shared? The Unlucky Expert, Mrs Guggenheim, Mr Smug, and Futile Willie will repeat typical mistakes as long as hands are bid and ill-bid, played and misplayed.

Your own *Aces All* is the most thoroughly thumbed and regularly scanned of all the books in my possession. Truth to tell, it sits on the chair in the bathroom, easily at hand for the enstooled enthusiast. It includes a heartfelt tribute to Skid, as well as generous words about 'Konnie' Konstam, whom you brought, along with Edward Meyer and Jack Marx, to play against Cambridge in my crowded third court attic in St John's. I still wince when I recall one incident in that 1951 match. I was naive enough to compete in the auction when I might have passed out your part score. By re-opening the bidding, I gave your side a chance, duly taken, to bid a game you would otherwise have missed. Greater follies, of whatever order, have been overgrown by time, but that 'two spades' bid of mine is to me what 'Calais' was to Queen Mary.

Konnie is the only bridge writer ever to have mentioned me in print. In the *Sunday Times* in 1960, he featured a hand in which six hearts was the contract in both rooms; !!, as the chess writers say. How come? In an inter-college match, Konnie's son, Michael, no crack like his father, contrived to leave his partner in a cue bid when seven spades was a make. Pity. I had made a bold bluff bid (otherwise known as a 'psych') in the other room; little good it did us. Michael went on to be attorney-general of Kenya (one of the last Brits in that office, surely) and died before his father.

Old Harrovian – suitably blue chalk-striped, you sometimes wore the tie – you had been at Oxford with my father, though you did not stay to take a degree, did you? You were in the nimble, patent-leather-shod crowd with whom Cedric went dancing in those unrehearsed days and competitive nights, at the Hammersmith *Palais de Danse*, with its frosted and veiled windows, decorous and racy, depending on the time of day. It was typical of you to say that he was a worthy champion: dago when dancing the tango, when the waltz a Viennese courtier. You had a good enough opinion of yourself never to belittle anyone else. No wonder Ewart Kempson saluted you as 'sahib'.

The bridge world, to which you devoted much time, as player, journalist and committeeman, was riven with factional spite. While you could not avoid (or resist) involving yourself in the face-off which divided supporters of M. Harrison Gray (columnist of *Country Life*) from those of Terence Reese (*Evening Standard*), neither side ever accused you of opportunism, still less of malice. You told me that during the graceless debates between feuding principals you tended to favour whoever had not spoken last. At committee meetings, you were given to presiding in a fashion which the unsmiling Reese described as both genial and grandiloquent. Hyperbole was an aspect of your delight in life, not the overstatement of ill-feeling. You might pontificate; you never scolded. Your tribute, in *Aces All*, to Reese's analytic mastery lacked the adulation bestowed on 'Skid' (whose nephew, biographer and economist Robert Skidelsky, no great circulator of the pasteboards, is a friend of mine). What family with roots in Vladivostok was ever more articulately English? What would Skid have said when told of his nephew's peerage? 'T.L. be P.'? For 'The Lord Be Praised?'

Being incapable of malice did not deprive you of accuracy when it came to Boris Shapiro, Terence's regular partner in international competitions. While Boris played the fly lothario, Reese could be cruelly laconic. Double First in Greats turned professional gambler, Terence was always very civil to me, as classicists often are to each other. During the Blitz, so you report, someone came into the room after a particularly loud bang and said, 'They've hit the War Office'. 'Not on purpose', said Reese, as he continued to execute a complicated squeeze. You told the story of how, against predictions, Terence got married, quite late in life. On his honeymoon, the story went, with a kick-start from Boris, I'll bet, Reese had embarked in a conjugal embrace, when everything came to a halt. The recent Mrs Reese said, 'Anything wrong, darling?' 'No, no, I was just thinking, I had only to duck the first round of diamonds, rectify the count and make that six spades'.

Boris was a shameless amorist and, it is said, an able rider. His habitual greeting to ladies with robust appetites was 'Fancy a spot of adultery?' On one occasion you recorded, the company at dinner included a lady with a very low-cut, well-filled top. Boris passed his knife to her neighbour and said, 'Cut me a slice'. It is typical Ramsey also to report how, one day, you were tempted into making up a four in the pound room at Crockford's. You had the luck to cut Boris as partner but, after your opponents had made a quick slam, not vulnerable, you regretted playing at ten times your usual stake. Then Boris opened 'one diamond'; the next opponent doubled, 'for take out' as the jargon has it; you looked at a useful hand

and redoubled; the next opponent passed and so did Boris. The doubler looked at the scorecard, confirmed that even if the contract were made it would not give you game, and also passed. Boris played the hand 'through the quill' in your Regency phrase; five overtricks, redoubled, worth 400 points each. You and he went on to win a fat rubber.

Sans gêne, Boris was known to do all sorts of brazen things to intimidate or deconcentrate his opponents. If they 'tranced' for excessive periods, where there was no obvious problem, he would hum some operatic phrase or snore. Reese sat impassive and disdainful. Jeremy Flint, another of Terence's regular partners, scanned the racing pages in the paper. When my father and I played against Reese and Shapiro, in the Crockford's Cup, they behaved with sporting rectitude even though we went on, that once, to defeat their team. Something about Cedric's posture at the table deterred bad behaviour. He played a steady game; I supplied occasional flash. Mary and John Moss, our pair in 'the other room', had much to do with our winning silverware, that once.

Mary, born Polish, became an England international. John, a colonel in the occupying force, had nabbed her as the willing spoils of war. As lively as vivacious could ever mean, she was dark, sexy – 'Naughty!' her favourite exclamation – and a delicious cook. She and John went to live in the South of France and played bridge with *émigré* tax-avoiding lotus-eaters until, suddenly, Mary was afflicted with what no one then called Alzheimer's. Where the Mosses had been first on guest lists, their names no longer figured. John told me that, towards the end, the brightest moment of his day was when Mary first woke in the morning. She opened her eyes, smiled, said 'Hullo, darling!' and then was lost to him for another twenty-four hours.

After Mary died, John used to call me, mid-morning, not my favourite time for casual chat. I suppose he was slightly, as they used to say, touched. Jew by birth, it amused him to blame it all, whatever it was, on the Chosen. He told me how, while in the army, he was on a long-distance continental train bunked up with Mary. In the early morning, a conductor knocked on the compartment door and said he was needed urgently on the telephone. Did he have some I.D.? Colonel Moss put on his regimental tie and, otherwise naked, stepped into the corridor to take the call, standing at attention no doubt. John inherited a small fortune and a certain arrogance. One afternoon the telephone rang in the two-shilling room at Crock's and a voice asked for Cubby Broccoli (later one of the two producers of the first James Bond films). True to his time and class, John suggested that whoever it was should try the kitchen.

Did you ever hear how, one day, my father became conscious of one of his opponents, General Mirza, the then recently deposed president of Pakistan, glancing, almost shamelessly, at his cards? Cedric said, 'If you want to look at my hand that badly, perhaps you should come and sit on my knee'. The general replied, 'That would be an exceptional pleasure'. You always said that it was a player's duty to keep his cards shielded from opponents' eyes; 'As ye show, so shall they peep' your monitorial pun. Jack Marx was notoriously unguarded when it came to revealing what was in his hand. His play was so accurate that even his opponents knowing what was in his hand did little to prevent him winning.

Only Shapiro ever said anything unkind about the unassuming, unmarried Jack: asked where he was, on some occasion, Boris said, 'Try the gents Leicester Square', and got no laugh, I hope. Jack, who seemed always to be in the same sports jacket and flannels, pen and pencil in the top pocket, was one of the originators of the convention in which bidding 'two clubs' over partner's 'one no trump' asked for him to bid a four card major suit if he happened to have one. Jack's modesty was his one conceit. His invention is now known as 'Stayman', after an American player with better publicity.

You told me that Skid, the joker to whom Jack often acted as straight man, was opposed to elaborate precautions against unscrupulous play. Formality risked taking the fun out of the game. In duplicate, however, bids have now ceased to be made aloud, because so much used to be conveyed by intonation, taking undue thought and the like. Today, all bids must be signalled voicelessly by the display of a selection from the player's rack of bidding cards. Ingenious cheats have, no doubt, sharpened their trickery rather than abandoned its practice. How long it takes to choose a card, and how it is put down, can always be turned into a kind of code. Himself an ash-covered model of dishevelled sportsmanship, Skid argued, skittishly, for 'all-in' bridge. Let cheats kick each other under the table till their shins were black and blue, it could never make them skilful. The good player would always prevail, however long the run.

Neither you nor Skid lived long enough to observe the *cause célèbre* during the World Cup in Buenos Aires, in 1965. Reese and Shapiro were accused by their American adversaries of employing a set of unsubtle signals – how many fingers they were displaying and of which hand – in order to exchange illicit information, about their holdings in the heart suit, during the bidding. Can you believe a great master would choose such banal means to gain so petty an advantage? Yet Reese's own captain, if never his friend, Alan Truscott, was appalled by what he was sure he witnessed. Reese and Shapiro were withdrawn from further play. Some said that the Americans had rigged the whole thing in order to disqualify England's best pair. Taking sides opened another venomous rift in the British bridge world. Truscott went to live in the States.

Variant versions survive of what happened or was alleged to have been said, denial or confession, then and later. The most improbable, hence the most appetising, is that Reese incited

Boris to participate in an experiment which would serve only to prove that cheating, among experts, would procure little or no advantage. Their silly ruse was supposedly devised to supply sensational material for a book Reese was writing on the subject. Boris is said to have called his long-time partner a devil. Terence's acidity had gained him few supporters, especially among glad-handing Americans whom his *morgue* had already alienated. Boss-eyed Boris might be shameless, calculating never.

Reason insists, after revising the evidence, that if one wanted to test whether cheating helps (as opposed to card-sharping, which has no use in 'duplicate' bridge), only rare arrogance would impel a man to conduct the experiment in the World Championship. But then again, when better time for effrontery than when every *afficionado*'s eye was on the participants? The oddity of the whole episode is that, even if the pair did indeed use witless hand-signals, not a single instance was ever cited to show that they had derived any advantage from whatever they conveyed. Skid was vindicated in his view that cheating will not make you a more successful player. The curiosity remains that Reese was already as successful as anyone could well hope to be.

Did you ever come up against a cardsharp called Sandheim? I played sixpenny bridge with him, at 'Mrs Mac's'. Considering the negligible stakes and his own skill, his ingenuity could be classed as a kind of conjuring trick. He was clever enough to give his partner good cards rather than deliver them to himself. From time to time, he even dealt an opponent a fistful of aces and kings. Do I do him too much honour by recalling a hand in which he, my opponent, dealt me a hand including, among other goodies, a suit of seven hearts to the ace, king, queen, jack, nine? I fell like a *klutz* (otherwise known as a 'piker') into claiming the slam without playing out my top two or three trumps to be sure that the suit 'broke'. Sandheim, sitting to my right, challenged my claim and displayed five hearts to the ten. Had I first played out two or three top trumps, I could have contrived what is known as 'the *grand coup*', picking up Sandheim's trumps *en passant*. Once I had claimed 'the rest', I was denied recourse to any such ruse and had to be one down. Had he foreseen my Mister Smugness? How shall we ever know, save at the last trump?

The Scottish verdict 'not proven' serves but never solves the Buenos Aires case. Reese's tacit disdain made him no friends and lost him a few old ones. He retired from international bridge and took up backgammon (where all the 'cards' were on the table) with no marked success. Boris suffered little from his partner's *hubris*. He made out that it had all been Terence's idea and claimed that, in any case, it was never put into practical or profitable operation. The bridge world forgave its naughty boy because he was such shameless company. You and I, my dear Guy, would happily tire the sun with talking about this typhoon in a tea cup, though we should prefer to adjourn for a rubber or two or, as would almost certainly be the case, several more.

Boris continued to play in high-class competitions, if never again for England, and won his last major cup when eighty-nine years old. His column in the *Sunday Times* was never as good as the ones you took such pleasure in composing for the *Daily Telegraph*. Your style and enthusiasm made it unthinkable that what appeared under your name was not one hundred percent Ramsey. Shapiro was, in every sense, a card, but no writer: did he ever deny that a ghost added the finishing touches to his weekly stint for the *S. T.*?

The book you might have written on the Buenos Aires affair is a missing masterpiece in the history of the game. In Reese's published assessment of your contribution to the bridge world, you would see, beyond the Tacitean terseness, an unusual hint of warmth and respect. It notes with approval that your life was crowned, as you had always wished, by being 'capped' for England, at Palermo in 1959. Your last act away from the table was penning that nth loving letter to Celia.

You and she asked me to dinner, alone, at 3, Hall Road, Hampstead, several times during the months between my leaving Charterhouse and going up to Cambridge in October 1950. England was still a society in which children looked forward to being grown-ups. The middle-aged rarely took exercise or watched their figures. Your round pink face and bald head, with that fair quiff on the crown, and protrusive lips had something all but big-babyish about it, but you were a paunchy man of the world as well as the word. You had been not only to Harrow and Oxford but also to Hotchkiss and Yale. You were young enough in 1950 to have parents still alive. Who they were, or had been, might have explained why so much of your education took place in the States. You no more mentioned them than you did your first wife, who may have been German and by whom you had a son, Valentine.

You were pleased to be unembarrassed, if never crude, when it came to sexual matters. You may have sensed that Cedric, whatever his personal morals as a young man, was uneasy (as who is not, very often?) when it came to practical matters. You told me, with admirable clarity and good humour, that when in bed, or wherever it might be, with a woman, it was wise to rely more on the durability of the tongue, suitably and subtly applied, than on the penis. The tongue, you told me, had the advantage of a good alarm clock: it never went off too soon, a much more reliable member than St Paul may ever have known. You told me the probably very old joke about the difference between English women and their continental sisters. After sex, the French woman says, 'Jean-Luc was better'; the Italian woman says, 'Do it again'; the Spanish woman says, 'Betray me and I kill you'; the Englishwoman says, 'Feeling better, George?'

While your devotion to Celia was unmitigated, you often stayed at Crock's for one more rubber before taxiing home for a (late) supper. Celia's patience occasionally snapped. On one occasion, after you kept her waiting when you were due to go to some party, she remained seemingly cool until you were on the escalator going down to the tube. She then turned on you and said, loudly, in a shrill scrubber's voice, 'A pound's not enough'. As heads turned, you said, 'Celia, please!' 'Don't you Celia please me', she said, 'a pound's not enough!' It ended, with you red-faced and thick-spectacled Celia burbling nicely. I used the exchange in *Darling*, in a scene between Dirk Bogarde and Julie Christie.

You were a performer who played the part of himself with all the aplomb duplicated (to say the least) by the then famous actor and playwright Robert Morley. The author of *The First Gentleman* made self-importance a form of charm. It amused you now and again to receive the servility, on the part of head waiters, which his West End fame merited. He asked me, in the 1970s, to contribute, for charity, to a *Book of Bricks* which celebrities (a word unused in your day) had dropped. He was kind enough to say that my brick was particularly stylish. I thought of you, who taught me how much the *mot juste* mattered. It was typical of your appetite for playing 'top board' that you said that you would be Flaubert to my Guy de Maupassant. You published only one work of fiction, a detective story called *The Spike* about the nailing of a prize bitch of a journalist (based on Nancy Spain?) on the upright prong that stood in the middle of the subs' table, last resting place of condemned copy. I remember you carrying *The Spike* into Crockford's, title outmost.

Your greatest coup as a journalist on the *Daily Mail* was in 1941. You broke the scoop of scoops when you discovered – who knows through what *tuyau*? – where, in East Anglia somewhere, Rudolf Hess was being secreted after his solo sortie to Scotland. Is it true that he hoped to do the Führer a favour by getting in touch with the Duke of Hamilton, who was said to be in favour of a negotiated peace? Denied the welcome and the glory he had hoped for, the deputy-Führer was whisked into some obscure bolted hole where the ungrateful Hitler would be unable to have someone deal with him as he had with his earlier right-hand man, Ernst Röhm. Did you play the sleuth, with a roll of fivers (rare and white in those days), or did a tip-off from someone with a grudge against The Beaver lay Lord Rothermere the scent? You took to it like a bloodhound.

By the time the Allies invaded North Africa in 1943, it was beyond doubt that Germany would be defeated. You went with other accredited journalists (in uniform, were you?) to Algiers where the victorious top brass was disputing the honours gained for them by the blood of the rank and file. General de Gaulle's future was in the balance. Churchill, who could be as sharp as any journalist (and had occasionally been one), had said that of all the crosses he had to bear, none was so vexatious as (de Gaulle's) Cross of Lorraine. An all but unconcealed plot was afoot to replace *le grand Charles* with General Honoré Giraud, an old soldier as stiff in manner as he was malleable in practice. Having escaped from a *Stalag* in order to reach North Africa, he was paraded as a heroic man of action as against de Gaulle's military Richelieu. Giraud infuriated the self-styled leader of the Free French by addressing him as 'Gaulle'. The General's '*de*' was indeed not an aristocratic *particule* but, presumably, a family affectation. Giraud's formal rectitude was an attempt to belittle a man determined to make sure that France was treated, under his sole leadership, as a full participant in the *après-guerre* settlement. De Gaulle saw him off without looking at him.

Le grand Charles was averse to Anglo-Saxons in general and *anglophone* journalists in particular. None had succeeded in getting his notebook (every reporter had shorthand in those days) within range of the lofty paranoid. The 1968 students, with small deference, came to call him '*le giraffe*'. In 1943, you sent him a note, in that cursive hand of yours, beginning: '*Mon Général, tout homme a deux pays, le sien et la France. C'est dans cet esprit que je m'adresse au plus grand Français de notre époque...*' If in doubt, lay it on, you told me. You got your interview and another scoop.

When my father was sidelined in Shell and put in charge of Press Relations, you were invaluable in making him *persona grata* on 'The Street', as Fleet Street was then called. Cedric's lunches at the Berkeley were attended by most anyone who mattered in City journalism. One such was Alan Brockbank. 'Brocky' combined a number of activities on the *Sunday Express*, from 'Our Industrial Correspondent' through 'Our Naval Reporter' to 'Our Political Correspondent' and on to sensational cases demanding so much attention that he doubled as '*Sunday Express* reporters'.

In early 1950, my father told Brocky that I was eager to be a journalist. Having left Charterhouse at Christmas, I had nine months to wait before going up to Cambridge. The *Sunday Express* had a skeletal weekday staff: feature writers, subs and a few reporters. Thanks to Brock (who claimed, very generously, to need an assistant), I was given an appointment with the News Editor. Stanley Head was a dyspeptic with little inclination to take on a neophyte. He told me, with no encouraging air, to go and write a news story, never mind what about, and bring him the copy the next day.

That night, I showed you what I had written about a house fire in Putney. You looked at it with a jut of that judicial lower lip and then with a busy pencil. 'No semi-colons, ever; no sentences that aren't subject-verb-object. No paragraph of more than three sentences.' As you lectured, so did you perform nimble surgery and stitching on my Ciceronian verbosity.

The little piece became a parody of a smart squib in *Time* magazine, the Beaver's ideal. The next morning, Stanley Head looked at it for a moment, then at me. 'If Brockbank will have you, you can start on Tuesday.' 'Thank you, sir', I said. I did a lot of sirring in those days.

Since I was not a member of the National Union of Journalists, I had to be discreet about my job; so did Brocky. He wrote all his copy in pencil, no more than a few dozen words per foolscap page. At first, I was paid only for 'expenses' licensed by Brocky. After a few weeks, I wrote a page five which found its way into the Scottish edition. The old hands, Bernard Harris, Bernard Drew, even solemn John Prebble possibly, came and clapped me on the back. The piece – about Germans taking unfair advantages at the British Industries Fair – was spiked by the time the London edition was printed. No more virgin, I was granted an unofficial salary of four pounds ten a week, in addition to modestly inventive expenses, when licensed by a nod.

What looked more secure than your place at the *Daily Mail?* How many awards would you have won, had they been allotted in those days? Journalism was not yet the profession of choice for literate graduates. A byline was the best bonus a man could well hope for. Your qualifications, both as enterprising leg-man and master of general knowledge (no one spoke of intellectuals in those days, not in London), should have made you irreplaceable, not to say invaluable; but a change of editor, from the nice Guy Horniblow to Frank Owen, of whom it was said 'The editor's indecision is final', threatened all those whose status might overshadow him. I was innocent to be amazed when you were abruptly declared redundant. You wrote cheques with the Ramsey flourish (£30 the maximum available at Crockford's) and you took taxis when others might have taken a short stroll, but you had no pension and no fortune whatever. Jobs were not easy to find for a man with rare panache and just expectations.

I used to travel home on the underground with a 'Saturday man' called Ray Foxall. Saturday men were taken on to fatten the regular staff when the *Sunday Express* had to be fully crewed. During the week, Ray was a reporter on *The Daily Telegraph*. He and I would leave the Express building around eleven at night, brandishing the late edition and head for Putney on the tube. One night, he mentioned that the *Telegraph* was looking for a feature writer and also that the paper's bridge correspondent was not well. '*Les malheurs des uns font le bonheur des autres*' would, I am sure, have come promptly to your lips. I called you the minute I got home. By Tuesday morning, you had a new job, not only as bridge correspondent but also as deputy literary critic. I last saw the word 'limn' in a newspaper in a review you wrote of a biography about some what's-his-name or other.

When you took me to a celebration lunch at the Paternosters Club, you waved your umbrella for a taxi with renewed authority. Now defunct, the club must have been an association, all male I think, of journalists and allied tradesmen. There were after-treacle-pudding speeches of a louche order. I remember someone talking about the miracles of modern science and giving 'Snip, snip and Bob's your auntie' as an example. That expressive mouth of yours was bunched in unamused silence. God knows, you were no sort of prude but want of subtlety won small applause. The best Fleet Street story you ever told me was about Randolph Churchill coming into the newsroom and throwing his considerable weight around, especially at the expense of some cowed typist who had made some misprint in his copy. When she was reduced to scuttling tears, one of the garter-sleeved subs turned round from the long central table and said, 'Know your trouble, Churchill? Your name begins with C,h in Who's Who and S,h in What's What'.

You are the only person I have met who knew (and recited) the clerihew 'The earl of Chatham, William Pitt /

On the eighteenth green fell, in a apoplectic fit / All round enjoyed the joke / As Fox murmured, 'Beaten! By a stroke'. You once showed me a piece of paper on which was written 'Fun. Fun. Fun Worry, worry, worry'; which being interpreted yielded 'Fun period fun period fun no period worry, worry, worry'. A terse tract for the days of hit and sometimes miss contraception. Dirty jokes also have their periods. Date this one you told me, the one about the woman who was crossing Threadneedle Street and was almost hit by buses coming in opposite directions. They came so close that all her clothes were torn off and she collapsed unconscious in the roadway. A passing City gent, observing her nakedness, had the style to put his bowler hat where it could do its decent best. When the fire brigade arrived, the first fireman on the spot took one look at the scene and said to his mate 'Better get the man out first'. Dirty? Not really. Funny? Worth a smile. How about another of your Fleet Street vintage defining a physical impossibility: two Lesbians whistling while they work? Shame on me for remembering it?

Your ideas on sex were typical of *l'homme moyen sensuel* whom you so perfectly impersonated. Sex could mean nothing but that 'spasm in the loins' (not to be spermed, as you may have said) or the consummation of something beyond words. After you had met Beetle you told me that you had no doubt that I made her happy and that she would do as much for me. When Beetle was in hospital for some minor operation, you honoured the convention of those lost days and visited her, whom you had met but a couple of times, with flowers and the *Evening News. Le style, c'était l'homme même.*

Cher maître, je t'embrasse, très, très fort.
Freddie.

Dear Dudy,

I know, I know: you stopped calling yourself that; being her. Trouble is, I find it difficult, very, to think of you otherwise. Dorothy recalls only Dorothy Tutin, the actress. Dotty and I read Noël Coward's *Private Lives* together on VE Night. Do you remember Amanda? I was thirteen. I never kissed her, nor did she invite it. We did play tennis though and puffed Craven A ('For Our Throats' Sake') in the adjacent loo. She had a good forehand; so do lots of girls. Not you, I think. Dorothy is what you re-made yourself. My Dorothy was living in a houseboat on Chelsea Embankment when she was having an affair with Laurence Olivier. Vivien Leigh threatened to kill her. Olivier chickened out. Dotty had a breakdown. Then she married a comedy writer, had a family, was made a Dame. She died, of leukaemia in a ward where she was done no favours. The National Theatre made no medical provision for its resident company.

I see on your collected poems that I said nice things about you; them. I made no mistake there. The printer did: he added a 'k' to my name. I call myself Fred and Freddie and Frederic when I get the chance, but the writer is what I am. You, whoever you were and aren't any more, are the poet. No Dorothy to me, no 'Dudy' to yourself; a baby name stuck on you, after your own infant version of it, by one of those sisters you called Sister Bo and Sister Co and whoever the other one was, who didn't rhyme: sister Anne. It held you in a long grip, the Quaker family; its Thou tagged you.

I stood in a spaced queue at Waitrose this afternoon. There are queues everywhere these Covid days, everywhere that's open. In missionary mode, I said to the woman two metres behind me, 'Hell is other people'. She blinked above her obligatory mask. I had just shaved. I said, 'Do you know who said that?' She shook her muzzle. 'Jean-Paul Sartre', I said, 'it's better in French'. She had never heard of him. What had she heard of? Me? You? Fat chance. Does that make me feel better? Not much made you feel better; doing better perhaps, trimming beards, as sculptors say. Cutting is never wrong. Brevity; what's short for that?

At Cambridge you chose to pass for an actress, a star among few twinkling females. Mark Boxer (aka Marc) cartooned you as a sex fiend, or something of that dated order. Women were short and you a short woman, but outstanding. Mark advised you to find a smarter consort than John Nimmo. A very tall north country man, he walked you round Cambridge, hand on the top of your head. The Amateur Dramatic Club's leading actress, in a silk slip that stood for nakedness in Anouilh's *Antigone*, you said no to matrimony. She preferred to be walled up than stitched up. In life, you said yes, as soon as could be. John sensed no rivals. You played, it seemed, at anxiety, when he, skinny, with specs and high face, all but gaunt, seemed the lucky, unlikely man. His father was a senior police officer. You craved custody. 'Do you love me, John? John, do you love me?' I do not remember him answering.

I hardly knew you in your best Cambridge days; your starred First never in doubt, you published no poems in smart places. Did you write them? Claire Delavenay (later Tomalin) did, as long as she sounded French; she then became prosaic. You saved your cold fire; wished yourself other. Stanislavski's Second Home licensed leading ladydom. Beetle and I got to know you and John only towards the end of your third year. You took the room above ours in Montagu Road, the 'unlicensed digs' to which we were allowed to repair. Your bed had regular, conjunctive exercise; a one and a two; a one and a two. 'Do you love me, John?'

While I was away on a long journey of discovery in Europe and North Africa, thanks to a Cambridge bursary, Beetle went with John to Brighton to watch you in your first professional role, a fourteen-year-old cutie in *The Duchess and the Smugs*. You were the right height, nothing else. Beetle was embarrassed, John no less. You were replaced before the play got to London. You asked John Barton, son of a baronet and Peter Hall's bearded Etonian adjutant, what to do to be a success on the stage. He said, 'Get a new face'. When you turned to me for advice, I suggested Drama School. You went to the Webber Douglas, SW7, now a whited sepulchre.

London was a large, lonely place. We got into the habit of dining, the four of us, back and forth, once a fortnight. One night you served a large boiled onion, each, as the main course. You made coffee by covering grounds with water in a saucepan until it boiled up in brown froth. You had a lodger, later an RSC director, a lonely Jones, First in English. You found typescript pornography among his clean laundry. It gave you something silly on him. He went into the theatre as his grandfather might have into the Church.

Nimmo was bookish in the days when he took you to be the new Celia Johnson. After Brighton, he abandoned books (you both admired *Voss*) and took a job with the Zinc Marketing Board. When Beetle and I came back to London from winter months in the unsmart eleventh *arrondissement*, the manuscript of my first novel was in our luggage. We found a basement flat, *sans* daylight, below George Weidenfeld's waterfront spread on Chelsea Embankment. He asked me to a party to meet Saul Bellow. Beetle was not asked. I did not go. George had a fountain in his foyer. I saw it when the cleaner left the door open.

In the late 1950s, I ghosted a book by Colonel Maurice Buckmaster, wartime commander of Special Operations in France. I took over from a man called David Tutaev. He had been traumatised by the history of treachery and torture. When he gave me the dossier, he said that he had seen a marvellous performance on the previous evening's television, an actress called Dudy Nimmo in Turgenev's play. We had seen only Dudy; he had seen Natalya, and took you for Russian. You told us, more than once, that men pinched your bottom in the underground. I supposed they did. Strap-hanging, you were conveniently at hand for attention from seated males.

What other work did you have as an actress before you decided to become a serial mother, as your own mother Elfrida Vipont had been between writing successful children's books? I cannot recall you mentioning your father. Many years later, Craig Raine published the opinion that you had 'hated' your mother. You seemed to us to dote on her. Craig recognised your rareness. Prose cut bleeds poetry.

Your sister Co, not much taller than you, was a dark beauty, Lawrencian heroine, married to a man whose business was in Africa, perhaps Kenya. They went on safari, I think, with a local driver who went off the road and into a tree. Co's husband was killed; she and their daughter survived. I bided my time with Dotty T. When she was older and did not find much work, I gave her a part in a radio play. Kindness is the best revenge. When she was young, I sent her a play, *Come, Claudia, Running*, based punctually on Co's experience (I flinch from the cant 'tragedy'). A young widowed woman comes back to London and, her husband irreplaceable, has an affair with her daughter's nanny. Dotty never acknowledged it. I never showed it to anyone else. I used Co's husband's death thirty years later in an episode of *After the War*. Claire Higgins was superb. Anthony Valentine too; I never saw a charmless part more unselfishly played. Had he not lost his hair he might have been a star. Life (and death, I see).

In your later verses, you used your disarray as the old Rembrandt did his own ruin. Were you fair to John?

You didn't do fair; you did true. Meanwhile you had played the wife and mother. John found a new job with Rolex in Geneva. My novels were published. I had a film to write. Beetle and I, and Sarah and Paul, went to live in Rome. We passed by Geneva and visited you in your modern, third-floor flat in in a suburban enclave that began with V. Did we eat a meal with you? Were you lonely? You said you had a friend. After a season or two, John found a better-paid job, back in London. You lived in Putney, at the bottom of Dover House Road. We dined there once. In Geneva, you remembered, you had your friend. Female? You came to see us at The Wick, in 1970, your last child in a wicker basket, as if shopped for. I had not yet broken my little finger; luckily, I was not a violinist; is there a poem in it? For a poet, possibly. Leper-pale, you wore a wide straw hat. Co never married again. You did not utter your verses until you had nothing to hide; something to show for it.

I'm going to have to leave you, he said,
very politely. *Sorry.*

I stood up to riddle the Aga,
to draw the red curtains I'd bought
ready-made, marked down, to put out
the cat and I said, *Oh really? When
were you thinking of going?*

As if I might offer to take him
to the station. As if I didn't want
to make him angry in case he left me.
I wish I'd said, Get out. Now.
In his pyjamas. In the rain,
Scrabbling in the gravel for his toothbrush.
Begging for a change of underpants.

I wish he'd had to rent a room
in Peterborough, to take his washing
to the launderette, watch his shirts turn pink.
I wish he'd lived on pork-pie and pizza
and it had made him sick.
I wish he'd gone senile and forgotten
who he was and what he'd done
and every day I could remind him. I wish
he'd died and left my name
as next of kin. They'd ring me
and I'd say, *Never heard of him.*

Your poems, true as pain, are at hand beside me. My yellow post-its mark where accurate nails were driven into your own flesh. I think of you as bleeding white, Aphrodite's ichor; just the allusion you would never permit yourself; too studied. Self-torturer, exquisite in the pains you take, I flinch from your gaze even though it is not on me. The fish you fry are trawled from your own pond; a reader would take it you married a heartless boor.

… He gives her five gold rings, one in her ear,
One in her nose, one in her nipple,

One in her navel, one in her finger. He takes
a fine gold wire and threads it between

Ear, nose, nipple, navel and finger.
He twitches the end. She dances.

John wrote to me a few years ago. His quiet handwriting told me he thought I had been unfair to my parents in *Going Up*. I had said that, although I owed them much, I could not say that I had loved them. Who could guess, from your excoriations, that Nimmo was one of the nicest men I ever knew? When Beetle scalded herself in Cambridge, during one vac when I was in London, he drove her to Addenbrooke's and stayed with her. When we came back from Spain (where you had come to see us) for Beetle's father's funeral, I was broke. He lent us his car. He also offered to lend me fifty pounds. Who will now ever see him as anything but your disloyal husband, with the big feet? In another poem, he treads on your little plants in a rejected return.

You will not blush. Did you ever blush? Even your lips had no blood in them, pursed in an oral circle, let's say. You didn't do *gros mots*, as that friend in francophone Geneva might have said. You made old words new; simple your arsenic. Adjectives add nothing to, take nothing from, words on your pages. You may be hateful; sorry, no. You know yourself too well to like yourself. John hurt you and you wished him, literally, ill. What hurt you most was that, for a time, he tricked, tickled you into believing you could be happy; happy your verses, never you.

I made you no promises, kept none; John made none to us and kept them. Beetle and I were, like many, more embarrassed by the company of unhappy friends than able to comfort them. We ceased seeing you. You had witnessed us at a bad time and were reticent. I was not: you contributed, a lot, to that character in *The Glittering Prizes* who took to drink and, given a lift home by Adam Morris, walked towards a suburban front door calling out 'Mummy's home!' You forgave me; your revenge. Beetle tells me that you once sat on the beach next to her in Fuengirola and said, 'You can only live one life'. That shows how sincere you were. Otherwise you might have said, 'You can live only one life'. You were not talking about yourself; not that time. And this?

> ... I turn, the washing on the rack brushing my face
> with the smell of cut-price detergent, the Rayburn

comforting my left flank, and go upstairs. Get into bed. Hear him shifting the furniture back the way it was.

I feel sorrier for John than for you. You were alone with your wit; never left alone, he was your target. He had his women, no purpose, as age came on, other than one more conquest; he wrote to tell me so. I knew that you were living on the little you earned as caretaker of a Quaker meeting house, near Yealand Conyers. I suggested to a schemer, once a *Granta* poet, then a literary editor, that she get clever you to do some reviewing. She said, 'She never shared her essays at Cambridge'. Christian. No longer than two sides, handwritten, they were likely to say everything that needed to be said; and not another thing. You needed no help; you gave none; your words the trumps in a game you played only with yourself.

La Tomalin now has more honorary degrees than Edith Sitwell ever did. She recognised genius when she saw it. Malice was all her praise. Many have heard of her; few of you. None accuse her of genius. She needs others to dress what she is. You needed only yourself, to strip. You used to go with John to nudist camps, you told us. But you could never take enough off, not that way.

In the mid-1980s, I was asked to give a reading at a Literary Festival at Lancaster University. I am like the sorry flautist who never ducks a gig, lest he not be asked again. I drove north, never my favourite direction. Dreading the occasion, I was early for it. You had left word at the front desk that you were coming to my reading. How often do we do the least that we can do? I did it: I called and asked you to supper in the best restaurant.

You were wearing a shapeless brown macintosh and floppy hat. You resembled the funny lady, Miss Ireland, who used to come and do the ironing when we lived in East Bergholt.

You did the irony. As we went to our table, I hoped that no one would assume that I slept with this strange bundle. You had earthy hands. You told me that you had read all my books; the best compliment I could hope for, from anyone. Dudy you remain to me. When you were born, God said: 'Keep it short'. You were. You did.

Love? No. Something though, very much so. F.

Dear Jonathan,

In the opening skit of the 1954 Cambridge Footlights May Week show, *Out of the Blue*, you and I were cast as American soldiers. After I had stuck you with a medal, we overdid the snappy simultaneous salutes. Arms interlocked, we hopped off stage in what seemed an inextricable *pas de deux*. Symbolism had us committed friends. In the mangle of time, what we had in common was not severed nor its promise kept.

You had come up to St John's from St Paul's in the autumn of 1953, the beginning of my fourth year. Someone had the idea of putting on a college revue, a form of bits-and-pieces theatre now dodoed by television. You (and a chum?) had already written and performed a precocious programme or two on the radio. A posse of Johnian arties was deputed to call on you in your rooms in The Wedding Cake, in New Court, and solicit your participation.

Cross-legged on the floor, barefoot, tieless, in blue jeans, your low-level hauteur brought us to our knees. Hair a carroty tangle, your appearance, neither youthful nor mature, advertised singular asymmetry. I never saw anyone who looked at all like you, except for your sister Sarah, to whom it lent small allure. You asked Beetle and me to her birthday party in the later Fifties. Soon after, she was run over and killed by her own car. Its engine running, she had lain on the garage floor to see what was wrong with something. The banger must have lurched into lethal gear. Life has no shortage of comedy without laughs.

That forgettable St John's revue was largely improvised. The Goon Show at the height of its renown, there was a plethora of Bluebottles, my capitain. The Sellers/Milligan genius has not waned. Remember the sketch in which

Secombe is marooned in the western desert? His only hope of getting home on time is a number 34 tram. Fat chance! We then hear the unforgettable moan of, yes, a London tram. Salvation! It slows down as Sellers, the conductor, leans out and says 'Not this one, yocky boy!' Did you, at the time, know that 'yock' was a low synonym for 'goy'? Not I. If the BBC had, they would immediately have excised it. And today? Sooner. Staged in a college lecture-room, I recall only one exchange between Joe Bain and Tony Becher, as psychiatrist, who began with: 'I want you to say the first thing that comes into your head'. Bain: 'God, but you're ugly!' Becher: 'Is that relevant?' Bain: 'It is to me.'

Some months later, solicited to become a member of the Footlights, the then all-male university club, famous for its May Week Revue and coterie camp, you less joined the cast than suffered it to join you. In the Easter vac, you suggested we collaborate on some larky material for the imminent show. I was invited to come from Putney to North-West whatever, where your parents had a large, very-sunny-that-day, sash-windowed house (flat?) with a gold and green, never Golders Green, prospect. I arrived with some small sense of election.

We set ourselves to devise routines to tickle the grockles. Diligence in the vaults of memory coughs up but one specific coinage. In those days, the weather forecast was broadcast in accordance with climatic conditions on the Air Ministry roof. You had the idea that the said roof should sport a meteorology alien to the rest of the country: tropical winter heat, sub-zero summer freezes. On snowy days in the rest of the country, listeners would be warned against sunburn; on hot, advised to wrap up warmly. A pretty conceit? No harvest of hilarity resulted. I was relieved to go home.

Reading medicine, you were a prompt recruit to the fringes of the Moral Sciences Club. Becher and I were habitués. Along with polymathy, the insolence of your imitation of Bertie Russell soon recommended you to the Apostles.

Meta-Bloomsbury semi-secret, all-male in-group, it honoured no betters. Members past and present were yoked in mutual promotion. E.M. Forster, while proposing two cheers for democracy, said that, if he had to choose between betraying a friend and betraying his country, he hoped he would have the courage to betray his country. The Apostolic Blunt and Burgess put his dictum to the test. In no danger themselves, they betrayed several hundred unknowns to be executed by the Communists behind the iron curtain.

Johnian apostle Hugh Sykes-Davies, asked what he would do if the belatedly disgraced Anthony Blunt knocked on his door, said 'I should say, hullo, Anthony, come in and have a drink'. In the red-hot 1930s, red-faced Sykes-Davies wrote a novel called *Rats*. Its hero abandons the corrupt human race and goes down the drain to join the classless (?) society of rodents. I have Sykes-Davies to thank for allotting me the Harper Wood Studentship which sponsored both my post-graduate travels and my first novel.

You never made mock of Wittgenstein, who had been unflattered when invited to eminence, whether apostolic or professorial. The solipsist honours no call to be a joiner. W.'s gestures were regularly mimicked; did anyone affect to reproduce his speech or accent? He was taken to be as inimitable as Alec Guinness was until Peter Sellers cracked the code of his River Kwai diction. Guinness then sounded to be imitating Sellers. Iconoclast Wittgenstein may have been; *in absentia* he remains iconic. Mockery was all but blasphemous. There were no more laughs in the *Tractatus* than in the Gospel, which we all but took it for; W. himself *non plus*. He signed off by saying that philosophy left everything as it was; how he left philosophy was another matter.

You and your surnamesake, and future brother-in-law, Karl, accelerated into the fast lane. Semi-radicalised by Suez, Karl, no Marxist, was to leave the Treasury, chuck umbrella, briefcase and bowler hat, and become literary editor of first the *Spectator*, then of the *New Statesman*. Was authority ever more unsmilingly exercised? He invited me to write pieces for him when, evicted from the *Statesman* by Paul Johnson, he was reduced, temporarily, to editor of the *Listener*. Karl's *Granta* chum N.O. Tomalin nicked his vacated chair. In time, Karl Miller rose again to co-edit the laughter-free *London Review of Books*. After many a summer, he was evicted by the rich, hyphenated lady whose front-office legate he had been. He never again asked me to write for him.

In the middle of that protracted spring day *d'antan* when we tried to cobble laughs together, your sixteen-year-old schoolgirl *fiancée* Rachel Collet, comely and nubile, called in to see you. I was slightly surprised that a medical student, with a string of years between you and making a living, should already have made such a decisive commitment. Rachel was also sworn to medicine; it was either what brought you together or a way of anchoring her to you, heart to heart, stethoscope to stethoscope. Why not? I was already with Beetle; and still am. Rachel's sister, Jane, was a beauty of my Cambridge time. She had the nerve, and the form, to wear a tight sweater and leopard-spotted tights on the way to lectures. One day, on King's Parade, Tony Becher (later Professor of Education at Sussex) pointed at her and uttered a shriek which doubled for derision and desire. She stood there, embarrassed and beautiful. Later she accepted a first-class ticket and married Karl Miller.

You had your parents' solemn place to yourself that protracted bright day. I never met either of them, Manny Miller, eminent psychiatrist, and Betty, authority on Keats. I left to catch my 30 bus with reluctance and relief. I had failed to seal a partnership to which I was in no hurry to pledge myself. We had not touched on anything to do with Jews. In 1960, you made a taboo-breaking jest when asked, in *Beyond the Fringe*, if it was true that you were, as rumour mongered, one of the Chosen. 'I'm Jew*ish*', you said, 'I don't go the whole hog.' During that show's long run, Beetle and I were in Franco's Spain, then Rome, then Greece, before the Colonels' coup. We never saw the smartest alicks on either side of the Atlantic perform their house-filling drolleries. You played D'Artagnan, musketeer *pas comme les autres*. I wrote *Lindmann*.

As you might not remember (hence it's tempting to mention), Quintilian said, at the height of Roman power, '*Satura quidem tota nostra est*'. Satire, he decided, was the sole entirely Roman art form, quite as if Aristophanes' Cloud Cuckoo Land had never been invented nor Aesop's fables. Officers on the Roman bridge could afford to be ridiculed, if only by each other (yes, except on the Saturnalia, when slaves took brief liberties). Britain's satire boom followed the post-Suez collapse of red, white and blue vanities. Peter Cook, mockery's master-chef, affected dismay on returning to find England wall-to-wall in giggles. Looking back in anger had yielded to *That Was The Week That Was*. In bust Britannia, the piss was the only thing left to take. Bernard Levin, on a high stool, did sit-down, allegedly mordant, one-man causeries. That similarly enstooled Irishman made sitting there less modish, more droll; Dave Allen.

With the opportunism that Tom Maschler and I had blueprinted in our 1960 '*The S-Man, a grammar of success*', ex-Footlight president David Frost had flown the Atlantic, for the first of many, many times, hot on the scent of fame. One Sunday, so your den-mother Judy Scott-Fox told me, Frost pursued y'all to the Scarsdale retreat where you were relaxing in and around the pool. His bathing suit never got wet. Lunch called, he loitered. After several minutes, Peter Cook came out to bring him to table. Frost was foundering in the deep end. Having watched with interest for a minute or two, Cook helped the water-logged visitor up and out onto the verge. When Frost had done gasping, he found the breath to say, 'Why the hell didn't you pull me out? Couldn't you see I can't bloody well swim?' Cook said, 'I thought you were taking a satirical swipe at drowning'.

Being in the swim became Frost's forte. He masterminded larky shows, not a few fashioned from the Footlights archives, updated and supplemented by ambitious sidekicks. Kitty Muggeridge won immortality by saying of him: 'He rose without trace'. One line can do the trick. Who was it who wrote that Petra was a 'rose-red city half as old as time'? According to Evelyn Waugh, Enid Raphael, who I hope was a 1920s relation, is unforgettable for having said 'I don't know why they're called private parts. Mine aren't private.' Some time in the 1970s, the *Observer* held a competition for two line quips beginning 'I am the ghost of...' A one-off winner supplied: 'I am the ghost of David Frost / Hullo, good evening, and now get lost'. My unprized offering was, 'I am the ghost of Marcel Proust / Seldom laid but often goosed'.

Cut back to Arcadian Cambridge. *Out of the Blue* was a big hit. You became the prancing tenant of the Arts Theatre stage during two long, barefoot monologues, never quite the same on any given night, a six-foot antique wooden propeller your shining side-arm. Might you remember my number about Evelyn Waugh and Graham Greene? Fat chance. Met with torrential applause, we almost went back for an encore, David Conyers and I, but the stage manager, Peter Scroggs, waved us away. You got the stellar notices, one by Guy Ramsey, who came to see the show at my invitation. The deferential raves sealed our clever-clogged transfer, via Oxford, to the West End.

Danny Kaye, hair ruddy as yours, charm not unlike, if never sprigged with fancy allusions, saluted you from the Palladium where he was filling the huge house. At one point, he invited the audience to snap on their cigarette lighters and make a big kids' birthday party of the evening by joining him in some sucrose number. How many of any modern audience carry lighters? Ingratiation was never your style. Prolific director of opera, in all the great cities, the *haut du pavé* became your yellow-brick road. Candy kisses were not in your repertoire.

Odd thing about you and Kaye: at some stage, in later years, both of you ceased to be funny. It's been said that he and Larry Olivier had a passionate affair; you and Larry a chaste one. Why not? The last time I saw Olivier was at a parents' day at Bedales, in the late Seventies. Sleeves rolled up, tartan shirt open, no jacket, he looked like a jobbing gardener, akin to that bishop in whichever Buñuel it was. You directed him in *The Merchant*. By then an empanelled director at the National Theatre, you had his Shylock dance a knee-slapping triumph that aped Adolf Hitler's conquering caper on the terrace of the Sacré Coeur in 1940. Nice one? *Tu crois vraiment?*

Tynan grew jealous of your eclectic *pasticcio*. How better label your production of *Rigoletto* in which misty Mantua, although far to the north of their fiefdom, is re-dressed as a city dominated by sun-glassed Mafiosi? The title *Dramaturg* gave Ken the Brechtian presumption that he would serve as Olivier's Lord High Executioner (and card-marker), but he was never to direct a single production. It remained to be scathing about other people's, yours not least. Failing to turn the South Bank company into the Berliner Ensemble, Ken elected to hold Mao's China to be a model state with 100 percent full employment. Whether the toilers received a living wage for dawn to dusk activity was not mentioned. Did you ever advertise a political opinion?

Proteus with no original form, you paraded a retinue of possible selves, never decisively buttoned into any particular one. As Dr Miller, you became a physician for whom the television screen opened wide. Familiar with death, Jew *pas comme les autres*, the medicine man is not a dignitary to cross. I remember your slightly shocked delight in revealing that medics who could do nothing more for suffering patients were in the habit of administering 'terminal cocktails'. Militant atheist, to dismiss the divinity crowned your *superbe*. Cultivated adaptation your *forte*, you directed operas in many cities but, no more linguist than musician, the pharmacopeia was your Esperanto, universal language without nuance. I once heard it spoken, language unavailable to wit or subtlety, on a Colchester to Liverpool Street train.

In a flourish of Renaissance manliness, you wrote a pamphlet, in the *Modern Masters* series. Marshall McLuhan was denounced as a shallow shaman. You seldom admired other people: even Mike Nichols, I'm promised, incurred a charge of being overrated. As it turned out, McLuhan was durably prescient with regard to the message and the medium. When your admirer Peter Medawar put Teilhard de Chardin down, he stayed down. McLuhan bounced back, higher than before, and justly.

Had it not been for you, I might never have met Jock Jacobsen. He came, in a grey fedora, which he did not remove in the dressing room, to see you perform in *Out of the Blue*. He had been a ready-when-you-are saxophone player in a band with Norman Payne before they became partners in a talent agency. Coalesced by M.C.A., they were lodged in fancy offices at 135 Piccadilly, with white telephones already. Jock understood little of your allusive patter, but stayed to admire Leslie Bricusse, whose less-than-wisecracks – 'the Vienna steaks / stakes were high' – needed no footnotes. Leslie refused to sign for M.C.A. unless I was part of the deal. Jock acquired the habit of greeting us as 'Hullo there, Leslie and burble-burble'.

Glad to be admitted to a vulgar world which promised to pay well enough to finance fat chunks of solo time for writing novels, I went along in Leslie's tracks. You told Beetle, while backstage during the run of *Out of the Blue*, that I had better be careful with my smart remarks. She was acting as assistant dresser to Judy Birdwood, daughter of the Field Marshal who had a chest full of decorations after sharing the command at Gallipoli. They concealed just how disastrous the Dardanelles campaign had been. Everyone liked Beetle, you told her, but go on as I was, I should never have any friends. Why, your analyst father might ask, take the trouble to favour her with such sour news? Putting me down was as close as you came to flattery. Why was I so snappy? How about I always dreamed of trading comebacks at the Algonquin with Dorothy Parker and George S. Kauffmann? 1930s New York was my Old Country.

Soon the buttered-up toast of London, you were invited, Ken Tynan the pander, to go to some nightspot with Princess Margaret. You claimed not to own the necessary dinner jacket. In the wake of clothes-rationing, it was a not unlikely poor-little-rich-boy story, despite no lack of wardrobes in your parents' large premises. Kitted with the required cozzy and beau-tied, you played Hamlet-cum-Yorick at the best reserved tables. Ken was can-opener and cant-supplier. At one of his parties he introduced me to Frankie Howerd as a coming man. Howerd said, 'I hate talent'.

Leslie Bricusse and I scripted a half-hour Footlights radio programme. You elected not to participate. I recall only a line at the end of a parody of *Yesterday in Parliament*: 'At four-thirty, the House dissolved in a glass of warm water'. It must have been the way we told them. Not long afterwards, when Spike Milligan had gone into temporary retreat, Leslie and I were recruited to write an episode of *The Goon Show*. Our inadequacy was a reminder of Edmund Kean's words in his last illness. A visitor said, 'How are you?' Kean said, 'Dying'. 'That must be very difficult.' 'No', said the electric actor, 'comedy is difficult.' You knew.

That summer in which we were hot was followed by my departure, funded by the Reverend Harper Wood's bursary, on three months of site-seeing in renascent Europe and sullen, colonial Morocco. Alone in a railway hotel in Juan-les-Pins, I began the novel I came to call *Obbligato*. Jock Jacobsen was ill-disguised as Franco Franks, 'the agents' agent'. I had written no more than a dozen pages, biro on glossy unlined paper, than I realised, quite as if it had nothing to do with me, that my mockery of The Biz was bound to be published. I also began filling the first of dozens of Joseph Gibert's spiral-bound notebooks in which I have cached raw material for reflection and *recyclage*.

Life without Beetle, however instructive, offered little pleasure. She (in a green coat with a little fur collar that she loved) flew to meet again in Paris just after Christmas. We have rarely been apart since. We returned to London, briefly, in early January, to get married in a conventional, parent-pleasing way, and then back to the *Hôtel des Deux Continents* in the Rue Jacob. Jackie Weiss ceded us the rooms she had rented in a blind man's flat in the *onzième arrondissement*. Who she? A Ph.D. of quiet diligence; not your style. Not long afterwards, Beetle and I were surprised and touched by your handwritten congratulations, on blue paper, the only example of your script I can remember. I hope I still have it somewhere.

Were you and Rachel already married? We all tended to do it in those days, impelled by the pursuit of 'maturity', today's obsolete quarry. Until 1963, being man and wife was the Leavisite ideal relationship, based on the gospel (revelations omitted) according to D.H. Lawrence. 'Immaturity' was code for the homosexual revels of which *Scrutiny* held Wystan Auden to be the ringmaster. Rumour promised that Auden never wore underpants and was economical with loo paper. That his long, uneasy relationship with Chester Kallman was quasi-conjugal granted him no reprieve from scrutineers.

In his monastic anecdotage, the wittiest modern poet was shunned by the Christchurch dons amongst whom he retired.

Beetle and I found a roach-ridden, basement flat on Chelsea Embankment. Come in, snap on the lights and you caught them socialising. Were you and Rachel already installed in Gloucester Crescent? Thanks to you and your smart friends and neighbours – Alan Bennett, Nick Tomalin, and who all else – that address became *the* Oxbridge haven. It seemed to recoil from the shabby fringe of Camden Town and insinuate itself into the green environs of Regent's Park. Was it there that I observed that you had ranged your books on thick unpainted planks, starting at floor level, tiered on raw bricks? I imitated the arrangement when we moved to a garden flat in Highgate. You invited me and Beetle to your last amateur appearance on stage. In a terminal Bacchanal, you and other graduating medics extracted strings of sausages and gory ketchup from squirming, squirting victims.

Obbligato was published, in May 1956, by Macmillan, a few months before Anthony Eden installed himself as the deutero-Winston. Churchill had refused to quit Downing Street until he had, more or less, to be carried from it. Eden's long, long apprenticeship taught him little but impatience. By July, he was playing at Britannic defiance in the face of Gamel Abdul Nasser's gyppo deutero-Führer. I was writing *The Earlsdon Way*, an abrupt change from show-bizzy skittishness to something like Sinclair Lewis. Why am I telling you all this? The kicker is that my *alter ego*, the suburban quasi-rebel whose name I should have to go and look up, was based on Jonathan Miller.

It was neither compliment nor caricature. I had the innocent conceit to take the world as my sample cupboard. The writer was a freelance portraitist in the human comedy. Few people have taken offence at being depicted, more or less recognisably, in my novels. Celia Ramsey never forgave me, not for my affectionate version of Guy as Vernon Dorset, but because I said, *en passant*, that he had a plain wife. Have a few people been disappointed to rest unused? 'Mugs' Marber (the man with the lamp in our Footlights) is the only character I blessed with his proper surname. Brian was denied entry to the Hawks Club, even though the President of a half-blue sport (fencing) would normally have been a shoo-in. Guess why.

The Earlsdon Way culminated in the demonstration in Whitehall which Eden's cavalry clattered in to disperse. Unsporting marbles were flung under the horses' skidding hooves. Beetle and I may have been against Suez; we did not join in the 'Eden Must Go' chorus. How Old School was I when I thought, 'How can he think straight with this noise going on?' Opposite the Cenotaph, we lurched into some old Jordan's Yard habitués: the amiable, pasty Posnan and sharp-featured 'Stoyan' Danyev, a translated Rosenkrantz and Guildenstern. Woe-faced, they broke the news that Eden's folly had given cover to Khruschev's *realpolitik* in Budapest.

In which Marx Brothers' film did someone say, 'This means war?' Not in 1956 it didn't; England could no longer pretend to a place in the major league. Pillow-fights became the nation's sport. Your fame grew and so, according to *Private Eye*, did your head. One thing we know about satirists: anyone is good for a laugh, friends not least. Alan Bennett was shrewd enough to become a national treasure, certified by Yorkshire pawkiness: he imitated what he was. The only personal remark I remember him uttering, in some smug TV number, was when he extracted a book whose title, so he read, was '*The Wonderful World of Bryan Forbes*'. Playing the honest Tyke, he found a target that could be bullseyed without risk of horny comeback.

And you? Peter Cook and his *sous-chefs* put you at the bottom of the page in a strip entitled *The Sayings of Doctor*

Jonathan (geddit?). In their eyes for the main chance, you were the Grand Sham to Dr Johnson's grand Cham. Some might have preened themselves on up-market martyrdom (Mark Boxer cartooned me with, yes, a big nose). You came to resemble Jean Cocteau of whom Cyril Connolly said that, in his later years, he was interested in nothing but incense and burnt offerings. Bryan Forbes was the only celebrity I ever knew who became nicer when the god deserted him.

Good things came our way, in various forms, in the 1960s. Beetle and I bought a tall, narrow terrace house in Seymour Walk, SW7. Lionel Bart had the bastion on the left as we drove in. Stephen was born on the day the Israelis captured Jericho. I won the Oscar (congratulations came only from Leslie Bricusse). For a wide slice of Sixties slickers, things were certainly not what they used to be. You and I had secretaries. Our semi-basement, windowless dining room in Seymour Walk was lined with mirrors, a combination of interior decorator's illumination and reflective narcissism. I received regular bundles of Durrant's press cuttings, vanity's soft furnishing.

Publishers must have solicited you at least as often as they did me. It never occurred to me that we were rivals. Your success neither surprised nor challenged me. I remembered that back in the Fifties you had talked of writing fiction. Having published all of two novels, I offered to be of help. No doubt, the novel you might have written would have been as experimental as the sculptures composed in later years, when you had a minute or two to spare. This reminds me that you told me that Leslie Bricusse once met you in the street, unless it was somewhere more elevated, and said, '*Tiens!*' See what you could do to people?

Beetle cooked many fine dinners for the guests who were reflected on the glazed walls of our dungeon dining room in Seymour Walk. It was with no rare motive that we asked you and Rachel to dinner on whatever night it was. Brian Glanville was coming; so were David and Clare Deutsch. We looked forward to a lively evening. I had no doubt which night I had asked you for, though I made no diary note of it. The other guests arrived; you and Rachel did not. We guessed that she had had a late emergency patient and drank the usual champagne. Half an hour went by; then forty minutes. I called your number. Rachel answered. You had gone to the cinema. More vexed than apologetic, she promised that the invitation was for the same day the following week.

The dinner was dominated by its absentees, its comedy by your presence at a table at which you were not sitting. No solemn offence was taken. These things happen, not all that often. The next morning, your secretary telephoned and began to explain to Beetle that Jonathan was sure that the mistake had been ours. He was a very busy man and always had her keep his diary. Beetle cut in to say that however busy you might be, she did not think much of an old friend who deputed personal apologies to his secretary; goodbye.

Shortly afterwards you called. Accusation doubled for apology. You implied that Beetle might have known that your stammer made it p-particularly d-d-difficult to talk on the t-t-telephone. She may not have said that it was remarkable that, while nothing inhibited you from public speaking, private courtesy was such an embarrassment. How come the other guests arrived on what you claimed to be the wrong night? It might have occurred to you and Rachel to ask us back some time; you did not.

A few years later, I was directing a little film for the BBC at Ealing Studios. After *The Glittering Prizes*, my stock was high enough to give me a free hand with a very modest budget. Tom Conti's presence sanctioned boldness in a surrealistic squib which Mel Calman, a then well-known cartoonist, not a friend of mine, saluted by sending me an image of the TV with a balloon coming out of it labelled 'Art'. The mention of Conti recalls that you told him, after seeing his impersonation of Adam Morris, that he caught every aspect of my character, 'except for [my] piranha-like savagery when crossed'. Hang about and irony floats to the surface.

It happened that, on another Ealing stage, you were shooting one of your medical programmes, *solus rex* style. We had canteen lunches together during which we talked as easily as getting-older friends might. I recall your explaining the means by which renaissance artists enlarged and squared their purposeful sketches on the canvas before proceeding. I cannot imagine that you remembered anything I said, even if there was time for me to say anything. What was the name of that rare saxophonist who found a way of drawing breath while sustaining the continuo?

In accordance with the Maugham's principle of embellishing whatever chance delivers, I wrote a story, a year or two later, called *The Best of Friends*. Two estranged college chums are at first embarrassed to find themselves attending the same *kulturklatsch* but resign themselves to making the best of it, which turns to be much better than either expected. I was Maughamian enough to give the Jonathan figure the best lines as well as the haughtiest conceit. In the TV version, Norman Rodway made you over in his own image. I gave him the last laugh.

Not long afterwards, Jo Janni called me to say that you were interested in making a movie of Henry James's *Portrait of a Lady*. You had directed all sorts of things on the stage and TV; Plato's *Phaedo* for fancy instance, of which I remember only a scene in a carpenter's shop where Socrates' coffin was being nailed together. Did ancient Athenians use wooden coffins? Never mind, it was nice *hommage* to Stanley Kubrick's use of empty, soon-to-be-filled coffins in *Paths of Glory* (1958). The only movie movie you had directed was a version of Kingsley Amis's *Take a Girl Like You*. Wikipedia, although primed with a multiplicity of your productions, publications, articles and appearances, makes no mention of it. Stanley Price did a rather clever rewrite, so he told me, but you ducked confrontation with the producers and went ahead with the banality which, no doubt, you blamed on them when the movie was not a hit. How often does playing safe deliver safety? Wikipedia reminds me that one of your public allocutions was entitled *Born Talking*, not on the telephone presumably.

So, there was no doubt about that lunch date; at Bertorelli's, was it? One of your scholiasts will know. I took petty care to arrive just a little late. I found you talking without difficulty to Jo. I happened to have a fair knowledge of *Portrait of a Lady*, a quite conventional four-square novel whose virgin heroine, Isabel Archer, no *Daisy Miller*, is remarkably calculating in her innocence. You did not display any but a passing knowledge of the plot. That propeller you carried onto the stage in *Out of the Blue* stayed with you, metaphorically: you were original in all sorts of ways, but always by distorting and refashioning whatever antique prop you chose to lean on.

Rarely impressed by reputations, his own included, Jo was sceptical about raising money for H.J.'s old-fashioned number. You switched to what Biggles, my boyhood biplane hero, would call 'the gravity tank': how about Kafka's *Amerika?* A Vatican Latin prose prize winner, Jo preferred Anatole France, whipping boy of the Surrealists, to whose fraternity you might have craved dangerous invitation (you recall what happened to Salvador Dalí, of course: he had to take the knee, to André Breton). You, Jo and I went on talking but the leaven had gone out of the occasion. Lunch ended in polite fashion with the usual promises to think about what might suit us all.

As soon as you had gone to whatever the next thing was, Jo said 'What a phoney, I must say!' No, that is not at all what I think; no more, you might be pleased, if unsurprised, to hear, did Peter Medawar. Teilhard de Chardin was his idea of a pretentious fraud, as Arnold Toynbee was Trevor-Roper's. I met Medawar just once, at a dinner party given by Hilary and Helge Rubinstein. They were kind enough to tell me that he was particularly pleased to be about to meet someone he had long admired. Vanity's scanner sought some lofty essay of mine that might have caught his clever eye.

It turned out that he and his wife had seen *Out of the Blue* at the Phoenix Theatre, where I played Joe (Loss), the bandleader, in a number called *Joe and the Boys*, a clownish performance which derived from a surge of spontaneous invention when auditioning against Brian Marber. I never did anything similar before or after. So what? Medawar was quadriplegic, a model of sociable modesty that underlined his virtues. His admiration for you was based on your medical, not your comic, performances. They rarely overlapped, though I do recall a facts-of-life primer of yours, published by the astute Tom Maschler, which featured a pop-up penis in its midriff. Sold by the thousand I daresay; knighthoods are all very well but there's no accolade like cash, is there? Chips on the shoulder take various forms; grudges and captaincy seem to go easily together. Enough already, as we would never say.

The next meeting that I recall from fallibility's repository is when Sue Bradbury, of the Folio Society, invited us to debate the lofty literary claim that 'good books do not belong in front of a camera'; not a topic to engage today's knockabout celebs. I cannot be sure which side of the fancy postulate you had already elected to champion when I was enrolled. I am pretty sure that I was asked, for what I took to be fun, to oppose the motion. In truth, I had no urgent wish to do anything but amuse the diners and, if possible, you. If, as I am pretty sure I did, I took the devil's part, it was without the smallest missionary belief in it. You seemed amiable enough at the table, more pugilistic on your feet. Was Rachel there? I think not. Beetle was. In truth, I cannot now recall any good book that made a good or better film. I long admired and wanted to make a movie of Alfred Hayes's *In Love*, a quite perfect novellita first praised by Guy Ramsey, but it is indeed generally the second-rate that translates best. So you won the debate by much the same margin, I suspect, that I might have, had our roles been reversed. I was polite enough not to mention that to adapt mediocrity was no promise of cinematic superiority. Nor did I ask what unadapted work you had ever done on any screen. Bricolage was all your art. It did not occur to me that your victory in the debate was anything to cock a hoop for, but someone must have told the press how you had trounced me in our evening of intellectual ping pong. You would never have stooped to flagging trivial triumphalism of that order, would you?

Anything else? God, yes! However many years later, when Beetle and I were summering, unless it was springing, in the Périgord, as usual, our son Paul called, late one afternoon, and asked whether I knew you. Of course I did; why? He and his pregnant partner, Gina, later Spielberg's casting lady, had gone to an afternoon showing of *Godfather III*. The place was largely empty but then a couple came in and chose to sit close behind them. The voluble male soon began to explain to his companion, who had evidently not seen the first two fat episodes of the trilogy, exactly what various references back alluded to, his voice not markedly modest. This continued pretty well throughout the projection.

When the lights went up, Paul turned round, saw who you were, and observed that you of all people might have known that talking throughout the movie had spoiled it for those who happened to be near. Rather than apologise, you chose the philosopher's defence and claimed that 'throughout' was an exaggeration. Paul said, continuously or continually, you talked enough to spoil his and Gina's rare afternoon together. You then pulled out a £20 note and thrust and wagged it at Paul, saying, 'Take this'. Paul had the pride to wave it away, saying he would sooner have an apology. This kindled an explosion of rage on your part. As Paul and Gina made to go, you called him a cunt, and then a fucking cunt, while making that £20 note into a soft cudgel.

Once on the pavement, still in a fury, you continued your abuse as this unknown young couple sought to outpace you. Paul's refusal to take your money seemed to exasperate you more than his calm, unanswerable reproach. When he got home, he made the telephone call in which he described your all but incredible effusion of what used to be obscenities. It need hardly be said that Paul had not said who he was. You presumed that not yet Sir Jonathan had put some insolent nobody in his place.

As it happened (the title, who will remember? of Clement Attlee's memoirs), I was writing a monthly column for the newly founded *Prospect*, to which I had been seduced into making an investment. Bernard Levin, whose shrine will be all columns, said that it was easier to write three pieces a week than one. My next mensual piece seemed always to be due. Paul's encounter with you was a gift I did not refuse.

Without mentioning your name, I was quite explicit, with due asterisks, about what you had said. No garish outrage, it did supply fast food for my column. I made anonymity no secure mask for your performance. It was no surprise that the *Sunday Times* called and fished for further chips. I made no overt revelations, nor did I deny that your name was in the frame. There followed a big page-three piece, pictures of you scowling, me amused. It was sadly comic that I had nothing to do, personally, with what all but terminated the contact between us.

All but what? However many years later, I was writing an essay about antisemitism (yes, again) and remembered

Shylock's dance in that old production of yours. On a sentimental impulse, I dialled your forever unchanged number to check the details. It rang and rang and then it rang off. I was relieved and I was disappointed. I was pretty sure that I was right anyway. Shall we analyse that? Shall we not? I put the phone down. Ten minutes later, it rang. 'Hullo.' 'Who is that?' I said. 'I might well say the same thing.' 'You called while I was out.' 'How are you, Jonathan?' 'Who is that?' 'Freddie. Raphael. I wanted to check something about Larry Olivier's knee-slapping dance in your production of *The Merchant*. Your idea, was it, or his?' You said: 'Mine, of course'. 'We should have been friends, shouldn't we', I said, 'you and I?' 'Yes', you said, 'of course.' I said, 'And all we were was…ish'. I gave you the last smirk; why not?

Tante cose, but never quite enough. Freddie.

Dear Larry,

I have not seen you for sixty years. I remember you more vividly, certainly more affectionately, than hundreds of those I have known, bumped into, in the intervening decades. During the first six years of my life, most of them in New York, I do not think I ever spoke to a black person, except for a large nanny called Fleggy. Saks Fifth Avenue had no shame in selling handbags advertised as 'nigger' in colour. In London, in the later Fifties I met and interviewed, for BBC radio, several of the first West Indian writers to make a mark in England, Derek Walcott among them, Naipaul not (*A House for Mister Biswas* was no place for me). Educated in schools with a curriculum determined in Whitehall, the Caribbeans' written language was marked more by the King James Bible than by any native idiom; intonation something else. That I took care to talk as I would to any other writer suggests conscious courtesy. The last time I saw Naipaul, he was being carried down the stairs from a publication party, bundled like burglars' swag, by a quartet of helpers. I have never enjoyed anything he wrote; all of it seemed corroded by bitterness accelerated, as can happen, by vanity.

Did my mother's origins infect my childhood attitude to 'coloured' people? Kansas City, MO, was not a place where blacks and whites enjoyed any common space. When I was there in 1949, I overheard a coloured man mowing the grass, with an unmotorised machine, say to himself, 'I'se not doing this because she said to. I'se doing because it needs doing.' Yes, of course, my grandmother Fanny's friends referred to black people as '*schwarzes*'. They took Yiddish to be an incomprehensible code; it is to me, *schlemiel*. When my

British father was in India, in the early twenties, he was instructed to signal 'natives' to clear out of his way with a commanding sweep of the arm. It would be letting the side down to treat them otherwise. East and West, white men were hoist on a balloon plumped with their own hot air.

We did have a Ghanaian called Johnny Quashie-Idun in the cast of the Cambridge Footlights revue, *Out of the Blue*, in 1954. J.Q.-I. sang some songs and took part in a sketch, later scrapped, in which we counted it a scandal that the Savoy Hotel had denied a room to a black person. It hardly went to the heart of the matter, but it put us virtuously on side. I had previously been denied a place on the Footlights' committee on the ground that no Jew deserved that elevation. Such was the goodness of the good old days.

After Beetle and I and our infant son Paul were abruptly evicted from our Highgate flat in the summer of 1959, we stored our furniture, strapped everything else we had to the roof of PLD 75, our green second-hand Ford Anglia, and set off for Franco's Spain, where we could be passing rich on forty pounds a week. Calle Tostón *diez y seis* was on a lane parallel to the *Carretera* that ran on to Marbella, through Estepona, to Algeciras and Gibraltar; Malaga in the other direction. The houses, stern and flat-faced to the street, were tight, undetached bungalows, most of them let to *estranjeros* of various stripes. Once inside, we found a sun-bright, bougainvillea-purpled patio with an unimpeded view, over a low white wall, of the Mediterranean. Twenty years later, it was three blocks from the sea.

We had been advised to pay Salvadora Martín no more than three hundred pesetas, four pounds, a month. She was a rare cook (ah those *rizzoles!*) and diligent bucket and broomer, but we should not spoil her. A widow with four daughters, *hoy so*, she sang sunny songs with a plethora of *corazón*; if there was rain, *lluvia* (pronounced *juvia*), she came mantled in a black cloud. She arrived, most mornings, with an opaque bag bulging with provisions from the market. She left in the evening, sack still bulging, with what was left of the very large lunch she served us with the command '*Todo!*'. It would have required a platoon to finish it all. Her daughters no doubt supplied it.

You, Larry, the painter, were our neighbour, one doorstep to the right. Little Fuengirola's foreign colony, poor enough to pass for bohemians, was mostly American. We first met, Harry and Charlotte Gordon, Paul Hecht – poet son of a New York hack driver – and Joan, his black lady friend, and who all else, at a drinks party at your house, next to what was now ours. When I asked you what Joan did, you said, 'She sleeps a lot'. I was wearing an orange turtle-necked sweater which Beetle had knitted for my recent twenty-eighth birthday. A then famous English 'Angry Young Man', Colin Wilson, had made such gear a sign of rebellion. Beetle knew only that orange was then my favourite colour.

Charlotte, full of breasty swagger, bouffant head of incurable curls, gathered a handful of my sweater and said, 'What's this?' She had, until a few months earlier, been art editor of *Seventeen* magazine. Harry had quit a similar job in New York to come and paint, for as long as their accumulated salaries lasted. He had been promised a classy show in NYC if he returned with a suitable cargo of canvases. The Gordons rented a tall house in the Calle José Antonio, roomy enough for them to have separate studios. They had no children, then.

You and the other Americans were the first I lived among since I was extracted from New York City in 1938 and transported to England, lengthened my a's and acquired a new language, social and educational. Vestiges remain: I still say 'nuts' and 'sonofabitch' on expletive occasions. In Fuengirola, I was pleased to hear American accents again. I played poker a couple of times with a bunch of veterans. One of them, Bill somebody, used to say, on teased occasions, 'Up yours with a hay rake, Jack'. He had been a commander in the US navy. I never heard anyone else use that expression. Did you know that 'snap' is the only card game in which luck plays no part?

There was another G.I. veteran, Chuck, with but one, wheezy, lung; a disability pension to go with it. He was divorced. When one of his stateside children sent him a pair of socks for Christmas, he refused to pay the few pesetas duty. 'What kind of present is a pair of socks?' He later married a Malaga *putana*. He did not have long to live and what the hell? Did she inherit his pension? She had earned it. I used to take tennis lessons in Malaga. One day, when I was having a beer at a café on the *avenida principal*, a correctly dressed middle-aged man came and proposed that I enjoy a clean young woman he could take me to.

Hans, aka Johannes, and Juliana Piron, your neighbours on the far side, were also at your party. She was on the verge of having been beautiful: fair-haired German lady, fearing forty, *pobrecita*, appeal in brilliant blue eyes. Her Jewish husband had, we were told, been in 'the Resistance' in Holland during the war. Without malice, you deglamorised that as meaning he stole coal. As Christmas approached, Hans asked me to help him poach a fir tree from a big orchard on the Marbella road. Devoted to the *Stille Nacht, heilige Nacht* tradition to which German Jews often subscribed, he needed PLD 75 as a getaway car. A heavy cold spared me being an anti-Franco Yuletide resistance fighter.

When she married Hans, Juliana was cut off by her father. He had escaped to Argentina, fat fortune intact, as the Third Reich foundered. Hans and Juliana's fair-haired, blue-eyed daughter Claudia received regular bounties from her South Americanised grandfather. Her brother Pauli was denied similar favour. Hans and Juliana made their living, just, as translators; he was about to set off for the Frankfurt book fair, confident of picking up enough work to keep them going for another year. Juliana assumed that he would also pick up a few 'flirts'. A few years younger than she, Hans was tall, with plenty of pepper and salt hair and almost all the charm required for social and amorous purposes. Both spoke fluent English, with the odd Germanic eccentricity. Having seen Harry Gordon's recent paintings, Juliana declared that he would one day be hung in a Muse-you-um. Hans's large, loud laughing father Max (in black beret and cape) and wife Elsa lived in Malaga. He called Juliana his 'daughter-incest'.

You had been a student at Cooper Union in NYC and particularly admired Juan Gris. You gave us a sketchbook of watercolour drafts in his style. Whatever your experience of being black in post-war America, you had no public wish to be categorised as anything but an artist. One of the unlikely guests at your party was an English spinster called Miss Anderson, a provincial headmistress in her later fifties, chairperson of her local Conservative Association in Axminster. You treated her with hospitable attention. As she made to go, you kissed her on both cheeks. She was sufficiently enflamed to say, 'What would my committee say if they saw me being kissed by a black man?' She called you *Mister* Larry Potter. You were gracious enough to be gratified.

It would not have occurred to anyone at the time to describe you as African-American. You were articulate, well-read, slim, charming and asthmatic. You showed no urge, defensive or aggressive, to be defined by your negritude, an about-to-be-fashionable Parisian term. Your wide reading must have included Ralph Ellison's *The Invisible Man*. If you had any notion of being visible, it was by declaring yourself in your work. It did not occur to me to wonder whether your slimness had anything to do with having nothing much to eat. We were poor enough for me to take it that we were equally poor, which was not the case. That party in your place, when we met the arty *Fuengirolistas*, seemed to imply you were not short of money. Did we all bring bottles? I'd like to remember doing so. When my mother, not yet fifty, came to stay with us, she told you how she went to art classes (and did pretty good work). You gave her the fine etching of a sleeping woman which hangs in the hall outside where I am writing this.

In those days, psychoanalysis, largely Freudian, was an American national addiction. It was common to read physical characteristics as having psychological sources. You and Juliana both suffered from spasms of stifling breathlessness. Did your blackness have anything to do with it? Juliana had renounced access to her father's fortune in order to marry a Jew and refused to regret her decision. Did it choke her? Anxiety about age was her only admitted sign of stress. I remember her at the street door, no bra to support descending breasts under her black dress, saying it was her birthday. When Hans went off to cull work and, she did not doubt, kisses in Frankfurt, we were slightly shocked, Beetle and I, to hear that you and she had had a quick, why-not affair. True?

The rapid clicks and cursed jumbles of my manual portable typewriter began after breakfast and did not cease until Salvadora gave that peremptory call, '*Señorito, la comida!*', at any time between two and three in the afternoon. You told me that other inhabitants of the Calle Tostón were disquieted by my diligent keywork. Most of our books were in store, but I did flaunt Wittgenstein's *Philosophical Investigations* on the table in the living room, to put visitors in their place and advertise me positively pale blue. No one looked at it.

Soon after we arrived, I wrote a play called *The Roper House*, based on the character of Sir Oswald 'Tom' Mosley, the virile, leather-belted, black-sweatered Leader of the pre-war British Union of Fascists. I embellished him by making him an architect of undoubted quality. In haughty post-war disgrace, he is visited by a young man who has something in common with the bourgeois character in Sartre's *Les mains sales* deputed to kill the 'Trotskyite' Hoederer, but somewhat falls in love with him instead. Squeamishness renders him *'irrécupérable'* (beyond salvation). Like Ernest Hemingway's Swede, in *The Killers*, he makes no effort to evade the Party's hit-men.

Sartre was more eclectic (Heidegger his misunderstood *maître-à-penser*) than his puffers allow: his trilogy *Les Chemins de la liberté* owed a debt to the innovations of John Dos Passos. In those days a socialist, Dos's skill and success rendered Hemingway jealous enough to acquiesce in his proposed murder, never achieved, by the Communists during the Civil War. In 1960, Hemingway was commissioned, fatly, to cover the series of *mano-a-mano* bullfights featuring Dominguín and Ordoñez. The author of *For Whom the Bell Tolls* was not reluctant to be the celebrity guest of Franco's Spain. Dos, if not a McCarthyite, became an outspoken anti-Communist.

When you heard that I had written a play, you urged me to give a reading. One evening you and a dozen or so others in the foreign contingent brought chairs to our house. I played all the parts to an audience which proved promisingly attentive. Afterwards, there were questions, polite and less polite (Harry Gordon was of competitive temper). You amazed me by being able to recite quite long passages of dialogue after a single hearing. Your comments were as intelligent as your quotations were accurate. *Ach so*, Larry Potter!

We should have talked more and more often than we did. I was too polite to ask about your background, whether you came from New York, as I assume, or what your prospects were for a show of your work. You had a fine smile, but I can't recall you laughing a whole lot. You were alone, but you did not seem lonely. You kept your troubles to yourself. Hans and Juliana were easier to know. Hans had a nicely incised ivory Mah Jong set, which he would bring into our house, along with a suitable table to play on. His regular, insinuating remark was, 'Now I finish it quickly'.

You did come to Christmas lunch in our patio. We had clubbed together to buy a large turkey which was cooked for the necessary hours in Fuengirola's communal oven. We paraded it in a hungry procession to where our table was empurpled with bougainvillea. Harry and Charlotte Gordon were invited, but didn't come. Harry, lapsed Catholic, said he didn't even know what day Christmas was. We were all running from something, except for Beetle; she has always been easy in her skin.

While Harry had been all-but-promised a one-man show in NYC, you had no such prospects even of disappointment. Being a painter was a form of courage and of presumption: you were daring the art world not to treat you like any other postulant, knowing all along that it was likely to do so. You were, in that regard, as much Jewish as black: with small hope of overthrowing the established way of things, we had little choice but to play out our chances, different as they might be, on a warped board. In those days, Jews were in the forefront of the struggle for the rights of, as was then the done thing to call them, Coloured People. In that famous 1965 march to Selma, a rabbi would walk side by side with Martin Luther King all the way. He was cut out, except for a quick glimpse of him among others, in the film which has become the authorised version of the occasion.

You had the wit to hear the undertones of *The Roper House*. When I sent it to my agent in London, she said (her name was Betty Judkins) that even if it went into production, it would soon be found to be unperformable. By the time she delivered her verdict, I had finished *A Wild Surmise* and, with a weekend in between, started *The Trouble with England*. Much of what you had remembered of my dramatic dialogue became the foundation of an episode in a television series I wrote fifteen years later. The Mosley talk-alike was played by Eric Porter, the very best of the kind of actor who always guesses that he has been cast, late in the day, because someone more famous (Paul Scofield) has proved unavailable. His grudge supplied a chip that lodged perfectly on my character's shoulder.

You're right: I wish I had more to recall about you before confessing that I have run dry of direct reminiscences. We left Fuengirola in the spring of 1960, soon after Jack Kennedy entered the White House. Beetle was pregnant; she flew home, with Paul, from Gibraltar. I drove north alone, with our stuff, at twenty-five miles an hour in the waning, lop-sided PLD 75. It boiled if I went any faster. When I called in to say goodbye, you gave me the sketch book, bulging with pages that proved your abiding admiration of Juan Gris. I keep it in the drawer in front of me as I write. Yes, I do look at it; I like the work and think of you.

We returned to Fuengirola in the spring of 1961, with Paul and five-month-old Sarah and a new, grey Standard Ensign. Charlotte Gordon thought it looked like an American car. We needed a bigger house. She had found us the Villa Antoñita, on the *Carretera*. You had left for Paris. We heard later, not directly, that you had there fallen in with another crowd of expat Americans, including Jimmy Baldwin. You are thinly disguised as a character in *Another Country*, one of the first books I reviewed, enthusiastically, for the *Sunday Times*. When I met the author, I found him a whole lot shorter than his photograph, more jockey than titan, a raging cutie. Saul Bellow called him Martin Luther Queen. He shouldn't have, but he did.

Sometime early in that second period of ours in Fuengirola, I came across Harry Gordon at one of the tables outside the Casino bar in the *plaza*. He was looking, more dejected even than usual, at a copy of *Time* magazine. When I asked him what was going on, he turned the folded back pages towards me. The headline was 'Hard Edge Is Dead'. I did not understand what that had to do with him. The answer was everything. He had accumulated at least a hundred large, once modish, hard-edge canvases in all those industrious months in the Avenida José Antonio Primo de Rivera (no trace of that name on today's map of Fuengirola, or of anywhere else). Now he had no prospect of showing or selling a single one.

I was, and remain, somewhat innocent when it comes to the arts. I assumed, when I started, and still believe that true artists should do the work they want to do, not what the market wants. I had thought Harry did hard edge because that was what his Muse dictated. He never did have a show in New York. I wonder where all those paintings are. I showed some photographs of his work to a well-known London critic, not John Berger, the other one. He said only, 'I don't like his paint'. Harry went back to being a designer in the advertising business. He and Char came to London and she gave birth to two sons.

I guess you must have corresponded with Harry, unless it was with Juliana. Somehow we heard that you had written, with grim lightheardedness, that things were not going well for you in Paris. You were, you said, 'flat on your black ass'. We should have done something; weakest of all apologies. That you remain unforgettable is my lame, true, last word. Here am I trying to do all a writer can in the way of sketching from memory someone not seen, not at all forgotten, during those fleet sixty years.

Abrazos muy fuertes, Frederic.

TO LUDWIG WITTGENSTEIN.

'W.', in the vocative, best serves to summon and summarise your mythical personality. In 1951, when I was first intrigued by Moral Sciences – as Cambridge formality (following David Hume) then termed philosophy – you had just left the scene, a messiah whose apostles took him to have relegated metaphysics to the old curiosity shop. I was a callow twenty-year-old, adept with parodic proses and verses in Latin and Greek, bent on fiction, hot for the exit of ideology, religion not least. The end of the war had seemed to promise a freshly levelled playing field. You were cast as Reason's referee, decisive with the whistle at any flash of supposititious fancy. I took Freddie Ayer, author of the razor-edged *Language, Truth and Logic*, to be your linesman.

You had been barely twenty in 1911, when Bertrand Russell was approached, in Trinity, by a shriven Germanic pilgrim and, pretty soon, disconcerted by him. G.E. Moore suspected your rare quality when you alone looked puzzled in his lectures. Not long afterwards, the author of *Principia Ethica*, Bloomsbury's secular gospel, went with you on a Norwegian retreat on which he, a full professor, played your *amanuensis*. What other incursion into Britannia's philosophical élite has matched yours for disruptive intensity? I read you as possessed with passion for once and for all truthfulness, the stripping out of fancy. Philosophy, you said later, 'leaves everything as it is'; but you left philosophy quite other than it had been (Bertrand Russell too).

Displacement of morals and ethics in favour of engineering, aeronautics and the totalitarian dream presaged the Great War; mechanical progress pandered to press-button ruthlessness, mark of the twentieth century. You did your duty in the Austro-Hungarian army but took no loud pride in it.

Was there a pinch of insolence in volunteering for that solitary steeple-high perch from which to co-ordinate artillery fire on enemies with whom you had no personal quarrel? Your entry in *Zettel* for Christmas Day 1916, when you may have been up there on duty, jingles no bells. Higher mathematics knows no holy days. In logic there are no surprises, you said, and no God – I took you to imply – to spring them. Then again a suicidal strain ran through the Wittgensteins and marked a blaze it would be coy not to link with Semitic origins; self-denial can be self-destruction's double. We shall, as academics say, come back to that.

Calamity for the Central Powers and its ruling houses dashed the patriotic pride you might have scorned, had the double eagle never been cropped of one of its hawkish heads. Your pianist brother Paul lost an arm, Austria lost Hungary; the Wittgenstein fortune emerged intact. Post-Versailles, you left no longer imperial Vienna and returned to Cambridge, as if after a sabbatical, to say 'Where were we?' When it came to qualifying for the PhD., necessary to academic advancement, Moore and Russell sat as examiners you chose to patronise. 'You'll never understand it' you told them about your thesis, joker trumping aces. Did any other such submission ever resemble *The Tractatus Logico-Philosophicus*? No sooner was it construed as a work of genius than its composer discounted it. Your programme for a grammar congruent with a reasonable world was a post-armistice casualty of the Great War. Common decency died of wounds. The Jabberwocky came, left and right, in the wake of the old order.

Whatever your second thoughts, the *Tractatus* was seminal in post-Versailles Vienna; philosophical *klatches* prowled and prowled around your numbered bastion. Deserted by its architect, impregnable and undefended, it resembled that castellated octagon built in Apulia by Friedrich II of Hohenstaufen. Did you ever sight-see? What fails to interest genius is always interesting. Did you whistle while you worked, or only afterwards, or before, at faultless length, a one-man orchestra? Playing your clarinet, were you ever tempted to jazz? You seem, in biographies, as austere as that centimetre-perfect steel and glass house I visited in Vienna's Kundmanngasse; no place like home, as they say, no place whatever in that instance. You helped Paul Engelmann engineer it for your sister when in retreat from a petty reverse. See below; Freud's place to look.

Translated to 1930s England, you came to accept a Cambridge professorship, with small gratitude, even less collegiate zeal. You offered no welcome to 'tourists' at those seminarian huddles in your rooms in Whewell's Court, across from the Taj Mahal restaurant where, in the 1950s, we Johnians clustered over three-and-sixpenny curries. Celebrity-hunters were advised to knock on other oaks than yours. Like Archilochos' hedgehog, you bristled with singularity. Did adroit Isaiah, Berlin that is, ticket you in that uncuddly form, himself the versatile fox? As if scorched by your unaccommodating heat, Berlin abandoned philosophising in favour of *recyclage*, black coat, striped trousers, carnation buttonhole, rich wife: metic as local toff, the first Jew to have been elected a Fellow of All Souls, the English language his neatly buttoned carapace.

Unlike the devil, you had no nickname. Never Witters, disciples furnished a pedestal for your five feet, six inches. Didactic solipsist, archetypal one-off, 'Wittgenstein' branded the ladder you supplied for trammelled escapees from the metaphysical fly-bottle; once out, they would be wise, you said, to fling it away. Philosophy had no heights to scale, no lofty furniture, no celestial rewards. When Pompey the Great invaded the temple in Jerusalem in 63 B.C. and unveiled the Holy of Holies, its lack of treasure left him robbed. Vacancy was content; zero a mystery the Romans never plumbed. Latter-day Spinoza, you ground metaphorical lenses the more clearly to see less and less.

Russell was sometimes called Bertie, behind his back, by the few undergraduate Moral Scientists of my time. I attended his last series of lectures. So many people came to the first that the overflow overflowed, into Mill Lane. Russell declared that he suspected that many had come 'for the wrong reason'. 'Accordingly' subsequent lectures would be 'more difficult'. Uncomfortable was he, the mandarin, with the popularity he had helped to publicise? Or proud? You had your secret apprehension; did he have his? Imagination was not your field, unless dread, cousin to menace, was its crop: scourge and fruit confounded. The nearest you came to self-revelation was in that paradigm hybrid, the rabbit and the duck; Jew and Gentile, as you never said, in an Orwellian farmyard, Napoleon and Snowball. Freddie Ayer wondered whether or what sheep were thinking. His master, Gilbert Ryle, affected to discount 'mind' altogether. You spoke or did not speak. Did your silences ever lose their foreign accent?

Ayer, for all his wartime Guards' officer rig, Old Etonian tie, knightly embellishments, dreaded that one day they might come for him, another *Jud Süß*. Bluebeard's castle loomed; Kafka's too; and *The Trial*? A palace and a prison on either hand, Freddie's nimble-mindedness toted a secret ball and chain. Had he not said so, who would have guessed? Because he said so, was it true? Even apprehensions can be self-important. Something is missing in all biographies; otherwise they would be lives. It was said, in my days as a *habitué* at parties at 5, Jordan's Yard, that there was a knock at the door on one such occasion and, when some lit *au pair* girl opened it, a grey head craved entrance. She took a look and said, 'Old people's home is number eleven' and shut the door, on Bertrand Russell, *dit-on*. There is a nine of diamonds in every suit.

However straight your face, or aghast John Wisdom's, you and he treated philosophy as a litter of often insoluble cryptograms rather than as any coherent system; disassembly was the way to make its elements intelligible. You came to call philosophising 'the game', as whores their 'Are-you-coming?' activities. In Attic drama, the same *topos* could accommodate solemnity and frivolity. 'The modal child', Wisdom used to say, 'is the child around whom the others cluster'. If ethics are equated with aesthetics, as you said in the *Tractatus*, your dictum entailed that Leni Riefenstahl's 1935 *Triumph of the Will*, glorifying a Nazi rally, was beyond criticism; beauty its goodness. Might that dispose you to think again about that brisk equation?

Logic has something in common with Talos, the hot-chested, tireless Cretan automaton invented by the crafty Daedalus; any intrusive exception, clapped against the grill where it might have had a heart, was toast. As the Jews of Europe were being consigned to extinction, Heinrich Himmler (another one-time schoolteacher) asked a blonde, naked, beautiful Jewess merely to swear that she was not Jewish. He could then spare her the gas chamber. The twentieth century's anonymous Antigone denied him the divine right, died for what she was. So? So suppose that you had surrendered your family's tons of bullion to save her life, as you did for your sisters' sake, never mind that it armed the Nazis. Would that blonde Antigone not have looked at you with contempt? After Auschwitz, you played the British game: reticence muzzled the unspeakable. You quizzed, but did you ever embarrass, yourself included? Fencing goes around the minefield, never ventures inside, protects what those skulls and crossbones warn against. Philosophers also fence; thieves too.

Your notion of repairing to the USSR stands as one of the few callow moments in your life. Lenin, in his Zurich days, had propounded dialectical materialism as a doctrine that denounced the Vienna Circle's polemic neutrality. However briefly, you bought Soviet communism, the prospectus if not the savage practice, quite as if the old world and its suite of clerics, *rentiers* and hypocrites deserved eclipse, never mind the conduct of its ravenous replacement. That 1935 visit of yours to the Soviet Union coincided with the beginning of the Great Terror, whereof, so far as I know, you kept silent, as you did, when the time came, about the Holocaust and the logics applied to sanctify inhumanity. Not your field? I took you for the moral authority I craved and you never affected to be.

How did you see, or not see, yourself? In Greek iconography, only women look in mirrors. Are human beings not sometimes perceived more accurately by other people than by themselves? Lewis Namier, in the Athenaeum, asked how he was, responded 'Am I a physician?' He shared your *morgue*; ironic masks are common to scholars.

Austria-Hungary's post-Versailles dissection docked a measure of the pride that came from deleting yourself from the gilded order your family enjoyed. How else shall we read your decision to secede from metropolitan wrangling, and play schoolteacher in a mountain village? Your intolerance of error was not effaced. Pupils responsive to your urgent teaching made remarkable progress. Inattentive ears were boxed hard enough to excite rustic indignation. Disdaining to be chided, you returned to Vienna to work on your sister's house. The story is that you found the steel window frames to be three millimetres out of specification and insisted that they be re-made. It is taken to show how implacable your applied mathematics. Is it unjust to read your demanding accuracy as typical of a rich man's son? Giving away your money gave you away in other regards. Before long, the lure of philosophising at the centre table uncorked your bottle. Can you deny that the dated expression has fizzy pertinence? Discussion has violent roots: *discutere* to shake apart. You resumed bending first-class ears while what was left of Austria came unglued. Oh yes, another pun lurks, brutal and artless.

The oddest *fait divers* in your life was having been in adjacent classes with little Adolf Hitler when in primary school at Linz. Was he Adolf Schickelgruber then? Did anyone box his ears, or yours? The former is easier to imagine; it happened or it didn't. Another nine of diamonds! You became solipsists of opposing orders, rant and reason, urgent to prevail, dictators literal and figurative. Imagine if... Never mind. Did you hear the story about Bob Boothby, a maverick Scottish Tory MP, a regular in high and low circles, when some time in the 1930s, he was presented to Adolf Hitler? The Führer greeted him with his selfish upraised arm and 'Heil Hitler'. Boothby replied, with similarly upraised arm, 'Heil, Boothby!' Humour has little place in philosophy. Democritus saw the funny side, but it was not catching. In speculative verbosity, are the dancer and the dance ever one?

Being 'difficult' was not your mark, not during your Second Coming anyway; uncompromising, yes. The story goes that you were once approached by a lady who said she had a problem: she did not feel at home in the universe. You are said to have said, 'That, madam, is not a problem, it is a difficulty', implying 'next window, please'. Freud might have helped her; you not. Russell had a similar experience with a lady who maintained that the earth was flat and sustained on the back of a gigantic tortoise. Russell inquired nicely on what the tortoise reposed. 'Another giant tortoise; as far as we're concerned it's tortoises, tortoises all the way.'

Odd that the method still ascribed to your mature self is termed 'therapeutic positivism'. Is it therapy? Is it positivism? Their seen-through ghost? It is not the answers that come at the end of your book, but the questions. The crux of philosophy: it never supplies what we want, unless a charlatan propounds it. Difficulty doesn't make anything true; the clever wish it did: why else did George Steiner fawn on Heidegger? The hope of being admitted as exceptional to the Aryan rule, as Allen

Ginsberg with Ezra Pound? Your name was neither mocked nor abbreviated, despite faecal possibilities; no Nietzsche, no feature rhymed with you; what would it be to falsify, trade on, pervert, toy with your thought? Made curricular, it furnished tracks, and points, for trains carrying aseptic cargo, powerless engines. I met a man recently who affected to be a philosopher as well as a publisher. He said he had no time for you. That was his right. He turned out to be a con man.

Is there any recording of your Cambridge seminars? You uttered no Joadian catchphrases; only your gestures – bracketing sidelong hands, advancing or retreating, boxing clever, it seemed – were cadged by latter-day apostles who affected the arcane fellowship which select disciples had enjoyed in your presence. Your manual code composed a waggish semaphore; caution primed distinctions, straitened gates; your scowl a shutter: poor Friedrich Waismann, common ground his trespass! Possessiveness did not vanish with possessions, did it?

Did you ever value despatches that saluted you? Some people take praise for insolence, reserve no welcome for men from Porlock. Isolation prompts outspokenness, prison liberties: Boethius, Sir Walter Ralegh, Antonio Gramsci. When did Leopardi and Montaigne have more to say than on their own? Solipsism and egotism are not the same thing. Contrast your parable of the man who read something in the newspaper and then went out and bought another copy of the same paper to verify its truth. Imagine having nothing to lose; is that, to some degree at least, what impelled you to give away your share of the Wittgenstein fortune?

There was at least one thing of which you never divested yourself: nettled respect for Otto Weininger, the raw rash he raised. Carlo Michelstaedter, another suicide at twenty-three, enough said, did you ever find time for him? Consider rhetoric and its false floor, Trieste and *tristesse*, spectrum and spectre, fostering Claudio Magris and the biggest synagogue in Europe. Shucking Jewishness can narrow horizons without erasing its mark. Why else did you label the philosopher a solitary without a place to call his own; sly reference, was it, to the Son of Man? Windowless monad, ghetto for one, bare bed of *nihilismo*, are they not elements of what Julien Benda celebrated in *Exercice d'un enterré vif*? *Vif* suggests *Juif, n'est-ce pas*? Silences pun in different languages.

By the time you took up permanent residence in Cambridge, Russell's singlemindedness had dissipated, thanks, in the first place, to Lady Ottoline Morrell. His public renown came from popular texts on morals (one advocating 'experimental marriage') which you held should be clapped in red jackets to advertise their unworthiness. Blue would distinguish works rated (by you) as having intellectual merit. Diffidence outgrown, you were the master now. Did Russell ever honour you more unequivocally than by omitting any mention of you in *A History of Western Philosophy*? Did you ever rate, or berate, Heidegger, whose metaphysics furnished absurdities for the Vienna Circle's lighter moments? Heidegger's brother read him for a straight-faced Dadaist. Reichsmarshall Hermann Göring's brother helped to smuggle Jews into Switzerland. Saint or seditious sibling? Both? What would it be to know the answer? Decision may classify; it is not a form of knowledge.

That deckchair in which you sat during Cambridge seminars furnished a canvas throne, as Diogenes' tub his palace. When young you were racked by what Russell called your sins and by their purge: dread of not measuring up to your ambition to be a philosopher, was that? Or of 'something coming out', as they used to say? Is motive ever only one thing? No such thing as the self, John Gray claims in one of his buy-me pamphlets; self-preservation is there though, anything but still, scissors and pasting against the odds, dressing the void. Only the soul has no colour. When you proclaimed that philosophy lacked exclusive authority, you docked the once 'Queen of Sciences' of its regal coat of arms. At the same time, warning apprentices against its glitter conceded its lure. As you wound things up, you restored their tick.

Whatever you may have confessed, or given away, ducking or rabbiting, there were elements you kept to yourself, unless you deceived yourself as well as those who took you for a 'Christian' and proposed, as the Geaches did, to bury you with a cross marking the spot. Thanks to them, was it, that you have a headstone in Cambridge's Ascension parish church? Your *Tractatus*, mantic and misconceived, as you concluded, posted Baruch Spinoza, Russell's 'noblest of philosophers', as your nominal cousin, Benedict. The convert lives more comfortably in translation than in the original.

Weininger's shamelessness made a trimmer out of you, did it not? Were you a little ashamed to discount him merely because he was wrong? You dared to say that his work expressed 'a great truth' provided one preceded it with Russell's wavering dash, which symbolised negation. Did that not all but concede that being correct, formally, is never everything; the rub, the rub? Weininger discussed vexed matters from which, unlike physical danger, you chose to absent yourself. His sense of cloven pre-destination, like the synthetic *a priori*, was not rational. It remained fatal; Christian stigma led to selection; goats this way, sheep that. Detach divinity, stigmata stick.

That first visit of yours to Cambridge, before the Great War, to sit at Russell's feet, before snapping at his heels, had a licensing effect; so Jesus when endorsed by John the Baptist, Eliot when Pounded. Apollo warned against the oracle over which he presided: *gnothi seauton* implied the futility of looking other than within for the truth about oneself; within what? The sign over Dante's hell was matched over

Auschwitz. During the long Calvary of European Jewry, you absented yourself from Cambridge to become a hospital orderly in Newcastle. War work allowed you to be yourself, unless it was someone else.

William Bartley III's account of your younger days alleges that you had indulged yourself with the 'rough trade' available in Vienna's Leopoldstadt park, implying that Newcastle had similar pleasures available. He has been accused of muck-raking, yet he was, in other regards, a respectable philosopher. What impelled him to spill wanton beans, what source delivered them? Renan's *Vie de Jésus* was regarded as scandalous in its day, because – like Thucydides – it eliminated the supernatural. Bartley's Wittgenstein revelled, as if rejuvenated, in wartime obscurity. If true, does whatever you were alleged to have got up or down to damage your integrity? For all your interest in Freud, you never played the moralist; what individuals chose to do, or found they dreamed about, was their affair. I wonder what you would have made of D.H. Lawrence, he of you. Better than he did of Russell? Lady Ottoline Morrell, absurd as she may now appear, had unnerving effects on all three of you. There's a topic.

Once anointed a philosopher by Russell, you began a long parade of detachment and disdain. Your conceit declared itself in that parenthetic exit line, after you and Popper indulged in a retrospective Viennese coffee-house barney, in the Cambridge Moral Sciences Club, in October 1946. The grandee and the prodigy in you banged the door on your 'What do you know about philosophy, Russell, what have you ever known?' Michelangelo Antonioni was given to not calling 'cut' when the actors expected it. He let the camera run when the scene, as scripted was over. Then the truth would show up, he hoped, for want of confected words. Actors, he imagined, looked more true in a panic void. Would that some angelic vigilante could deliver footage of you going down the steps from Richard Braithwaite's rooms into the courtyard! How did you look, where? How did you walk? At what angle was your chin? Popper's *The Open Society and Its Enemies* has proved durably canonical.

Although most reputable sources do not quote your naughty-boyish exit line, it has a plausible ring: Russell after all had not even allotted you a footnote in his recently published and popular *History of Western Philosophy*. We may be sure you would have had it bound in red. From the beginning, your pronouncements had a stinging effect on him. How much pleasure did you take when demonstrating, in the last lustrum of Edwardian Britain's complacent *imperium*, that his (and Alfred North Whitehead's) long attempt to make mathematics the basis of transcendental knowledge amounted to a horizontal Jacob's ladder runged with elaborated tautologies, its end no higher than the beginning? Russell had the nobility to honour your dismissive rigour; that does not entail that his pride forgave it. Logic makes few friends.

Some say Russell never again did work of fundamental importance in philosophy. A fierce disciple might say that there was no such work to be done; would you, wholeheartedly? Delete the fraudulent, the fictional, the dramatic, the practically meaningless, who can argue, or deny, that writing remains on the wall, invisible or no? The unnecessary (logically) can still, and often, make humans wear and bear their stripes and stars. Is that Jean-Jacques Rousseau's point? Was he right? Shall we ask Voltaire? Philosophers compete for a crown with no known kingdom. They also do their share of careerist crawling. Forty percent of German academics heiled Hitler.

Empiricism's puzzle: why must it be logically unavoidable and practically absurd to be only as we are? I Am That I Am: God's boast or His lament? 'Why not?' trumps 'Why?' as fundamental. Hence G.E. Moore took your puzzlement for a symptom of rare intelligence? Jesus did not spring God from His loneliness; never a Christian, He was tagged as one; seal of Roman imperialism, universal deity posed as irreplaceable. No wonder Plato, faker and fakir, was embraced as Christianity's adjutant! Was Jesus ever tempted to make a getaway, once on earth, from celestial bloodlessness? Is that what the devil was up to during that dialogue on the pinnacle of the temple, displaying the sweets of here and now? Suppose, as D.H. Lawrence fancied, Jesus dreamed of shedding divinity, finding sweet mutability in being uncapitalised he, the son a father. No such luck? *Moira* lives, *Tyche*'s plain sister.

John Locke's plausible claim that the human mind was a *tabula rasa*, ready for education's scratches, served to warrant universal suffrage, falsely: DNA, no sort of leveller, pitches humanity into a hazardous mixer, irrational desire the whisk. Nice that DNA's discoverers were laurelled shoplifters, Watson and Crick; some of the jewels in their Nobel crown were filched from Rosalind Franklin. I once saw a sign in a Madison Avenue costumier's window: 'Everything in this store is guaranteed fake'. The Cretan question: including the sign? The Cretan's question can never be the Cretan's to ask; it can only be put to him; and then he cannot answer it; neither truthfully nor falsely. So what? The potter pots until he elects to do no more; the work detached from his wheel, however sweetly, has its navel, mark of its human source; done and dusted is never immaculate. No work of art is ever finished, they say, only abandoned, like hope.

Your return to Cambridge, ten years after the Armistice, was sometimes referred to, if not in your hearing, as 'the Second Coming'. In every class there has to be a naughty boy. You published no New Testament to supplement or disavow the *Tractatus*. The circulation of the manuscript blue and green notebooks made your apocrypha available, on loan, to warranted insiders. 'Not many laughs there, dear', John Schlesinger might have said: has anyone a record of your laughing at anything anyone said? Your warmest acknowledgment, one guesses, was a frown. We can be sure only that you were scornful when it came to sentimental assumptions. After Norman Malcolm, your American (significant?) buddy, claimed that assassinating Hitler would be contrary to the British character, you derided the idea that there was any subterfuge, or shortcut, from which the British were too fine, by definition, to abstain. Maurice Buckmaster told me that, during the war, the British launched seemingly shipwrecked boxes to drift ashore in occupied France containing large size condoms, labelled SMALL. Good one? Ian Fleming's idea? Who he? You're probably right.

The notion of national characteristics touched on matters you seldom chose to broach. How good was your English? Part of your rare reputation depended on the Sibylline delivery with which we were quick to bless you. It is not unusual for aliens revered by Englishmen as masters of literary profundity (Conrad by Russell, for instance) to lack conversational fluency. The great classical scholars never affected to *speak* Greek or Latin. Eduard Frankel's edition of Aeschylus is a scholarly masterpiece and a translation into gobbledegook. If German backed your mental agility, you elected to limit your thoughts to a quite specific field; Betty Grable's nimble charms on the sunset side of it, 'Can you do a flick?' your slang proposal when her legs were on a local screen. I remember a German on our Greek beach stopping to say 'I've got a bum knee'. Characteristic of German speakers, fluency that promises lumpen foreignness?

Casimir Lewy was a Cambridge philosopher of your period and – unlike you, the anticipator – an all but just in time refugee. When Anthony Rudolf thought of becoming a Moral Scientist, Lewy told him to go away and read, among other books, René Descartes's *Discours de la méthode*, but not in French: an English translation would lack seductive garlic. Tutored by Wisdom, Lewy had become a logician who stayed in his lane. Formal logic supplied the fence over which he could pitch rotten apples, but never reach for good. Far-fetched double-talk? Cf. skid-marks, their silent screech. Did Lewy write, say, *feel*, anything about what came to be indexed under *The Holocaust?* Wasn't there a clerihew 'What Dr Ewing / claimed to be doing / was a load of hooey / said Casimir Lewy'? There is now; what whitewashed wall long lacks writing on it? Logical possibility warrants ruthlessness. Once the premisses are in place, and the lather, Occam's razor knows no pity. What Socrates knew: you never know.

You too questioned doctrine, impersonated quizzical procedure. 'A thing is what it is', Bishop Butler said, 'and not another thing.' Or so we wish; if we do. Can life go on without double-dealing? Nice that bishops' head-dress has a cleft in it! Your later work, akin (you implied) to psychiatry, was devoted to unravelling vexed complexities; dissolving knots, spinning out clear threads; thin stuff, some say. Oh that rabbit and that duck! Nursery analogy – Donald Duck, old Mrs Rabbit – bring Disney and Beatrix Potter into the index. You played the oracle from which neither instruction nor prediction could be expected. Philosophy became a training ground for an austere caucus race; none are promised prizes.

John Wisdom was disposed to a kind of larkiness; unlikely that he learned it from you; perhaps it taught you an English you never spoke. Did your acolytes Miss Anscombe and the sockless Peter Geach ever set the table on a roar? The seriousness with which you are so often credited, your disdain for the much-too-niceties of the High Table, suggests you had no time for donnish distractions, but who knows what pleasure you took in the impersonation of uniqueness? How apt that you were a flawless one-man bandsman, able to whistle all the parts in your selection of Brahms, Beethoven and who all else. Mahler? You filled a private auditorium with the ensemble of yourself.

Can a genuine article ring false, a false ring true? Weininger jumps back into the frame, the dreaded – because undisguised and unblinking – Other who recognised in you, *for you*, what your own mirror was cleverly enough cracked not to deliver full-face. You thought to shuck yourself of what, later at least, you saw to be the thing that, in essence, you could not dodge. How am I so sure? Because your philosophy, as Cambridge marketed it, promised escape from specificity, the triumph of choice. The philosopher claims, again and again, to serve only, especially, Christianity's substitute, truth without a mythology or a saviour; yet even you, like Descartes and who all else, grew pettish when others (yes, including your honest acolyte Friedrich Waismann) appropriated ideas which, in texts or lectures that delivered them, were paraded as common knowledge. Can truth have an owner? The bourgeois proprietor caught *in flagrante delicto*, were you, on occasion? When you gave away your money, you gave yourself away, or so you hoped; duplicity nodded, Butler blinked.

Your claim, mimicked by John Wisdom, not to have read many curricular philosophers, seems less modest than a promise of originality. Byron said he had never read Shakespeare. I have only recently come across the work, in translation, of Georg Simmel. Did you ever? I was struck by the confident erudition and decorous outspokenness of a Jewish philosopher who suffered the usual malice in Wilhelmine academic circles but seemed to accept them as little more than an irritation. What is remarkable is the freedom with which Simmel drew attention to money as an ingredient to be reckoned with in human ethology. Before you used the cute image of the rabbit and the duck, Simmel argued for the impossibility of pinning down a comprehensive analysis of the human condition; there was no escaping a variety of readings on different scales, a theme germane to the uncertainties declared by Heisenberg, following Heraclitus' *panta rei*, everything is on the move.

Your renunciation of wealth calls for, or rather generates, a more subtle account of the contingent of motives that induced it. After washing your hands of lucre, you considered emigration to the Soviet Union. You went on a visit just before the Great Terror, but not, as noted earlier, before the diabolisation of Trotsky, *né* Bronstein, and the murderous onset of Stalinist antisemitism. Did you suppose that a penniless penitent would be easily assimilated? Had you offered Stalin your fortune, you might have been welcome, for a while. What else could he want of you? Were you surrendering yourself in order to be a registered nobody, Odysseus' other? Bertrand Russell had been one of the first westerners keen enough to be appalled by the vindictive Vladimir Ilyich when he gloated over the execution of hundreds (soon thousands and thousands) of alleged impediments to the inevitable classless society. How could you have missed the blood-stained decks of the latter-day Potemkin's ship of state? Why were so many German philosophers recruited to antisemitism and so few historians (Mommsen, however 'fascistic', despised Treitschke and company)? Did that question ever interest or perplex you?

In the 1950s, we believed that you had written the last chapter in western *philo*. Implicit in what passed for agnosticism was hope for what could not be specified: retreat of a questionable deity from miraculous influence on human affairs. Spinoza made logic do something similar when he equated nature and the divine. If a negative could not be proved, might its subject be deemed irrelevant without anyone having to say so? Thanks or no thanks to you, this is what my twenty-year-old self imagined philosophy to establish or at least concede. Does the self age, do souls? Impossible, surely. As you lay dying, the story is, Mrs Bevan came in and said that you had visitors. This prompted your last recorded words, 'Tell them I've had a wonderful life'. Did saying so mean you meant it? Or, knowing the credulity of your mourners, was it the solipsist's last laugh? Can it be that all the public events of your lifetime, the horror, the horror, left you unaffected? Death, you said, in the *Tractatus*, 'is not an event of life, it is not lived through'. Whereof we choose not to speak, much remains to be said.

Yours sincerely, F.

TO VLADIMIR NABOKOV.

Cher Maître,

Today, when every tease and tout writes 'Hi, Fred', Shelley's antique courtesies retain their call on me. My father recommended that, if in doubt, call a man 'Sir', never a woman 'madam' (despite Macaulay's famous first words). Born in the same year as yourself, named in honour of Little Lord Fauntleroy, Cedric had been a world amateur champion tango dancer. His dago turn served him better than small talk. When it came to the ladies, he offered no advice save Spinoza's *caute*, rubberised. I discovered much later that he had failed to honour it; hence the appearance, in middle age, hers more middle than mine, of my half-sister Sheila, no Augusta Leigh. I never heard my father say 'fuck', with or without a screamer, my wife's early term for an exclamation mark. In *Speak, Memory*, you recall your father saying – fifteen-years-old were you? – 'You threaded that girl?' Neither reproach nor praise, was it? A *constatation*. Lightly flossed shins did she have? Life is one story; story another life.

I associate getting little things right with those sketches, in one of your critical compendia, of the disposition of seats in the old Russian railways. Again in *Speak, Memory*, you say that you received a 'college blue' for tennis while at Trinity, Cambridge, in the 1920s. I have never heard of anyone else being honoured in those terms but hesitate to cross words with a man whose eye for aberration led to several sub-species of *lepidoptera* being tagged *Nabokovensis*. When you posted nature's oldest law as being 'the survival of the weakest', you saluted the catch-me-if-you-can't specimens that eluded your prehensile passes. Divide through by motive, ignore excuses, withhold explanations, is that the lesson of mastery?

In your books, caressing the details delivers the art of the matter. Branding Fyodor Dostoyevksy a 'journalist', you rated him a case of scribbler's rush. You conceded that his manic tendencies came of having been subjected to mock execution by the Tzarist authorities, but in your aesthetics, as with Henry de Montherlant when it came to *fautes d'orthographe*, sympathy procures no remission. Then think of Raskalnikov. Genius, *quand-même*, Fyodor?

In the smart New York crowd into which, thanks to Bunny Wilson, you came to be translated, who else was heard to mutter that the Romanovs' don't-do-it-again mock execution of Decembrists was a cruel, all but mere, parody of ruthlessness compared with Communism's murder of millions of innocent citizens? *Invitation to a Beheading*, the Red Queen's speciality, put your loop around the smirk that Bertie Russell observed on Lenin's face when, in power, he gloated over what Auden was trendy enough to call 'the necessary murder' before he had Christian second thoughts. Osip Mandelstam alone of those within Stalin's grasp scorned him, openly, as a black beetle.

Enough of the Georgian poet still lodged in Josef Vissarionovich's Kremlin for him to ironise at Boris Pasternak's hedging – as good as ditching – when quizzed about the suddenly toxic Osip. After listening to a spasm of vicar-of-Braying, Stalin said 'Is that the best you can do for your friend?' He then ordered that Mandelstam be untouched, for a while. Did you ever have a good word to say for *Doctor Zhivago*, Paster/nark's swank apology for want of outspokenness when it might have cost him dear? Nobel Prizes too can hang around a man's neck. You, we may guess, were never a contender. Irony rarely strikes gold. Who last heard a Swede laugh?

You always insisted that Russia's *ancien régime* never descended to the mass transports of the slaughterer at the centre of our wartime pin-up trinity; cigarette, pipe, cigar their fuming markers. Was close reading ever more dandily validated than in your prognosis that the Soviet State would disintegrate because the Russian language was bound to get its own back against the *apparat* that degraded it into New Speak? The English journalist Bernard Levin is the only other scribe I remember to have diagnosed the Soviet Union as doomed to dissolution.

As you pointed out, Levin is an odd name for Tolstoy's conjugally virtuous *alter ego* in *Anna Karenina*. Can it be that Levin's indexed proximity to Lev – as Tolstoy was liable to be addressed – deafened the Master to the Jewish ring of Levin? Do any Jewish characters feature in Tolstoy's work? You advertised no ear for music, he no nose for Jews. Bernard Levin lacked *solus rex* dandyism, but you and he fought the good fight, albeit ('all bite' an English M. Jourdain called it) *separatim*. Bernard's prose alone was handsome. Who ever wrote more studiedly on water? Most western intellectuals, few with wider experience of the Soviet State than Potemkin-style tours afforded them, hedged their bets and softened their buts; Orwell and Malcolm Muggeridge excepted. You pouched your words as David that quintet of smooth stones before slinging Goliath.

The conceit that jumped Vladimir Nabokov into the world's literary limelight was, *bien entendu*, *Lolita*. You had already shone, locally, in 1920s Berlin. In the *émigré* press, those reduced to the rancorous were treated to consolatory caviar. Sirin's salted tales were stuck on the great ass of Soviet pretensions. As for the Viennese witch-doctor, scorn for Sigmund's oedipal schematics certified your unambiguous love for your father, shot by a Kremlin hireling whose target Vladimir Dmitrievich, true gentleman, shielded with his person. I remember reporting to you how Leon Trotsky, in his *History of the Russian Revolution*, spoke of your father as the most intelligent of the Kadets. I am not sure how welcome you took his compliment to be.

When did you start to teach yourself the English which garnished your first stories enough to appeal to the *New Yorker*'s Bunny Wilson? There was an English Bunny, whom you never knew, I think: Bloomsbury's David 'Bunny' Garnett. I went to see the author of *Aspects of Love* when he was eighty-six. Separated from his wife, Angelica, he was living *tout seul* in a cottage with an earth floor in the Lot-et-Garonne. He had first seen Angelica Bell in her cot. He looked at the pretty infant (and her mother Vanessa) and said 'I shall marry her one day'; and so he did. Who denounced Bunny as a double-dyed wanton, except for the bride whose freedom he had filched? Many years and three daughters later, she divorced him. *Aspects of Love* was one of the first books I ever reviewed; for all Bunny Garnett's erotic experiences (wide-eyed Tiresian and buy-sexual) he made mish-mashed potatoes of their fictional cookery.

You had only your recherché wits to live on when you and Véra first landed in NYC. I see you in that tight rented bathroom, brown suitcase for knees-up desk, translating yourself into a professorial author, Pnin and ink, his what-the-Dickens English with implications more arcane than natives were liable to decipher. Destitution never dented your *superbe*. Comedy, with a twist, followed whatever befell you. Making America yours (as Kafka did *Amerika*, though he never went there), you chose to be more amused than affronted by Roman Jakobson's casting-out vote when rejected for an Ivy League literary professorship. While you found a niche at Cornell, you disdained to put down roots. You and Véra bowled from one sabbatical absentee's house to another.

Had it not been for Graham Greene, *Lolita* might never have crossed the Channel, then the Atlantic, from its lodging, alongside other, naughty, books published by Maurice Girodias in his Traveller's Library, apt to be read one-handed, as J.-J. Rousseau had it. Those commas enclosing 'naughty' exempt me from implying that you supplied a catch-penny contribution to the pornography amongst which you were softly shelved. Hard-backing came after you extracted yourself from that blue Parisian range. Greene furnished you with a ticket to the *via dollarosa* which wound up leading to the Grand Hotel, Montreux, whither I was seconded to find you.

Time was that any number of hot books, in English, were on sale in Paris. They were liable to confiscation if found among the luggage of returning Anglo-Saxons. Back in 1929 Chicago, my mother Irene (silent latter 'e') took pride in parading down State Street reading about James Joyce's Cunty Kate, assuming she got that far (how many do?). Her copy of *Ulysses* – odd/issues concealed within – was smuggled in from Paris by Buddy Cadison, one of her *beaux*, after he had visited Sylvia Beach's Shakespeare and Company. In the second lustrum of the 1950s, some of my Cambridge contemporaries made a louche secret of contributing erectile material, *Thongs* among them, to Girodias's Travellers' Library. I scanned them in the *Librairie La Hune*, in the Boulevard St Germain, adjacent to the *Café de Flore* where during the war Sartre and the Beaver hogged the stove. Not so *braves Crillons*, their camp fieriness parodied the resistance Albert Camus and friends were actively pursuing on the *chemins de la liberté*.

During the Occupation, Sartre took artful care that his play *Les Mouches* passed the Nazi censors. It opened on the Right Bank, to an audience of *le tout* Paris *collabo*, on June the Sixth, aka D-Day 1944. Only after the Germans had departed did he come out in valiant style, against France's capitalist liberators, as de Gaulle soon did against the same allies, entitled in his case 'Anglo-Saxons'. Has anyone construed the plague of flies in Sartre's play as being not so much the occupying Fridolins as the seething Jews? How else did it pass the German censors? It's no great surprise that Sartre's *copain* Camus came to be shot down, in *Les Temps modernes*, as a phoney *philosophe*; what was insupportable for Sartre and his go-get-him marksman, François Jeanson, was that Camus had been *engagé* when it was a matter of life or death, not a politic flourish.

Did Graham Greene light on *Lolita* while cruising at *La Hune*'s wide, slightly tilted display table or did some specialist pusher mark his card? G.G. relished the mackintoshed anonymity he impersonated in François Truffaut's *La Nuit américaine*. I remember, when at Cambridge, hearing that he was known as 'Grim Grin' *chez les Français* amongst whom he later tax-exiled himself. Greene's Catholicism – whatever its origin (was he not seeking to bed, if need be wed, some rich American R.C. beauty)? – seemed to offer access to the dark side of life, quite as Willie Maugham's medical degree had to the back streets of Lambeth where his Liza languished. The success of *The Third Man* may have derived more from Carol Reed's movie (and Orson Welles's sinister gleam and beat-that Swiss roll on the Prater's Big Wheel) than from the intrinsic merits of Greene's sketchy novel. Did you ever mutter an admiring word about him?

While they toyed at privileged access to hellish depths (Scobie's the deepest, in *The Heart of the Matter*), Greene's 'novels' were calculated, no less deliberately than his 'entertainments', to excite but never shock. He hinted at impropriety, treason too, as luridly as the market might relish. Faith unfaithful went but so far. Grim greenery was his trade. You, I recall, took pride in the colourful alphabet in your cerebral font. G.G. played at being something finer than a commercial author but never risked confounding his public. Catholicism was his wubber wing, as childish swimmers have been known to say. Has anyone yet undertaken a profile of the divinity as depicted by post-Auschwitz English writers? T.S. Eliot and Greene are conspicuous in advertising His abiding salvationary powers. *The Family Reunion* and *The Living Room* bore witness that, for the right people, He had survived the Holocaust and remained at the receipt of custom.

More naughty schoolboy than Byronic wanton, Greene's choice of *Lolita* as a book of the year – 1956, was it? – applauded a recklessness he never emulated. His terrestrial father was a housemaster at a minor public school where Greene himself had been a pupil. While his characters flirted with damnation, their author was wary of exciting a bad report at home. His cheekiest excess came when, as grub street film reviewer in the 1930s, he made play with the idea that Shirley Temple's cute little girl was a Hollywood prototype of your little Lo. The good ship Lollypop might have featured the pair of them as part of its welcome on board. The damages it had to pay for Greene's upskirting of Shirley T. bankrupted the publication he wrote for, but her innocence was never retrieved. That plug for *Lolita* was in line with G.G.'s paying habit of tickling the nonconformist conscience. Wilful, prolific and pseudonymous as he had been in Weimaresque Berlin, Vladimir Nabokov was suddenly a hotshot *in propria persona*.

Kingsley Amis, still a young man but scarcely angry, stood in an *alt*-English corner at the time that Greene put you in his Christmas box. The author of *Lucky Jim* was at the peak of reprint-on-reprint fame. Victor Gollancz had hesitated to publish Orwell's *Animal Farm* and *1984*, but what danger was there of Kingsley ruffling important feathers? Oxonian iconoclast, alongside the soon to be waning Wain, young Amis was no champion of Beowulf nor yet of Leavis's po-faced Great Tradition nor, when yetting on, of experimental innovation. He came to exemplify the post-Suez style of aggressive modesty. Making a diet of hands that fed him, he accepted a Somerset Maugham Travel bursary and wrote *I Like It Here* by way of no thank you letter.

The old *New Yorker* rubric 'No Fine Writing Please' could have furnished a badge for The Movement Kingsley consorted with. Its wry writers and viceless versifiers embodied the neo-brutalism of Utility Furniture. Commercial and critical, Kingsley's early work Yoricked at the expense of the literary tradition dodo plumage had served to dignify. I happened recently on a jaundiced cutting from the *Daily Telegraph* in which, at the end of a slew of novels, *Lucky Jim* is seen off, by some double-deckered Julian, as of small and perishable wit. I listened on my bulky-batteried portable radio as Jim Dixon cut up his host's cigarette-burnt sheets, harbinger of the *anarithmon gelasma* of England's protracted self-deconstruction. Was sat/ire ever more aptly sectioned than in Kingsley's I'm-all-right-jacketed fiction?

You were, no doubt, promptly alerted to the repel-boarders tone of the Amis review of *Lolita*. Larry Durrell used to say that if an author was deep in some remote jungle, his best friend would make sure that a runner came toting bad reviews in a forked stick. Kingsley switched, with ease, from being Jim Dixon to a critical Dixon of Dock Green (no, I do not at all expect you to take the dated reference). With Jack Warner's black and white TV copper's cry of 'Oy, what do you think you're doing?', Kingers nicked Humbert Humbert fair and very square. What conforms more self-righteously than the non-conformist conscience? *Lolita* as *Alice in Wonderland* in erotic travesty shocked the family man that Kingsley impersonated before Jane Howard tripped in to play the wicked witch of the Cheltenham Festival.

Why deny that you came out as the sublime Reverend Charles Dodgson never did? That *Lolita* should also ring changes on the shamelessness of the old hot book has to have been part of the Petronian fun of writing it. Did you ever claim, as addled admirers reported, that the adventures of little Lo satirised your initiation in the US of A? Such spurious insights announced their chefs to be the very type of foot-notaries you satirise in *Pale Fire*. When did you claim that *Lolita* was not scandalous, Humbert not a humbug? What Movement could ever have welcomed you as a member? Promising that second-rate was as good as it was prudent to be on the tight little island, Kingsley won many English prizes. One example is enough to prove that your imagination composed on a scale beyond his. No, not *Laughter in the Dark*. I am thinking of that simple short story, set in an alley of trees in the Luxembourg Gardens, in which a couple are having a tart-tongued, gesticulating quarrel when one or other realises that, at the far end of nature's archway, a green child is watching and listening. The couple are ashamed to realise that they are fouling his memory with ugliness.

In the autumn of 1970, I was commissioned by Columbia Pictures to go to Montreux to convene with you (and converge with handsome producer John Van Eyssen) to discuss writing a movie script from your latest, tubby novel, *Ada*. Stanley Kubrick's movie of *Lolita*, with the incomparable James Mason, had been little more than a *succès d'estime*, but your fame remained such that, *Ada* still in proof, not yet a pudding, you were able to oblige Hollywood studios to send plenipotentiaries to the Grand Hotel Montreux. Seated in the big, quiet main reception room, they were handed advance copies and invited to consider their verdicts and the zeros attached to them. Only bids sealed there and then would be entertained. What hospitable device was ever more exacting? No one was obliged to make a bid, but each delegate dreaded missing the Big One and the reproaches of his studio if another turned it into a hit. Now or never paid a sweet dividend: something of the order of a quarter of a million dollars was promised before the Byronic prize was taken home to L.A. and laid before its new owners. Victory proved sweeter than its fruits. On unexcited studio reading, Ada was no naughty chick nor did her story promise golden eggs; no Humbert hummed.

The Sixties and my Oscar had made me well off and the brief darling of the biz. My 1960s fee had, however, like that of anyone on the A-list, collapsed with the market. Luckily, we had nice houses, here and there. I was happy to take my winnings and revert to writing fiction. A copy of my latest, *Like Men Betrayed*, was in the boot of my Cambridge blue Mercedes 280SE as I delivered Beetle and the children to Bordeaux airport for their flights back to England and, we presumed, the right schools. No deal had yet been struck for me to write a screenplay of *Ada*, even for a slump price, but I was promised fat expenses for my excursion *en Suisse*.

My selection as putative screenwriter was capped by my parodic eulogy of *Ada* in the *Sunday Times*. Unlike the producers, I appeared to have some idea of what it was all about, Byron's daughter Ada (inventor of a prototypical computer) in particular. The Columbia brass needed someone whose ingenuity would justify the price they had paid for the rights. I had relished the wit of your remake of a miscreant world, but I had no prompt sense of a hit movie shambling towards Montreux to be born. Had it not been for the lure of meeting you, I should, as bridge players used to say, have passed in sleep.

Beetle's flight was in the late afternoon. I was instantly lonelier than fancy had proposed. With Flaubert's warrant, I scanned the whores, some transvestite no doubt, stilted on steep heels on the *trottoirs* around the glass-bracketed market in the centre of Bordeaux. In conscience's custody, I made for the big bookshop where I furnished myself with *un peu de lecture*, Vidal-Naquet and company; Greek scholarship made appetising in the French style. I happened on a copy of the *Tri-Quarterly* which included a segment on your work by whoever they were.

Armed for head-down solitude, I went, with none but a timekeeper's appetite, to a modest, stiff-chaired restaurant where I remembered there was a *table d'hôte*. Salesmen and other solitaries traded the small change of their quotidian pursuits. There was only one female in the company. Neither girl nor yet middle-aged, *bien poitrinée*, she was eating modestly before repairing to wherever it was that she danced other people's nights away. She had worked, for however long and when, in L.A. Our conversation was spiced with insiderishness. Before she got up to go, she told me, with no manifest flirtatiousness, where she was strutting her stuff; last show one in the morning. As soon as she had gone, one of the other men at the table said, '*Vous auriez dû la suivre, monsieur. Vous aviez des fortes chances.*'

I walked back to my respectable hotel. The next morning I set off to drive across the Massif Central to Lyon. Stranger in my own car, parcel and chauffeur, I cannot remember stopping for lunch. As evening drew its October drapes, I made for Beetle's and my favourite one-star Michelin restaurant, at *Les Halles*, a one-street village in the loopy hills ahead of Lyon. Perhaps Monsieur and Madame Rigaud would recognise that I still was who I had been. Shutters closed, pinched light outlined their exclusivity. How could they do that to me? The lonely man takes the world personally.

I drove down towards Lyon, fat, cold city. Too late for a restaurant, I stopped at a *voyageurs* hotel on the far side of a humpbacked bridge in a sorry suburb with a handsome name. After she had shown me to a room, I asked the landlady whether there was anything to eat. How should the scene be shot to convey what failed to happen? Did she watch me peel her apple? Was I detaining her with my small talk or was she loitering? Neither young nor old, she seemed at home with her solitude as I was not with mine. Nothing took its time. No, she did not stay. No, I did not want her to.

My sleep changed gear as the *poids lourds* did, catarrhally, as they got over the humped bridge. It was Sunday morning.

I was not due to see you (and John Van Eyssen, our delegated producer) until lunchtime on Monday. Fettered in freedom, I chauffeured myself to the bank of the Saône and parked outside the three-starred Restaurant Paul Bocuse, where Beetle and I had lunched a few times. Seated one file from the windows looking over the river, between two hooped families, I pretended to be hungry. How long I seemed to wait for my *moules marinières*! I instructed myself to take note of the conversation between two businessmen adjacent across the aisle. The writer had better be an eavesdropper, a spy, a voyeur, a double-dealer, had that not been your theme more often that once? I lent so much ear to the two men that I put my fingers in the sauce where the *moules* were basking, not the fingerbowl. *'T'as-vu ce type qui se baignait les doigts dans la sauce?'* Do you know the story of Duff Cooper, when put down as *'espèce d'objet de valeur'* by a Parisian taxi-driver, responding saying, *'Écoutez le Belge?'*? I lacked the ambassadorial gall to give it weight.

No, inspector Javert, I cannot remember what I did for the rest of that day, nor where I stayed the night, in France or *Suisse*. My next sighting of myself is at the Château de Chillon, Montreux's sentinel, stone toes sandalled in Lake Leman, on Monday morning. I shivered where Bonnivard was chained for nine years before Byron and Percy Bysshe stopped by to underline his fame. For all my pious dawdle, I was early for lunch at the Grand Hotel. I settled on a blanched bench to revise the *Tri-Quarterly* until it was time to go in and register. John van Eyssen had not arrived. I was soon being shown into a room no wider than a single-car garage. Its terrace had space only for an upright, armless, metal chair. There was a shower, not a bath; and no bath towel. *Ah les bons Suisses!*

Memory cuts to a round table on the glassed terrace at the right front of the hotel. My strip of memory has you and Véra and me being served with veal and vegetables. Did we have something to start? Did we drink wine? It was not long before you found occasion to accuse me of being fond of anagrams. I recalled John Fowles' snaffled phrase 'I denied the soft impeachment'. Nevertheless, as people rarely say but often write, you scribbled a Russified jumble, ending in -ski, on a paper napkin (can it have been? At the Grand Hotel, Montreux?) and turned it to me. 'Do you recognise the author?' I had the wit to look from you to Véra, implacable examiners both, and then, but a calculated tick or two from immediately, I swivelled the paper back and said, 'Kingsley Amis, isn't it?' Matching my beats, as your admirer Stanley Kubrick would put it, you said 'This is a very interesting young man'.

I said, 'Is it interesting to be well prepared? I can still rehearse the main provisions of the Sullan constitution if that will get me anywhere; no future in being a tribune of the plebs, you may remember.' I listened to myself without pride but with a certain amusement as I played your bowling. No, I cannot remember much else that was said at that blanched table. Did we have cheese? If so, it too was blanched. As you left to have a rest upstairs, you warned me that you were going to take another look at my review of *Ada*. Did you imagine you might find some unexploded squibs *là-dedans*?

The lunch may have been an audition; I had no expectation of a scholarship to follow. My interest in the matter was meeting you. Usually, I can reproduce something of the vocabulary and accent of memorable personalities. I am sure you delivered excellent English, with a where-did-that-come-from timbre, but you seem to have retained the patent. You were courteous, you agreed to be amused as you allowed me to clear the hurdles you set, but no voice comes back to me, only the Cheshire smile.

I may have flattered you with an account of the duration of my motorised pilgrimage to Montreux. Perhaps that evoked your account of travelling to some upstate New York university in mid-winter to deliver a consignment of vintage arcana. The professor deputed to welcome you had a prompt confession: owing to some sorry maladdress, your lecture had not been signalled in the college press. He led you into the wide lecture room and, with an apologetic hand, waved at the dozen students he had managed to cull. 'A choice company', he said, 'and, you will notice, nicely distributed in the available space.' That had been then, now – as Véra was prompt to say – you filled halls to overflowing, when you cared to favour them. She, it seemed, was company enough for you and your imagination.

When nothing-but-handsome John Van Eyssen arrived, flushed with frustration at having been late for lunch, I reverted to being the scribe who was there to save the sum of things for pay. *Ada* was a fat version of that tricky paper you swivelled to me, challenge to which I had no prior riposte. I did have one good idea, which I produced as if it were an example of copiousness to come: my opening shot was of the White House, seen at ground level. The camera would then tilt and widen to include the flagpole on the roof topped by the Union Jack in proprietorial mode. This chimed sweetly with the parallel world, without internal combustion engines or portraits of George Washington, in which you set your incestuous romance. Do I remember flying sleighs, somehow propelled by super-horsepower, or is that my *père Noël* confection? You listened to my busking with indulgence, saying at some point 'This man is like a good doctor. Whenever anything seems a serious problem, he promises that it can be taken care of.'

Quack as I might, I was quite sure, by the time Van Eyssen took me out to a handsome dinner, that no ingenuity of mine, however neatly dressed, would ever induce cash-strapped Columbia to, as they used to say, divvy up. When I paraded my wit, it was in the hope of no better reward than your conniving slope of a smile. We were there, Van Eyssen and I, in tribute to your gambitry in extracting all those dollars by means of a sublime bluff. At some point on that next morning, you and I were armchaired in one of the grand reception rooms in which I cannot recall seeing a single other guest. Sharing the knowledge that neither of us spelt out, that we had conned Columbia without the least dishonesty, we talked of other things.

You told me, in particular, about the explosive rupture you had had, quite recently, with your one-time sponsor Bunny Wilson. His review of your labour of patriotic love, the translation of *Eugene Onegin* which you affected to pass for a superbly groomed pony (your term), had something in common with Sartre's procured panning of Camus: revenge for a quality beyond the critic's competence, except to deface. The effrontery with which Bunny challenged your command of Russian put rouge on his cheek. Exile was said to have tarnished your vocabulary. In particular Wilson ridiculed your translation, as 'Kinkajou', of some native Russian beast Pushkin had laired in his text. There was, I suspected and did not say, at least some justice in ridiculing the translation of a small tree-happy mammal, unique to Central and South America, to the Siberian veldt (let's say) where it was never seen to swing. Were you teasing? Even your alleged howler had to be something like a *hapax legomenon*.

I was conscious, oh God yes, of not having been invited to your apartment. I could make no secret of my commercial motive, but liked to presume that there was now something father-and-sunny in our dialogue. Certainly, we were close enough for you to tell me how, when you had done rallying with him, Bunny W. sent you a Christmas-time envelope from which, in lieu of a card, a black butterfly flopped. The attached note told you that its author had 'never enjoyed a literary duel as much' as your altercation when Pushkin came to Shovekin.

You looked at me in telling silence. I should be cheating if I claimed that your eyes grew lustrous or your throat thicker. You did pause. Then you said, 'I did not enjoy it in the least'. That rare moment put the capper on our encounter. Oddly, we did not talk about *Pale Fire*, a masterpiece I enjoyed much more than *Ada*. Mary McCarthy, the twentieth century's Madame de Villeparisis, judged *Pale Fire* a masterpiece, not wrongly but also, surely, to ladle derision on Bunny Wilson, her overripe ex-husband, by implying that he had a defective ear for genius. Her calculated folly in marrying him excited no self-mockery in Hannah Arendt's New York oppo. No more, we might go on, was Arendt ever likely to have seen herself as fortune's fool when she became Heidegger's virginal doxy. There is no end of paper loops in the Great Chain of Being.

I left you a copy of *Like Men Betrayed*, as apt, title-wise, a tribute as I could offer. I must have driven away, fast, before lunch, but memory's tape flutters on empty. Did I hope that I might have a line from you about my novel? Perhaps you were never much of a correspondent. We have yet to see your Collected Letters, if such a collection can be made. Spontaneity was rarely your style, was it? You always wanted to have the questions ahead of any interview, I seem to remember; so too did Heidegger. I recall the story of how you challenged the philosopher Max Black to a game of chess when you were first his colleague at Cornell. He beat you quickly the first time, after which, in polite style, he offered a return game, and won almost as swiftly. Is it true that you never again played competitive chess, but established unchallenged mastery in devising problems of diabolical ingenuity? You must have told the story yourself, which is excuse enough, I hope, for recalling it. Did Ingres ever play in an orchestra? We know that you were deaf to music (you said so yourself pretty well). Were you also blind to painting? I do not remember a single reference, although Balthus all but prefigured *Lolita*. Cinema was the art closest to yours. Odd that no good movie ever came of any adaptations of your work.

A year or two after you and I failed to tire the sun with talking, Beetle and I drove through Montreux on our devious way to Italy. I halted outside the Grand Hotel, but feared embarrassment, yours or mine, if I claimed acquaintance. It had been no surprise that nothing came, then or later, of the project to make a movie of *Ada*. Despite that publishing scoundrel who bloated some antique flirtation of yours into something all but adulterous, you and Véra seem to have been content, never contentious, whether in that bathroom study in NYC or in the sequestered luxury of the Grand Hotel. Did you ever own a motorcar? I see you either on foot, silent and reticulate, or helping yourself, and Véra, to a car and driver.

There is always a detail that the keenest researcher's diligence cannot caress. For small instance, one summer's day almost ten years after our meetings, I was called from the tennis court adjacent to our French house to take a call from the Canadian Broadcasting System. Some guy, in Toronto was it?, thought I should want to know that you had left us. I thanked him for the courtesy but wondered why he had bothered to call me. He said that Véra had told him that, of all the writers you had known, you had had the keenest sense of rapport with me. So? So damn.

Mes hommages, cher Volodya, si j'ose dire. Frederic.

Dear Ken,

Our first meeting was on the Bedales lawn on Parents' Day, 1974. I had hurried to thank you for giving extra tuition to our son Paul. Your colleagues read his cross-lateral reading difficulties for laziness; you had the empathy to encourage, not chide. Hearing that we had a place in Greece, you coached him in Classical Studies. You were in your earlyish thirties; not young; nor ever old. As we ambled around that vacant tennis court, it was clear that you were never likely to be quick to the net. In all the time we were friends, did you ever mention playing or watching games of any kind? Our common ground was established in peripatetic style. You were a Bradford Grammar School boy with a First in Mods at Worcester College, Oxford, before switching to study music under Edmund Rubbra. Latin and Greek were our playing field.

As we did our rounds, I told you that I was in the middle of translating Catullus. I had admired his salt ever since his verses were all but proscribed at Charterhouse. More than a few of his pieces of below-the-belt and up-yours vituperation were omitted, as recently as 1960, in C.J. Fordyce's prim Oxford edition. How sweet indeed that 'Fordyce spots', in medical terms, are to be found on the female *labia*! My Johnian supervisor, Guy Lee, was already supplying applauding ticks (one or two) and deprecating crosses (ditto) in my Catullan margins. In his own version of the *Amores*, he glossed Ovid with tart brevity that depended on readers' familiarity with the Latin. Years later, translating Horace, he chose to be literal; he could no longer rely on a readership of classically primed bookworms.

When I mentioned some Roman sexual practice, you queried whether I had a text to justify it. I cited the wall paintings in the Pompeii brothel. I had had my first sight of them twenty years earlier, when they were locked behind slatted peekaboo cupboards. Key-holding officials extracted tips from male tourists hot for a sight of the stew's mural menu. You reacted with a *'moment de déclic'*, rather like the *'Ach so'* General Kreipe had occasion to utter, high in the Cretan mountains, when his captor Paddy Leigh Fermor capped him by coming up with a concluding slice of Horace's dawn ode, after the general dried in mid-quotation.

'Après ce moment-là', I had heard Leigh Fermor say on French TV, in Stratford-atte-Bowe tones, *'nos rapports étaient magnifiques.'* Nice story? Several hundred unnamed Cretans were executed by the Germans in revenge for Paddy's swaggering coup. No doubt you remember that the great Pericles planked rebel Samian commanders and had them slowly beaten to death for ten days. Resentful allies, they had reacted against Athenian *hubris*. Did Bowra mention the incident in his exaltation of the Olympian? Pericles is said to have had a cephalic oddity; hence the helmet in which he chose to be portrayed. Kreipe's fellow-officers drank champagne to toast his abrupt transportation. He spent the rest of the war in Canada. Leigh Fermor became an honorary Hellene, the Mani his manor. Your ex-pupil Paul has recently taken up residence in the Cyclades and is learning modern Greek.

By the end of however long it was, you agreed to have a look at my Catullus versions so far; and then further. In the age of typescripts and waiting for the post, I seldom lacked punctual *corrigenda*. Our subsequent friendship was sustained, span on span, by regular prosaic flyting, often on the Sunday telephone; long, rich chats, their wit vanished *ceu fumus in auras*. You told me that you had a wife, Valerie, and two sons. Valerie taught extra-curricular music at Bedales; she was also a cook. Your accent carried no Oxonian intonation, nor any mark of class or location. You labelled yourself, and Valerie, as 'working class'. How so when your father, a Marxist, was a Glaswegian professor of mathematics? Perhaps his speciality had driven you to another, distant field. Ah 'perhaps', the speculator's flimsy licence! You told me how, at some public launch of one of your books, you were introduced, as 'Professor McLeish'. Your father stood up to the applause and announced, 'I, in fact, am Professor McLeish. My son Kenneth is the author of the book in question.' With support like that, any tit may sag.

Something about your excellences provoked deflation: Rubbra recognised the merit of your musical compositions (some later played on Radio 3), but remarked that, if there was nothing wrong with the notes, you misgauged the pauses between them. The comment was undeniably astute: you raced time's chariot from one project to the next. Your comments on my accelerating Catullus continued to be courteous, magisterial, *more Latino*. I had had no mercantile purpose. The versions had been a matter of keeping up appearances, to myself, and loose attachment to the classical fraternity. Thanks to you, I began to think of publication.

I have always known that there is a gulf between winning scholarships and the serious scholars on whose graces I have long depended. Simon Raven, a Carthusian who wished he had been an Etonian, told me that he did his 'bit' of Latin or Greek every day, a form of knocking up, a less solitary activity of his in another sense. He was sacked from Charterhouse early in my first quarter (term). Our *amicitia* was sparked by his amiable review of *The Earlsdon Way*, my second novel, in the *Observer*. You may remember that Simon came to salute our eventually collaborative Catullus, especially *in malis partibus*, as he put it. My friendship with him was never as close as that with his Carthusian contemporary Peter Green, who reviewed

The Earlsdon Way with even greater enthusiasm. Carthusian classicists are a *coterie à part*, Robert Graves *en tête*.

The more thorough scholar, Peter had small respect for Simon's flash. Was he irked by Raven's popularity when he arrived at King's, after a short spell in the wilderness? Behind the gates to which the Provost, J.T. Shepherd, controlled access, Morgan Forster was a privileged resident, his sexual appetite unexceptional while still illicit *coram publico*. He took his latter-day lover, a London policeman, to dine in college. Simon deplored the chipped glasses in which the author of *A Passage to India* dispensed Cyprus sherry. Was *Maurice*, that doleful cup of Hippocrene, the off-his-chest result of Forster's seclusion? He wrote one brilliant quasi-sci-fi story in which, as if in a pandemic, people lived in delivery-served hermetic cells and took TV for reality.

Simon's abiding grievance was that he had been deprived of a last season in the Charterhouse first eleven cricket. Oh those enviable pink-striped, cable-stitched hashers, the click of the scoreboard on Big Ground as unsmiling Peter May served up his regular Saturday century! Simon combined being a rogue with playing every other ball with a straight bat. Despite wanton imbroglios, sexual (with a younger Carthusian during school hols, a nice woman impregnated at Cambridge) and pecuniary, he incurred more *réclame* than obloquy. When he had to be cashiered from the smart regiment to which he had had recourse, it was to the regret of the fellow-officers whose mess funds he had mounted on the wrong horses. After he fell into deeper debt in smart, bad company at the Clermont Club where John Aspinall buttered up the toffs and made a meal of them, Simon was bailed out, *in extremis*, by Anthony Blond.

A rich, bisexual publisher, hot for the profitably *risqué*, Anthony had Marks and Spencer resources and Etonian nerve. He offered to clear Simon's debts on condition that he retreat to rural Kent and work week-daily at the outrageous novels (*The Sabre Squadron*, etc) for which he had developed Waugh-like facility. If Simon had occasion to come to London, he had to promise to be on the train to Lewes by nine p.m., before the casinos opened their chandeliered traps. Despite that sullied escutcheon, having given his word he kept it. Classical scholars were drilled to mimic whatever ancient author or poet was liable to procure prizes. Trainee vicars who came to bray like Sophocles or Ovid, Demosthenes or Tully, we shared a pre-Christian culture. We could quote, not crib, bluff not cheat, pay homage not kneel.

Simon's novels were brazen with caricatures. In the *Alms for Oblivion* series, William Rees-Mogg, scarcely disguised as Somerset Lloyd-James, was the prime butt. Simon suspected the Mogg of having procured his expulsion from C'house (the H.M., 'Bags' Birley, regretted he had 'no alternative') in order that he, the Mogg, should become head of the school. Although some kind of 'closed' scholar to Oxford, the greater spotted Mogg was neither Blood (sporting hero) nor – despite his Roman faith – any brand of classicist. Nostalgic for an England that never was, as editor of the *Times* he advocated return to the gold standard. That hyphen of his stood for some kind of quasi-peerage. Later, he backed David Cameron as Prime Minister. Aristocratic origins were held to guarantee high-mindedness and lack of mercenary purposes; the Old Oligarch's humbug was recycled in witless *Times* leaders.

In *The Rich Pay Late*, Simon Raven turned from whacking the Mogg to ribbing rubicund Jim Prior, a C'house fast bowler in Simon's day, and later a rising Tory politician, as the upright, uxorious, Jim Morrison MP. Declining to be tickled and with opening bowler's directness, Prior went for the middle stump and dismissed Simon as a raging pansy. Simon took publicity for applause and, having gone too far, went further. He skittled his own rumpled looks no less than the delinquencies of his contemporaries. He also disclosed at some point that he had appetite neither for penetration nor for being penetrated. M.M., as Fifties' *argot* had it, was not uncommon among monastic adolescents hot for what Kinsey listed as 'outlets', never mind whose pretty touch procured them. In later years, for pre-nine p.m. pleasuring, Simon frequented a lady whose handy business was just off Pall Mall.

Gentle expulsion from C'house had allowed Simon to take his laurels with him and sport the O.C. tie. In due time, he fell off the light blue rigging, without losing his popularity as a Kingsman, and took up soldiering. Dumped from the army, he continued to parade, in the amiable ex-urban society of Lewes, as 'the captain'. His younger brother ran a nearby prep school. Peter Green was not caught doing anything disreputable at Charterhouse and did his national service, in the RAF, without lurid incident. While Simon neglected to feature him in his *Alms for Oblivion* decalogue, Peter served as model for a subtle character in his friend Paul Scott's *The Raj Quartet*.

Simon's only comment to me about Peter was that his great mistake, when it came to post-graduate preferment, had been bolshie reluctance to be an officer. To cap his First in the Tripos, he then won the Craven scholarship. When 'the uncle' A.J. Irvine, legendary C'house sixth form master, happening to be adjacent at some dinner, asked, with no marked warmth, whether congratulations were due, Peter 'owned the soft impeachment', as John Fowles once said, and once too often. 'In that event', said The Uncle, congratulations.' Peter acknowledged his debt to Irvine's tuition, but came to dispute the certainty with which he resolved every crux.

Contrariness was Peter's never silly, rarely popular habit. He was one of the first of today's ancient historians to check out the topography of Thucydides' Syracuse *in propria persona*. He discovered that steep, rock-ribbed Epipoli, which stay-at-home bookmen had construed as some kind of Sicilian proto-Hampstead Garden Suburb was in fact not inhabited in the late fifth century when Demosthenes, the Athenian general, never the orator, all but succeeded in a bold night attack; in other words, he failed to achieve a quick knock out, as Churchill did at Gallipoli. The war went on and ended in the elimination of what Peter entitled the 'Armada from Athens'. I am referred to in the grateful introduction as 'Mr Frederic Raphael'. *O tempora, o mores.*

Had Peter conducted himself with timely deference, he would have glided into the academic circles which required squaring if a man was to be enrolled as Fellow or lecturer. Once in, he could have turned with irrevocable licence on John Raven and other grave, overrated seniors. As it was, his precociousness lanced those on whose votes preferment depended. He served for a while as a stand-in director of studies, but neither college nor faculty cared to enrol him in its permanent company. Doubling as editor of a proposed Yearbook for the publisher Robert Muller, in 1951 Peter was the first person to accept a short story of mine for metropolitan publication. He was glad to say that his wife Lalage, *née* Pulvertaft, admired *The Lacquer Set* as much as he did. The Yearbook foundered before it was launched. *The Lacquer Set* has never been published. *Habent sua fata libelli.*

No less versatile than heterodox, Peter repaired to London, where his journalism was as swiftly mimetic as his sapphics and iambics. He had your meticulous speed: needing the money, he contracted to translate six French books a year for the then avaricious market for naughty uncut pages! He allowed himself no more than an hour to review his clutch of fiction for the *Daily Telegraph*, where he shared the slot with John Betjeman and my mentor Guy Ramsey, whose Street argot he relished ('see you next Tuesday' called for no rare lexicographer). Like another famous Carthusian, Robert Graves, Peter soon said goodbye to 'all that', meaning Byron's 'tight little island' and repaired to Lesbos, where burning Sappho loved and sang (and recently became trendy). Before very long, Lalage sang, and loved, along with her. Larry Durrell was swank enough to call his daughter Sappho. She too suffered an unhappy love and threw herself off a cliff.

This Proustian loop may have its snobbish side (then again, what genuine snob ever boasted of being a Carthusian?); it is also a reminder of the common ground that Classics supplied when grammar and prosody, not trendy opinionating, got the marks. Today's students are not expected to know the optative of *hieemi*, or what accents to put on it, but to serve up *crambe repetita* in the jargon that makes it appetising to the examiners who coined it. Back when, opinions had little to do with Lit. Hum.; grammar and scansion ruled. As Dr Johnson proved, the Classics were a leveller.

The best undergraduate classical scholar of my generation in Cambridge was John Patrick Sullivan, son of a Liverpool docker determined not to follow in paternal footsteps. Sullivan was adroit in ascending the prosaic face of Parnassus. Excellence beaten into him by the Jesuits' tawse, he retained their instruction, abandoned their faith. His Scouse accent made him all but unintelligible to me in our first term; later, he reserved it for parodic nostalgia: he told us how, when his mother asked him where he was going, he said 'Out' with Liverpudlian conclusiveness. He soon adopted a classless middle-English accent for social purposes. The Church's farewell unction had been to dispose him more to Latin than to Greek, though he did come to see us on Ios. The sole Greek phrase I recall on his lips was an exaggeratedly pronounced '*mee tie ge dee*'.

With starred honours and rare prizes, the graduate John Patrick had little difficulty in gaining academic office, first as Dean at Lincoln College, Oxford; then professorially in the US, first in Buffalo, NY, finally at UCLA, where his rank was upped to 'professor six' to discourage him from yielding to Ivy League lures. His publications included a daring appreciation of Ezra Pound's 'Propertius' (Robert Graves *contradicente*) and a vindication of 'Silver Age' Martial's art. The Spanish on-the-maker had long been held more disreputable than Catullus: he lacked the autobiographical anguish which spoilsports like to read as self-pitying fantasy; *moi non plus*. Martial was the poet as scanning *arriviste*; he made a fortune and no waves and headed home.

Soon after you and I met, Sullivan invited me to do a week's lecturing at Santa Barbara. My credulity concerning the mutual respect of academics was ruptured by the animosity with which he was regarded by some Californian colleagues. He wore a two-piece, fawn cotton, many-pocketed leisure-suit and subsisted for mental acceleration on very powerful Martinis. A translated Celt, gin was mother's milk to him. Mutable, never pretentious, loyal friend, eager symposiast, he invited you and me to contribute to the Martial translations he edited.

When dying, in increasing agony, of cancer of the oesophagus, he asked me to send him the tapes of *The Glittering Prizes*, in which he was affectionately portrayed as Bill Bourne. I was told that he watched them again and again until, one night, when the pain was insufferable, he asked his wife Judy for the exit treatment which an academic medic had supplied. How typical that he chose his own time for a Roman death; more Petronian than Senecan! Where was he going? 'Out!'.

It is just as well, I like to tell myself, that I did not get a First in Moral Sciences, as my friend Tony Becher did. Had I been so lucky (not that luck was needed to supplement Becher's thoroughness), vanity might have impelled me towards the academic hurdles. I should soon have stumbled. My addictive attention to philosophy has been of an unphilosophical order, better expressed in informal terms. This deviation, seemingly remote from your case, is not irrelevant to what happened when you quit Bedales after you failed to be listed among the candidates to replace Tim Slack as headmaster. Tim is the only man who has ever apostrophised me as 'mate'. Beetle and I had donated a new washing machine for the pupils' use.

His successor, Mr Nobes, scarcely stood out as an unquestionable choice. Bedales' fame derived from the co-educational style which distinguished it from the monastic, allegedly great public schools. Mr Nobes, never known by any less formal or lumpy title, deplored Bedalians (Daniel Day-Lewis among them) going so far as to hold hands in public. Would you have been a better headmaster? You would certainly have been an immeasurably better *teacher*. But diplomat and plausible Round-Robinite? You had none of Peter Green's insolence; you stand out, modestly, as one of the least boastful high intelligences I ever encountered; yet you, like he, it seems, did not fit the officer role.

Your next job was at a state school in Lincoln; scarcely a happy post. Your sons were bullied by their classmates and you, I suspect, lacked friends in that grim city. It had not taken long for me to realise that your contributions to my Catullus deserved more than thanks. When I suggested that we become co-authors, you told me, with more candour than tact, that Andrew Best, your literary agent, warned you that since I was a Jew, you were bound to be cheated. Among the silly coincidences of life, I had been at prep school, in North Devon, with Andrew. His younger brother Jeremy was regularly reduced to tears as copious as Niobe's. I cannot recall occasioning Jeremy's grief nor yet of much personal contact with the freckled Andrew. His *Guardian* obituary remarked on lordly inflections and sharp tongue. Of course, you told me, you were not going to pay any attention to what he said, but you were not slow to tell me about it. Was Best's hostility personal or principled?

Not long after we met, *The Glittering Prizes* made me, so Bernard Levin said, 'the most famous man in London'. Buonaparte's mother would have murmured, '*Pourvu que ça dure*'. It lasted long enough for me to have something like *carte blanche* at the old BBC TV centre at White City. Mark Shivas, my producer on *T.G.P.*, asked me to lend my name and pen to enhance a project to make a trio of films. Did I know Geoffrey Household's *Rogue Male*? I had turned down writing the next Bond movie for half a zillion, but I said yes, immediately, to *Rogue Male*. Peter O'Toole said that I gave him his favourite, toffy part. Geoffrey Household wrote, in longhand, to say that my version trumped his. A gentleman's compliment hardly matches riding in triumph through Persepolis, but it beats the rigged trophies of today's show-biz.

When Mark Shivas asked what else I should like to do next, I made bold to suggest that you and I collaborate on a new translation of the *Oresteia*. It's evidence of my spell of fame that the commission came through without delay. The fee was small change compared with what I was being paid for movie scripts, but your half was enough to enable you to move from sullen Lincoln, its cathedral a monument to Christian malice. In the twelfth century, the small Jewish community had been subject to a pogrom *à l'anglaise*, after a small boy disappeared and it was assumed, greedily, that the Jews had made his blood part of their ritual recipe. In truth, if that has any place in the old, old story, blood of any kind is specifically forbidden in the Jewish diet. Ah, but... etc. To think I used to imagine that Reason had a remedy for human vanities and religious quackery! Lincoln made so sour an impression that twenty-four autumnal hours there spawned the *donnée* for *Heaven and Earth*, which some amiable critic took to be emblematic of the Thatcher years.

Mark Shivas shunned confidences and declined invitations to stay with us in the Périgord. His father was a public schoolmaster; neither young nor old, Mark had the wariness of that profession. It was thanks to him that I had written *Daisy Miller* for Peter Bogdanovich, while he was high on Hollywood's slithery totem pole. Generous or calculating, Mark delegated production of our *Oresteia* to Richard Broke, who had been script editor on *The Glittering Prizes*. Bogdanovich told me that Mark had the most unattractive girlfriend he had ever seen. One of Peter's prize ladies had been a Playboy centrefold. She killed herself.

Richard was an Etonian with whose proper parents I used to play two shillings a hundred bridge at Crockford's. In a burst of maternal honesty, Mrs Broke told him that Mr Broke was not his father. During the war, she had had an affair with an American. I was about to write 'officer', but that is a snobbish reflex. That same night, Richard was in a collision as he was driving home. His back broken, he was to spend the rest of his life in a wheelchair. His smiling fortitude was such that I presumed on my charm and nicknamed him 'Ironside'. He told me that, on some petty occasion, he reminded his mother of that cruel night. Perhaps she had forgotten. She said she had never laughed since. Richard's good humour was remarkable; reduced to that wheelchair, he conducted himself like the six-footer he still was. When someone offered to help him stow his wheelchair in the car which he drove with manual dexterity, he said, 'Very kind of you, but I'm in a hurry'.

I had the confidence to undertake the first draft of *Agamemnon*. My prime ambition was more cinematic than stagey. I did not 'modernise' the text, but abstained from word-for-wordiness. I had Agamemnon, the conquering hero, arrive in a limousine and then step out into dusty ancient Mycenae. My version would remain true to Aeschylus' words but the visuals would be cinematic. I imagined that television could be the basis of a new 'language'. I can't remember how you responded to my conceits, but you kindled to my breach with translationese. With typical versatility, you went along with me. Unlike the great Eduard Frankel, I was determined to have the translation fit in the actors' mouths. My 'cinematic' visual fancies were deemed arty (and expensive) by Richard Broke. I don't think you were ever hot for them. I can't remember at what stage Richard brought in Michael Hayes as director. Did he have anything useful or critical to say about the scripts of the three completed plays?

Eager to do something 'big', Hayes was a workaday theatrical director of the RSC school. His imagination went only as far as to imagine the trilogy in quasi-operatic terms. Diana Rigg liked the script; her only question 'Will there be cozzies?' Oh, yes, there would indeed; encouraged by Hayes, they were outlandish enough to give Clive James, never happy when others succeeded, the chance to fire his first torpedo at a new target. Hayes was so determined to make a great show that he paid more attention to the parade than to making the words audible or precise.

The first rehearsals alarmed me, Helen Mirren's Cassandra not least: she would wave her arms about and make free with the text. Everyone seemed encouraged to declaim, rather than keep their voices down, consonants sharp, not least because, on a spacious stage, microphones were ineptly distributed. Your first venture in what seemed the big time made you reluctant to criticise, however helpfully. I was hobbled: the text was ours, not mine. I did have lunchtime sessions of some frankness with Hayes. He had the alcoholic's inability to assimilate anyone else's ideas even after he claimed to agree with them. The enterprise had been cursed with a director with little sense of the Greek world. Aeschylus became an overdressed, minor Elizabethan. I did us no service by ceding the last word to Master Hayes. I should have remembered Clive Donner's old pro's advice: 'When they tell you you'll like it when you see it, you won't.'

We both know what happened. Clive James supplied the iceberg in our Titanic's course. He had already made known his dissentient dislike of *The Glittering Prizes* when he alone wrote a sneering notice of the first episode in the *Observer*. Clive's road to fame was paved with distributed brickbats. He went for anyone, Peter Hall another, who seemed to need toppling in order that he become the master of cultural rankings. At the time, I knew nothing of him personally but suspected that he was vain enough to take my randy showbizzy man Alan Parks, played by an Australian actor, as some kind of slur. Clive went so far as to point out that the supposedly dated lettering on the staircases was in some modern style. All his barrels were for scraping. He somewhat retracted in the face of his public reproaches, but returned with recharged torpedo tubes when *The Serpent Son* (your clever title for our *Oresteia*) came within his gabby range. Ossa on Pelion does fill a quick column.

Diana Rigg's cozzie question was answered in a style apt for derision. I am not sure what guns, pop or otherwise, C. turned on our text, but he blew the whistle to rally his colleagues to go over the top. You were deeply wounded by your first experience of critical scorn. How posh journalists do dread the culture they affect to yearn for! I had enough experience of ups and downs to retreat to France and solitary endeavour. I never watched the *Eumenides*, which you reported the best of the trilogy.

I did have a bit of fun appending a satyr-play to the trilogy. The original, whatever its topic, probably went up in some righteous Christian bonfire, along with the Torah, Mayan holy books and who knows what other despicable expressions of dissent from Trinitarianism. My satyr-play imagined, with deutero-Aristophanic boldness, the home life of Helen and Menelaus in their middle-aged domesticity. Menelaus had the loudest shout of 'Fore' on the Tiryns golf links. If you ever watched it (I never did), you would remember that blousy Helen was played by Diana Dors, who in her starry days had carried all, and then some, before her. She was not popular among the cast because she tended to turn up late for rehearsals. Helen was the last part she ever played. Fate, with its aptitude for cruel ironies, had her die of mammary cancer. In the Hellenistic Age, more temples were built to *Tyche*, Chance (Luck, if you were lucky), than to any other deity. Between *Tyche* and tee-hee there is but a giggle of difference.

If you were stunned by the gleeful virulence of Clive and kindred marksmen, I rated their pellets no more than a clutch of sour grapes. Peter Hall soon announced an RSC production of the *Oresteia*, translated by the peerless whoever-it-was. Hugh Lloyd-Jones, who had been as smug as may be about our version, published his own (has it ever been performed?) with a dust-jacket of *la* Rigg in our cozzie. Meanwhile, Jonathan Cape was all set to publish our jointly credited *Poems of Catullus* when the National Union of Journalists, enraged by Rupert Murdoch's blowing the whistle on their shameless finaigling, went on strike. You had encouraged me to write the introduction, which Guy Lee saluted, perhaps with his left hand, as 'very professional'. There was something in you which backed away from striking noticeable attitudes. You left that, I learnt, to your professorial father. An avalanche of Catullan *variationes* followed ours. The N.U.J. strike deprived us, if deprivation it was, of any noticeable press. Our best review was supplied by Tony King, professor of politics at Essex, who used to read out the cheekiest of our squibs by way of a *digestif* at his dinner parties.

After a break for lamentation, we proceeded to translate a slew of Greek tragedies. Our *Medea* and *Bacchae* were staged all over the place. When Fiona Shaw won the *Evening Standard* Best Actress award, using our version of the *Medea*, she thanked most everyone in the unit by name, but had no word for the translators. You have to laugh, as Aeschylus used to say. We went on to collaborate on all of the latter's extant plays, but I was happy to leave the majority of the tragic canon to you, and all of Aristophanes (your speciality). Our Sunday talks continued to spice the Sabbath. You learned Norwegian, Danish and Swedish on the quick as a way to translate Ibsen, Strindberg and who all else. Our sad experience with the televised *Oresteia* had the happy consequence of funding you to move from Lincoln to the Fens.

You bought a house next door to an amiable Pole whose antisemitism you were prompt to report. Malice had no part in your character, but you had a tendency to tactlessness. Having failed to stall your tongue, you called me back to say that I was the least Jewish Jew you had ever met. On reflection, that was not the nicest thing anyone ever said, so you called back yet again. All this can be filed under comedy. I was not in the least offended at any point. Why mention it? Because it honours what a Dublin friend of Brian Glanville (*né* Goldberg) once said to him, 'Whenever I scratch a Gentile, I expect to find an anti-Semite underneath. And oi'm rarely disappointed'. Colour that Irish, it takes the curse off it. I never imagined you antisemitic, but did you dump Andrew Best after he said what he said? Quite right: none of my business. That Galilean '*Eppure...*' does mutter on though.

A few years later (there goes life in a trite phrase), you were invited to take part in a symposium at Delphi on ancient Greek literature and allied trades. George Steiner was among the symposiasts and seems to have singled you out for an afternoon of two-sided triangulation: you told me that I was the missing hypotenuse. George had a habit of putting everyone down without realising that jealousy diminished him. His own lecture was due that same evening. Halfway through it (aha!), you passed out. The usual *post moram* collected around you.

Someone asked if you had had too much sun. Your reply was barely audible, and unforgettable: 'Too much Steiner'. Famous words, fortunately not your last. Geoffrey Kirk, ex-British officer, took command and had the clout, and the demotic, to summon a helicopter to take you to the best cardiac hospital in Athens. Valerie, who always referred to you as 'Kenneth', called me because no one who spoke English was available. My own demotic was never better than when I managed to get through to the consultant who responded in the negative to my list of sites for possible organic catastrophes, *kephale, kardia, eepar, kai ta loipa* [head, heart, liver and the rest].

What they did discover was that you had indeed suffered from the heat due to the fact, ascertained by x-ray, that you had an impacted vertebra at the back of your head. What had been treated in England, for years, as some kind of psychological 'problem' (what else?) was in fact anatomical. While tutoring some rich child in Mallorca, you had been a passenger in a car that went off the road into a concrete culvert. The drop drove your spine upwards and created a small pocket in which liquid accumulated. According to the consultant, Delphic heat caused the liquid to expand, press on some vital installation and made you pass out. The Greeks had the right words for it, and the right remedial work, but you were left shaky and shaken.

Steiner was not moved to sympathy. He thought you had been outclassed by the academic company and added no lustre to its constellation. You had, he was pleased to tell me, embarrassed the distinguished company, less because you lacked their scholarship than because you were a callow socialite. His condescension did little to explain why he had spent that hot afternoon with you. Can it have been in order to cull things to say about you which would sever my attachment to you, make his and mine more precious? Never seek the motive; note the details. Even George did not bring himself to tell me of any disparagement that would ring true enough to drive you and me apart. His lecture that night was, no doubt, suitably pitched, if not overpitched like a sophisticated yorker, to dazzle the Delphic company. Your own contribution was never delivered, your Latin and Greek resources would have outdone Steiner's, in scholarly quality, if not in sonic booming. The comedy, cruelly in tune with Eliot's 'objective correlative', is that George's crumpled ear stood sweetly for his inability to speak any language as if it were his own.

Your capacity for cracking languages like a code prospered when you turned to Ibsen and others. You found enough of a welcome at the National Theatre to make boast and apology one when it came to doing translations for them, *Peer Gynt* not least. I was happy to see your talents employed. You were bold enough to send Frankie Howerd a comedy which you thought might appeal to him. He seemed interested enough to invite you to come and see him in his flat. Someone else must have answered the bell. You were shown into the bathroom where F.H. was harboured, main mast erect. He asked you lend a hand to what he was up to, quite as if that had been the purpose of your visit. You declined; so did he. Should I not have repeated the story? It hardly reflects any kind of discredit on your character and, given his shameless reputation, hardly damages his. I cannot imagine that you made the story up nor, to tell the silly truth, can I imagine anything of the kind happening had I been the visitor.

Our friendship continued; our partnership not. I had an opportunity to recommend you for a Fellowship of the Royal Society of Literature and the small wit to appear surprised when you told me of the pleasure it gave you when you were elected. I did not tell you that when, in 1975, I told Michael Ayrton that I had been a Fellow for over ten years, he said that he had been recruited at some point but decided that it wasn't worth three guineas a year, the then subscription.

A Fellow for almost sixty years, I have never been invited to participate in any of its *soirées*. Its ethnically distributed initials are now scarcely more of an honour than being addressed as esquire.

Recruited as a translator by the National Theatre, you were never short of work, though shorter of breath. When I checked to see what you had done in the following years, I was dazzled by your prolificity, as listed in Wikiwhatsit. It reported that you had been especially proud to have completed translations of all the surviving fifth- and fourth-century Attic classic dramatists. No mention is made of my participation in any of them. No doubt through no agency of yours, I was less worsted than Bested. That's show business. *Sto kalo, phile mou*, Freddie.

TO MICHAEL AYRTON.

Dear Michael,

The first time I remember hearing of you was when Peter Green showed me your dustjacket for his first novel, *Achilles His Armour*, about that master of ambivalence, patriotic, political, sexual Alcibiades, most modern of ancients. I may, however, literally have heard you previously, when you were a member of the wartime *Brains Trust*. Still in your early twenties, you were the youngest pundit in the programme's history. The now legendary image of wartime England in which all pulled together, lords and proles, Etonians and oiks in the same boat, like antique Athenians, occasionally, is scarcely borne out by close inspection, but the programme was a weekly presage of the Open University.

Clever-clevers (Julian Huxley, Bertrand Russell etc) and the odd clever-silly (Commander Campbell) or odder silly-clever (C.E.M. Joad) played meta-Socratic roles. Sophisticates took it as scarcely better than an audible version of *Reader's Digest*; those who had left school at fourteen, or earlier, could listen to a quality of discourse previously unavailable to them. Nothing did more than the BBC to assure the British that Browning had it right: 'There is a new tribunal now / Higher than God's – the educated man's!' Joad's mantra 'it depends what you mean' (by x, y, or z) became as famous as it was infuriating to Russell: invited, at some later date, to review Joad's latest book, he declined with 'Modesty forbids'.

Joad was eventually disgraced for having repeatedly and seigneurially travelled without a ticket on the railway. His recurrent attribution of the world's ills to the internal combustion engine seemed cranky at the time, but has had more practical durability than many of Russell's mantras.

You may well have outboxed and outfoxed the polymaths in the ring with you, but you had no phrase or accent that solicited mimicry, least of all from a schoolboy. Did milling away left and right with your elders, and bettering them, win you any fond reputation among your peers?

In the 1960s, the *Sunday Times* offices were at 200 Gray's Inn Road. The literary department was a Tuesday-to-Friday club. Initiates were welcome, under Jack Lambert's sometimes baleful eye, to browse the green tin shelves where new books awaited a reviewer or, if not pounced upon for a week or three, met the fate of the *neiges d'antan*. All of us, except Cyril (Connolly) and Raymond (Mortimer) had to take care not to be presumptuous, but cruising was not forbidden. I spotted and extracted *Fabrications*. The handsome, cellophaned volume, with your élitist style and subject matter, reminded me of P. Green's high opinion of you. I asked whether perhaps, etc. Jack said, in his literally sniffy way, 'No more than seven hundred words'. As he entered the title in his ledger, he added, 'No one much likes him'; licence to pan.

The text did indeed prove what insular spirits would call pretentious. Glorying in abstruse fancy, you stiffened the wind for those who shrank from your gale of erudition. What more promptly uncorks a reviewer's acid than the whiff of a kindred spirit? My first temptation was to play *picador*, but I soon chucked my cape and skewers. How not confess unusual pleasure in the book's conceits, those elastic Giacomettis not least? On the same Sunday that my eulogy appeared, *Fabrications* was knifed in the *Observer*, under the headline 'A Bit of a Borges'. Your father had once edited the paper. Nice people literary journalists, one or two of them.

Your parents together or, more often, separately, offered the key, or keys, both to your complexity and to your sense of election. At the Savile Club, you were renowned for having little practical time for its sociable motto, *Sodalitas*.

Exclusive conversations were deplored: any member, boring or antipathetic, was supposed to be accommodated. If, however, someone not to your taste presumed to intrude on your company, Ayrton was known to say, quite often, 'Bugger off'; no charmer's slogan, charming though you could certainly be. Rudeness flatters those not subject to it; victims bide their time.

Having discovered that you lived not many miles from our house in North Essex, I wrote to confirm how much I had enjoyed your book and invite you to lunch. The prompt reply was typewritten; evidence, I learned later, that it had been dictated to Elisabeth. You did not care to type. Did your prolonged little fingernail snag the keys? Or was handwriting an ancillary art, as typing could never be, not to be lavished on strangers? That nail was a mandarin stiletto reserved for winkling wax.

You and Elisabeth preferred that we come to lunch at Bradfields. A week or two later, we drove along the Cambridge road from Colchester and turned left. A long drive passed under the swoop and rise of electric cables slung between gigantic pylons. Having watched them bestride the long valley, mammoth skeletons, and swagger in to breach your privacy and seemingly to intimate your datedness in insular rankings, you referred to them, with small possessive affection, as 'our Lynn Chadwicks'.

A wary, bearded face came round the doorpost as our red Mercedes 280SE snubbed the gravel. What had you got yourself into? Beetle's long-legged elegance as she swung out of the car had an encouraging effect. One step down from the broad, unremarkable slate-roofed ex-farmhouse, you were shorter than expected. Now in your early fifties, you suffered from spondylitis; impacted back, hunched thick shoulders racked you like one of your own muscle-bound Minotaurs. The crouched example we bought squats in our sitting room, glowering in horny puzzlement at the palm of one of his all-but-human paws.

Literally and metaphorically, you had stood taller in precocious youth. Over six feet, a handsome, domineering prodigy, in 1941 you teamed with John Minton to design sets and cozzies for John Gielgud's production of *Macbeth*. During the production, an exasperated senior theatrical lady asked whether you thought to prove your genius by being offensive. Was your recklessness at once camouflage and advertisement? What did you have to hide or wish you had? When called up, you opted for the RAF. An initiating sergeant asked your religious affiliation. You responded, 'Gnostic'. The sergeant's mouth slid to one side. 'I'll put C. of E.', he said.

You were co-opted as a war artist before you had occasion to prove yourself Daedalus or Icarus (today's Greek air force trainee pilots are known as *Ikaroi*). Many of those selected by Kenneth Clark – Paul Nash, Laura Knight, Henry Moore (whom you came to call 'Old Henry'), Graham Sutherland, David Piper, David Bomberg – made patriotic reputations. Subway slumberers, poignant ruins, kerchiefed factory girls became totemic. You scorned agitprop; prig, never snob, you furnished a one-man raree-show. Your politics a shade of timely red, your art for the ages, more at ease with illustrious elders than with contemporaries, in the Broadcasting House canteen, with its cliquish congestion, you rubbed leather-patched, age-of-austerity elbows with 'Gloomy George' Orwell. What ages a man more quickly than being a prodigy? You went on from the *Brains Trust* to art critic of the *Spectator*. Keen eye and supercilious severity won you a lifetime of unforgiving peers and grudge-ridden gallery-owners.

At your progressive co-ed school, your name had been, like that of many English middle-class persons, hyphenated. Your alcoholic father, Charles Gould, was a literary journalist with, so you told us, unfailing taste, except when served with a work of genius. Young Ayrton-Gould's schooldays came to a sharp end when, aged fifteen, you were caught being progressive with an older girl equally eager to discover whether the unlikely anatomical information each of you had gleaned was feasible in carnal practice. Following paternal congratulations and footsteps, you enjoyed uncommon entrance into the *gratin*: Chelsea pubs and Soho drinking clubs became your precocious university. Out-clevering the conventionally erudite was to be your lasting pleasure.

In the late 1930s, you went, garnished with suitable introductions, to Paris for apprenticeship *chez* Eugène Berman. Having occasion for further erotic experiment, in the comely form of a BCBG *petite amie* with bohemian appetites, you discovered that, given coitus without interruption, one and one was liable to make three. As war clouds thickened, you beat a retreat from *mons veneris* to England with small apology. More than thirty years later, on a visit to Paris, so you told us, you were in *Dupont* in the Boul'Mich, when a young man, in a proper suit, carrying a rigid briefcase, came in and was hailed to a table not far away. Your companion said, '*T'as-vu ce mec qui vient d'entrer? C'est le fils que tu as eu avec ta petite amie d'avant guerre.*' You considered the collar, the tie, the close shave, and said, 'I don't think I'll go over'. *Chez Dupont Tout Est Bon* flashed red on the white china ashtrays. I stole one once.

Having set up your easel in phoney-war Chelsea, you decided that a hyphenated artist sounded ridiculous (despite or because of Gaudier-Brzeska) and dropped the Gould. It sounded Jewish although, in your father's case, it was not. Your remarkable grandmother was, as they will say, of Jewish origin and a prodigious scientist. The one public Jew with whom you acknowledged a link, on your mother's side, was the then celebrated Isidore Zangwill, to whom Percy Wyndham Lewis referred, in the *entre-deux-guerres*, as 'Yiddle' Zangwill. In those days, antisemitism was modish *un peu partout*: George Orwell was astonished, when on imperial duty in the far East, to hear some native say 'I am a Joo, sir' quite as if he was proud of it.

Lewis is ticketed as founder and captain of the Vorticists. Ezra Pound signed up to be in the first eleven of his proto-Fascist casuals. The team had a fraternal source in Marinetti's Futurists. With scorn for bourgeois traditions, in a hurry for the fast lane, they were hot for tomorrow and a bit of rough. Saline as Céline, blasting and bombardieering, Lewis swivelled his fire on the Bloomsberries, whom he regarded as 'the enemy' and by whom he aimed to be taken as such. You may well have long admired him, his draughtsmanship at least, though you had gone sharp left where he chose to swing right. Willie Maugham wrote a story, set in Malaysia, about a character called 'Powder Puff Percy'; Wyndham Lewis was not, we may be sure, the target, but he dropped the foppish Percy as you did the suspect Gould. Who is ever wholly at ease with his given name? Michelangelo Antonioni, perhaps.

After the war, when Lewis – 1914 veteran, 1931 admirer of Adolf Hitler, 1940 war artist, polemicist for all seasons – was going blind, you stepped in to be his *amanuensis*. Your little drypoint of him in a whoremonger's slouch hat hangs on our wall. He might be aping the frustrated rapist he was accused of being. What else did you see in him? His art, like yours, was his character; the fascism more Bloomsbury-baiting party-piece than programme; the draughtsmanship, like yours, immaculate and fat-free. His adversarial self-advertisement had something in common with the Sitwellian theatricals of the same period. Unlike Harold Nicolson, all style, no man, Lewis did not fall for Oswald Mosley. I suspect he never quite got over being Canadian. Fear of being nice nettled him. If he was a shit, he was a shit who could draw, and scribble.

When you tried to enrol in the Republican army in the Spanish Civil War, aged fifteen, they turned you away. Did you know anything about Spain? How many of those who rallied to the International Brigades ever spoke Spanish? Does it matter? The scoundrel passivity of the British government led volunteers to raise two fingers to appeasers at home by clenching fists abroad. I remember you saying that you would sooner have been shot by Communists than by Fascists because your death would then make some contribution to a worthwhile cause. I have played that remark back to myself several times, wondering why being shot by Fascists would not have made you a more useful martyr. Did the fancy of being executed by your own side appeal to your appetite for irony?

Did you see yourself in contradictory mirrors, a bourgeois who resembled Hugo in Sartre's *Les Mains sales*? Deputed by the Party to assassinate Hoederer (a Tito/Trotsky-like heroic infidel), Hugo falls under the spell of his charismatic victim and cannot go through with his mission. In the last scene, knowing that the Party has sent agents to dispose of him, he waits resignedly for them (shades of Hemingway's *The Killers*). At their approach, he runs into the street to meet them, crying out that he is '*irrécupérable*'; admission and boast. Sartre had the common vanity of writers; assuming the victim's place makes martyrdom the proof of quality. All attitude, no drudgery, it avoids committee meetings.

Your attention to Wyndham Lewis was a double bind; each of you did some kind of service to the other, generous and grateful, loyal and perverse. Was your devotion not a form of domination, a way of having him in your power and not taking advantage of it? He was the bully masochist who said 'Beat me', you the sadist who said 'No'. Is something close to the reverse also in the characteristic chiasmus? His misfortune enabled you to act out a fantasy of exemption, as if you needed it, from the malice he had levelled at Zangwill. At the same time, you could flatter yourself that you were entitled to it. Applause from the ranks of Tuscany can be sweeter than any chest full of honours from one's own camp. You declined to be made an A.R.A., did you not, when a young man? It smacked of deference to the old guard. Later... you rather wished you could press the rewind button. As for the R.S.L., you deemed Fellowship not worth three guineas a year, even in the days when I thought it a rarish honour.

There was a chiasmic aspect of your devotion to Wyndham Lewis in your competitive attitude to Picasso, with whom you had enough common ground to double for a wrestling mat. Your sense that Picasso had so dominated twentieth-century art, had had such a Midas touch, that he must have been corrupted by a faculty that became a facility, led you to suggest to John Berger the idea that grew, not very grandly, into his *The Success and Failure of Picasso*. Berger was possessed, it seems, by a rage fuelled by adversity. He wanted criticism to be a creative activity, if not a kind of directorate. Did he seriously think that the Hungarian revolt, in 1956, against Soviet rule was a counter-revolution? Or did it amuse him to tease the western bourgeoisie by threatening that it had been a mere kink in the inevitable progress of the Marxist dialectic, a means of flushing out the counter-revolutionaries by seeming, like Mao's fake tolerance of the thousand contending flowers, to allow them to raise their heads, if only to make it easier to lop them off?

On that first visit of ours to Bradfields, you led us into the big sitting room where George and Zara Steiner were already waiting. Elizabeth greeted us with experienced courtesy. As everyone in the know knew, she had been married. His popularity made you (and Steiner) unlikely to have been among his keenest readers. Balchin's wartime bestsellers had the unadorned line of utility furniture. One was called *Mine Own Executioner*. *Verb. sap.*, as our friend Peter Green used to say. While lacking his mercantile renown, as a fellow-Savilian you became Nigel's cultural tutor.

A story of choice triplicity remains to be composed about the excursion to post-war Italy on which you conducted Balchin and his ripe wife, mother of their three children. Had you already written your monograph, skimpily introduced by Old Henry, on Giovanni Pisano? You were certainly as qualified a guide, and charmer, as any couple could be so guileless, unless it was so bored, as to enrol. Licence as genius unrevoked, if not quite fulfilled, you had the old young bohemian's presumption that females were fruit to be plucked; if married, ripe for rupture. Your scowl threatened passion; affection, its small change, was never your style; your smile complicity.

How nice the scene, or succession of scenes, in which young Ayrton can be seen acceding to presidency of the trio! How much he knew and how perfectly apt Elisabeth was, being both educated and, we can guess, weary of the conjugal clutch, to kindle to him! We can imagine, easily, how you first addressed yourself to mastering Nigel. Your generous guidance doubled as evidence of how deficient your senior was in the recondite. The more you exuded knowledge, the more you reminded Elisabeth that her best-selling husband, however mechanically well-informed, was no rare spirit. Your intelligence paid your fare; when it evoked a small smile from fair Elisabeth, it proved seductive. I see you dosing your patrons with information at once grateful and divisive. She knew a thing or two more than you may have guessed at the outset.

I follow the three of you, in 1950s Italy, Nigel bulging with those big, soiled, brown 10,000 lire notes, power passing to you; your attention, first concentrated on him, more and more alert to Elisabeth. By all but ignoring her, you conveyed how keenly you came to wish to be alone with her. If less of a fool than you took him for, Nigel was a bourgeois it was a pleasure to pillage. I imagine your trio, together and distinct, in front of Barna's pitted frescos in San Gimignano (damaged by allied fire in the war, they had not yet been restored). One pocked panel depicts the drunken Noah lolling naked on deck, lank penis patent to his sons. What did you have to say about the *membrum virile* in art? Did you link it with *campanilismo*, the competitive architectural upsy-daisying of the local grandees, San Gimignano's stiff parade? How very English that 'boner' can signify both 'howler' and 'erection'!

Adjacent to your volatile Tuscan triangle, do I see the loitering eidolon of John Minton, his versatility so remarkable that he never arrived at a style of his own? You told us how you yourself, when going around a gallery, sometimes said, if your companion stopped before a striking work, 'Oh do you like it? I can do you one of those.' What is the real thing against a clever fake? Anyone can afford a can of honest Campbell's soup. Warhol's facsimiles fetch a fortune.

Your reputation as 'cocksman', as Steiner put it, with obsolete modishness, suggested that females were your regular, varied diet. That early relationship of yours with Minton (you shared rooms when studying in pre-war Paris) and continued partnership led Steiner to imply that you were sometime lovers. His moist and spatulate tongue relished the lubricious; why else did its operator make such a savoury meal of rooting out obscurities? I doubt whether you would have thought it a big deal to do Minton a quick favour; it saved time. (Philip Toynbee used to call women up and invite them to bed with the promising tag 'It'll only take twenty minutes'.)

Among the unedited apocrypha of old Bohemia is a story of how Minton was said to have come one night, late, into the Chelsea Arts Club. He had been delayed in meeting some desirable male. The usual barmaid, Molly of course, was not on duty. Her stand-in knew none of the regulars by name.

The next late morning, Minton returned and asked Molly what had happened to his *bien-aimé*. She said, 'Oh he waited and waited and seemed very disappointed, so I took him home with me.' 'Did you do the business?' 'What do you think?' Minton smiled, went home, killed himself.

What was your expression when told the news? Compare Picasso when told Matisse had died, Hutton when Washbrook was out (there's a figure to stump Steiner), Daedalus when his clever nephew fell, or was pushed, to his death. There is no end to it, is there, the gloss, the reinvention; the bond, the malice? Art conceals what Steiners expose. As seldom short of stories as the Irishman you sometimes sounded to me to be, you told us of a bibulous evening with Augustus John in old, cheaply rented Tite Street. Lolling in Bacchanalian mode, you grew conscious of the great amorist's speculative hand working its way up an adjacent thigh, yours. When they approached what John O'Hara (one of your brief list of unread writers?) called 'headquarters', you removed the Master's reconnoitring fingers with decisive aversion. John said, 'Sorry, old boy, wasn't thinking, wrong sex'. Did this incident find its way into Michael Holroyd's protracted, reverential monograph? The apocryphya is always more unguarded than any version neatened by top-and-tailoring or fattened with authorial stuffing.

On another occasion, while in the tube, you found yourself sitting next to James Agate, once ace theatrical critic whose many reviews were collected under the unparadoxical title *Ego*. Cautious homosexual, as he had better be in pre-Wolfenden days, Agate made keen conversation with handsome young Ayrton. As they came into his station, the egotist asked whether you would care to come up and see his collection of antique and modern nail scissors (as you will recall, Ashburnham, a character in Ford Madox Ford's *The Good Soldier*, had a similar fetish). Did it convey some coded message or – more probably – imply no more than angling loneliness? Why did you tell us about it? Any seductive pass was a score of a kind, even if, as in this case, the quick single was declined; another duck for Steiner.

Among the many conquests which gave you enviable allure in George's eyes was the young Elizabeth Jane Howard, whose sexual appetite seems regularly to have been stimulated by famous studs, Arthur Koestler not least, you, Ken Tynan and Kingsley; their fame, I suspect, counted for more than their potency. You told me that Jane Howard, although beautiful beyond question, was a disconcerting mistress. It was less than flattering to discover that what she wanted was so precise as to render her lover more caterer than object of desire: her masochism was at once demeaning and demanding. Can it be that all her life she thought she merited punishment for a child she abandoned in her youth? In other regards, she was quite the grand lady. She undertook to give Nick McDowell, our daughter Sarah's husband, weekend master classes on how to write novels. Sarah told us how, in thanks, Nick invited her to come with them on holiday to Ios, where our house had grown large enough to accommodate her. She played the great lady and made no attempt to be either useful or agreeable.

Cut back to San Gimignano. In fiction, I should hint that your seduction of Elisabeth combined with an increased show of manly matiness with Nigel. By ignoring Elisabeth, you procured her wish that the attention lavished on Nigel were being directed at her. Indirectly, then; was it not? The heat you generated found no vent in flirtatiousness. You charmed *la donna* with the recondite until the moment came, when and wherever it was, that you and she were alone. Then that light squeeze on her shoulder, which a dated screenwriter might guess (plagiarising Trevor Howard in *Brief Encounter*) triggered conflagration. *La donna diventata mobile.*

As director, I should hold on the doorway; that clipped moment when Nigel was there and not there. How better convey than by a glimpse of vanishing shadow that he had been very quick to – what? – duck the issue, avoid embarrassment or, my choice, profit from what he had somewhat schemed for, expected, dreaded (all can be simultaneous and synonymous) from the very beginning? Dwelling on emptiness until it means something to the audience, Antonioni was the master of *rallentando*. As in *L'Avventura*, the low road and the high road can lead to the same destination. Take a bow, Heracleitus. At the outset, what did each of your trio have in mind, other than a sense of possibilities? Which was the beast, unless it was all three, but not at once?

We can cut to you and Elisabeth having dinner alone, perhaps at that *trattoria* in Campagna, outside Virgil's misty Mantova, where – since menus are not offered – guests are first served with a suite of farinaceous courses to take or leave. Alone at last, are the two of you not conscious, each differently, both furtively, that Nigel's absence is there too, cellarless salt on the table? The passion you were so keen to sate or appease sits with you, hot to be served. A waiter, bringing the main course, might convey the satyr's smirk as he looks at the couple that three minus one makes and then at a waitress who has seen it all before, most of it.

Nigel has left for home. Ayrton has a ripe woman in his bed, spoils of a civil war; her caresses as much command as reward. Does she show any intention of retrieving her husband or of wondering what to tell her all but grown-up daughters? Gotcha! You had loved married and unmarried women; in the spirit of those days, and nights, irrecoverable today (however accurate costumes and hair-dos, the chat is never as old), the odds were that the wives a man bedded, or who bedded him, would return to the conjugal home. Where was a woman so free as in pampered bondage from which she could have recourse to a private him if she wanted something hot, pleasure and punishment? Legitimacy is pleasure's snuffer;

husbands never do the things brute lovers do, even when it is the same. Revenge alone, the liberator, gives the married man leave to resume the beast.

Were I to poach or scramble the story, my Elisabeth would not blame Michael for betraying Nigel, but she will know he has, she has. The betrayal is doubled and redoubled: both have given what each lover fears, just a little, Nigel may have been after, when he matched them. How soon did you realise that Elisabeth was quite expert in the art and mythology of ancient Greece? Did she grow older by being wiser when it came to Daedalian craftiness? Is getting what a man wants always what he wants? How many lovers want the same thing? The question sits differently on either side of all but very few couples, does it not? She grew younger; you aged. Remember the mother, in Fellini's *Giulietta degli spiriti*, who was springier than her daughter?

Did it occur to you to wonder whether Nigel had been as much schemer as victim, ace as fool, plot his forte? Had the cuckold made you his fool? Was the best-seller already back in London, saying amusing things about the two whom he has left behind, to another woman perhaps? Free at last! You and Elisabeth look at each other. Which had the key? In the silence, you read the future, together and several. Michael the Pyrrhic victor, victory will cost him his liberty. Is it not a plot that a writer, shadowing Joseph Albers, might rehearse again and again, in different tones? Morandi arranged and rearranged bottles on the never-quite-the same shelf. Why do people tell writers their secrets? Hoping to be stuffed, they hail the best taxidermist they can find.

When George and Zara had departed for Cambridge, you remarked, without malice, that she was the most unattractive woman you had ever seen. American, I did not quite agree. Her accent took me back. It was a compliment of a routine sort, your comment, was it not, to Beetle? Elisabeth proposed to show us some of your work. Did the fiery Mercedes in the driveway signal prospects she had not failed to spot? We went into the barn that served as your studio and there were all manner of brazen marvels.

Artists often do more work than any writer can well believe. Were any of the pieces for sale? Were they not? Elisabeth was unembarrassed to produce a prompt catalogue: cellophaned pages and brow-raising prices. Did we buy anything there and then? I cannot remember, but probably. While I like to think that my wit and Beetle's beauty (intelligence's wise camouflage) made us welcome, Elisabeth offered friendly discounts. How long was it, after we became irregular visitors back and forth, before you told us how Steiner had suggested, since reduced energy was limiting the scope and scale of your projects, that you design and make a chess set, each piece a hefty bronze?

Daedalian mutability spared neither pains nor expense. You had him right: however uncivil his genius, the artist thrives on commissions, works harder in bondage than when free of it: Michelangelo served his pious sentence racked under the Sistine ceiling. Without Minos, Daedalus might have been lolling at the beach (an eye on Ariadne, hers on him?). By the time the chess set was done, in due style, the price for bronze pieces, board and inlaid box had to be, complete with sighs, six thousand pounds. Both smiling, slightly differently, you showed us George's Jacobite (as if from H.J.) handwritten reply. It began with allusive homage to the Master: 'Ah…'

In anguished apology, G. wrote to decline the opportunity to acquire what would no doubt become a much-prized curio. You may remember how Evelyn Waugh, appearing on John Freeman's TV *Face to Face*, decried the vulgarity of the medium, upon which Freeman asked what had induced him to appear on it. Waugh replied 'Poverty'. Steiner avowed similar lack of specie. His Swiss-franked stipend shrivelled before us. Vanity led me to step in to redeem his unfunded commitment. Generosity has its greeds. Bishop Butler was not right: nothing is ever only what it is. My gesture dismissed Steiner, cheaply, hat-tricking him on the way. You and I, Michelaki *mou*, share a self-destructive urge to infuriate the, so-to-say, if never aloud, *goyim*. There were, we were told, only six castings of the heavy set. I have no notion whether it has grown in value. Your knights and castles were of a weighty idiosyncrasy that deterred chess nuts, for whom Hammond pieces were and remain standard issue.

Waning energy was a symptom of the diabetes your good old GP failed to spot. As pain wracked you, you spent more and more time in bed. I used to drive now and again an hour from Langham to Cambridge to have lunch and conversation with Guy Lee, a Latinist content to spend the whole of his life as a Fellow of St John's. He did not care to go to Italy or to Greece. He thought the ancient Greeks overrated: for all their genius, they lacked the wit to invent the arch or to mix concrete. The Classic texts were autonomous for Guy; he had seen enough of the world during the war, part of which he spent in Iceland, where he learnt the local language. I am told that he ventured abroad only to Bowes and Bowes, not for books but to charm a comely woman who worked there. He translated Ovid's *Amores* all but allusively, presuming that his readers would be amused by his liberties; later – working on Horace and Virgil – he became more literal, conscious that he could no longer rely on readers knowing the Latin he had previously glossed. Your visual play on Greek themes called for no such caution.

On my way back to Colchester, I would call in at Bradfields with some petty treat; once a *chirimoya* which you, never a *señorito*, had never tasted; once some soft earphones which I hoped would enable you to listen to music at no disturbing volume. When you asked me to bring some books you might not have read, three of the more abstruse volumes on our shelves supplied no novelty. Had you really read Kenneth Burke's *The Philosophy of Literary Form*? And *A Grammar of Motives*? Wittgenstein's *Zettel*? How not?, as that overrated ladies' lady Sybille Bedford too often said in an overpraised novel. I see she received PEN's Golden Pen award. Who dared to tell her where to stick it?

In the late summer of 1974, when you seemed to have some relief from prostrating pain, Beetle and I suggested that you and Elisabeth come and visit us in France. Whether through tact or glad of a chance to have time to herself, Elisabeth claimed that it would be better if you came alone, with no doting witness to hold you to invalidism. Kenneth McLeish and I had done a new translation of the extant poems of Catullus and invited you to do a set of drawings to accompany publication. You would bring your first *esquisses* with you. The plan was for you to fly to Bordeaux, hire a car and drive from there to Lagardelle.

The hour came and went when we expected you. I had sent a very clear map. We called the airport and were told that the flight had landed on time. Could it be that something, as they say, had happened? Were we more vexed than worried, vexed to be worried? An hour or more later, an Avis Renault 5 came up the hill. You told us how, as you picked your suitcase from the snaking belt, some quick hand had abstracted your briefcase from your trolley. All your travellers' cheques and the set of drawings were in it. Time spent on the telephone to the airport culled little cheer.

The stress of that delayed arrival and infectious concern about the briefcase led it to becoming my headache. Pounded by a migraine attack, I took two codis and my painful head to bed. Lying there, I could hear murmurous conversation and the odd gout of laughter from the kitchen. Had some masochistic strain led me to leave you and Beetle together? You were no more likely to be inhibited by our friendship than you had been by Nigel's. As it happened, you could do no better than to tell Beetle that you were not yet well enough to make love again. You hoped soon to be in a position to test the resurgent equipment. Having known a few Chelsea men, Beetle was not, so far as I could see or she cared to say, dazzled by the courteous postponement.

I followed my usual routine of working all morning, revising and decorating *California Time*, a somewhat experimental novel about the Biz, Julie Christie and Stanley Donen in the mix. You came up for breakfast from the flat beneath the house, where we had stowed you, shaking with cold, although the weather was mild. You huddled close to the wide fireplace in the kitchen while Beetle did her culinary stuff. You laughed together often enough, but I doubted your chances of 'storming her cool fortress', to retrieve the splendidly dated phrase of Celia Dale, a novelist rarely given to such castellations. After a day or two, we had a call from the police in Bordeaux. The missing briefcase had been found. The travellers' cheques were gone, but they were, of course, insured; the Catullus drawings were still there. 'Not unduly flattering', you said.

The week passed with enough laughter to foster the illusion of chaste intimacy *à trois* and – to stretch the implicit *donnée* – leave Elisabeth not quite up to speed in our association; the unspoken charm of the week. You amused us and yourself. We drank more than we were used to, you less, because we would not match you in whisky. You read my work in progress and, wisely, urged deletion of a plethora of inverted commas. You seemed to have left your agony in Blighty. We had such a good time that, on the day of your booked flight, you said that you would like to stay with us for good.

Thanks to my continued employment by Hollywood, Beetle and I bought several more of your bronzes, as generously discounted as Elisabeth chose. The grandest was an Icarus, about five feet tall. We proposed to mount it in the garden at Lagardelle. The following summer, you offered to drive it down to the Périgord in your Volvo, Elisabeth with you (she did the money). We sited the bronze Icarus so that he would be clear for take-off into the wide valley below us. This time, there was no extended stay. One afternoon, you and I and fifteen-year-old Sarah went and sat on a concrete wall across from Belvès and sketched the hill-topping town.

We had been at it for half an hour or so when you said that we might as well go home and finish it, glass in hand no doubt, from memory. You looked at Sarah's work and were kind enough to frown and say, 'She'll probably be better than me'. You told her that models were useful sometimes, but that she should not forget that she had one with her all the time: her arm, *mutatis mutandis*, was enough for any arm she cared to imagine. She smiled and paid little attention. Might it be that, unintentionally, you were confessing why your work, finely observed as it might be, was essentially autographic? Its mythopoeic remoteness was allayed by its proximity to you, your own Pygmalion.

Over one of our meals at Lagardelle, you proposed that the four of us make an expedition to Kenya, where you had been on some previous occasion. The attraction of the wild was not so much the animals, though you did very good monkeys, as the fact that there was absolutely no local art that demanded attention. You were off duty in Africa as you never could be in Europe. During one of your days in the South-West, you felt obliged to drive to Moissac to see the twelfth-century church and its sentinel saints. A sacked synagogue is featured on the famous portico. Christians are often bad winners.

The compact was that we should all go on safari in the following January. As you know, it never happened, whatever 'it' might have comprised. Your advice to Sarah lingers with me: we carry the anatomy of all sorts of unrealised schemata with us. My arm can also be your arm, whether or not it serves, as Nigel all but foresaw, as one's own executioner. Yes, your charm was your threat, threat charm. You were never the man you wished to be, but what you never became was also you. Like Daedalus, never Midas, you were scorched by the heat of the shower you yourself had the wit to turn on. Hating and loving Picasso, a subject you told me you wished on John Berger, you sought rejection and election. And achieved both, did you?

I miss you. There's a simple-seeming, monosyllabic triplet apt for some lancet-tongued Steinerian marksman to unpack.

Love, Freddie (surely not my true name).

TO ROBIN JORDAN.

Dear Robin,

At the beginning of every academic year, you may remember, each Carthusian was issued with a thick, pocket-diary-sized 'school list', tabulating the names of pupils and members of Brooke Hall, the beaks' common room. Like those of professionals on the Card of the Match at Lord's cricket ground, surnames came first, alphabetically; initials followed. Yours were J.F.R.; Randall's the most memorable: B.S.C.G., for Brough Stuart Churchill Gurney. He was third monitor in September 1945, when you and I arrived at Lockites. He used to take the 'locking-up time' roll call standing naked in 'toshes'. Since the ruling habit was that new bugs call each other by our last names, what initials hid was our *petit bagage*. R.E. 'Tubby' Gladstone's Ewart soon boasted him a direct descendant of William, Queen Victoria's declamatory Prime Minister, unsmiling foe of Benjamin Disraeli. I had nothing to hide, but I still hid it.

Except for gig-lamped Master Gladstone, I have never known anyone called Robin who was not in some respect a pretty, slippery fellow. Leslies form another sub-class, not always pretty, generally amenable, seldom aggressive. Randall's fancy names suited his handsome *hauteur* (Gurney did not yet summon up the image of a hospital trolley). His way of carrying a dip pen clenched in his teeth, like a pronged cigar, honoured his 'Churchill', whether from family pride or wishful conceit. I used to imitate him, until the chewed wood gave me a sore throat. Your J.F. initials were never unpacked in public, to my knowledge. Whatever family quirk they may have masked, Robin's chirpy ambivalence suited you well. Not easy to be angry with a Robin. Gladstone of that ilk is the only one whom

I have regarded all my life with unabated hatred, not least, but not only, because his name reminds of my own cowardice.

There was something apt in your being an Exhibitioner, an intermediary step between commoners and scholars, the only one of our year in our House. I was the only Junior Scholar. Jeremy Atkinson, seemingly very sure of himself, was the sole (soon to be senior) scholar of the year ahead of us. We were assigned to Lockites to leaven the lump. It failed to rise in any noticeable manner. Scholars earned scant respect: C'house slang called them 'Hash (for work) Pros (for professionals, i.e. needing the money)'. Jeremy's father, a captain R.N., posted in Singapore, had gone down in a Chinese tug he was trying to guide to safety, when it was bombed by the Japanese in 1941. Atkinson J.J.W. was the arbiter of intelligence in younger Lockites. You and I were rated eligible.

Even at fourteen, you seemed tall and well-proportioned. If amiability masked a less secure secret self, it did so in comely fashion. You were bright, but never 'festive' (Carthusian slang – need I remind you? – for cheeky to one's betters), quick with a smile, never 'groisy'. You admired 'spo-ey' (good at sports) Lockites and were one of them yourself; I remember you testing Buchan-Hepburn's biceps in an admiring way. Our best fast bowler, he became Sir Alastair B.-H., Bart. Fifty years after we left Charterhouse, I had a friendly letter from him, written in a shaky hand. He asked me to intercede in a misunderstanding he had had with his new French lady. Touched by the implied compliment, I promised him that he was doing me too much honour: a letter, written in French by some strange scribe was unlikely to heal the rift; better to blunder sincerely in his own hand. *J'espère que tout s'est bien passé. Pas un mot depuis.*

You turned away schoolboy curiosity with good humour; you knew how to raise topics congenial to any who crossed your path. A few salty details emerged about your background as time went by. Your father, you let it be known, owned a pier – or was it two? – in some south-coast resort(s). The war cannot have been good for business. He must have had other irons in the fire: C'house was not cheap. Your sister was called Cassandra; you had a half-brother with some kind of criminal record. Was he on the run, did you suggest, in foreign parts? You glamorised him as a modern Heathcliff, a bold buccaneer, without concern for rules. You yourself rarely broke them, did you? Yet that smiling wariness of yours doubled for dissidence, rendered conformity ironic.

The docile were conscripted into the house platoon of the Junior Training Corps. Every Tuesday afternoon, we changed into hairy khaki, complete with forage caps, blancoed belts and gaiters and brassoed metalwork. I worked polish into the toecaps of my kick-their-heads-in black boots with the bone handle of an old toothbrush. While we left-right-left-left-lefted around with our Lee-Enfield .303s, you exercised the right to conscientious objection, up on the house gardener's metal-seated tractor, as if fresh from digging for the victory the Allies had just celebrated. When privates in the J. T. C. were set a 'Promotions Exam', veteran scribbler Raphael leaped to the rank of acting-corporal.

At once correct and just slightly off-centre, you made no enemies, joined no cliques. Like Gladstone, you liked music; like Sinha, son of the only Indian peer, you played agile pingers (with a Victor Barna bat); like Cellan-Jones, you admired George Bernard Shaw (the complete plays sagged his shelf). Brainy, you refrained from being a swot. Good at sports, you were eventually in several school second elevens and a boxer with a Corinthian straight left. Since we all wore similarly patterned suits of (rationed) tweed, how is it that I have a memory of individual flair in your vaguely arty wardrobe?

Latin and Greek not your territory, you were segregated in a class for students of French and German, your subjects for school certificate. Our housemaster, H.A. March, witlessly known as Ham, a man of nervous disposition, with quick-licked, thin, prefatory lips, given to saying 'in point of fact', while underlining the obvious, taught French and, understandably, thought well of you. Whether or not he had any kind of authentic French accent, I am sure his liaisons were impeccable. *C'était son truc.*

You sang in the choir and attended voluntary Friday Evening Service. Yet you were not entirely the onward Christian soldier you impersonated, were you? You introduced me to W.H. Auden's *The Age of Anxiety* and scanned my sorry verses. I never heard you talk dirty or use obscene language. You had an aura of chastity. Did you masturbate? Who did not? Ay, there's the rub! If slightly unearthly, you were not quite convincingly Christian. When I finished one slab of free verse with 'The sum of all experience: muck!', you proposed a rhyming emendation beginning with f.

During our year in Long Room, you sported a yellow paperback fat with stories of Slapsy Maxie Rosenbloom, Max Baer (wearing trunks with the star of David on them, he beat Max Schmeling), Joe Louis, Jack Dempsey, champions all, none English. Pacifist, you were not unwilling to box for the house. I watched you in Armoury going three rounds with Jenks, a thuggy Bodeite. When he got through your guard and smashed you in the face, you grinned at him with bright red teeth. He might have done you a cruel favour. That rouged smile claimed victory of a kind, even when you had lost.

I had a sense that it afforded you amusement to be taken for a conventional Carthusian. Possessed by a humour older than you were, you seemed to live adjacent to your contemporaries. You and I were outsiders of different stripes. I was the house Jew. I saw Jewishness less as a faith than as a fortuitous condition, like a birthmark or being left-handed, as I was at my t'utherun – prep school – when I first played cricket. Later in that summer of 1940, I was put right by that baleful beak Mr Crowe as German bombers throbbed overhead on their way to London.

At C'house, I dreaded anyone else seeing the fortnightly beige envelopes, rubber-stamped STUDENT'S EXERCISE, which came from the Liberal Jewish Synagogue. My parents had enrolled me for confirmation. What was Hosea to me? Nuts to Gilead. When Robin Ewart Gladstone led a group of our contemporaries (Sinha among them) in what he called a 'Jew-bait', my reaction was stunned, if not pathetic. I had thought myself quite popular. I became a pariah. I had a tiny study and shut myself away most of the time. I still do.

You were my only caller. We never spoke of the reason for my isolation. Like a prison visitor, you did not discuss the justice of the sentence, but offered neutral, consolatory company. Your decency was discreetly weighted so as not to mark you my ally. Is it significant that there was another Jordan in the school? He was a Saunderite whom I later joined in the Classical Sixth, a cross-country runner in the school team and, yes, a thuggy Jew, good at Latin verses which he claimed to compose in his sleep. After two or three weeks, my stay in Coventry came to an end. It would be nice to suppose that it stopped only because I threatened to fight each one of my persecutors in turn, starting with the weakest (a shrewdly divisive proposal). I suspect that, in point of fact, Ham heard of what was going on and, licking his lips, put an end to what was no longer amusing. None of the participants seemed to bear me any subsequent ill will.

A year later, I became a monitor; before you. The comedy of ambition and opportunism was served because Jeremy Atkinson, as head monitor, was going to be too busy to go lefting and righting as Commander of the Lockite Platoon. When he asked acting-corporal Raphael to become house commander, I refused unless I was made a monitor. I feared having no punitive rights if faced with festive once-a-week squaddies. I was duly embossed. Monitorial standing armed me with the punitive *'post te'* (privilege) necessary to procure obedience. You were still driving around in that tractor next to the green-baize-aproned gardener with the silver rimmed glasses. I detested him, as people do the witnesses of their humiliation. In my first Quarter, Harry March sentenced me, for failing to send for my Ration Book, to be the gardener's serf for a number of hours. There has always been some small thing I have failed to do.

With the licensed bark of a suburban Napoleon, Putney my Corsica, I led Lockites to an unusually high place in the annual Field Day manoeuvres. I was promoted to acting sergeant and, as other successes followed, culminating in Lockites being joint winners of the Drill Competition in the Oration Quarter of 1949, I rose to be a Junior Officer, complete with swagger stick, Sam Brown, and officer's peaked cap. My silly triumph might have been complete, had I not been conscious of your veiled observation of my snappy imposture.

In that same Quarter, my platoon-sergeant Jim Cellan-Jones (Laertes) and I (Osric) persuaded you to play Hamlet in the school play. Comely reluctance did not long detain you. Why did we suppose you the right casting? You were though; imposture was part of the curriculum. Charterhouse, the cynics said, was a school for the fathers of gentlemen (Eton for the sons). The one thing the Carthusian disciplinary system never tolerated was sexual activity with younger boys. 'My boys', a famous inter-war headmaster once said, 'are amorous but not erotic'. You showed no inclination in that direction; no more did I. Narcissus made do with his pool.

Jeremy Atkinson had also become a senior scholar. He had had nothing to do with Gladstone's group of Harris-tweedy stormtroopers, nor had he indicated disapproval. Like you, he refrained from loud laughter and was unamused by dirty stories; a characteristic caw subbed for amusement. In the Oration Quarter of 1948 (there were only three Quarters in a year, but there they were), Jeremy, soon also to be head of the school, was one of a handful of candidates for the Holford scholarship to Christ Church, Oxford, endowed especially for an annual Carthusian worthy of preference. George Turner, the headmaster, made the selection. His favourite went to Oxford, among predestined also-runners, to be quizzed by Hugh Trevor-Roper. Jeremy returned victorious, as in truth he had departed.

It seemed to me that he had cleared no very high hurdle. My father had been at Oxford. I supported the dark blues with due piety. Why should I not be a candidate for the following year? The only two Sixth Formers who were better classicists than I, Bryce Cotterell and James Rennie, were so precocious that, at sixteen, they had already won open scholarships to Oxford. I had reason to hope that I would be, as we never said, a shoo-in. My confidence that I might follow Jeremy to Christ Church was never greater than when I was summoned to see the headmaster early in the Oration Quarter of 1949. Could that be why he wanted to see me? At the end of the previous academic year, I had won the prize for Latin Verse in the exams supervised by Christ Church's Hugh Trevor-Roper. He had offered beady congratulations. It seemed a happy augury. Lord Randolph Churchill 'forgot Goschen', they say. So did I you.

I approached my audience with small respect for George Turner. He had taken it upon himself to teach Latin to the Sixth Form and had us work on Caesar's Gallic Wars, a text more suitable for beginners. Caesar wrote his history to commend himself to Roman voters. Its prose was a conqueror's election manifesto with little rare vocabulary or turn of phrase. No Latinist, Turner liked to have the Loeb edition, Latin on one page, English on the next, at his elbow. Your namesake, Tony Jordan, was clever but idle; on one occasion, to avoid puzzling out Caesar's meaning, he had early recourse to the school lib's Loeb, which he had open on his lap, below the level of his desk, when the H.M. came into the Sixth Form Room. Turner asked, as if it had just occurred to him, whether someone would go and get the Loeb from Library. Tony Jordan was quick out of the blocks and, the Loeb under his coat, went and came back with it on show. Turner thanked him politely and was now armed to take on the Belgians.

At the stipulated hour, I presented myself to Turner without apprehension. He then showed me the reason for my summons. I had written a letter to the Provost of Guildford denouncing him as, yes, a Nazi for what he had said in a recent Sunday evening sermon about the shopkeeper to whom the apprentice carpenter Jesus sought to sell his work. 'The shopkeeper, being a Jew, tried to give him as little for it as possible.' Had I been a man, I should have walked the length of the chapel and slammed my way out. As it was, and has often been since, I bided my time and then took up my pen. If I had not expected a reply from the Provost, it never occurred to me that he might forward my letter to his fellow-Christian. Turner began more in sorrow than in wrath. I had elected to live in a Christian country. Did I think I should make friends by writing this kind of abuse to a guest of the school? The implication was that, if unable to support local prejudices, I had better wander on.

Somewhat choked, I said that neither my first intention nor my last was to befriend the Provost. The conversation turned to the immediate future. What were my plans or hopes? Humiliated and outraged, I mentioned the Holford scholarship to Christ Church. Turner told me that it was up to him to declare the boys he considered eligible. I was not among them. When I went up to Cambridge, I discovered that Turner had a brother, a fellow of Magdalene. He had lost most of his nose in the Great War. A horizontal clean white plaster bridged the spot.

With no signs of pushy ambition, you were apt to be on hand when stardom was forced upon you. In Oration Quarter 1949, you must have been amused to discover that, although a new monitor, you had been bumped above me in seniority, having been designated a school monitor by George Turner. This sign of high favour was heightened when, after the customary pilgrimage to Oxford, for ritual grilling, before the prescribed award was announced, you became Jeremy's successor as the Holford scholar. You did not crow any more than you wished that the cup should pass from you. Turner's Christian spite pursued me to the very end. I was the only Oxbridge scholar of our year not to receive the customary adieu of forty pounds worth of books. I did win the Latin Verse Prize, however. I used the book token to buy Keats's poems, for piety's sake, and Willie Maugham's *A Writer's Notebook*, for the sake of example.

We went our separate Oxbridge ways. I do not know how we happened to see each other, certainly not by any pre-arrangement, at Hyde Park Corner, when Beetle was about to catch a 52 bus to Willesden. She and I had just had our last evening together before I went back up to Cambridge for whatever term it was. She was in tears and you were, as was not unusual, an interested witness of others' distress. I never saw you in any such condition. She took her bus and I was left talking to you, wishing that you had not seen what you did. Was I not also just slightly proud of her distress? *On n'arrive jamais au bout de la vérité*, as you were never heard to say.

Over the years, you wrote me a letter or two, never quite as clever as expected. Your handwriting was oddly characterless, like a banal disguise. Your speciality was sudden, silent incursions, like a spy who chooses, from time to time, to disclose his presence as reminder of his furtive vigilance. When the Footlights Revue of 1954 went to the Oxford Playhouse, before proceeding to London, you must already have gone down. Having done his National Service in the Navy, Jeremy was still in residence. I had tea with him and his fiancée, Janet. She flattered and embarrassed me by asking, on a solicited walk across Christ Church Meadows, whether I thought she, a comely blonde, of solid build, would be 'good for Jeremy'. Cast as the witch of End/or, I said, with discreet bluntness, that I knew nothing about her and not much more about Jeremy. It occurred to me that the whole Carthusian ethos was hostile to any form of genuine relationship between the boys. The system was calculated to make all ambitions public and vertical. While advocating the team spirit, it made every boy the rival, in some regard, of others. Jeremy and Janet married and had six children.

I had heard somehow, perhaps from you, that you planned to break free and go to Argentina. Did you have some kind of rendezvous with your romantic scoundrel half-brother or merely an appetite to emulate his *picaro* life? French and German might be of small use to you *là-bas* but I was sure that you would soon achieve fluency in Spanish. Meanwhile, what you learned from Charterhouse's German beak, Dr Gerstenberg, came in handy in the circles into which you insinuated yourself with customary agility. No few Nazis, Adolf Eichmann included, had been subtilized out of Europe into Argentina, with the help of charitable Benedictines. Their fugitive faction may have been exclusive; it was not at all furtive. Juan Perón, although more Musso than Adolf, had nothing against Nazis. Paraguay's General Stroessner, more Adolf than Musso, welcomed them. He did nothing that I know of to persecute the Jews of Asunción who had a street full of shops Beetle and I visited fifteen years ago.

You were, I am sure, amused to happen on company which never questioned your Aryan credentials and took your secret amusement as deference, its counterfeit. I had no keen wish to see you again, yet you haunted my imagination. I thought you cursed with goodness, a Christian halter that you might not be sorry to shuck. I imagined Argentina as Conrad depicted it in *Nostromo* and Luis Borges in his brief stories, a place of Latin manliness and knives, where galloping gauchos brought down stampeding cattle by flinging their *bolos*.

The first of the novels I wrote in Fuengirola had the Keatsian title *A Wild Surmise*. It was set in an imaginary South American country called San Roque (a village of that name was on our way to Gibraltar, where Lipton's was the only place on the coast to find fresh butter). My anti-hero was called Carn but I dwelt, without animus or affection, on Robin Jordan as my model. Carn, with its fleshy connotations, was taken from a quiet, tough fair-haired boy with whom I had been at prep school. I feared that I should never be so calm and meatily sure of myself. Carn in my novel was and was not you. Years of separation pitched you in a new, more tricky light. I described what I saw and reported what I heard in my *fort intérieur*.

The need for a plot required me, as Gilbert Ryle used to say, to 'unpack' you. I wrote you as a loner, slightly dangerous, watchful and, for fictional purposes, sexier than you had seemed at C'house. I avenged myself on you out of curiosity not rancour. I always enjoy playing a character utterly other than myself. I/you landed in San Roque, with a few pounds, and toyed with seducing a well-spoken ex-pat oil man's beautiful wife, more for something to do than out of lust, easily slaked with a local whore, Chatita; love did not come into it, but Carn dares to think that Chatita likes him.

The story involved the sale of refined machine oil to the 'natives' as cooking oil; implausible but based on truth:

something that had happened in Morocco not long before. Carn is last seen on his way out of San Roque, heading up stream towards Paraguay. On the way he sits down with some gauchos and shares their meal, knowing that the oil in which the steaks were being cooked could well be poisonous. Carn bore some resemblance to Hemingway's Robert Jordan, in *For Whom the Bell Tolls* (which rings scarcely truer to republican Spain than my San Roque to South America), but he was undoubtedly my you, your me.

Two years later, Adolf Eichmann was smuggled out of Argentina in a packing case by Mossad and put on trial in Jerusalem. Somehow – your hint or my fancy – I had the impression that you might have known him. I have often toyed with making a fiction of it. My negligible German put the necessary impersonations beyond my scope. When was it, I wonder, that you sent me that brown foolscap envelope with some thirty pages of handwritten fiction? I opened it with a surge of antique apprehension. I had published several novels, but I feared that your text would pulse with genius. It did not. I cannot remember what it was about. One more amateur scrawl, neither silly nor revealing, it was a cover story.

I could easily imagine you, in another dose of Carn, treasuring the knowledge that you were socialising with the pseudonymous Eichmann. Polite as you needed to be, you doubled as a vengeful and a complicit nemesis, excited not by the possibility of being the vessel of justice but more, much more, by the power you had over a man who had no idea that his life was in your hands. The sweetness of that power disposed you to postpone its use. You might well in truth have met the publicly pseudonymous Eichmann, either by chance or as a result of your curious aptitude for being adjacent to singular specimens, as to me in my lonely study. Your neutrality was a form of compassionate sadism. Might you not have been tempted to give Adolf the impression that you sympathised with his fears, if not with what warranted them? Your smile could be read as a sort of promise even as it stood for the power that encouraged him to see it so. Threat and reassurance all at once, you were the considerate blackmailer, the more unnerving for wanting only that twitch of grateful apprehension at the sight of you.

In 1976, the *Sunday Times* threw a warm good riddance party for my patron Jack Lambert, the long-serving literary editor. I was among a select company invited to a barge on the Little Venice Canal to raise a glass to a man who, in unspoken, well-known truth, was being eased out of a job he had had no wish to renounce. He was kept on the strength, as 'chief reviewer', but relieved of his selective clout. Hugh Trevor-Roper was of the company. When I reminded him of Charterhouse, he winced. How many distinguished O.C.'s thought well of the school? Like Simon Raven, T.-R. wished he had been an Etonian; colleger, of course. I suspect he would have been happier as a classicist than as the historian he became. Seemingly unaware of the arrogance he displayed, in his early time as a history don, he made bold to correct Maurice Bowra's Greek and was surprised when his emendations were ungratefully received. I suspect that he had hoped to be embraced, socially at least, by the Warden of Wadham, whose homosexuality was no secret and could be practised with immunity, even (if not especially) in those days, within Wadham's locked gates.

When I mentioned you, Trevor-Roper said that granting you the Holford had been the biggest mistake he had ever made. He had not yet endorsed the Hitler diaries as authentic, an error blatant enough to sink an outsider, but which did little to damage his reputation, much as it delighted his enemies. I tell you this, please believe me, not because I was convinced that you had committed any very scoundrelly act. T.-R. said only that you had 'gone to the bad', whatever that might mean.

I suspect that you neglected your studies and took to the louche, perhaps boozy, company of theatricals, females even. I smiled, as you might, and guessed that you had veered, with that emulative skill of yours, towards a life more like that of your brother, whose name was never disclosed. Trevor-Roper was, I suspect, seduced, nicely, when he interviewed you, with George Turner's eulogy at hand. What he abominated may have been not so much your conduct as his own gullibility, the downside of conceit. Hitler's ghost worked the same trick on him, revenge for the book which made T.-R.'s name, *The Last Days of Hitler*, a work of masterly, precocious, detective work.

In the early twentieth century, Beetle and I made a trip to Buenos Aires, then to Montevideo, before flying up to Paraguay. After visiting the ruins of the settlements created by the Jesuits in the wild lands between Asunción and the Argentine border, we crossed the long bridge over the Paraná between Posadas and Encarnación (scene of *The Honorary Consul*, that not very entertaining 'entertainment' by Graham Greene, complete with cute pooch). We drove north across the wide pampas towards Iguazu, where the air over the junction with Brazil scintillates with spray from a suite of waterfalls. On the way, we passed a brave, a procession of resigned, indignant country people, protesting in the void against some regulation that, no doubt, favoured big landowners.

Quite suddenly we saw a hedged property with a stilted sign in front of it: HOTEL TYROL. It needed little wit to guess that its brazen, inappropriate name (flatlands spread on all sides to the horizon) was wished on it by some unapologetic Nazi. His pensioners would be suited by a sequestered property in a setting unapproachable without clear notice. I thought immediately of you. How had I learned, as I certainly had, that at one point you were hired by a set of *émigré* Germans – i.e. unredeemed Nazis – as an armed watchman? You carried a pistol, you must have told me, and rode a horse around the perimeter of the property, an equine Talos. So much for the conscientious objector you played when avoiding C'house khaki.

I doubt that you ever had cause to fire the Mauser with which you were loaded, but I could imagine your duplicitous pleasure as you protected men like Eichmann, perhaps Eichmann himself. You could smile and charm your employers while knowing, as they never guessed, that you could as well turn your weapon on them as on any avenging intruder. You were, I fancy, superbly bolstered by what no one guessed you might do. The vanity of those who were still hoping for the fourth Reich was trumped by a mounted hireling privy to their history and easy with their language. Conformity doubled with dissidence, in no matter what context you figured; deutero-Rimbaud, proto-Rambo, your *je* was *un autre*. How long did you stay in Argentina, what women did you enjoy, as you later indicated you did? Did you ever fire that gun? Chekhov's dramatic principles would require its use; life abides by no such aesthetic.

In the early Sixties, I was writing novels and became, for a while, a star screenwriter. Beetle and I had three children and were basking in more money than I had ever imagined or wished to make. In the spring of 1968, *Far From the Madding Crowd*, directed by John Schlesinger from a script by me, was due to open in New York. An ad in the *New York Times* promised that he and I would in the big city for the première. Before we left England, you called us, having obtained our number, I don't doubt, by a dose of your usual charm. I am sure it was not beyond you to smile effectively in the telephone. You said that you were now living on Staten Island with a wife that was not your first and your two, was it?, children. You proposed to drive to Kennedy Airport and meet our plane. I was flattered and pleased, I fear, that you had been alerted by so brazen a trumpet.

We flew first class, Schlesinger, Julie Christie, Terry Stamp, and who all else and arrived to be met by a posse of newsmen and publicists. Confident that you would be waiting for us, Beetle and I declined to go into the city in one of the waiting limos. When we came through customs and immigration (quite quickly thanks to my American passport) we scanned the concourse for your smiling welcome. We waited, we wondered. You never arrived. We took a cab to the Plaza and were soon being shown into a large suite, the wide sitting room with two bulky televisions. The assistant-manager took a look round and announced himself embarrassed. I assumed that he had realised that this was John Schlesinger's suite. His embarrassment was because there were no flowers. A little while later, the telephone rang. You were downstairs in the lobby. I seem to remember that I went down to find you while you were already on the way up in the elevator.

You offered Beetle small apology for not having been at Kennedy to meet us. There had been a problem at home. Living on Staten Island made it impossible to hurry. We understood, of course. I think you were married to your second wife. You were wearing an off-white macintosh. We talked for a while and then you left. Did we discuss meeting on another occasion? You were working for an advertising agency in Manhattan, weren't you? You seemed to be parading something, but we were not sure what. How much you had changed? Although more worldly, you seemed not very different. There were few critical bouquets for *Far From the Madding Crowd*. The première was no sort of success. Hardy's rustics were unintelligible to American ears; Julie kept her clothes on; what was there to like? A turkey then, the movie is a classic now.

I do not think that you ever wrote to me again. In 1981, I agreed to do an evening about Byron at the Queen Elizabeth Hall in a Festival of the Romantics. It would be more accurate to say that Alan Bates was going to play Byron and I was going to supply text and continuo. It was no big deal. I spent most of the day reassuring Alan that he understood B.'s verses perfectly and would perform them with his usual cleverness. By the time we were in the improvised greenroom, getting ready for the reading, I had had little time for the nerves which suddenly possessed me. Alan proved as calm as professionalism required.

As we prepared to go on, someone clapped me on the shoulder. I looked up with some kind of irritation, unless it was apprehension, looked and looked again and then, of course, knew who it was. Once again, you had seen the announcement of the Festival in the paper and were impelled to make contact. Living in London, you had a new, beautiful Argentinian wife on your arm. You were amused, if not slightly patronising, when I told you that I was still married to Beetle. She was, I think, already front of house. There was no time to talk. Did we exchange addresses and numbers? I think not. You were, I suspect, touching wood. In my notebook there are a couple of pages describing Alan's bravura performance and the rather good notices which followed. You are not mentioned at all. I never saw you again. I cannot say that I am any sorrier than I imagine you to be. We were never truly friends, but we were truly something: witnesses? Never of quite the same things.

Bien a toi, Fred.

TO WILLIAM SOMERSET MAUGHAM.

Dear Mr Maugham,

Am I the last suburban innocent for whom certain writers were distant demi-gods? Are you the last of those who replied in handwriting to a callow correspondent unknown to you (and who, as you remarked, omitted to date his letter)? Today, the deconstruction of literary fame is a noisy industry. Biographers are as quick to muddy renown as to displace attention onto their own verbiage. Yesterday's masters totter on pedestals that double for pillories. For all their disparagements, you continue to be more readable than your critics. Literary assayers have rarely rated you highly. I recall that in 1944 Cyril Connolly spoke up, against the current vogue, for *The Razor's Edge*. Thirty years before, an earlier pundit had been surprised by the merits of *Of Human Bondage* after a sight of the proofs you were reading on the way to the Front.

The latter title does not promise that you had conned Spinoza's work *de bout en comble*; it does intimate the range of your culture. Has any delving Ph.D. student yet sought out what you read or learned while a student in nineteenth-century Heidelberg? Odd that you never, if I remember rightly, created a German character or parodied a German phrase, as you did *par bleu* (as 'by blue') in a short story? Did your want of Oxbridge provenance have something to do with the Establishment's reluctance to embrace you? Morgan Forster, neither as prolific nor as varied, never as amusing, was welcome both in Bloomsbury and, for many years of residence, at King's College, Cambridge. 'Dadie' Rylands, the *arbiter deliciarum* of King's, entertained you gladly, and no doubt relished your porcupine wit; but you were never embraced in any quasi-Apostolic clan, though you were, as you put it, three-quarters

315

more queer than straight. You became too successful for your own standing among the literary élite. When Edmund Wilson 'made shift' to read your short stories, his sneer was primed by your theatrical successes. Which of his plays was ever staged on Broadway (or off)?

Doubleness served you well where it mattered most: in the work. A British subject, born in the British embassy in Paris, your first language, until you were eight years old, was French. You recall being shipped to England after your parents' deaths. You called a taxi a *fiacre*. Your mother's disappearance left a lifelong trauma; her picture always at your bedside. Was her involuntary desertion relevant to a lifelong apprehension of female *mutabilité*? It was matched, whatever your dominant appetite, by the disconcerting and delectable otherness of so many of your female characters. Neither Forster nor Conrad, Hemingway nor Faulkner created such a lively variety. Your novels, stories and plays – from *Liza of Lambert*, through *Of Human Bondage, Rain, Home and Beauty, Theatre* to *Cakes and Ale* and *The Painted Veil* – have women at the heart of things, never submissive, seldom conformist, often wantonly unpredictable, rarely foolish. The only woman you confessed to having loved was an actress who became pregnant by another man. Poor Syrie loved you, but that was another story.

Your medical training (Evelyn Waugh is alone in being recorded as addressing you as 'doctor') armed you for case by case annotation. Biographers have made little of the significance of your time at St Thomas's, not least when dissecting cadavers. The clinical requirement to be unfeeling, the better to deliver a clear diagnosis, underlies the realism of your first novel, *Liza of Lambeth*. How typical of you to report that Edmund Gosse, that dominating Edwardian pundit, continued to greet you, after you had published any number of other books, with 'Ah my dear Maugham, I so admired your *Liza of Lambert*. How wise you were never to write anything else!'

The apparent callousness of what some critic called 'the medical mode' confronted what other English writers found distasteful or – key word – unnecessary. You contrived to be outspoken without using a single vulgar word. Ignoring ideology, you peddled no cure for the human condition, money the best placebo: you rated it a sixth sense which made it possible to enjoy the other five. The doubleness of the doctor, who guards against involvement, let alone excitement, was the key to your unblinking manner. Others elaborated; you looked, listened, took note.

As a small, lonely, foreign-seeming boy, translated to Whitstable, where your uncle was the vicar, you were deprived not only of parental affection but also of the *netteté* of Parisian *argot*. Your tendency to cliché in English was an echo of French writers, *dans ses oeuvres*, having recourse to standard phrases. One of the early drafts of, I think, *Of Human Bondage*, has the Gallic expression 'natal day' corrected to 'birthday'. It has become a commonplace to compare you with Guy de Maupassant. Your stories, often with a sardonic twist – 'today she weighs twenty stone' – tend to be drawn, unfiltered, from the bottomless well, if not pit, of life. Your humour rejoiced in that moustachioed face, unsmiling ossature. Playing at starchy, you were amused to portray smug first-class passengers on the ship of fools who lacked the grace of those they were pleased to mock. 'At that moment I did not entirely dislike Mr Kelada' was as far as you went to side with the outsider. It was, typically, further than it seemed.

Your longer stories owed little to anyone. *The Alien Corn* was remarkable for its treatment of Jews. Is there any other English author of the 1930s who dealt so candidly or so amiably with the Chosen? Here again, your sympathies were salted with paradox. The quasi-hero is a handsome, fair-haired, straight-nosed young man who could easily pass for a Gentile. The twist is that he wants nothing other than to be a first-class pianist, an allegedly common Semitic talent. His brother, whose origins are stamped on his face, wants only to play life with a straight bat, sport the old school tie, inherit what passes for the family seat in parliament.

With sly angularity, you tell the story from the point of view of Ferdy Rabenstein, a rich, cultivated Jew. Proust's Swann crossed with Benjamin Disraeli, he disdains to conform, in dress or ornament, while being as cultivated as any Fellow of All Souls. You are pleased to relish his company and, by doing so, pass comment, without a direct word, on another batch of 'betters': the *literati* who, following Mr Eliot and who all else, affected Christian contempt for Jews. What classy English writer, from Dickens and Trollope, to Greene and Priestley, failed to scorn and caricature Jews? You remarked only that 'tolerance is another name for indifference'; an epigram more shrug than smirk. What better proof of unbiased realism than to entrust your investments to that Californian Jew, beginning with A, who amply rewarded your confidence? You did have a pompous lawyer character in *Home and Beauty*, I think it was, called A. Braham. Why not?

Your believable accounts of the misdeeds of British planters in Malaya during the *entre-deux-guerres* summoned a lasting black mark against you. Only a cad, it was said, would let the side down by revealing his compatriots to be prigs and adulterers. As for *The Letter*, based on a notorious actual case, it should never have been posted. Not only did you tell salacious tales; you were said to have abused the hospitality of guileless colonials. Who can doubt that they rejoiced in entertaining famous company? Were you greatly dismayed to be ill-regarded by face-savers in the UK or its imperial possessions? You left it to Kipling, whose work you told me you admired, to endorse imperial conceit. Whatever tributes he paid to Gunga Din, he also gift-wrapped the white man's burden. You not only cracked the code by which the

British kept certain things to themselves, you also rejoiced in mocking the pretensions it mantled. You had been the first to say, before the Great War, that the British would discover the flimsiness of what they took to be the deference of lesser breeds when they ran out of money. Constantine Cavafy warned Morgan Forster against what happens to people if, as the Greeks had, they lack the gold to subsidise their vanity. Now we know.

Noël Coward, who succeeded you as the West End's darling, was pleased, in his later days, to denounce you as a spent force, unloving and unloved. His sugary version of *Our Betters* had been his 1938 play *Cavalcade*. Flag-waving ingratiated him with the public and flaunted Britannia's dominion over palm and pine. His cinematic maritime captaincy, in *In Which We Serve*, made him a celluloid war hero. Staying up with his ship, he was rewarded with a knighthood. Your only published war work was an unsentimental story set among French peasants during the Occupation. To be made a Companion of Honour, if not measly, did more to emphasise your not receiving the O.M. than to celebrate your qualities. When Jack Priestley was granted the latter sign of royal favour, Rebecca West told me that it debased the last of those posterior initials worth having. Who else, I wonder, is or has been a Companion of Honour?

Despite (or was it because of?) his pinpricking references to your obsolescence, you asked Coward to lunch, one hot midsummer day, at the Villa Mauresque. Guileless, not to say smug, enough to accept the invitation, he was allotted an unshaded place at the head of a long table, the rest of it cooled by a lowered awning. While you and the remaining guests were served with *salade niçoise*, summery delicacies and chilled wine, Sir Noël was enthroned in the full sun of a Riviera noon where he alone was favoured with roast beef, horseradish, roast potatoes, Brussel sprouts and a full-bodied claret.

The true blue knight, you told him, deserved a genuine English Sunday lunch.

Coward's sexual appetites were more discreetly, and more thoroughly, indulged than yours. Thanks not least to his loudly advertised, if chaste, passion for Gertie Lawrence, he and his lovers escaped the kind of scandal which your 'secretary' Gerald Haxton excited, back in the 1920s, by making blatant advances to some young person in – can it have been? – the Natural History Museum. '*Tous les goûts sont dans la nature*' was your seemingly impersonal apology for what had done for Oscar Wilde. You had the courage, at the time of his martyrdom, to be a signatory to a petition on his behalf. It left you forever alert to how society can enjoy a wit's Yoricking for a while and then, as you put it, crumple him like a piece of wastepaper and chuck him in the bin.

Haxton's arrest was not publicly connected to you. There was a gentleman's agreement – engineered, was it, by your insufferable barrister brother Frederic, later Lord Chancellor? – not to make too much of it provided he, an American citizen, left England and never came back. You already owned the Villa Mauresque; it now became your permanent home. When married to Syrie, the mother of your only daughter, Liza, you had a smart Mayfair address: Hill street, was it? Once Haxton had been denied entry to the country, you visited London alone, quite regularly, but never again had an English residence. Might it be that Max Beaverbrook's diplomacy had some part in saving Haxton's bacon? Years later, the Beaver was blamed for having lured you into the revelations, hardly startling by today's standards, in the volume you called *Looking Back*. It was loudly serialised in the *Sunday Express. Donnant-donnant*?

Born abroad, as were Cavafy, Lawrence Durrell and Kipling, whatever pride you took in your nationality, you lacked nostalgia for home ground. Embarrassed by your poverty, even after you began to be successful and were invited to vivify the company at Edwardian country house parties, you regarded the vanities of your compatriots, grand or parochial, with persistent scorn: 'We see life in the raw at our golf club' (*For Services Rendered*). Your diction and style were indelibly in period – you are the last person I ever heard use 'omnibus' to designate a form of transport – but rectitude doubled for irony: the more proper your tone, the more scathing the nuance.

Brother Frederic was a particular target. Deny that you had him in mind when you wrote that judges should have a roll of toilet paper on the haughty desk in front of them, to remind them of what they have in common with the rest of humanity. Did someone tell you of the occasion at the Savile Club when Frederic, a man of no great stature, was being wontedly self-important? Maurice Richardson, an amateur boxer of some strength, picked him up and sat him, legs dangling, on the high mantelpiece and said, 'Sit there and tick away till someone comes and rescues you' and left the room.

When I was lucky enough to be your guest for tea at the Villa Mauresque, you quoted Kipling's 'What know they of England who only England know?' At the time, October 1954, he was out of style, but you did not doubt his qualities. Although *The Razor's Edge* dealt, with surprising and sustained respect, with oriental philosophy (the long passage bracketed to allow incurious readers to resume further on), you renounced India as a topic Kipling had made his own. You never mentioned Forster, so far as I know, in essays or in conversation. *A Passage to India* may be an undoubted classic but I suspect that its adroit squeamishness, when it came to what happened, or not, in the Marabar Caves, you took to be as much artful as art. Subtlety and funk can be heads and tails of an author's wish to tease the knowing while offering no offence to the censorious. Tired of concocting heterosexual romances, Forster renounced publishing fiction. His one 'gay' novel, *Maurice*, a squeamish expression of coming out, was withheld until after his death. It is no great argument for candour. You were unstinting in your praise of *The Old Wives' Tale*: 'Arnold (Bennett) has written a masterpiece'.

Medical training, crossed with admiration for the tartness of French prose, disposed you not to flinch from any aspect of the human comedy. *Powder Puff Percy* was a brief example of your ability at once to pander to readers' appetite for deriding suspected pansies, as my father's generation called them, and to deplore their narrow-mindedness. The Leavisite charge of 'immaturity'– meiotic for queerness, especially regarding W.H. Auden – was never your style, but you conceded something by declaring El Greco's genius to be decorative, not to say camp.

Scrutiny, the Leavises' school mag, paid no heed to your novels, but it went out of its way to dismiss *Don Fernando*, a memoir of youthful travels in Spain. It was said to show how superficial your knowledge of the country and its culture. *Don Fernando* never pretended to be other than a distant cousin to *Old Calabria* by Norman Douglas. You knew the old rascal, I recall, in Capri: was he not the subject of your story about a man who decided to spend everything he had and then commit suicide at sixty-five and then, at sixty-five...? *Don Fernando* is memorable for your description of going with a young prostitute who, when undressed, proved to be no more than a child. You asked what had led her to go on the streets. She said, '*Hambre*'. Hunger. You gave her money and went back down the stairs.

George Steiner liked to quote Paul Valéry on '*la profondeur de la surface*'. Your disinclination to describe the inner lives or thoughts of your characters endorsed the view that noting word and deed trumped affectations of psychological insight: better Stendhal than Virginia Woolf. Your preference for following characters around, rather than building crenelated verbal castles, disposed you to find Henry James's fiction so stuffed with refinement as to lack any relevance to the come-and-go, rough and tumble, of human intercourse. H.J.'s snub, when he failed to include you in that pre-Great War list of young writers he deemed worthy of attention, was repaid by your disdain for his stories. You declared them so swollen with nuance that next to nothing happened; he canned beans but never spilt them.

You saved your sharpest shafts for H.J.'s darling, Hugh Walpole. You less depicted than picked him to pieces in *Cakes and Ale*. The character of Alroy Kear (how many people recognised the pun on *Kir Royal?*) nailed best-selling Walpole as a literary climber of shameless agility and small wit. That you did yourself no favours in your first-personal guise was at once candid and prophylactic: portraying yourself as a crosspatch, you anticipated the knockers by knocking yourself. Walpole is said to have been mortified by your scorn for him and his work. After happening on his *The Inquisitors*, I was surprised to find how eerily entertaining it was; sorry about that.

The nicest story about Walpole as a handsome young person is that he as good as invited Henry James to, as they used to say, take advantage of him. H.J. is said to have responded, 'I can't, I can't'. The brevity was as ambiguous as it was untypical. Was the denial moral or physical? That 'obscure hurt', incurred when James slid down a fence in his Bostonian youth, was never specifically diagnosed. Did it render him literally impotent or did the obscurity lie in the neutralising effect on his appetites? Max Beerbohm sentenced him to be remembered, with a smile, as the stout stooper in the *Hotel des Trois Couronnes* – scene of *Daisy Miller* – sniffing the shoes left outside doors for cleaning, in order to deduce what was happening inside. You told me that you had recently visited Max in Rapallo. 'I was sh-shocked at the change in him. He seemed a very old man. Of course he *is* a very old man. He must be at least eighty. But he l-looked a hundred and fifty.'

Unlike Forster, Henry James was never silenced by inability at least to imagine heterosexual passion. *Portrait of a Lady* was a transvestite fantasy of the beautiful Isabel surrounded by vivid varieties of male beastliness or inadequacy. H.J. subscribed so thoroughly to the conceits of the British that they could not but think well of him. Unlike the raffish Frank Harris, he dined many times more than once at the best tables in London and took care to be so replete with refinements that manners passed for manliness. There was sweet irony that you can but have relished in the fact that H.J.'s humiliation on the 1895 first night of *Guy Domville* coincided with that of Oscar Wilde's triumphant *The Importance of Being Earnest*. Having read most of James's work, I remain slightly surprised that Leavis should have made him the culminating master of the Great Tradition of English fiction. I ain't much of a Janeite either.

Your successes in the Edwardian West End were capped by that *Punch* cartoon showing the shade of Shakespeare sulking at the sight of playbills advertising your work in four theatres in the same season. Many writers have been pleased to assume that theatrical and cinematic success amounted to something little better than prostitution. It may pay well but, they like to hold, it requires no more than a willingness to be what H.J. called (after his thudding failure) 'base'. That rare Jamesian monosyllable said it all, but not quite enough: in neither theatre nor the movies is success as easy as it is convenient for the condescending to presume.

You were Tiresian enough to bat for both sides. That passion for a beautiful American actress, with whom you broke only when she became pregnant by another man, may have been decisive in disposing you to play safe, though never as safe as you hoped, by relying on your own sex for pleasure, if never for love. When Haxton died, you were, it is said, deeply bereaved. In public, you said only that he had been 'useful', not least because he had a facility for luring strangers into revealing conversation, which you were not slow to record. It became a regular lament of yours that you had never known reciprocal love (scarcely Syrie's fault, was it?). Your house guest Cyril Connolly was bold, and charming, enough to dare to greet your lamentations with '...although the night grew chilly, no one cared to poke poor Willie'.

The young Paddy Leigh Fermor earned no laurels when, seeking to entertain the company, he imitated a stammering man. You were touchy enough, on that occasion, to say 'goodbye' rather than 'good night'. He would, you explained, be on his way to the station before you came down to breakfast. Stories of your sarcasm are the small change of small people. Beverley Nichols, in blazer, neck-square and white flannel bags, affected to be hurt when you greeted him, as you were on your way to your desk (I was at the auction where Godfrey Winn bid £500 for it), with 'Good morning, B-Beverley. You're looking very s-s-spruce!'

The story I like best is of when you went with Alan Searle, in the long evening of your days, to the Hôtel de Paris, in Monte Carlo, for dinner. On the way in, Alan Searle spotted George Axelrod sitting in the foyer. With his usual (as I experienced it) grace, Searle whispered to you that it would be appreciated if you were to say a word or two to the author of *The Seven Year Itch*, a current Broadway smash hit. You went over to George and said, 'I am t-told that you are a very brilliant young p-playwright and you have just had a g-g-great s-s-success. All I can say is, thank G-god I'm too old to g-give a shit.'

I like to imagine that George agreed to be amused. We went with him and Joan one evening to have dinner with Christopher Isherwood and Don Bachardy in Santa Monica. Isherwood opened the door and apologised for not having put us off; he was afraid he had rather a bad cold. George said, instantly, 'My dear Christopher, any cold of yours is a cold of mine'. *Chapeau?*

You have never been accused of being a writer of the first rank, still less did you ever claim to be. A diligent worker, you were sometimes surprised by the speed with which the best novelists (Stendhal not least) could dash off their work, even in longhand. You yourself ceased to write books because you suffered so painfully from arthritis that you could no longer hold a pen for sustained periods. Unlike Henry James, you never had recourse to dictation. The stammer, I guess, would come between you and the fluency which gave your imagination its scope. Why did your facility, when it came to dialogue, never incline you to use a typewriter?

A stammer seems an odd affliction for someone who so swiftly put words into other people's mouths. Dialogue your forte, you were garrulity itself in printed and performed work. You shared your misfortune with my contemporaries Ken Tynan and Jonathan Miller. Both spoke with little hesitation when publicity and acclamation were available. You had the wit to turn what seemed a disability into some kind of asset when, at the dinner at the Garrick to celebrate your eightieth birthday, you got to your feet to respond to the toast to your health. You began by saying 'C-c-contrary to what others might fear, reaching my present age had its c-c-compensations'. The Old Party, as you came to call yourself, opened his mouth to go on, it seemed, but no words came out. The silence became all but embarrassing. You stood there and stood there and then you said, 'I'm just trying to think what they c-could p-possibly be'. Relief and admiration charged the ovation that followed. Timing is of the essence in stand-up.

I have a notion – a phrase you used more than once – that your stammer was the result of a kind of mental chicane: the multiplicity of voices and languages in your brain raced, collided and jammed when it came to speech. I advanced this theory, rather generously I thought, when taken to lunch, by one of today's Alroy Kears, with one of your imminent biographers, a titled youngish lady. In the style of today's allegedly classless Britain, she appropriated my contributions but her bibliography did not mention my several times reprinted monograph about you and your work, a pretty compliment, as you might have said.

One evening in the late 1950s, hearing that you were in London, I arranged a game of expert bridge for you at Crockford's. Kenneth Konstam, Edward Mayer and Guy Ramsey made up the four. You wore careful glasses and played with modest competence. My little tribute did something to repay a long debt. *Of Human Bondage* changed my life. In the days before television, a fifteen-year-old flat-bound suburban only child had little to do but read. I went through my parents' library (except for that complete Dickens) with greedy curiosity. When my mother had mumps, I was banned from going in to see her. I had literally all day to read that illustrated edition my parents had brought from New York.

It included an image of the lusty Miss Wilkinson undressing down to her stays. She was supposed to look a fright, but I saw her as quite stimulating. Your Philip Carey spoke directly to me as no other fictional character ever had (though C.S. Forester's Captain Hornblower furnished wartime fantasies of life on the ocean wave). My miseries at school could, you taught me, be turned to literary use, provided – the proviso was of the essence – what was made of them was self-deprecating. One had to make a model of oneself and then be sure to be merciless in the moles-and-all department. I had always wanted to be a writer; you taught me how: work, work, work; and never wait for inspiration.

Is it graceless to remark that, when I went back to *Of Human Bondage*, after my mother gave me a handsomely bound copy, I was dismayed at some of the awkward locutions it contained? I had something of the same surprise when re-reading *Le Rouge et le Noir*. In both masterpieces, the vividness of the characters made grammarian's quibbles irrelevant to the pleasure they continue to give. Flaubert said of Balzac, '*Quel écrivain, s'il savait écrire*' [What a writer had he known how to write]. So much for Flaubert, you might have said, while never denying him to his place in the sun.

Merci, maître. Frederic Raphael.

Dear Jack,

Who save his family and a very few others will remember Pat Murphy? It was thanks to that substantial Irishman, broad chest, few medals, that I gained access to your attention. As amiable in practice as he was pitiless in theology – while all Jews were deemed perfidious and meet for roasting, Peter Shaffer, Brian Glanville and I were among his favourite writers – Pat was a managing editor of the *Sunday Times* in Roy Thomson's time and an acquaintance of my father Cedric when he was in charge of Shell's relations with the Press. I played cut-in bridge with Murphy at Crockford's. In any celestial team selection, he will not be among the chosen.

Complacency was as characteristic of the 1950s as patriotism. At the cinema – not yet 'the movies' – nice undergraduates – not yet 'students' – waited and stood at attention for the national anthem to be played (and made no polite way for curfew-dodgers). Until the humiliation of Suez, we managed, through narrowed eyes, to believe that Britannia still ruled most of the waves. In the humanities, clever boys impressed examiners by a capacity for accurate regurgitation. Doubling on the spot was a very British exercise. I owed my Cambridge scholarship not least to having been able, when asked, to spell out every detail of the Sullan constitution. With lucky foresight, I had learned its sullen provisions – disqualification of Tribunes of the People from future office, etc. – by memorising a crib my father had underlined at Oxford. Learning by heart, prose and verse, was known as 'repetition': saying the right things, again, in the right accent, was central to advancement. Syntactical rectitude held society together. I recall your wince when a contributor wrote 'photos' for 'photographs'.

In a time of formality, the only Mr in English studies was Mr Eliot; it might have been short for Monsignor. He had declared *ex cathedra* that we lived in 'an Age of Criticism'. As the Sixties began, he retained archiepiscopal dignity among aspiring *literati*. They had his word that pundits trumped journeymen. Karl Miller, my Cambridge contemporary and sometime Leavisite, quit the Treasury and shed his bowler over Suez. By 1962, he was literary editor of the *New Statesman*. When I presented myself in the hope of admission to the critical ranks, he asked, with no sort of a smile, what qualifications I might have for reviewing fiction. Unimpressed by my having published six novels, Karl handed me a thin volume by Erich Fromm on which to prove myself worthy of passage through his straitened gate. I was sighing over its lustreless pages when Pat Murphy called to say that you were eager to enrol me among your reviewers.

In your later forties, you had the handsome profile and modulated voice of a greying matinée idol. By way of *rite de passage*, you commissioned me to write a few hundred words on *The Dark Monarch* by Sven Berlin, a memoir of his days as a painter in the hot beds of St Ives. My notice, miming the going mandarin style, was prominently boxed on your pages just before the book was withdrawn for fear of libel. I had the small wit not to return my review copy when asked for it. It is quoted at £220 today.

My advent as regular fiction reviewer was saluted with monthly deliveries of all the yellow-jacketed new books on Victor Gollancz's list. V.G., who had named Beetle 'Sheba' when she worked for him, knew very well that I should review no more than one or two. The others, he surely guessed, while sweetening his house's reputation, would go to the bookseller next door to the *Old Cheshire Cheese*. The proprietor could be relied on to divvy up half of the published price, a welcome tax-free supplement to my £30 honorarium. When double yellow lines were introduced in Fleet Street, it became unprofitable to load the boot of our Vanguard with saleable volumes. I still have a good few of those too ponderous to tote. Laziness is every librarian's assistant.

Your editorial tutelage was vigilant and instructive. I remember you querying my use of 'whipcord' when ignorance had presumed it to have something to do with a ringmaster's disciplinary equipment. I was at liberty to applaud Jimmy Baldwin's *Another Country*, but you deplored excess of scorn when it came to Sybille Bedford. Her Sapphic provenance and international hook-ups had procured classy puffs. Her titled characters said 'How not?' to prove their Italian sources. Your scissors went into my ironies. You did not doubt that *A Legacy* was overrated, but if a book had little to be said for it, why denounce it at length? Another lesson learnt.

You seemed content, not to say complacent, in your literary editorial chair. Cyril Connolly and Raymond Mortimer were your page-topping stars, Julian (*né* Alphonse) Symons, Hugh Trevor-Roper and Charles Snow among middle-order players. Once in the team, I did a thousand words on four or five novels every two or three weeks. If it made fewer friends than enemies, I relished instant print and petty renown. My ambitions were without careerist purpose; I wanted merely to shine. I did notice, however, that my novels received more amiable attention in other papers once I was in a position to reciprocate favours, even if I did not. I received a note from a renowned publisher, whom I had never met, signed 'yours aye'. Better, I had a hand-written letter of thanks from Ivy Compton-Burnett (where the *hell* have I put it?). She lived in Oakwood Court, the same block of flats as my great-aunt Minny. If I have always thought it a matter of honour to be implacably fair to the work of those who have written ill of me, I rejoiced, quietly, in the sheathed menace which your favour bestowed. You announced that I was one of two reviewers you were proud to have discovered. The other was John Metcalfe; now a candidate for the 'Who he?' file. They all go into the dark, do we not?

You gave the impression of being content with your literary fiefdom. I seldom heard anyone in 200, Gray's Inn Road mention that you had had, as they used to say, 'a good war'. You never spoke of it yourself, but we all knew it. Roy Thomson's viceroy, Denis Hamilton, whom I never met, proclaimed enough pride in his war-time rank to be known, behind his back, as 'Major Major'. Your unmentioned D.S.C. and D.S.O. promised greater entitlement to respect. Heroism had left you, by the end of the war, in a state close to nervous and physical collapse, all but unable to speak. Who now knows what you saw or endured on the cruel sea before Nicholas Montserrat bottled it? The only story you ever told me was of when your M.T.B. was on patrol in the North Sea and the seaman on watch reported 'Heavy breathing on the port bow, sir'. Trained vigilance was rewarded with the sight of an errant whale's spout and sleek back.

Your return to Fleet Street came only after Catherine, speech therapist as well as comely lady, nursed you back to articulate self-assurance and into marriage. Passion for curative *bel canto* resonated in the tones I came to associate with you, even on the telephone. Did naval gallantry dock you of silly greed for top places in journalism? The prizes of peace called for more energetic guile than you cared to summon.

Your one abiding ambition was to succeed Harold Hobson (his wheelchair had exempted him from wartime service) as the *S.T.*'s drama critic. His regular deputy, you claimed to be content as you were, but that nasal double snort of yours – a hyphenated intake of breath in the middle of a sentence – smacked of swallowed pride. I never heard you speak ill, or particularly well, of anyone. Loyalties mattered more to you than standards: you were embarrassed by my scornful review of a poor novel by your former contributor Charles Snow, but you did not deny it publication. Your favourite writer was Saki in whose style, I suspect, your own short stories were pitched. They have never, I think, been collected. You mentioned, rather often, how gratified you were not to have been to university (i.e., to Oxford or Cambridge) after Tonbridge.

When I first worked at the *Sunday Express* in 1949, journalism was no target for graduates. Ten years later, Ken Tynan's insolence had given Beverley Baxter the heave-ho as the *Evening Standard*'s drama critic. Oxbridge smarties of my generation grew hot for by-lines. Set to leap from literary editor of the *New Statesman* to more rewarding perches, Nick Tomalin proved his nerve by writing the first loud article about the nuts and bolts of the Vietnam War. 'Zapping Charlie Cong' was a front-paged, first-hand account, in the *Sunday Times*, of going on a chopper-borne turkey-shoot conducted by US troops, black and white. It did something to endorse Harold Wilson's wisdom in keeping Britain out of the war. Peter Cook, you will remember, said that the British preferred the role of honest broker: no one was more honest and no one – boom-boom! – was broker. For all his insular fame, in time, Peter became charged with resentment at his friend and double-actor Dudley Moore's success as movie-star and ladies' man. When was enough ever enough when more was enjoyed by others? *Private Eye* became the vessel in which Cook brewed *ad hominem* sat/ire, mark of the deskbound crusader.

Nick's arrival at Thomson House warned of the insurgent threat to your greying eminence. He bumped into me in one of the corridors of editorial power just as he had heard that you had given me John Fowles's *The Magus* for review. He warned that it was overrated, less to support high literary standards than as a hint that, if I wanted in among the *gratin*, I should shy from enthusiasm as well as from irony which, he advised, never works in journalism. Having lived for some months on a Cycladic island, I did not need my card marked before declaring Fowles's fat account of being a schoolmaster – Nicholas Urfe, if you please – on the island of whatever he called Spetsai absurdly inflated. Fowles/Urfe had taught French, a language in which he made howlers of no rare order. If his Greek was better, he never flashed it (I did, a bit, in *April, June and November*). Fowles's trio of bestsellers, culminating in *The French Lieutenant's Woman*, was the soft fruit of pseudo-modernism grafted onto the trunk of the English novel.

Fowles impersonated the low-brow's idea of a highbrow. Didactic merchandiser, he made sure that his compositions, artfulness as art, never puzzled those at the back of the room. One phrase – 'I own the soft impeachment' – brags his modesty. Bearded and *superbe*, he flirted with audacity while taking no risk of losing the common reader. His first published novel, *The Collector*, a U-certificate precursor of *Lolita*, made erotic promises that its author, unlike Nabokov, was too squeamish – or was it too British? – to keep. It reminded me of a wartime fairground peepshow-machine, which promised sight of a nudist colony for those who inserted a penny. Click and a narrow ant-heap was disclosed. Did you know, Jack, that Nabokov's Humbert Humbert was originally named Lambert Lambert? What difference might that have made to how people read or smiled at you? Beetle was once in a minor road accident with a man called Fagin. Charles Dickens authorised me to deal with his demands for payment with split-the-difference disdain. Funny, I hope.

John was as unamusing in company as in print. So was Elizabeth, the stringy wife whom he had filched, with sublime self-righteousness, from a schoolmaster colleague on Spetsai. Common guilt can keep couples together; some revel, some are as John and Elizabeth were. All Fowles's novels, and *The Ivory Tower*, a novella about another mini-Aleister Crowley, made witless movies. No invented *maître-à-penser* can rise above the intellectual level of his creator. Fowles, like Henry Williamson, was an eager naturalist with suburban vanities. Pleasant enough to me in person, in his notebooks – they just happened to come to me for review – Fowles portrayed me as a latter day version of Proust's Bloch, little Marcel's *alter ego* who wore the Classics like a blazer of the club that wouldn't have him as a member. Maschler, Wiseman and Wesker were among Fowles's familiars. Hands up anyone who remembers him buying a round of drinks or supplying a bottle.

The best-sellerdom of *The Magus* promised that the convergence of publisher and pastrycook was upon us. Nick Tomalin was as critical of merchandising the word as he was its accomplice. Had things developed otherwise, we might have seen Nick contest Harry Evans's place. The latter was an *arriviste* from a different source. Apprenticeship in the *Northern Echo* gave him an education in practicalities, as editing the *Fruit Grower, Florist and Market Gardener* had you. Roy Thomson, a Canadian without the Beaver's lust for metropolitan eminence, was more at home with Harry than with Nick, though he recognised the savvy of the graduate musketeers (Joyce might say 'must-get-theirs') amongst whom Tomalin played d'Artagnan. He called on me, as a colleague, to help track down John Profumo when he had gone into hiding near our house in north Essex after being rumbled as a bald-headed liar to the House. Did he prefer expulsion from Westminster to humiliating his wife, Valerie Hobson? I hope I wasn't a help.

Nick's father Miles, who once wrote amiably to me on a topic that may have been Charterhouse, belonged to the C.P. An O.C. poet and Spanish Civil War veteran could be taken to be hardly worse than eccentric; connivance with alien cut-throats left no domestic trace. For Anthony Blunt, treason had a piquancy no single allegiance could ever supply. Straight-facedness mocked the institutions which second-order toffs served with all the groomed scruples of imposture. Kim Philby made Janus a traitorous adulterer; every false gesture had to ring true. Guy Burgess's outrageousness drew attention away from darker secrets. The nicest apology offered for Blunt's implicit endorsement of the Gulag was, so George Steiner told me, his alleged outrage, as a Poussin expert, at the sequestration of the latter's works in private hands. Mastery of the Queen's pictures was public distinction, furtive irony. The motion that, once exposed, he be expelled from the British Academy was rejected, just, by a majority that set intellectual resource above politics. He was, however, docked of his knighthood. Burgess could never be deprived of the O.E. tie he wore when on parade with western visitors to Moscow.

Nick Tomalin's inherited scorn for bourgeois society warranted ruthlessness to shine in it. The zest with which he displaced his Cambridge friend Karl Miller as literary editor of the *New Statesman* gave notice to those who tenanted enviable rungs. Claire, *née* Delavenay, boasted of marriage proposals from both Karl and Nick, before opting to love the latter. Karl, she told me, regretted that she was no longer the 'giggling armful' she had been when on show on King's Parade. Her French father had long since deserted her English, piano-teacher mother (now Wiki-billed as a composer), but Claire's *moeurs* had Gallic practicality: the prime reason, she told me, for having children was to be sure to have someone to care for you in old age. Her mother had told her how lonely it was to know that no one would ever again put an arm around her.

Mark Boxer, aka Marc the caricaturist, was another insurgent star of my generation, eager for come-on-in access to Thomson House. Simon Raven, my fellow-Carthusian, if only for a few months (before he was expelled for 'the usual thing'), was just old-fashioned enough to envy those who had had a war as good as yours; Tomalin, like Karl Miller and Boxer, being younger, had small respect for patriotic gallantry. Once bowlers were obsolete, none owned a hat to tip. Dr (later Sir) Jonathan Miller and chums stuck out their tongues at dated heroism in a sketch in *Beyond the Fringe*. When Peter Cook called on Jonathan, dressed as a wartime aeronaut, to feature in a 'futile gesture', involving self-sacrifice, he implied 'more fool them' when it came to The Few and those like yourself who had risked their lives for our soft living.

Satirists never had it so good as in the England that paid them to take the piss. When Harold Macmillan went sportingly into the front stalls as he had, in 1914, into the front line, where he was twice wounded, Peter Cook took prolonged pleasure in mowing him down again. No loyalties were reliable. In due course, Stephen Fry and Rowan Atkinson redug the trench warfare of the Great War and unearthed a protracted source of laughs and revenue. I went to a chiropractor who, in his teens, had been buried in mud for three days on the Somme. He advised me against heading the ball in the park games supervised by Brian Glanville, who parked his car with rare insolence under the edge of the park police station. When challenged, he declared himself 'Glanville of the Yard' and was duly saluted.

Semper fidelis was no sort of motto for the Sixties as against the sexual artilleryman's *ubique*. Karl Miller is said to have been startled to discover that a beautiful wife did little to abate appetite for other women. Beetle and I were soon meeting Cambridge wives in various states of disillusion. When Nick was taken with 'the Jay twin' (I never knew which), Claire called me and Beetle 'lucky things'; it presaged that we should not be forgiven.

Dr Leavis had sold his 'connection' the meta-puritanical myth of mature relationships. Back in the solemn early 1950s, I bumped into a bridge-playing research student called Hitchcock on Trinity bridge. Applying a Swan Vesta match to his grown-up pipe (it had a little lid hinged to the bowl), he asked me with urgent directness about the mechanics of sex. His lady love was coming to see him and he was innocent of anatomical expertise in the *meum-tuum* department. When I proceeded directly to the ins and outs of two-backed beastliness, Hitchcock (that was indeed his name) chose to go back to his rooms and re-read *Women in Love*.

For all his want of Oxbridge gloss, Harry Evans proved more threat than fellow-spirit as far as the old guard was concerned. He was a lean, short, un-young figure, given to quitting his editorial chair in order to patrol his new domain, like Henry V before Agincourt, in quasi-incognito. I met him several times on my way in and out of the lit'ry department (as your secretary, Miss Pomphret, aka *Pommes Frites*, pronounced it). On each occasion, not least because he was wearing a different style of glasses, I failed to recognise him. He would then say 'Harry Evans', quite as if he himself needed to confirm who he was. His off-the-peg rig was in discreet distinction from Mark Boxer's black four-buttoned, single-vented jacket and the *m'as-tu-vu* finesse which had the buttons covered in the same material as the jacket.

Mark's experience both as editor of *Granta* and as fashionable cartoonist qualified him to be founding editor of the *Sunday Times* colour supplement. Determined to be a shaper of things to come, Marc was the first post-war caricaturist to realise that satire and social climbing could be teamed in the haulage of fame. Never to have been clamped in his Osbert Lancastrian pillory was a demeaning exemption; my grateful nose grew longer under his pen. The satirists' common assumption was that English institutions were capable of sustaining, and rewarding, any amount of derision. They were daring children, calling out 'I hate you, England' (was that Jonathan Miller?), while collecting the rewards, social, sexual and financial, which patriotism once culled.

If they aped John Osborne scowling back in anger, they looked forward to prime places in the Almanack de Gotcha.

Boxer's camp might not have been to your taste; it scarcely threatened your status as literary satrap. Tomalin was a looser cannon, capable – it seemed – of being in at least two places at once, as he had been at Cambridge where he doubled as President of the Union, although no great speaker, and as an editor of *Granta* whose tenure was marked by no smart scribbles of his own. Like his *frère-ennemi* Karl, Nick had been wise enough to play the master of writers before being called on to deliver any evidence of wit in that domain. British justice rated judges higher than performers. 'Judge that ye be not judged' is the creed of on-the-makers. Nick once promised me, with as straight a face as he could compose at short notice, that he remained young because he had no executive ambitions. When the editor of the *Statesman*, Paul Johnson, bounced Karl Miller off the back of the book, Nick willingly took his friend's place before hop-step-jumping to a better one.

In my early pride as a published author, I sent Karl copies of my novels, to which he never responded with more than one typed line of acknowledgement. We lived in adjacent streets in Fulham, but never met. One day, Beetle heard that the Millers' son had had a serious-sounding accident in the playground of the Bousfield school to which our son Paul also went. I telephoned to ask how he was and, on hearing all was well, invited Karl and Jane to dinner that night along with Jim and Monica Ferman. Actually I asked Jane, who said she would have to check with Karl, who assented.

This was soon after he had been resigned, so to say, from the *Statesman*. At a time when a selection of the quasi-peerage (not yet called 'celebrities') were being canvassed for views on the Vietnam War, Kingsley Amis and Bernard Levin were in favour of the American mission. I had yet to articulate my position. At the dinner table, with no motive other than to stir the sluggish conversation, I asked, as I carved Beetle's much-too-good-for-them *filet de boeuf en croûte*, if Karl had strong views on the Eastern Question. I just happened – as Freud would never allow – to mention Nick Tomalin's Charlie Cong article on the still quite little war in Vietnam. I dared to say that it had tipped me towards turning down my thumbs on righteous zapping.

'What does he know about it?'

'Well, he has at least been there.'

'For twenty-four hours', Karl said.

'Twenty-four hours more than I have. First-hand experience has to outrank anything the rest of us may base our...'

'I don't think you have any right to say that.'

'At my own table', I said, nicely, 'I'll say what I fucking well please.'

We remained the Karl Millers's neighbours for many years. Our invitation was never returned. By the time Karl became editor of the *Listener*, however, he was eager to have me write for him. After being elevated to the *London Review of Books*, he ceased calling.

You and Catherine became our friends, of a kind. When we invited you to lunch at the Wick, you hired a car (an old-style Citroen, wasn't it?) to come to us in style. Living in Belsize Park, you elected not to run a motor, as you might still have called it. You enjoyed naming the uncommon flowers in Beetle's garden as well as her cooking and the St Emilion 1953 which I had bid for in Restell's wine auction. I had been alerted to the frequent bargain parcels by Robert Goodden, principal of the Royal College of Art, who lived in Dedham. Executors were obliged by law to dispose of cellared legacies by public auction, but not to advertise the sale at all loudly. Discretion allowed the *avertis* to benefit from their reticence.

Did you and Catherine ever ask us to your house? I remember that you took me to lunch at Scott's immediately after the Six Day War of June 1967. I had appeared for the first and only time in pole position on the BBC nine o'clock news when I handed in a petition at Number 10 Downing Street, soliciting the government not to dump the threatened state. Afterwards, Harold Pinter told me how pleased he was that 'we' had given the Arabs 'a bloody nose'. Idolators will accuse me of making that up, evidence of its now embarrassing truth. I gather that Harold was considering, in his later years, conversion to Roman Catholicism. That Damascus road is forever being resurfaced.

On the way into Scott's, you warned me, in an-honest-word-in-your-ear style, against triumphalism after Israel's victory. In the same season, since I had just won the Oscar, you were kind enough to warn me that my books would never again receive good notices. I was still innocent enough to believe in British justice; you were wise enough to know better. It was as close as we ever came to any sort of intimacy, though I do recall your speaking of 'thumbing it in softly' when engaged in conjugal activity. I never doubted your affection for Catherine, but you were not immune to female charmers. When Adelle Donen had made a well-timed solo entrance at a rather smart party of ours in 1964 (Stanley was shooting elsewhere), the large, loud room fell silent at the sight of her chic. You were soon in conversation with her and, when she made to leave, were quick to offer to see her, presumably, home. Why not indeed? I doubt whether, had she known of them, your D.S.O. and D.S.C. would have enhanced your chances as well as L.S.D. might have.

The office politics of the *Sunday Times* interested me only as gossip. I continued to enjoy your favour and came to the office now and again, to keep my place warm. On one such occasion, I was followed out of the room by one of your lieutenants. John Peter had escaped from Hungary in 1956 and, thanks to linguistic agility and sharp wits, graduated a few years later as an Oxford Ph.D. His intellectual credentials could not be questioned but, so he told me, you were rarely civil to him. What should he do? I asked whether he was willing, by making some bold complaint, to risk being ousted from his situation. He was not. In that case, I told him he had little choice but to play patience and bide his time. He was grateful, he said. Licensed cowardice always feels like prudence. Sometime later, you saw fit to tell me that Harry Evans, now editor of the paper, had referred to J.P. as 'that pushy little Jew'. Bernard Levin had written, back in the Fifties, that antisemitism was dead 'in this country'. You had been right to guess that Israel's triumph was likelier to sanction than to repress its return.

In 1969, Beetle and I bought a hilltop house in the Périgord *noir*. No sort of *château*, Lagardelle is a conflation of three cottages in what had once been a hamlet of some eighty souls. That its beams were eaten out with woodworm explained the price, some £18,000, much the same as Willie Maugham had paid for the Villa Mauresque. When his centenary came along, you seconded my suggestion that I write a 'front' about him for the weekend section of the paper. By 1972, we were sufficiently into an unended series of improvements to the place to invite you and Catherine to come and stay for a week, if you happened to be in France during the summer.

I drove the hour and a bit to Saulieu to meet you off the train from Austerlitz and carried your bags to the car. *Normal!* You were tired and in need of a rest. After inspecting the renovated apartment overlooking the swimming pool, you asked, as you presented Beetle with a small, unfinished cellophane bag of chocolate walnuts, whether you might stay ten days. As Sybille Bedford might have said, 'How not?' What else was there to say? The dejection which you had brought with you may have been alleviated by the attention, not least the sumptuous meals, which you received, but memory has you in a white sleeveless vest, sitting on the bench overlooking the pool, slumped in no officer-like posture. During the whole time you were with us you never set foot in the warmed water. Nor did you speak one word to Paul, Sarah or Stephen, although we all sat at table together. Catherine went out of her way to be very nice to them. Commissioned to write a mini-book (typical of the times) on Antonin Artaud, you had brought with you a copy of his manifesto on the Theatre of the Absurd. I recall your asking what the phrase '*en demeure*' was supposed to mean. Were you still auditioning for Harold Hobson's place as drama critic? The little book never appeared.

When I mentioned that I was going to go into Sarlat for the market early on Saturday morning, you and Catherine were promptly on parade. I parked on the threshold of the medieval town and suggested that you take an hour to enjoy its charm while I culled the week's fruit and vegetables. I had already stored my heavy purchases in the boot of the Mercedes when you returned. Back at Lagardelle, I was opening the boot as you were going into the house. On top of the groceries, I had laid the bunches of flowers which, in the days before we grew our own, cost very little in the market. 'That's lucky', you said, with that characteristic double snort of yours.

'What's that?'

'We almost bought you some flowers.'

A better man than I might have said, 'Almost thank you'.

Beetle cooked dinner as well as she knew how, which was very well indeed, and you came dressed with almost suitable formality. All went well, if never swimmingly, but we were quietly determined that you stay only for the week stipulated in our invitation. I was able to say, with truth, that we were expecting a call from our next guests about their date of arrival. You had mentioned taking us out for a meal, but the news of the Wisemans' arrival, just a week after your own, meant that you had to move on, to your next scheduled hosts before there was time for such an outing.

While I flattered myself that I had served you notice with credible regret, my original invitation had not been without diplomatic purpose. I managed, at one meal or another, to mention that my last two novels had both been reviewed, with no sign of favour, by the left-arm slow bowler, Symons, J. You said that I need not worry with regard to the forthcoming *April, June and November*: you never sent the same author's book to the same critic three times in a row. *Ouf de soulagement.*

We returned to England for the autumn term and publication. I opened the *S. T.* on the publication of *April, June and November* and saw that it had been reviewed by Julian Symons. He compared it, with small collegiate courtesy, with Simon Raven's latest naughtiness. When we repaired to Lagardelle for half term, we found that Michel Quéroux, the local landscape gardener, had cleared the bramble thickets from the unkempt half-acre of our land. The ground was now suavely shaped and grassed. We collected many baskets of walnuts from under our trees and to hell, so to say, with Burgundy. Your future as literary editor did not, I confess, feature among my anxieties while I, mute inglorious Montaigne, was writing (Clive James would have said 'composing') *The Glittering Prizes* in sweet isolation. I decided to stay in France for as long as possible; no place like not being at home.

The fame of Nick Tomalin's 'Zapping Charlie Cong' led directly to Harry Evans prevailing on Nick to go, well subsidised no doubt, to cover the 1973 Arab-Israel war. Nick had lunch with David Pryce-Jones, at the American Colony in 'Arab' east Jerusalem, as fighting flared on two fronts. They agreed that there was more to be learned about what really mattered by staying where they were. Next day, Nick hitched a ride to the Golan. He stayed in the lightly armoured truck while others got out for a communal piss. When a Syrian missile hit the truck, Nick was killed. His companions with weaker bladders all survived.

Being conscious-stricken is not a common characteristic of journalists, but Harry Evans had a bout of it. Nick's death had been a direct consequence of his demanding persuasion. Claire's grief doubled as *réquisitoire*. You had had no part in what happened, but you paid a large part of the price for it. Harry combined hair shirt with knight's armoury, penance with ruthlessness. If he had hesitated to change things, he now had just cause. Claire was installed in your place as literary editor and you were budged into a fine-sounding backwater as 'Chief Reviewer'; a room of your own doubled as solitary confinement. You did, however, find occasion to say very nice things about my little biography of Byron, going so far as to say, so memory claims, that I had the rare nerve to treat him as an equal. I took it well.

John Whitley and Master Peter remained as Claire's deputies, soon supplemented by the subtle Julian Barnes. I responded to Nick's death by an immediate, sincere, hand-written letter to Claire. She was kind enough, for the moment, to rank it the best of the bunch. Not long before, I had resigned to her, with no motive but kindness, a commission for writing a brief life of Shelley for Thames and Hudson. My situation on the literary pages, scarcely essential to my livelihood, though a brace to my vanity, seemed secure. I had, however, rendered the new literary editor a few services, not least in speaking well, at her invitation, in the *Statesman*, of a blandiose mini-*Tractatus* composed by Michael Frayn. I had not at the time known that he was her *cavalier sirvente*. The game of musical chairs following Nick's death soon promoted Frayn into the role of consort. With solicitous despatch, he deserted his wife and three daughters to lend comfort to the new widow and hotter ticket.

You suffered most from the fall-out of events in which you played no part whatever. I remember having lunch with you at the Garrick, for which I never dared to seek membership, and meeting Harry Evans in the queue to pay. Your civilian wound hurt badly enough for you to accuse him, as if joking, of having sacked you. He replied, as if joking, that he had given you a promotion without administrative obligations. Your salary, it seemed, was not diminished; your pride was. Your dated decency was never better illustrated than after Cyril died. It turned out that that master of bluff had left debts of £29,000, for which, in avuncular style, you thought should be paid, to save his reputation as some kind of a gentleman. I confess that when you called on me for a contribution, I did not feel the vocation. Cyril's ability to live on tick was proof of his charm but had no claim on me. I hope the *S. T.* rose to the occasion; but I bet it didn't.

Once enthroned in your place, Claire seldom invoked my services, preferring to recruit academics whose gratitude would express itself, in time, with electing her to more honorary degrees than even *la* Sitwell had been draped with. Beetle and I were spending most of the year in France, where Stephen went to the local school and then to the *collège*. When Claire sent me a book about China, about which she was sure I knew nothing, I recognised it as a not particularly sly way of giving me notice. I had the consolation of writing quite often for Christine Walker on the Travel pages; her generous commissions took us on many enjoyable trips and paid better, but Claire's angular pebble remained in my boot.

Three years later, you and Catherine invited us to a party in Belsize Park. The startling success of *The Glittering Prizes* just may have qualified us for the guest list. Bernard Levin came up to me and said, 'What does it feel like to be the most talked about man in London?' 'I was just going to ask you, Bernard', I said. John Vaizey accused me of being a genius.

Julian Symons was not of the company. Such, such were the consolations of Warhol's fifteen minutes of fame. When John and Marina Vaizey gave Beetle and me a lift home, I heard myself asking them to come and visit us in France the following summer. John died before he had the chance to bring us a few flowers. I wrote to Marina with due, dated propriety. She did not acknowledge the letter. As *Sunday Times* art critic, she never deigned to print a word about our daughter Sarah's exhibitions at Agnew's; nor did she write to us when Sarah died. Among certain people, nothing excuses having had more luck than it is in their power to allot.

Your little delayed retirement from the paper was celebrated by a party in a barge in Little Venice. The occasion resembled an Agatha Christie convergence of villains and victims. After it culminated in nothing more lethal than congratulations on what you had so long dreaded, *la* Tomalin continued to dispense patronage and sugar lumps for however long it was. One of your successors as drama critic confided to me that when he failed to applaud what she wished to have admired, his piece was axed and another taster invoked. My own books escaped attention on her pages. Her pink pride was crowned when Michael Frayn was made one of its ten Companions of Literature by the Royal Society of Literature, where she occupied a key position on the committee. It is not clear which of his books elevated him to that honour. Claire proceeded to write many books about classical authors, sowing tributes to her sources as she went; they flowered as awards and doctorates of all colourful sorts.

When Claire made it clear to John Whitley, your sidekick who had acceded to the role, if never the power, enjoyed by Leonard Russell in the *bon vieux temps*, that I should not look to her for any further employment, John was embarrassed but powerless. Harry Evans was keener to make an impression on the London in-crowd than to honour someone who shared his provincial origins. At some later point, the post of drama critic, which you understudied for so many decades, fell vacant. John Whitley proposed, in the mid-1980s that I should fill it. I was, as so often in my nervous life, flattered by the offer of what I never much wanted or needed. Promotion, rather than living well, sometimes feels like the best revenge, even when inconvenient.

We were living in London, while our son Stephen (to whom you never spoke) was at the *Lycée* in South Kensington. He had but to remark that he supposed that he would now never see me in the evenings for me to realise, when the appointment was as good as sealed, that to play George Sanders in *All About Eve* would be more servitude than *sacre*. John Peter, who had taken my antique advice and hung on to his place with patient diligence, had agreed, with good grace, to be one of my deputies (Robert Hewison the other). When I withdrew, with a proper show of regret, John stepped into the role which eluded you for so, so long. Harry Iredale's bedbug, if you take the abstruse reference, had got there just the same.

Claire's departure from the chair from which Harry had budged you procured a change of regime which, as such things can, brought a recall of exiles. Penny Perrick, whose mother, Eve, was a renowned columnist in the Beaverbrook press in the days when I was playing boy reporter, called me in France to ask me to resume the role as regular reviewer that I had enjoyed under your captaincy. Although I scarcely needed the work, I accepted, as much for the pleasure of getting my silly own back on Claire as for any worthy bookish reason. My resumed tenure in the place occupied by Cyril and Raymond long ago ended only when Andrew Holgate, the deputy lit. ed. (whom I had advocated as Penny's successor in a handwritten letter to Harry Evans) became literary editor. After I called him 'Anthony' on the telephone, there was no way back. There is never a shortage of candidates for the Clare Booth Luce award.

John Peter had honoured my advice, drained his sour medicine, and bided his time. Having become *S. T.* drama critic in my stead, he remained in office for all but twenty years. On the only occasion on which he had the opportunity, he gave a bad review to something I had translated. When he met me in the street, however, he was as genial as if truly grateful to me for my advice to keep on crawling. 'The bed-bug has no wings', said Harry Iredale, a Charterhouse French master not at all *de mon genre*, 'but he gets there just the same.' John Whitley was soon edged out by rough'n'tough Andrew Neil, who was enthroned in Harry Evans's stead by Rupert Murdoch until, having been duly celebrated with raspberries by the forever wrinkle-nosed editor of *Private Eye*, he was replaced by another uneasy head.

You would, of course, be quite right to read this letter as being not a little like those plays, of the second or third order, in which characters exchange information of which both are well apprised but which the audience needs to know in order to understand what comes later. Ionesco made farcical comedy of that kind of thing in *La Prima Donna Chauve*. Quasi-New York wisecrackery was never your style. The world that conscripted you to be courageous lacked the stable power to deliver due rewards in the years that followed. What never ceased to impress me rendered you obsolete, like all good examples, to my contemporaries. I hope that my affection and thanks are not soiled by this resumé of journalism's bumpy roads. If you were to take offence, that would be your right. If you managed to smile, or even to snort, that would be my reward.

Vale, Freddie.

Dear Jo,

An e-mail clicked up, late in 2015, to say that Beth Rogan had died. My female correspondent, name unknown to me, said that Beth had told her that she and I were friends. Would I write an obituary? Beth had written to me, quite recently, asking for advice about her autobiography (how to sell it, not how to write it). I had not seen her since October 1962, when you invited the ex-Rank starlet, *demi-mondaine* turned society lady, to give me and John Schlesinger the low-down on the high life. Beth came to lunch at Bentley's oyster bar, at the top of Queen Victoria Street. Stilted on tall stools at the narrow counter, we inclined together to cull scarcely lurid details about jet-setting with her current, much older husband, Tony Samuel, grandson of Marcus Samuel, Lord Bearsted, founder of Shell Transport and Trading.

I remember you saying that Beth's maiden name was Jenifer Puckle and how, in the mid-1950s, maiden no more, she was extracted from a queue for the Wimbledon tennis tournament by your friend Charles Riconno, London correspondent of *Corriere della Sera*. He escorted her, too pretty to be allowed to wait her turn, to the press box. Charles's companion happened to be a friend of the head of production at Pinewood Studios, Earl St John; his nominal earldom bestowed at his christening in Baton Rouge, Louisiana. Until Charles came into her life, Jenifer was a part-time Latin teacher married, in her early twenties, to a suburban art teacher called Ted Draper, his company preferable, just, to that of her military family in Walmer, Kent.

Jenifer was not reluctant to be translated to Iver, Bucks, where the Rank Organisation ran a parody of Hollywood in what had been a panelled country club. After enrolment in 'the Company of Youth', she was re-titled 'Beth Rogan' ('de Bess' in Janni-speak). In the studio's Charm School, a converted Church Hall, comely females were taught to appeal to the camera and career-enhancing executives. To prove what could happen to a duly re-shaped girl (falsies part of the kit), John Davis, the head of the studio, a bald, weighty, no less thorny than horny accountant, married Dinah Sheridan, the pick of the nursery's English roses; less understandably, Dinah Sheridan married him. Beth played small parts until culled by Mr Samuel.

Many of the long-serving actors spent their time in uniform, re-enacting brave British moments. At lunch time, officers (Johnny Mills, Jack Hawkins) messed at one table, other ranks (Dickie Attenborough, Bryan Forbes) at others. In the medical section, Dirk Bogarde and Donald Sinden, Michael Craig and Kenneth More impersonated white-coated students of russet-bearded consultant surgeon James Robertson Justice, the studio's senior cocksman. Nigel 'Paddy' Patrick was his laddish other in the how's-your-father department. Norman Wisdom fell about, pulled profitable faces and was pals only with John Paddy Carstairs, his knockabout director. Virginia McKenna's classy cheek bones made her the good wife for all seasons, never for all ranks. David Lean's lady-for-the-time-being Ann Todd was the unsmiling vamp. His rolling home was a large Rolls-Royce.

You and I first met in 1955. You were prepping *The Big Money*, with Ian Carmichael. Leslie Bricusse and I had been hired to inject hilarity into an already multi-coloured, tutti-frutti script. Each new draft, from a different writer, had a distinct tint. While Leslie had smarter things to do, I delivered our contribution to your first-floor flat, 36 Burton Court, adjacent to the Royal Hospital, Chelsea. You asked me, years later, whether I remembered the first thing I ever said to you.

I said, 'Probably, good morning, sir, I hope I'm not late'.

'What you said, Fred, was: what do you want to make diss piece of shit for? You were quite right, I must say.'

No yet forty, married to Stella, who owned seventeen houses in Wales, and with a son called Nicholas, you envied Charles Riconno his amorous liberties. When did you tell me how, while weekending in Geneva with Beth, Charles proposed that they find another girl to stimulate their erotic revels? On a Sunday evening, they went to the railway station. 'De Bess' was sent to approach an appetising arrival. Did she have a hotel? No, why? Told that they had a spare bed, the stranger blinked; she did not turn away. Charles suggested they go to the station café and have a drink. Calvin's rules ran: no alcohol could be served. Charles bought several boxes of liqueur chocolates, broke them open and made sucrose knock-out drops of the contents. 'What happened after dat, Fred, to tell you de truce, in many ways, I don't know exactly.'

Your slurred aspirates disposed me to see you as a joke, a hangover from the war, when Eye-ties were intrinsically funny, rarely warlike. In the early 1950s, at the Cambridge Arts Cinema, I admired the post-war realism of Roberto Rossellini's *Roma città aperta* and Vittorio de Sica's *Bicycle Thieves*, but film producers too, of whatever provenance, were by definition figures of fun. What was the name of that Pinewood Hungarian who, suspecting that his team was scheming against him behind his back, was heard to say 'You think I know fuck nothing; but you are wrong: I know fuck all'?

Had I taken the trouble, I might have discovered that, a year earlier, you had produced Renato Castellani's *Romeo and Juliet*, with Laurence Harvey and Susan Shentall (who she, indeed?). When the film won the Golden Lion at Venice, you were accosted, you told me, in the lift of the Excelsior hotel by a Roman producer who proposed that you do some co-productions together. Since the man's name meant nussing to you, you asked what kind of films he made. 'I will tell you de truce,' he said. 'I do four productions a year. Two of them are, to be honest wiz you, low-class *merda*. The third one, if possible, slightly higher class *merda*. But de fource one! The fource one... *merda con zucchero*!' Shit with sugar.

To be very honest with you, Joseph, a lot of people wonder how many of the stories I (and John Schlesinger) told people that you had told us were true. I am innocent enough to think they all were, the least likely the likeliest. Am I right? I don't at all think that you were a liar (except, of course, to Stella), but it always amused you, didn't it, to deceive people? Deception can serve as a life-jacket that, as in your case, is best inflated with charm.

During the years before we met again, you made some good films for Rank, the best *A Town Like Alice*, with the young Peter Finch, directed by Jack Lee. Quality came at a price which did not commend you to John Davis. Your contract due to lapse, you were summoned to lunch in the boardroom. Over Cyprus sherry, Davis warned that he had some bad news for you. When the bell rang, at 1.45pm, to announce that shooting was due to resume on the floor, you stood up and said, 'I must go to work, so now I ask you: what is de bad news?'

'I thought I'd made myself clear. The studio is not going to renew your contract.'

'Dat I know; but what is de bad news?'

You formed your own company with Jack Lee, making commercials for the nascent independent television industry. Your undying ambition was to produce films better than *merda con zucchero*. You spotted John Schlesinger after he made *Terminus*, a documentary about Waterloo Station, shot in black and white, in the patriotic tradition of the war-time Crown Film Unit. In the prize-winning scene, you remember, a London policeman went to comfort a child abandoned in the concourse. The kind-hearted bobby reassured the weeping child and established, supposedly, that British truth was warmer than cinematic fiction. In fact, the encounter had been confected, with a uniformed actor and John's small nephew. The only moment of truth was when the little boy failed to weep on cue. John was quick to stand in for cruel necessity and had the words to turn on the tap.

You called John and said, 'I want to discover you'.

John said, 'Be my guest'

Jack Lee went to live in Australia. He never directed another movie. In the early Sixties (not yet the Sexties), you and John made *A Kind of Loving* and *Billy Liar*, back to back, on location in Bradford. Butt and buttress, you became John's father-in-cinema. Denied yet another take, he was not above calling you 'the refugee', was he, or even, in vexed cases, 'the enemy alien'? *'Ma* John…', you'd say. He also relied on you to handle emergencies. He and his friends joked about 'Mavis', a generic term for the police ('Mavis Polizei' in full), but in pre-Wolfenden times, no active homosexual was immune from risk of arrest and ruin. Marooned in Bradford, you sometimes felt excluded by the complicity between John and Alan Bates: 'De way they whispered together, Fred, I must tell you…'. On the other hand, John was glad to cover for you when Stella became suspicious of what pudding might be alleviating your Yorkshire celibacy.

In 1961, during a week in Paris, Beetle and I saw Michelangelo Antonioni's *L'Avventura*, twice; on the same day. Its lingering discontinuities seemed proof of the director's genius. In practice, they were a sublime remedy for budgetary shortfall and the defection, sick, of Lea Masari. Luminous Monica Vitti saved the day. I wished that I could work on films with Antonioni's lingering intensity.

After David Deutsch happened to see a play of mine on ITV and commissioned a movie version, Beetle and I moved to Rome. I wrote the script of *Nothing But the Best* in a small flat on Monte Mario, leased to us by the usual Contessa, who had a double-buttoned chauffeur in a cap to drive her Fiat Millecento. In 1962, when we returned to London, the film was about to go into production, directed by Clive Donner, with Alan Bates, Millie Martin and Denholm Elliott. David told me you and John had had enough of honest soot. You now wanted to make the English equivalent of Federico Fellini's *La Dolce Vita*, 'sophisticated like hell'. David promised that I was the man you needed.

I remember John's suspicious first look round at me before a supper party at the Deutsches. Peter Sellers was one of the guests. He laughed generously when I was persuaded to tell a long story about my great-uncle Jessel. Peter and I later crossed a few times at Douggie Hayward's in-group tailor's shop in Mount Street. He used to say, 'Still getting away with it, Fred'. The lack of a question mark indicates that he said it as if as true of himself as of me.

A Kind of Loving had been denounced, by Lindsay Anderson and other New Leftists, as bourgeois commercialisation of British Working Class Life. Its success ensured that you went straight into production with *Billy Liar*, starring Tom Courtenay. In a luminous sequence, the girl in the piece ambled down the provincial high street, dreaming of London. At the end of her amble, reflected in a shop window's wedding dress, the young Julie Christie was a nascent star. You put her under contract before she could twinkle elsewhere. John's friends told me that she looked just like his actress sister Susan.

By the time you and I met again, I spoke fair Italian and was in love with Italy. When I announced my passion for *L'Avventura*, we were as one. You told me you and Antonioni both attended the *Centro Sperimentale* cinema school, sponsored by Mussolini. You were given your first cine-camera on your eleventh birthday, in 1927. You had a photograph of yourself, in a pepper-and-salt suit, plus-fours, baggy peaked cap with a black bobble on the top, white socks, black and white shoes, and the camera. I asked did you remember the first film you ever shot. 'To tell you de truce, Fred, it was a porno film in many ways. I had a friend, Mauro Benedetti, eighteen, nineteen years old, he had a girlfriend, quite beautiful I must say, he wanted to have film of her, you know, in de nude in many ways. So… we went to dis field near Lake Como and she took off her clothes and did this and that he asked her to while I shot de film. Not porno porno, but… eleven years old, you can imagine… interesting, I must say.'

During the 1920s, you told me, a good many Jews were enthusiastic fascists. Unlike Venetians, Neapolitans and Florentines, with their local exclusivities, Italy's *Sephardim* had rallied patriotically to Garibaldi's *Risorgimento*; their sons and grandsons often signed up to the Duce's swaggering nationalism. He even had a Jewish mistress. In due time, the summons came for the adolescent Giuseppe Janni to report to the town hall to be inducted into the Fascist Youth. At the usual baize-skirted table, a plumed Maresciallo was checking names and addresses. When you stepped forward, the official looked up and said, '*Ma*, signor Peppino what are you doing here?' Without his plume, the Maresciallo was a foreman in one of your father's mills.

'I was told I had to come. I came. What else can I do?'

For a few weeks, you went regularly and reluctantly to parade. One day, the Maresciallo took you aside. 'Signor Peppino, tell me, do you really enjoy doing the drill?'

'In many ways, I have to say, not.'

'*Senta, faremmo così*: every week, you telephone, ahead of time, you give me a good excuse in case anyone ever asks and I put a tick in the book next to your name. You go and do whatever young gentlemen like to do in the evening.'

Every week, for a year or so, you called the Maresciallo. Every week a tick was put in the book against your name. Meanwhile, your worldly uncle Bernardo introduced you to the clubby Milanese brothels where rich young men learned sexual manners from clean, well-paid, smiling girls. Initiation involved being blindfolded and obliged, with other young men, to dangle your penis into a bowl which, according to the master of ceremonies, contained a sow's sex, and then... 'I don't have to tell you, Fred, what we had to do...' In fact, you discovered, your fleshy target had been a slice of pig's liver. Then it was time to go upstairs.

One day, you made the usual call to the Maresciallo and did not receive the usual response.

'I am sorry, signor Peppino, this week, no excuses. You must come to the parade. Full uniform.'

'Listen, I give you an extra hundred lire, you put the tick in the book...'

'No, Signor Peppino, you listen: this week is the parade to award the sword of honour to the Young Fascist of the Year. You absolutely have to be here.'

'For God's sake, one person missing who has never been there, who will notice?'

'On the contrary. They will certainly notice. You have to be here. No excuses...'

'Why? Why?'

'Because you, signor Peppino, are the Young Fascist of the Year. The only, only one in the whole class with, every week, a tick in the book.'

That was before Hitler became Mussolini's malign genius. Till the late 1930s, you told me, you and your family – your mother a Montefiore – lived in cosseted seclusion, not unlike the Finzi-Continis in Giorgio Bassani's novel about Ferrara, where Antonioni was born (and now has his own, ill-attended museum). Events in Germany first impinged on the Jannis in 1935. The Jewish multi-millionaire who had been your father's keenest German customer was dispossessed and came to Milan seeking work. You told me how you stood with your father on the terrace of your house as Max, whose two chauffeurs had made sure that he never walked an unnecessary step, trudged down the drive with a suitcase of Janni and co samples in each heavy hand. Your father said, 'One day very soon, that will be me'.

Before the Great War, your Janni grandfather had been a ship-builder in Trieste. In those days, oil was shipped only in metal barrels. After Marcus Samuel acquired substantial rights in Middle Eastern petroleum, he toured Britain's shipyards in search of someone to build him a 'hollow' ship. He had seen how much more crude a 'tanker' could carry and how quickly it might be loaded and unloaded. No British shipwright considered such a ship feasible. Samuel went to Trieste – then still part of the Austro-Hungarian empire – and found his man. Since he lacked capital to pay for the vessels he needed, he offered stock instead. In exchange for ten percent of Shell T. & T., your grandfather's yard built the first tankers. Had he put the shares in the bank and awaited dividends, the family would have become increasingly and uncountably rich. The success of Marcus Samuel's fleet excited the envy of its constructor. *Nonno* Janni invested heavily in the Lloyd-Triestino line. In the post-war slump, he was bankrupt and had to sell all his Shell stock.

When Mussolini licensed Italian fascists to emulate Hitler's antisemitism, your father, Rudi, feared disaster. It was impossible to export capital. The only recourse was to sell up, before things got worse, and smuggle as much money as possible abroad. The price had to be paid in cash. It could then be passed to underworld people who had their ways of exporting it. As you put it, 'De only people you could trust in dose days, to be honest, Fred, were de criminals'.

Your father was ill and resigned; your uncle Bernardo strong and resourceful. He made contact with the Camorra in Naples. Yes, for a fat percentage, of course they could move money to London. Bernardo was being watched. You had to be the courier with a suitcase solid with cash. The trains left on time in Mussolini's Italy, but the journey from Milan to Rome, Rome to Naples was long, and slow. During several nerve-racking checks on the way, your papers were seen to be in order. After eighteen sleepless hours, you were met at Naples station by a man of a southern breed you had never encountered before. 'You know what dey say, Fred: after Rome, Africa'. You were in a hurry to hand over the suitcase and be gone, but the man insisted on counting the money. You rented a closed horse-drawn carriage and drove round Naples until the tally was concluded.

Soon after that, your father was told that he needed an operation. The likelihood, they warned him, was that he would die on the operating table. 'In that case', he said, 'we do it at once.' They did; and he died. Your mother went to meet the money in London. You followed, in the autumn of 1939. The train to Ventimiglia was thick with Italian peasant conscripts on their sorry way to camp on the frontier. 'When I told zem I was going to London', you told me, 'all dey said was, my God, if only we could go wiz you!'

'I didn't speak English; who did I know in London? I went to dis big bank, in de City, and asked to see Lord Bearsted, de son of my grandfather's friend. Imagine, Fred, what I looked like. The doorman told me, not possible. But I had a desperation beyond... so I said please to tell de Lord I was de grandson of Janni from Trieste. A few minutes later, Marcus Samuel himself came down to the lobby. How he could help me? Oll what I wanted, I told him, was to work in de films. So he asked his assistant, did they have any film producers were clients of de bank? Yes; sreee of zem.

Did any owe the bank money? Oll of them. Who owed de most? John Sutro. So… he called John Sutro and asked, could he give me a job? Sutro, a very nice man, I must say, had a film about to start shooting, June 9th 1940. I was welcome to come and be a surd assistant. June 10th, Italy came into the war. June 11th, I was arrested as an enemy alien and sent to de Metropolc camp, on de Isle of Man.'

No manifest threat to national security, you were released after a short time, you told me, and 'lonnly like hell' walked the London streets. In the blackout, a woman standing in a Bond Street doorway flashed a quick light on her face as you came by. 'I went up to her and said "good evening" and she said "It's three quid". Quite a lot I must say. I said, "Listen, I'm sorry, but in Italy, when we say good evening, you don't just say what you just said". She said, "Are you coming or not?" I said, "in many ways, yes, possibly, but you could say good evening…"'

'She led me up de stairs by the side of a shop to a dark little room at the top of the building. I asked her at least to tell me her name. She said, "Never mind dat, give me de money". I said, "For God's sake, we're young people, we could at least have a bit of a talk". I told her how, in Italy, when you went with a girl like… she was… you could still have a good time, have a drink even, or a laugh. She lay down on de narrow bed, coat on, her legs in de air. "Get on wiz it". I said, "Listen, for sree pounds, you could at least take your cloths off". She said, "What do you think I am?" I said, "In many ways, I know what you are. In Italy, you go with a girl, you can still both enjoy it, for God's sake." Legs still up like dat, you know what she said? "Welcome to England, ducky!"'

I wanted to emulate Antonioni; you wanted to be 'modern like hell'; John outrageous, but successful. Our common ambition was to stick it to the audience in a form they would applaud. Each of us had a different, kindred sense of alienation: I was a bit of an American, John was queer, you were an exile.

By geographical good fortune, we all had survived a horror we never mentioned.

In our many, many meetings, you could be inconsequential and interminable; John outrageous but deeply bitten by the documentary fetish of BBC's *Monitor*, fronted by the lordly Huw Wheldon. I preferred to make things up. In pursuit of de truce, on New Year's Eve, 1962, Stella and you, Beetle and I and John went to a supposedly chic fancy dress party. Tite Street, Chelsea, promised orgiastic licence. I was a pirate; John was a Cardinal; you I don't know what.

By the time tedium drove us to leave, not a fig-leaf had been removed, not a nipple of impropriety revealed. London was not yet swinging. We went on and on talking. After many fruitless weeks, I proposed that I go away and write a script about a syndicate of businessmen and showbiz people who, thanks to the elasticity of current law, had formed a company which allowed them to keep a *poule de luxe* in a Mayfair penthouse (what else?) at the taxpayer's expense. I had had word that the comedian Max Bygraves was a member of just such a syndicate. You said, 'In many ways, not bad, I must say'.

Beetle and I rented a cottage at Le Rouret, a few kilometres north of Cagnes-sur-Mer and I set out to astonish. My first image was of a birthday party with a recumbent life-size nude statue of Our Lady, embodied in suitably toned ice-creams. Shareholders arrive and eat her with delicious satisfaction. Ah, that secret strawberry slash! After a few weeks, John came to stay. There was still snow on the ground, but the weather was warm enough for him to sit, in pink shirt and bulging cream-coloured trousers, on a garden bench and frown over my already fat, if unfinished, confection. His first comment, when it came to any original suggestion, was 'How do we do it, dear?' Was there ever a better or more entertaining guest than Schlez? He took Beetle and me to dinner at the Hôtel de Paris in Monte Carlo, famous for the roof which opened, during the *plat de résistance*, to disclose the stars, and entertained us with pitilessly affectionate imitations of you. He also told me how lucky I was not to be queer.

My Riviera pages primed the many scripts that followed, but hardly a line survived into the quarter-final draft. Our tripartite conferences resumed in London. One day, John did not come. His sister, actress Susan Maryott, had committed suicide, following the death of her lover, the playwright John Whiting. After the funeral, John joined us again. The clinching moment came on whatever day of whatever week, before or after we went to lunch at Franco and Mario's Soho trattoria, when I said that what we needed was a title and then supplied it: Darling. You said, 'In many ways, not bad, I must say'.

Franco and Mario's 'trat' was Soho's in-place for show-bizzy people. The menu was as thick as a tasselled missal. Every time we went there, you looked through it with a Harlequin face, short eyebrows canted towards the centre. You would sigh, and then, as John and I hoped that this time you would not, you always said 'Do you have anysing else?' When the waiter looked embarrassed, you said: 'Tell de chef, oll what I want is a white rice, no cream, no salt.' You were once again the Milanese rich boy who had to have what was good for him; and then a cigar.

When you had other things to do, I would go to see John in his neat house ('an upper and a downer' he called it) in Peel Street, W8. We imagined that we made quicker progress without you, but when we rehearsed our latest ideas, your not unusual response was, 'oll what you're saying is, if you don't mind my saying, nyah-nyah' an intimation of mediocrity beyond appeal. You were usually right. Then you would say, again, 'We need an image'. One of your favourites was of our heroine, alone in de smart flat wiz de white telephones: 'She has everysing and she has nussing. She walks to the window, she lights a cigarette in a certain way… we know everysing!'

Real life caught up with our fantasy when John Profumo's affair with Christine Keeler became public. In any other society, her uncommon beauty might have procured her a place at least as nicely padded as de Bess Rogan's; in Macmillan's England, her victimised accent did for her. The meatier Mandy Rice-Davies (aka Randy Mandy) survived in outspoken shamelessness. John was staying with us in our house in Langham when Harold Macmillan resigned, quite as if his prostate cancer was terminal (he lived for more than another twenty years). The emergence, in the cabalistic Tory style, of the pre-war appeaser Alec Douglas-Home as Prime Minister seemed to make satire superfluous.

A few weeks later, tragedy succeeded farce: J.F.K. was assassinated. Even John found nothing subversive to say. The spring had gone out of the year. What was the point of making films? Our long faces did nothing to lengthen yours. You said, 'Let me tell one thing: de world will not change in de slightest. It is not any worse today dan it was yesterday and it was never zat much better. Nothing matters as much as you sink. To tell you de truce, so what honestly?' Then he looked at the new pages which I had brought to the meeting. 'Not bad, in many ways, de scene on de underground escalator.'

Not long afterwards, you told us about your friend Luigi, a producer (you still pronounced it 'poducer') morbidly afraid of flying. Many months earlier, Luigi had had a call, when he was skiing, insisting that he fly, at once, to Rome, to a meeting about financing his new movie: now or never. He was being driven, in the snow, down to Geneva airport, when the road became impassable. The flight took off without him and crashed into the mountains. Everyone was killed. 'And de film, of course, went ahead a bit later. Luigi swore he would never, ever fly again, because my god... But then, one day, he was in Pantellaria, he had a call: he had to come to London to see I don't know Carlo or Dino, somebody. He missed the flight,

I don't know why, and... yes, de plane went into the sea and everyone was killed. You know the old saying, "No two wizout a sree". So zat was it: no more flying for Luigi, ever.'

'But den – of course – a while later, he was in Paris and Carlo called again, maybe Dino, probably Dino, he had to fly immediately to Los Angeles and he could have de deal of the century and I don't know what. So he said no, because... and Dino said he would pay for the ticket; Luigi said that wasn't the point, but he went to the airport, you know, certain dat dis time... because... So, de plane takes off. They are flying and flying and all de time Luigi is waiting for something bad to happen. Four, five hours out, de captain says he has an announcement. Owing to unforeseen circumstances, de plane had to make an unscheduled landing at Boston. Unforeseen, unscheduled! Luigi looked out of the window, right, left: no flames, not yet. He asked the steward, what's wrong? He looked at his first-class neighbour. He was asleep, for God's sake. After I don't know how long, it was de captain again: "Ladies and gentlemen, I am sorry to say, I have some very bad news... President Kennedy was shot and killed in Dallas, Texas earlier today". Luigi put his arms around his neighbour: "Sank God!"'

By the summer of 1964, we finally had a viable draft of 'de Darling'. You and John went to Pinewood, seeking finance. When a writer is no longer in the loop, he can guess he has done a good job. The Rank executives told you that de Ralph Thomas had recently made *The Wild and the Willing*, a film very like the one we had in mind. It had not been a hit: good afternoon. The way John reported it, the real problem had been my script. You promised that you had uzzer places to go. So did I: armed with Stanley Donen's commission to write *Two for the Road*, Beetle and I headed for Greece.

While we were in our cottage on Ios, in the Cyclades, I received a telegram from John. A deal to make *Darling* had come together, at last. After all those months and months of labour and garrulity, we had Julie, we had Dirk Bogarde and we had Larry Harvey. After a few weeks in Greece, I was eager to work on *Two for the Road*. Beetle and I decided to go back and live in Rome. Soon after we had rented a flat in Vigna Clara, a modern suburb to the north of the city, John wrote me a neat, handwritten four-page letter. Casting was complete; shooting would start shortly; he hoped I would not be surprised to learn that a few things on the script had needed attention. You had hired Edna O'Brien to do a polish. The script would 'of course' be credited entirely to me; love, John. All those foolish, unpaid weeks when I thought we were friends! Did a single one of Edna's expensive contributions escape the dreaded shears at the final cut?

I composed *Two for the Road* on a stack of cards and juxtaposed them in non-chronological order on the floor of our flat. It went, as they used to say, like cream. After not very many weeks, I sent the completed script to Stanley Donen. He called late one night to say that he had just finished reading it and it was going to be 'the best thing I ever did'. Would we come back to London to talk about a couple of things? He had a place we could stay.

John had been shooting for two or three weeks. You invited me to come to the cutting room and see the footage. It had been roughly assembled by Jimmy Clark, who drove a white Jaguar, proof of independent means. I watched with disenchanted eyes. When the lights went up, you and John looked at me. I relished your white faces. I said, 'You can't use much of that stuff, can you, if any? Apart from anything else, what does she look like?' John said, 'You should have been here'. I said, 'If I'd ever been paid, I might have been'. You said, 'You should have asked'. I said, 'I just hope nothing I've seen so far has to be in the movie'. You said, 'It was your idea, Fred, to have dem go to de cricket'. 'And it was Edna's idea to have them say the things they say.' Jim Clark was watching and listening. I said, 'I suppose you think it's all wonderful stuff'. He said, 'As a matter of fact, I agree with you'. His tone did not make us allies. It promised only that he had no fear of John's displeasure. For many years, he and his wife, Laurence, made a show of being our friends, Beetle's and mine.

John said, 'Freddie, while you're here, that scene where Dirk sends Julie off with the car when he wants to work, he feels he looks very weak'.

'Ask him why he thinks we cast him.'

In those days, agents, lawyers and accountants had not yet become the lords of The Biz. Although I had worked with you and John for more than two years and had been paid several small sums, no formal contracts had been drawn. Once *Darling* was actually in production, our common agent and friend, Richard Gregson, was charged with getting the paperwork in order. Until I signed a contract, my script remained, in legal terms, my personal property. The film could not be distributed until I made over the rights to Vic Films, after which I would receive my final, not very large payment. With casual tact, Richard mentioned that you and John thought you deserved some kind of credit on the screen for your contributions to the script.

I said, 'They're the producer and the director. They'll get all the credit anyway. Tell them about Naboth's Vineyard.'

'Tell them about what?'

'Put it this way: tell them about going and fucking themselves.'

Richard said, 'Things went very well with Audrey, I gather. Stanley's very happy.'

A few nights later, at one in the morning, the telephone rang.

'*Pronto*.'

'Fred?'

'Yes.'

'What time is it?'

'What time is it? You called me at one in the morning to ask me what time it is. Fuck you.'

'Listen, Fred...'

'I don't want to listen. Fuck you.'

'De scene at de flat when de Dirk Bogarde comes back...'

'It's one in the morning. You're supposed to be Italian. You know very well what time it is. I don't want to talk to you.'

'Fred, for God's sake, de scene, we are shooting it in de morning and I have to tell you, I said it before, it's not right. It needs work. You are de writer.'

'Am I? You and John seem to think you're entitled to put your name all over the publicity and mine never appears. Now you want my credit, I hear. So... have a good idea. Get him to have one.'

'He can't. He knows dat. Fred...'

'Ask Edna O'Brien. Or can't you afford her?'

'Fred, for God's sake, de film is going very well in many ways...'

'Well it can go without me. And, as I may have mentioned before, you can go and fuck yourself.'

'Dat may very well be true, but de scene needs you and you are the only person who can do it. So please...'

I said, 'What page is it on?'

'It needs a line. It needs....'

'An image?'

'An image is exactly what it needs.'

I said, 'I'll have a look at it. One in the fucking morning.'

You said, 'I call you in an hour. It needs a line, maybe two. And, yes, an image.'

'She can light a cigarette in a certain way.'

'Or not.'

'Are you going to pay me?'

'Listen, Fred, de film is a success, they will all pay you all you want for de rest of your life. Now please…'

You were right, as so often: the scene did need improvement. It gave me venomous pleasure to have the required two or three neat new lines ready in a few minutes. I called you and asked you what time it was.

You said 'What?' as if it were composed of several syllables.

I said, 'Have you got a pencil or something? Because please write this down exactly as I say. Otherwise it won't play. Just take it down. If you and John like it, fine. If you don't, you can think of something better. Whatever you do, don't call me back.'

I dictated the scene, with malevolent precision.

'Much better, I must say. I was right, Fred.'

'You were absolutely right and now piss off and let me go to sleep.'

You said, 'Should Julie not say something?'

'She's more effective with her mouth shut.'

'Iss true. But she is going to be a big star.'

'Good for you. Good for her. Goodnight.'

'Fred, while you're there, de scene in de hospital…'

'Fuck off, Jo. Preferably forever, will you, please?'

The next morning, the doorbell rang. A messenger in a peaked cap handed me a thick box. Inside was a copy of Richard Lattimore's handsome, if fattened, translation of the *Iliad*. The enclosed card carried the message, in your singularly slurred hand, 'This is the story of a much bigger war'. I sighed and I smiled and I went to call and thank you. You were glad I had, Joseph, because there was one line…

By the time the unit arrived in Florence to shoot the Italian sequences of *Darling*, you had heard that 'the Americans' were excited by 'de word of mouse'. Beetle and I came to watch some of the shooting. We had never before stayed in a hotel where the front door opened automatically as guests approached. John was glad to see me, not least because he might need an idea. I said, 'Oh but you and Jo have all the ideas, don't you?'

He said, 'Freddie'.

Later, in Rome, he asked me to come with him to the press conference at the new big hotel, named for Julius Caesar. I said, 'Go by yourself. I'm tired of playing the elephant to your Hannibal.' Stanley Donen had told me that he hoped Paul Newman would be playing the male lead in *Two for the Road*. When the *Darling* caravan moved to Capri, Beetle and I, with Paul and Sarah, took a thumping ride in the *aliscafo* across the wind-swept Bay of Naples to spend a few days at the Quisisana Hotel. The previous afternoon, the mayor of Capri had taken exception to John's indecorous parade of sexual eccentrics around the main square. 'You'd think we were in Bournemouth, dear!' During dinner, word came down from John's suite, 'Come up. We need a line.' When I went up, Julie looked at me as if she had not seen me before. The writer is never quite one of the company, unless he is also the director.

The next morning, they were due to shoot the scene in which Julie/Diana comes down to breakfast on the terrace with Malcolm, the queer photographer friend (Rowley Curram) with whom, in the story, she is taking a sex-free holiday to recover from an abortion. Julie was supposed to be displeased because, the previous night, she had seen Malcolm going off on a Vespa with the same handsome Caprese waiter with whom she had just alleviated her chastity. John's scheme had her take her place next to Malcolm at the table and then not speak to him. I suggested, sotto voce, that she collect her cutlery and sit at another table. After which Rowley's 'Darling!' would have more snap.

You said, 'I buy it at once'.

John conceded that the scene played much better that way. I asked, nicely, whether I would now get credit for directorial ideas.

You said, 'Fred, I come to Rome in a few days. Would you and Beetle come and have dinner with Michelangelo and Monica?'

We met at the restaurant *Il Bolognese* in the *Piazza del Popolo*. Tall and narrow, with a face that appeared drawn downwards by angst, Antonioni was in his early fifties. He wore fame like a shroud. You told me that he and Monica were known in movie circles as '*un lung' in espresso*': he was never in a hurry; she always was. Monica had been a light comedienne when Michelangelo first saw and cast her. *L'Avventura* made her the personification of rare and fragile femininity, touched with a Virgilian sense of the tears in things. You took the reference; you had told me that, as a student, you won first prize in the Vatican prize for Latin composition. You were, in many ways, not a joke.

In person, unlike many stars, Monica was at least as beautiful as Antonioni had made her on the screen; and more cheerful. Over dessert, Michelangelo told the story about the movie director who dies and goes to heaven. He is given a very nice apartment and, a day after his arrival, he is told that God would like to see him. Since his films have been not entirely reverential, he goes with a little trepidation, but the big door is open and, when he walks in, God gets up, embraces him, invites him to take a seat and immediately asks whether he would be willing to go on making films. The director asks if there are any, well, limits on what... 'Not at all', God tells him, 'not at all. This is heaven, isn't it? I happen to know that all the best writers want to work with you: Tolstoy has some big ideas, Chekhov some smaller ones, Marcel Proust loved your last picture. For the music, Beethoven's hearing is now perfect and he's... much happier... Verdi is still Verdi. As for the actors, we have everyone back to, oh, Roscius, you know. Leading ladies, we have them all. Cleopatra, by the way, is looking wonderful these days. She is on the short side, but… it all depends how you shoot them, doesn't it?'

They talk movies for a while and then God gets up, comes and puts his arm around the director. 'Decide what you want to do, talk to Gabriel and you have all the time and means you need to make your masterpiece.'

The director says, 'And there are really no… conditions?'

'Conditions, of course not.' God is walking the director to the door, still with that arm around him. 'Ma, as you ask… when it comes to casting, you could perhaps do me one small favour: *c'è un piccolo angelotto…*'

You said, 'You understand, Fred? There is one little angel…'

'I understand.'

When we had finished dinner, Monica said, 'Now you come to my party.'

You turned to Beetle and said, 'Listen, I don't know what de party is exactly, but dis is Rome, you know? I don't want to get you into anysing, I don't know what, with the *spogliarello* possibly and when people take dare closes off, that is only the beginning… you can imagine. So…'

Beetle said, 'We can always leave'.

'Or you can olways stay. But don't say you haven't been warned.'

We drove across Rome to a tall new apartment block. Monica rang the bell of the ground floor flat. A small lady of no great age opened it. 'This is my mother', Monica said. 'When you have a birthday, who is more important than your mother?' The marbled flat was furnished as it might have been for one of the 'white telephone' films of the 1930s. There were big books and many sets of Chinese Chequers. No one seemed likely to take their closes off.

Beetle and I went up the spiral staircase to Antonioni's flat. The large sitting room had a mantlepiece with a tall, transparent cabinet above it, shelves filled with fumed glass bottles as if it were a three-dimensional Morandi. You told me later that happiness made Michelangelo feel guilty. People from Ferrara could be like that. Later I learned that, during the war, when he was a young critic, Antonioni had admired Veit Harlan's *Jud Süß* unreservedly. Seventy-eight Jewish pupils were deported from the primary school in Ferrara and murdered in Germany.

Antonioni's first film was, like John Schlesinger's *Terminus*, a documentary: *Nettezza Urbana*, about municipal dustmen. *L'Avventura* was an unmatchable masterpiece. Its sequel, *La Notte*, lacked its unnerving asymmetry, but it did contain one unforgettable exchange. When Marcello Mastroianni meets Monica, in a black wig, she is playing shuffle-board on a black and white marble floor. Marcello says, '*Quanti anni hai?*' She answers, '*diec'otto anni e molti, molti mesi*'. ('How old are you?' 'Eighteen years, and many, many months.') As directors will, Antonioni claimed a wide share in the screenplay; can you believe that line came from anyone but Tonino Guerra?

Darling opened in New York before it came to London. John sent me a telegram saying what a hit it was: lines around the block. Julie was a big star. We had to find something else for her to do before her contract with Vic films lapsed. There was no time to go through another long process in quest of what might be our version of *La Notte*. Woodrow Wyatt had suggested to David Deutsch that Julie was perfect to play Bathsheba Everdene in Thomas Hardy's *Far from the Madding Crowd*. MGM were prompt to commission the screenplay.

You and John and *Darling* went to the Moscow film festival. The Soviet Union was at its paranoid peak. Visitors were at once cosseted and suspect. Every floor on the huge, slow hotel had a vigilant concierge. The surly officiousness reminded you of fascism. You did not appreciate waiting three hours for food you never wanted to eat. No one would make you a white rice. As soon as the film had been shown, and taken to be both a condemnation and a symptom of capitalist decadence, you asked the large, five-by-five Intourist guide to get you on the next day's flight to London. She took sullen pleasure in saying that the flights were all full.

You said, 'In dat case, get us onto a flight to I don't care where.'

'Not possible. You must wait.'

You then said, 'I must tell you one thing, you are wizout doubt the ugliest woman I have ever seen in my entire life.'

You and John were on the next morning's flight to Oslo.

When *Darling* came out in London, the critics were riled that it came garlanded with American superlatives. Ken Tynan headed his Observer review 'Identikit Girl'. It seemed disparaging, but I was not sure how. On reflection, Ken's rubric was shrewder than I cared to admit. Like the society it affected to satirise and hoped to please, *Darling* was a confection of vanities. So what? It was also an unsinkable hit. It hardly seemed to matter that Paul Newman was not going to do *Two for the Road*. Someone else would. Audrey was the one that mattered.

When Ken invited me for a drink in his Mount Street flat, we white-wined in front of a spot-lit photographic mural of Bosch's *Garden of Earthly Pleasures*. He told me, in an instructive tone, about a film that Albert Finney was about to do which seemed refreshingly original. It took place in several time frames, cut together to make a single composite journey from England to the South of France. 'That sounds as if it could be very good', I said.

Ken was usually of a blanched complexion. Was there was a hint of a blush as he looked at me? Or did he go paler than pale? No one will ever know. 'Oh my, g-g-God', he said. 'You wrote it.' He looked round and up at the balcony at the back of the room. A beautiful blonde woman came from wherever she came from, smiling. Her name was Kathleen Halton.

I worked more diligently than inventively on *Far from the Madding Crowd*. Since the novel is very long and full of incident, my activity resembled that of a charcutier. I sliced cumbrous hunks of Hardy's Latinate prose and stitched his dialogue into palatable parcels. You and John had busier things to do than to slow my progress with your help. I did not doubt that the film would be made or that John would make a worthy period job of it, in the David Lean manner. At the same time, I was conscious that we were slipping back, on a gilded slide, into playing safe. When we might have done something 'modern', I had agreed to put a thatched roof on old Wessex.

I delivered a script of just over hundred and forty pages. Three weeks passed before you called.

'Fred.'

'Yes.'

'Listen… de script.'

'Arrived, has it?'

'One thing worries me very much.'

'What?'

'Page one hundred and sirteen.'

'Page one hundred and sirteen. What about it?'

'Do we need de scene wiz the I don't know what because I don't have it in front of me.'

'If you don't think so, probably we don't. What about… the rest of it?'

'It oll seems to be quite good in many ways, I must say.'

That first draft became, *grosso modo*, the final draft. The logistics of producing a period film of such scope were demanding and complicated. I had small wish to attend the shooting, though I did make one sortie to Dorchester, when the three of us were photographed in complacent colloquy. You called me, when you were in London (probably without Stella knowing it), to tell me that Visconti's favourite writer, Suso Cecchi d'Amico, had written a treatment for a film about Byron. Would I be interested?

'Does John want to do it?'

'Byron, for god's sake! John...'

While shooting went on, and on, in the west country, I researched Byron's life and filed key scenes in a big box. I had the idea of a vast montage, not always in chronological order, a Regency version of *Two for the Road*, which had indeed now been cast with Albert Finney in the part of Audrey's husband. He had just had a big success in *Tom Jones*.

You were now a producer in demand. Even Joe Losey was willing to work under your aegis when Monica Vitti decided to seek fame outside Michelangelo's control. The chosen vehicle was *Modesty Blaise* from a newspaper strip cartoon. Were Losey and Vitti happy choices for whimsical rococo sex and violence? Joe was a stranger to humour, Monica to being quick on the trigger. Having given her leave, Antonioni regretted his masochistic generosity and offered, too late, to direct the picture 'à la manière de'. Losey's standing with *Cahiers du Cinéma* inflated his vanity; filching Monica was as near as he could come to sapping Michelangelo's genius. When they were making the movie, Dirk Bogarde, who played an evil part, went about saying, 'Miss Vitti is a pitti'. Losey proved to have no genius for comedy. There was one good scene, if you remember, when Dirk, camp as Aldershot, is staked out in the desert by the villains under a baking sun. He croaks out, 'Champagne, champagne...' Credit Evan Jones.

After the success of *Darling*, your only modest luxury was a new Jaguar. Restless in the office and at home, your unlikely, patient hobby was fishing. You often went as far as Wales for a promising river bank. On the way home, patience was abandoned. On one occasion, so you told me, you overtook and were then overtaken by the same vehicle, which veered across you, forcing you to brake, and then quit the motorway. You twitched the Jag into the off ramp and followed. The other car went some distance and then, through gates, up a driveway to a large house. You followed. The other driver looked at you with apprehensive alarm. You said, 'Do you know me?'

'Know you? Why should I know you?'

'If you don't know me, why do you want to kill me?'

You were now aware of a man in a peaked cap, wheeling a bicycle, who had come down a path from behind the house. The cap indicated that he worked for the Gas Board. He was writing, with an official air, in a notebook.

'This is private property', he said. 'I'm taking your number.'

'In dat case', you told him, 'I take your height.'

In town or country, you drove as fast as the road, not the law, allowed. Some years later, you were stopped by a motorcycle policeman while speeding down Park Lane. The policeman walked back from his parked vehicle and indicated to you to open your window.

'Did I do somesing wrong?'

The policeman said, 'Do you know what speed you were going, sir?'

'In many ways, not.'

'You were doing sixty-five miles an hour.'

'It's possible.'

'And do you know what the speed limit is in a built-up area?'

'Tell me?'

The cop frowned. 'You're not English, sir, are you?'

'In many ways, not.'

'Well, sir, in this country, in the city, the limit is...' He drew a large three and a large zero in the air. 'Thirty miles an hour.'

'Sanks for telling me, I must say.'

The policeman said, 'Enjoy your stay in England'. As he walked back to his motorbike, the policeman glanced at the front of your Jag and saw the English registration number. He came back. 'If I may ask you, sir, how long have you been in this country?'

You said, 'At dis point, about thirty-eight years'.

Fishing was your prime pleasure, but you also liked going to the races. Coming back through Liphook, with Charles Riconno and two other men, you were flashed by another motorcycle cop who asked him what speed he had been doing through the village. You said, 'About seventy-five miles an hour.'

The cop said, 'You're very... honest about it. I'll give you that. And do you know what the speed limit is?'

'Tell me.'

'Thirty miles an hour.'

You said, 'That's all right then'.

The policeman said, 'All right? What do you mean all right? You said yourself you were doing seventy-five.'

'Dare are four people in de car. Four sirties are a hundred and twenty.'

You went quite frequently to Italy, often in the Jaguar, on business and a little pleasure perhaps. Might it be that you relished time without Stella's supervision? On one occasion, you told me, you were driving in the Jag to Franco Zefferelli's villa out on the narrow old Via Appia, when you were followed, very closely, by an Alfa Romeo. The driver flashed his lights demandingly, even though there was no room to overtake. When the road widened, there was a red light. The Alfa driver came close to your window and shouted angrily. 'You shouldn't come to Italy, if you don't know how to drive. When an Italian driver flashes his lights, you pull in and let him pass.'

'As a matter of fact', you told him, 'I would like nothing better.'

'Meaning what?'

'Meaning, I have a certain problem, as a matter of fact. In the sexual... which means, as a matter of fact, de only way I can achieve any pleasure in... dat department is for someone to go past me in de car as fast as possible. So listen, when de light changes, please, put your foot down, because when you go vroom, only den can I...'

The light changed. The other driver stared, frozen. And off you went. True? Are you smiling? I am the sceptic who believes every word.

Far from the Madding Crowd was a success in England. In America, audiences had no ear for Wessex accents and no interest in antique rusticity and little for Julie with her clothes on. The première in New York was unapplauded; a similar screening in Los Angeles was cancelled. John immediately withdrew from interest in the Byron script on which I had been working: 'period' didn't work. He asked you and me to get involved in what would become *Midnight Cowboy*. You were sorry to see him go, but 'To tell you de truce, Fred, what do I know about dose kinds of people?' I felt the same way and chose to work on my new novel. When John won the Oscar, we both telegraphed the right things.

Still eager to sponsor me as a director, you had the idea of doing a three-part movie, in the Italian style: we would produce it together and I would direct one segment, from a story called *A Roman Marriage*, commissioned from Brian Glanville. One of the other stories, also about marriage, came from an article by Kathleen Halton, now married to Ken Tynan. She had interviewed me on the BBC when I won the Oscar for *Darling*. When she came to the office, you said: 'Fred, I must tell you, she is just my type.'

I said, 'Jo, I must tell you: she is everyone's type.'

Everyone's, as it turned out, except Ken's; poor Kathleen.

Two for the Road came out in America in the same year as *Bonnie and Clyde*. Stanley Donen enjoyed the praise, but he was not deceived: we won the *Concha d'Oro* in San Sebastian, but our movie was not enough of a hit to win Audrey the Oscar she deserved.

When Dick Zanuck and David Brown, who had backed us at Fox, came to London, Richard Gregson left me to entertain Natalie Wood while he negotiated a plump deal for me to write two screenplays, the first from a six-page outline entitled *Guilt*, which they agreed, in principle, that I should direct, with you as producer. When Faye Dunaway came to London, she asked to meet me. We talked and she said that *Guilt* was just the kind of thing she wanted to do. She was, in Stanley Donen's phrase, 'hot as a pistol'. I was set to write, and direct, the kind of movie which you and I really wanted to make.

By the time the script was written, the great economic bubble of the 1960s had burst. The stock market was diving. Hollywood was turning out fewer films than ever in its history. You were about to produce *Sunday Bloody Sunday* for John, script by Penelope Gilliatt. When Dick Zanuck and David Brown said that they wanted us to come to California to plan how, when and where to shoot *Guilt*, you proposed that we stop over in New York, to avoid jet-lag and kill de two birds with Fox's stone. You wanted to re-invigorate Penelope Gilliatt, John's *à la mode* writer, who was living in Mike Nichols's apartment on Central Park West.

Our flight was delayed. We didn't arrive at JFK till after midnight. I had only a light bag, but you had checked through a large one. We waited at the carousel until all the other passengers had collected their bags. By two in the morning, one sole suitcase was still in circulation. It bore four initials above the lock. 'Has to be yours, pal', the luggage guy said. You said, 'It's de same make as mine, but my initials are not C.K.M.W'. 'Take it anyway, because we're shutting down now. Guy probably took yours.'

We went to the exit. The customs guy said, 'Open it up'.
You said, 'I can't'.

'Open it up'.

'It's not my bag. It's like my bag, but…'

The customs guy jiggled the lock and opened the bag. It was a jumble of soiled clothes and various unsavoury articles. You said, 'Disgusting, I must say'.

There was a diary among the detritus. You called a number in upper New York state and a sullen person told us, reluctantly, where Mr. W. was staying in Manhattan. It was three in the morning when we arrived at the lobby of the St Regis. You had to prime the concierge with a buck or five before he gave us the number of Mr W.'s room. You called him and demanded he return your suitcase.

After another ten minutes, the man emerged from the elevator, in slippers and dressing gown, with your suitcase and without apology. All he said was, 'Why in hell don't you put your initials on your goddam suitcase?'

You said, 'For God's sake, you have your initials on your suitcase and you take mine. I assume that you don't know how to read.'

'You watch your mouth, my friend.'

I said, 'Jo, take your case, let's get out of here while we're still in two pieces'.

When we got to L.A. and checked into the Beverly Wilshire hotel, I was gratified to be told that I was described, in the clerk's ledger, as 'writer and director'. Each of us had junior suites. The town might be dead; we were alive. Dick Zanuck and David Brown had allotted us a studio limo, on permanent call. There was no difficulty in parking at Twentieth Century Fox. No new film was in production, but we, it seemed, were exempt from the blight. Faye Dunaway loved the script. No one doubted my capacity to direct. When I went to see the Head of Production, he asked whether I could find any use in my movie for thirty Zero fighters, left over from Dick Zanuck's *Tora, Tora, Tora*, a Pearl Harbour turkey which had done nothing for the studio's fortunes or Dick's own prospects with his father. On the raised desk in Dick's office, there was a bronze cast of a baby shoe.

We couldn't believe our luck, could we? And we were right: by the time we returned to London, *Guilt* had been deleted from Fox's programme. A day or two later, David Brown and Dick Zanuck were fired by the latter's father, Darryl. They lived to succeed again, royally, as the producers of *Jaws*, which did more than any other movie, until *Star Wars*, to revive Hollywood's money-making confidence and its now unalterable belief in 'no-brainers'.

Your son Nicholas was at Westminster by this time. You took paternity seriously enough to wish that Nicholas not turn out a *figlio di papa*. He, however, was eager to get out of Burton Court as often as possible. London was still swinging. One evening, when Nicholas was seventeen or eighteen, he was invited to a particularly enticing midweek party. You insisted that he be home by ten o'clock. Nicholas said that the party would not even have got started by that time. Jo said, 'All the same. Ten o'clock. Where is this party?'

'Oh come on, dad.'

'Your mother has a right to know where you are.'

'Does she have a right to know where you are?'

'Ten thirty. Now tell me the address.'

At eleven o'clock, you got into the Jaguar and drove to the address Nicholas had given you. The house was dark. You knocked at the door and a pretty girl, not over-dressed, opened the door. A sweet odour seeped out.

You said, 'Nicholas Janni'.

'Come in.'

'No, no, I have come to collect him. He is my son.'

'Why?'

'Why?'

'Do you want to collect him? The party's just getting going.'

'That's why. He has school in the morning.'

'So?'

'Please tell him to come.'

When Nicholas did eventually appear, you were in a paternal state. You pushed Nicholas into the car and drove, not to Chelsea, but towards the West End.

Nicholas said, 'Dad, are you drunk?'

'No. I am not drunk. I am taking you somewhere you will end up unless you're very, very careful.'

You pulled up outside West End Central police station, took Nicholas by the arm and led him inside. As you walked down the long corridor to where the duty-sergeant was checking his ledger at a tall desk, you said, 'You know what this place is? Dis is where dey will bring you when they catch you with de drugs and de girls and I don't know what. You are asking to be locked up with I don't know who and you'll end being I don't know what.' Your words were distorted and amplified by the white tiles on the walls and the arched ceiling. The sergeant did not look up until you had both reached him.

You said, 'Listen, I am sorry to say this is my son who has been doing I don't know what with I don't know who and I am afraid he is going to end up with the drugs and you will put him in jail for I don't know how long and his mother will go out of her mind so I want you to tell him exactly what happens to de young people who break de law with the drugs and I don't know what because in many ways... I don't know what to do...'

The sergeant looked at you and then at Nicholas's silent wince. He leaned down to Nicholas and said, 'I should take him 'ome, sir, if I were you'.

In the 1970s, you and I had quite a few projects, including the movie of my novel *Richard's Things*. Deborah Kerr was happy to have me direct the picture, but we couldn't raise the money for a movie about a love affair between two women. In 1980, my script was directed, listlessly, by Anthony Harvey, with Liv Ullmann, not at her best. She took but she didn't give.

Do you remember going with Beetle and me to see Visconti's version of *Death in Venice*, with Dirk in the part of Thomas Mann's wishful and wistful Gustav von Aschenbach? During one more prolonged, poignant pause while deck-chaired Dirk contemplated the paddling Tadzio, you said, with a deaf man's loudness, 'I wish he give him a kiss in many ways and we all go home'.

You were never a patient spectator. When you and Stella took us to see Tom Stoppard's *Travesties*, you booked seats in the front row. The curtain rose on an empty and gloomy set, illuminated only by a library sign which read SILENCE. We were, supposedly, in Switzerland in 1916. After a moment, the audience could hear the rumble of distant guns. Perhaps someone came onto the stage. You were then heard to say, again as loud as deaf men do, 'So far, I must say, I haven't heard a word'.

While John Schlesinger was engaged on *Midnight Cowboy*, you were producing *Poor Cow*, directed by Ken Loach, with Carol White and Terence Stamp, who had been less than tactfully handled by John when making *Far from the Madding Crowd*. You hoped that you had discovered another John in Peter Wood, who had directed *Travesties* on the stage. Julie Christie was set to star in *In Search of Gregory*, with Michael Sarrazin. A few weeks before they were due to shoot, you called me. 'To tell you de truce, Fred, we are still in search of de script.'

'You've got Tonino Guerra.'

'His English, I have to say, is not... Fred, listen, as a friend...'

'Who's the friend, Jo, you or me?'

'Will you look at it for me? Please. See if you have any idea for the beginning. You know how important the first minute is. It needs I don't know what.'

The script came round by messenger. It required little insight to see how badly it needed work. I covered it with question marks and scribbled a few improvisations in the margin and sent it back.

'Fred, listen, you are quite right, of course, but what can I do?'

'Peter Wood probably thinks he can write. They all do.'

'Fred, as a friend…'

'Jo, I'm writing a novel about Greece. I don't want to break off to do anything, crap least of all.'

'Fred, listen, you give me one week, oll right, maybe two, two weeks…'

'Give?'

'And I pay you ten thousand pounds. I don't have any more. I swear to you, on the head of my son.'

'No need to go that far.'

'Tax free.'

'How are you going to work that?'

'Listen, you do the rewrite and then…'

'I go to jail.'

'You go to Italy. I give you de ticket. You fly to, I don't know, Milan, and then you go Bergamo and in Bergamo, a man will meet you, at an agreed place very easy to find, and give you the money in Italian lire, cash. You take de money and then you get de steamer across de lake to Chiasso, Switzerland, where there are many banks. You choose a bank, change de money, you get a numbered account. You take the steamer back across de lake and you fly home and no one ever knows.'

I said, 'Jo, it's very bad, the script, and I doubt if I can make it any better. I have no intention whatever of going to Bergamo or anywhere else. Here's what I'll do. I'll give you one week and I'll try the best I can to give the thing a lift and a laugh or two, but I doubt if anyone can make it any good.'

'I can't get de money into England wizout…'

'Don't worry about it. Better if I do it for nothing.'

'Fred, listen: nussing is too much.'

I did the work, with strange pleasure and as well as I could, but it was of small use. When I had finished, you asked me to lunch. I took the pages to Bruton Street and he said, 'Fred, listen, about lunch…'

I said, 'That's OK, Jo, I don't need lunch'.

'No, Fred, listen. I have a bit of a… wiz somebody… so… I need to… But on de other hand, my wife may come to the office, because… I don't have to tell you… So, if Stella comes, den we have lunch. But if she doesn't come, I give you some money for you to have lunch I don't where, and we have lunch another time…'

'I'm off home, Jo. It's fine.'

'How is Beetle?'

'Beetle's fine.'

'I call you next week. We go to John's new restaurant.'

You never had another big success and I never wrote another script for you, alas. I took a fairly good-natured swipe at you and John and their presumptions of authorship when I came to write *The Glittering Prizes*. Jim Clark cut the relevant sequences together and showed them to you and some of John's friends after a dinner party. You seemed not to take offence, but you didn't ask me to write, or even re-write, *Yanks*. It could have done with, as they used to say, one more pass. It was close to a hit, but not very. Towards the end of shooting, in 1979, you suffered that crippling stroke.

When John went to see you in hospital, you were very weak and, for God's sake, frightened. You told John how, when you first came out of your coma, you looked through the window of your room and there, on the other side of the well, saw a priest administering the last rights to a patient. 'I must tell you, John, it was enough to kill me in many ways.'

John stayed for a while and then he kissed you and went back to the cutting room. The next day, he hired a soutane and a sacerdotal cap and went, with a crucifix on his chest, back to the hospital. The nurse told him, 'Father, Mr Janni is sleeping at the moment'.

'That's all right, I'll go and sit with him and say a few prayers.' I suspect that John tried out his Irish accent, but who knows?

He sat down by the bed until you stirred. Father John then got up and, as your eyelids fluttered open, leaned over the bed, made the sign of the cross and muttered suitably pious sounds, ending '...*in nomine patris, et filii, et spiritus sancti*...'

You said, 'You are a bastard, I must say'.

John said, 'Any sign of life in the...?' He drooped and then slowly raised his forefinger to pseudo-phallic rigidity.

'*Ma*, John...'

You lived for another fifteen years, but you never made another film. I came to see you, irregularly, in the Burton Court flat, a dutiful pleasure. You had recovered enough to sit in an upright chair by the fireplace in the living room, but seldom went out. You had a stack of Italian newspapers on the table beside you. Joe Losey was one of the very few British or American film people who called to see how you were. Ken Loach, no doubt, was too busy hoping for the revolution to have any bourgeois manners. If the telephone rang, it was more likely to be Federico (Fellini) or Michelangelo (Antonioni) or Tonino (Guerra) or Suso (Cecchi d'Amico). You grew fatter and fatter, stomach on your knees as if it was one of those awards you never cared much about. After winning the Vatican Latin verse prize, what did rigged showbiz trophies amount to? You endured without complaint. Perhaps you thought you were lucky, in many ways, to be where you were.

The last time I saw you, I came to tea. The big picture that had always hung over the mantelpiece was no longer there. I suspected that it had been sold. A maid brought tea, biscuits and Swiss roll on a trolley. The maid had her little girl of five with her. While we took tea, the little girl did hand-stands. She was not wearing any knickers: a scene from Balthus. As I stood up to go, you said, 'Fred, I like to think that we are really friends, you know? Because…'

I bent down and kissed your damp, stubbled cheek. 'And so we are, Joseph, and so we are.' At the front door, I dried my eyes and called goodbye to Stella. She did not reply. The phrase of yours that I remember best, and with great affection, was when you said, for whatever project's sake, 'In de last resort, Fred, we do it honestly!'

Tante cose, Fred.

TO J. RENFORD BAMBROUGH.

Dear Renford,

It must be over forty years since I last wrote to you. I cannot remember on what topics I fished for your opinions back in the 1970s; nor any warm response. Was responding as warm as you cared to get? I do have a vivid recollection of your manuscripts. Hand-written on stiff, emblazoned college paper, your texts wore the left shoulder higher than the other, *à la* Quasimodo. You may have begun close to the top of the page, as if you had a lot to cram in; you seldom proceeded further than halfway down before signing off. Did that blank half page closet sentiments you had had second thoughts about revealing? It was as if you had abbreviated, if not locked away, your boyish person in J., for commonplace John; Renford clamped you in mature formality.

Pseudonyms are a regular way of distancing childhood. Junius was never a kid; Stendhal *non plus*; Blair, see under Orwell, if you can; through him is another matter. Renford was not quite a *nom de plume*, but it served to baffle intimacy; so too 'Wittgenstein'? You were always a very dressed person. I cannot remember you without a proper tie. You looked big, never fat; strong, not beefy; always shaved, crisp hair flattened. Back in the conformist Fifties, fresh out of rationing, we almost all wore tweedy sports jackets, often with leather elbow-patches, grey flannel trousers, usually fly-buttoned. My zipped, fawn pants I'd bought in Kansas City, MO. Jeans came later. I doubt if you ever sported them; T-shirts likewise. We had weekly handkerchiefs, never Kleenex. Rough times, the Fifties: Bronco was no comfortable ride, was it?

I notice that I am addressing you in a dated manner, both sardonic and deferential. I once happened on Glyn Daniel, the College's first TV celebrity as presiding archaeologist, and a renowned oenologist, at a little one-star restaurant, *Chez Rigaud*, in Les Halles, a village in the often misty hills above Lyon. Ah M. Rigaud's *écrevisses à la Bordelaise*! Although I was married and had published two novels, I called Glyn 'Sir', in the manner of public schoolboys with beaks. We had both lived on E staircase Third Court. My neighbour on the third floor, David Wilson, was Glyn's pupil. He specialised in the Vikings. My other neighbour, Tony Becher, and I did not rate teetotal Wilson highly. He became Sir David, director of the British Museum, and never stopped smiling, even at Greeks demanding gifts. Glyn said that he and his wife were 'dawdling through the Dordogne'. Some dawdle! He was two hundred miles east of that province. The college's *arbiter vinorum*, he was better at vintages than geography.

When you and I first met, you were a twenty-seven-year-old, recently elected Fellow of St John's. Pub-crawling with John Sullivan and Tony Becher and me (*The Baron of Beef* rather than *The Blue Boar*, never *The Eagle*), sometimes close to giggly, you were careful not to allow alcohol to induce the confessional mode while we downed more philosophical pints than I had thirst for. I never liked English beers and dreaded matitudinal headaches. Guinness was not good for me; lighting up round after round of Players Number Three gave me a sore throat, though I liked the residual yellow smell indented on my right forefinger. You seemed in no hurry to get home to Moira and the children. Did you find yourself a little more grown up than you wanted to be?

Tony Becher was more your sort of company than I was, wasn't he? Tone – as he was sometimes called – and Sullivan rowed, as you had, for the Lady Margaret Boat Club second eight, unless it was the third. You sported a red-bladed oar on the wall in your rooms. The year I came up, the L.M.B.C. had six Blues in the university boat (Anthony Armstrong-Jones, of Jesus, was the cox). I never wielded more than a hockey stick for the college, once, in the second XI. I was some kind of a threat, with a fuse you did not care to light, or was it, more probably, that you did not care at all?

Tony and I became your acolytes quite soon after our arrival. We were not official Moral Scientists until our third year, after having taken Part One of the Tripos. You liked clever people, not earnest talk. The precocious often wind up wishing they had time to be young again. Becher gained an easy First in Mathematics; I got a shameful 2.1 in Classics. Taking a generous view, the College prolonged my scholarship to allow me a fourth year in order to read Moral Sciences Part Two. I may well have owed you thanks for this grace. I fear I never expressed them. Sorry about that, truly.

Philosophy was neither a popular course nor a good career move; Firsts were rarely allotted. A Moral Sciences team photograph that I have from 1953 shows faculty members outnumbering undergraduates. G.E. Moore, the emeritus professor whose *Principia Ethica* was published ten years before the outbreak of the Great War, sits like a modest grey ghost among us. The Bloomsbury Group took his unaggressive conviction that goodness was a 'non-natural' quality as the agnostic's gospel. We all knew the story of Russell saying to Moore, at some point, 'You don't like me, do you, Moore?' Moore allegedly thought for a moment or two before saying, 'No'. What, Gilbert Ryle might have asked, did that mean other than that he hesitated? How promptly we acquiesced in Ryle's *Concept of Mind* and the idea that there was no ghost in our machinery! There was certainly one in mine, and in yours, Renford, was there not?

Two of the regulars at John Wisdom's 9 a.m. lectures in Mill Lane were Andor Gomme, later an ardent Leavisite, and his then wife. In those days no one was privy to the sex of an embryo. It is said that Gomme *père* had called the unborn child And/or and left it that way when he was born. Andor's wife was addressed by John Wisdom only as Mrs Gomme. The regular, small audience was a caucus attuned to Wisdom's improvisation. He would occasionally throw a question at the company. One was 'Can anyone think of a metaphysical question?' A guileless newcomer, Piers Paul Read, was quick, too quick, to say, *en bon Catholique*, 'Does God exist?' 'Oh', Wisdom said, 'Oh. I was thinking of something along the lines of... is this really a table?' You've heard it before.

His categorical name, fit for *Pilgrim's Progress*, seemed to dispossess Wisdom of other characteristics. His conduct in the lecture room was both didactic and larky: he took himself off. Disdaining notes, he improvised in a manner almost suitable for the music hall. To illustrate the irrefutable nature of metaphysical entities (such as angels, devils etc), he asked us to look for snakes under our desks. 'Any signs of reptiles?' Playing proper stooges, setting up the pay-off, we shook our heads. 'Look again; any *invisible* snakes?' Again we shook our heads. Then the kicker (as none of us would call it in those days): 'You can't see them, but they're there!' Shades of the gods Wisdom didn't believe in.

As unsystematic as his teaching, Wisdom was too British for translation, too jocose for continental recognition. George Steiner would have no time for him, but there was anguish in Wisdom's humorous gasps; earnestness that dared not speak its name. You too? You could recall, as few now do, how Wisdom told a parable about a garden which seemed both beautifully maintained, in the luxury of its blooms and shrubs; yet elsewhere unkempt. The question was 'Is there or is there not a gardener?' The analogy with a loving or protective deity was prettily packaged. There was, however, an inadvertent bias, was there not, in the seeming fifty/fifty image? Whatever indicated a gardener's attentions did more, surely, to attest to his (His) existence than wilderness denied it. The moral?

Agnosticism was fine; atheism untenable. God could be ignored; not denied. Did Wisdom have a grudge against Him for not existing? When Pamela (an able water-colourist) died, he refused to go into the church where her funeral was held.

Years later, I met Bryan Magee, complacent pundit with a prompter's whisper, in the London Library, and quizzed him on why Wisdom had not featured in a prolonged TV series he had chaired on modern philosophers. He responded with a dismissive wince. Might the truth have been that he could not 'do' Wisdom, as mimics could not do Alec Guinness until Peter Sellers cracked it? Do you know who Patsy Hendren was? Pre-Great War Middlesex and England left-hander and mimic, of other batsmen, of amiable precision.

Thanks to your cautious campaigning, Part Two of Moral Sciences had been dilated to embrace a category comprising ancient and modern philosophy, somewhat like Oxford's Greats. It was just my size. I had been idle in my first two years, the first playing too much bridge (I had the very small honour of being in the Cambridge team), the second with second-rate theatricals. Having had quite enough of Latin and Greek prose and verse composition at Charterhouse, I had hoped that Classics at Cambridge would take some intellectually elevated form: philosophy. You led me to it, ancient and modern, prosaic hymnal: Anaximander to Zeno, Ayer to Wittgenstein.

When John Sullivan busied himself studying a handbook of Advanced Greek Prose Composition, I neglected to say 'after you with that'. Bent on scholastic eminence and livelihood, J.P.S. kept his eye on the specifics necessary for access to the higher rungs of the academic *cursus honorum*. I have spent no small part of a lifetime apologising, to myself, for juvenile sloth by acquiring shelf on shelf of books on the classics, doing translations, writing books on ancient topics. At Cambridge, bent on writing novels, I chose to read my way through modern fiction, from D.H. Lawrence, John Dos Passos, Hemingway and Faulkner, Henry James and Sinclair Lewis, Sartre and Malraux to Mann and Tolstoy, Turgenev and Zola, foreigners always in translation.

In the general election of 1951, halfway through my first year, the Conservatives under Winston Churchill were returned to power. Members of the Pitt Club wore flat caps with renewed officer-class presumption. During the following lustrum, cropped of the Indian jewel in her crown, Britannia affected to resume greatness. Civilisation had prevailed; values implicit in the English language were confirmed. Whatever turbulence lay beyond the light blue breakwater, Grantchester's clock promised to stand forever at ten to three; and, yes, there was honey still for tea.

After you recommended *Language, Truth and Logic*, I took it for a lay bible. It not only supplied polemic authority to claim that metaphysics was without substance, God non/sense, morals a matter of opinion; it also made it superfluous to read verbose German philosophers, especially those beginning with H: Hegel *mit* Heidegger, Husserl *und* Horkheimer. Arthur Koestler's compendium *The God that Failed* confirmed that, when it came to Communism, the only people who had all the answers were those who had not heard all the questions. George Steiner told me that Koestler kept a *cordon sanitaire* between himself and the Iron Curtain for fear of a snatch squad.

That punctilious Oxford pundit J.L. Austin held grammar itself to be the vessel of morality. His clipped prose not infrequently sported a comma after 'a', when an interruptive qualifier merited attention. Short back and sides trumped rhetoric. My friend Clive Donner, the film director, overheard Freddie Ayer, while at work on a French holiday, saying to himself, perhaps for fear of Austin's inquisition, 'That's very clever, but is it true?' Clive's wife, Jocelyn Rickards, had been Freddie's mistress. They were very grown-up and childless, as far as husbands and wives were concerned: Stuart Hampshire's son was widely known to be Freddie's too. When I called Clive and Jocelyn answered, and I said it was Freddie, it was never the Freddie she wished it was.

Over all contemporary philosophers, from Hampshire to Strawson, Ryle to Hart, the shade of Ludwig Wittgenstein loomed, like Mozart's *Commendatore*. W. had died the year before I came up. You talked about him, but never mentioned attending his causeries or even meeting him. Didn't you tell us that he had a birthday as he lay dying of prostate cancer? Mrs Bevan, his doctor's wife, brought in a cake and said, 'Many happy returns of the day, Professor Wittgenstein'. The patient is reported to have said, 'Would you care to rephrase that statement?' If so, it was odd; a wish is not a statement. W.'s categorising hand gestures were borrowed by his disciples when it came to chopping bad logic. No one was heard to imitate his voice. Did he speak fluent English? Like British royalty, he had been translated from the German.

Were you there on that now famous night when he and Karl Popper, two translated Viennese, of different social backgrounds, clashed at the Moral Sciences Club? Or another, on which, after Isaiah Berlin had read a paper, Wittgenstein responded with a protracted, dismantling monologue, after which he shook Berlin's hand, said 'Good discussion' and walked out of the room? Berlin decided to retire from Formula One philosophy and busy himself with retrospection: commentaries on Johann Gottfried Herder and other unfoolish, unfashionable topics. Incompatibles were reconciled, never resolved, in Berlin's diplomatic despatches. When he was seconded as a commentator on wartime Washington DC, his cool style brought him to Winston Churchill's attention. A practised toady introduced me to him once, in the Garrick Club. Berlin was wearing black coat and striped trousers, red carnation in the buttonhole, the image of an English gentleman of the kind none still resembled, if any ever had: first Jew to be made a Fellow of All Souls. He looked more like the head waiter who wasn't going to find me a table. Walking imitation of what he could never be, whose hauteur was ever more deferential?

The Moral Sciences Club was a symposium without drinks. I only ever said one thing. It earned a nod from John Wisdom, more for the quality of its mimicry, no doubt, than for its originality. When a visiting bishop sought to speak the local language, so to say, and called God 'a summit concept', he won no hallelujahs. Maurice Cranston, later a friend of mine, with a delightful wife, was all but reduced to tears by the light blue piranhas swarming to inflict lethal comeuppance. Until Ernest Gellner's 1959 *Words and Things*, who cared to remark that 'Oxford philosophy' was a symptom of victorious Anglo-Saxonry? Neither French nor any other contemporary continental philosophers were discussed, unlike St Augustine, whose namesake, nothing to do with Hippo, had crossed the Channel with what passed for good news.

The language in which I retrieve the complacency of those early Fifties carries a mixture of conceit and repetition typical of undergraduate essays of the day. We were expected to wear our gowns to lectures and supervisions, into hall, and out at night. The evening of November the fifth was a licensed-up-to-a-point Saturnalia. Hearties knocked off policemen's helmets, but always with their gowns on. When I first came up, I had been disappointed to discover that, unlike in the Oxford of the period, Cambridge scholars wore the same length black wraps as everyone else. That was the kind of leveller I was. Yet I did solemnly believe that rational patience could persuade humanity to renounce metaphysics and the theological castles in the sky which it foisted on credulous audiences. Science, of which I knew all but nothing, was to be the verifiable salvation of a world without rhetoric.

The 1950s world was not so much round as squared off: divided between what *The Daily Worker* – available in the Junior Combination Room – called 'the Socialist sixth of the world' and the Free World, in which we rejoiced to gambol. I glanced at *The Worker* where plucky Walter Holmes, signature reproduced in wobbly print, appealed for shillings and pennies for the 'fighting fund', but stayed longer with the *Daily Telegraph* because it contained Guy Ramsey's lively, two-handed bridge column.

Cambridge in the now old days is often portrayed as an enclave of privileged prigs. Smug we may have been, but the distinctions in which we rejoiced were not easily won: in your case and mine, they had been gained by unusual mimetic competence. Writing Greek like Demosthenes and Sophocles, Latin like Cicero and Ovid, plus knowledge of Periclean Athens and the Sullan constitution secured passage through the strait gate into Lady Margaret Beaufort's foundation. Once there, I was dismayed to be expected to continue in strictly copy-cattish mode. Professor Anderson, an antique don recalled to duty, waggled his red pen over a conceit of mine in some Latin elegiacs and said, 'Where did you get that phrase from?' I said, 'I made it up, sir'. 'We don't do that', he said and drove a shaky, stringent line through it. Innovation had little place in Part One classics. Anderson would have had no time for George Thomson or V. Gordon Childe but I found my way to their Marxist sub/versions of the ancient world, if not at your instigation, then whose?

1950s freshmen in St John's discovered themselves in no classy company. Many post-war undergraduates carried unlovely accents, often shed with wilful determination if they threatened social progress. John Sullivan, my manifest *miglior fabbro*, sometimes exaggerated his working-class Scouse tones, the better to efface them on his way to becoming, on his unquestionable merits, Dean of Lincoln College, Oxford.

After a brief parapause (a term he invented?), John Patrick was transatlanticised, via Buffalo and Texas, to the University of California at Santa Barbara. The quondam Scouser adopted a laid-back international accent and leisurely southland wardrobe: pale yellow cotton top and pants to match. Asked if he would ever return to England, he said with a brief recurrence of up-tilted Scouse: 'They couldn't afford me'. Might you be smiling just slightly, Renford? I doubt if being rich was ever your ambition. It would have been success enough to become Master of St John's, had that ever happened. I can be sure you will take the Tacitean allusion re Galba; how many would these days?

You did not conceal that you came from Sunderland, but would even Shaw's Professor Higgins have guessed it from your fastidious enunciation? Rarely mentioned, your National Service had been served in the mines as a Bevin Boy at Wearmouth Colliery, no cushy posting. Like Sullivan (Sergeant in the Education Corps), you came from a background to which you had small wish to recur. Were you not the first pupil from your grammar school to get into Cambridge? Becher's father was a colonel in the Indian army; Tony went to Cheltenham and became a second lieutenant while doing National Service. Given the choice, I remained an American citizen. I liked Ike: he didn't need me. Trust a general to keep his country at peace.

It would be a mistake, Michael Brearley's appreciation of you insists, to think of Sunderland as a quarry of rough diamonds. As the ex-Middlesex and England cricket captain and first-class Moral Scientist revealed, you met Moira at a debating society in your native city where Plato and Aristotle were regular topics. Loyalty to origins was vested in the home life your pupils were rarely invited to share. Moira, no great beauty, had enough to do bringing up your four children. It may be that the image of you, as priggish Thornton Ashworth, which I intruded in my 1960 novel *The Limits of Love*, wounded you, hence Moira, more than pride cared to disclose.

My book's title, with its playful reference to Wittgenstein's dictum re the limits of [my] language, just may have provoked a wry smile on those shapely, colourless lips of yours, even if Ashworth, a likeness of your didactic self, was an unflattering, though never malevolent, caricature. I cadged the name from a boy in my house at Charterhouse. Although plump, Ken once did twenty foot ten in the long jump, or said he did (my friend Jeremy Atkinson has his doubts). Ken's father managed the Yorkshire Penny Bank. As for Thornton, he was a skinny Lockite, perhaps fifteen years old, whom I heard saying, in the Matron's surgery, in a recently broken voice, 'I want a woman'. Didn't we all?

I had a notion, sincere as it was convenient, that artists should depict things and people truthfully, regardless of feelings. If I always preferred American novelists to English, my prose tended to be a form of English-tailored clothing. Tacitus and Hazlitt, Petronius and Willie Maugham primed me on how to write. I had put on Englishness, hurriedly, as soon as possible after arriving, in 1938, from New York to live in London. Unlike many of my friends among the Chosen, I was not a refugee, but a Yank. My father was British (his family's genealogy at one of London's oldest synagogues can be traced back into the eighteenth century); my mother a middle-western American who never shuffled off her accent. I remained a hyphenate of the powers that won the war. I can imagine the beginnings of that toothless smile on your face: why should you care to hear this? Does it not at all apply, if you mutate the *mutanda*, to your own public personality with its modicum of metropolitan impersonation? What Boeotian metic did not hope to be taken for an Athenian? Theophrastus, eloquent as a god, lived in the city most of his very long life. The *agora* stall-keepers never took his divine tones for Attic.

We all now belonged, it was nice to suppose, to a post-war society of equals, beneficiaries of Lord Beveridge's bracing prescription for the common welfare. A spoonful of the right medicine would make us undifferentiated subjects of a powerless monarchy escorted by a chorus of dated halberdiers and jingling horsemen. The public philosophy – Walter Lippmann's phrase – advertised a placebo which, in practice, left the privileged, you and me among them, if not very high up, in a position of modest priority. When was humbug, striped with minty duplicity, not a favourite British sweet, so sticky it had to come in a tin? In case you get a question on it at the final judgment, 'minty' used to be American slang for gay. Reminds me: 'Got a fag?' we used to ask.

It is difficult to reconstruct that period of left-then-right interregnum, between the triumph of 1945 – appropriated by Churchill, not without justice, as the horologist of Britain's finest hour – and the hubristic disaster of Suez. The devious ineptitude of British and French diplomacy when Nasser seized the Canal would have had Sykes and Picot shaking their cunning heads. The radicalism of the emblematic author of the time, George Orwell (pseudonym devised to efface an unwanted childhood?) was itself, in the nicest sense, duplicitous: 'gloomy George' – Michael Ayrton called him – wrote copiously for *Tribune*, the leftest wing of the socialist press, mocked the BBC, a habitual safe target of quondam employees, himself among them, and concluded, inconclusively, that a mixed society like that of post-war Britain might not be the best of all possible worlds, but was probably the best of all practical fractions of one.

Aneurin Bevan was the mast-headed editor of *Tribune* (before Michael Foot, who was kind enough to ask me to write for it), but after 1947, while Bevan was bludgeoning the medical profession to accept the NHS, the editorial hand in practical charge was – for a time – Jon Kimche, one of those clever, little-mentioned journalists who made respected names for themselves among the knowing, especially, in Jon's case, when it came to the Middle East. *Seven Fallen Pillars* (1950) made him a modern Laocoön, futile prophet of a catastrophe which would embroil the West in general and the British in particular in disastrous involvement, again and again, in what used to be called the 'Near East'. It has receded, in common parlance, to the 'Middle East' but continues to disrupt and besmirch the moral and practical conduct of the West.

Jon led an honourable double life, at once a journalist whom even the Arabs, some Arabs at least, read, with whatever wince or scowl, and a vigorous advocate of Zionism. He was fired from *Tribune*, in 1947, for taking time out to help get two shiploads of European Jews breach the British blockade and reach Eretz Israel. He once drove me and Beetle up to Cambridge in his open Austin 40. What his mission was he did not choose to disclose. I am sure he had one.

Once again, Renford, I seem to depart from anything that concerns you and me, but what is never talked about can be the underside of any conversation, philosophical or otherwise. Kimche's activities were manifestly in the real world. He was at once unselfish and committed to things which were never, to my knowledge, certainly not in my presence, broached in Cambridge. I never heard anyone refer to the young Wittgenstein as anything but an Austrian officer in the Great War who later renounced his fat share of the huge family fortune. His courage had been both exemplary and solitary. Posted in a tall tower, on the Italian front, he directed artillery fire on targets which he alone could see. He was, no doubt, a regular target for fire which failed to hit or deter him. His *Zettel*, notebooks of the time, carried no mention of the war, nor yet of what he much later called his 100 percent Hebraic methods. Moore was once asked, you told us, how he recognised that Wittgenstein was a rarity. The advocate of plain speech and common sense replied, 'He was the only one who looked puzzled during my lectures'.

I need scarcely tell you that, after the Great War, W. returned to Cambridge, where he had, before 1914, shown Bertrand Russell his *Tractatus Logico-Philosophicus*, a catchy title that tracked Spinoza's *Tractatus Theologico-Politicus*. I am telling you things you know already in the hard-to-lose spirit of the eternal student hoping for ticks in his margin. At the same time, though I never heard anyone say so, W. was acknowledging, as cryptically as may be, that he, like Spinoza – noblest of western philosophers according to Russell – was a solitary stylite. Despite the fact that he abandoned a fortune, the better to play the modern Diogenes, Wittgenstein's *superbe* had something to do with the gold he had renounced, would you not agree? But then again, were what he chose not to be, rich and a Jew, indelible elements of what he was? The spaces between the columns of the Parthenon are part of what the Parthenon is.

One of the less noted remarks of W. was that the philosopher was essentially a loner, the citizen of nowhere, somewhat like both the wandering Jew and the Son of Man who had nowhere to lay his head. This apology for the solipsist may also be a sideswipe at Plato who posited that he and his unnamed philosophical equals would be sole rulers of the ideal republic unconvincingly blueprinted in the so-called *Republic*. His politeia was a rigged oligarchy, complete with phoney mythology. Did you put me onto Popper's *The Open Society and Its Enemies*? It has to have been you who told Tony Becher and me that Popper was generally regarded as his own worst enemy. Someone is said to have said the same about Nye Bevan. Ernie Bevin replied, 'Not while I'm alive, he ain't'. I heard that story in The Hole in the Wall, a Fleet Street pub favoured by *Express* men in 1949. One recalls another: 'Where', someone asked, 'is the smallest airfield in the world?'

'Athens?' Fred the patsy suggested. 'Under a Scotsman's kilt: just enough room for two hangers and a night-fighter.'

Despite the pioneering merits of Popper's great book, written in the war which did something to restore to Soviet communism the brave allure, in some dazzled eyes, which it had lost when Hitler and Stalin signed their knavish concord in 1938, its author was accused, by diehard classicists, of misunderstanding Plato. That he had learnt ancient Greek, in order not to be misled by tendentious translators, did not spare him the scorn of the established pundits whom you, Renford, had the cautious intelligence to charm when you set out to reconcile ancient and modern philosophy. Spinoza's wary motto, *Caute* (mind your step), might have been yours; never Popper's. With none of his belligerence, you did admire and recommend him.

Wittgenstein's shade hovered over the Moral Sciences faculty which he had dominated. At the time when you opened our ears to him, he had published only the *Tractatus* which dazzled Bertrand Russell and which, on returning to Cambridge, the post-war Wittgenstein appeared largely to abrogate. Recent reconsiderers have taken the view that W.1 and W.2, as we used to divide him, overlap more than was previously thought. That Becher and I had never seen the man added greatly to his lustre; vatic utterance and cribbed manual gestures lent themselves to apostolic emulation. You never explained what W. might have meant when he wrote, in the *Tractatus*, as translated by C.K. Ogden and Frank Ramsey, 'Roughly speaking all objects are colourless'. Despite and because of its inexplicable nature, we recited it as if evidence of Heracleitan abstruseness. You cannot step in the same Cam twice.

'We' included David Gore-Lloyd, whom you may well not have supervised or even known. He died of testicular cancer (now routinely cured) a few years later. I have a callow essay of his entitled 'Intention', given Ryle's ironic treatment. David had been a dutiful old-school Roman Catholic. His father was the (part?) owner of Wills' Gold Flake cigarettes and had owned a steam yacht before the war. We all tended to smoke Players Number Three, with small pleasure in my case. After falling among therapeutic positivists, David deserted the church. When he was diagnosed with that soon terminal cancer, I somewhat feared that I had separated him from the God Who might, whatever Spinoza said, have saved him, if suitably solicited by candlelight. I visited David several times in hospital and was shocked by the indifference with which his agony was greeted among Johnians. I had learnt from my father that it was a duty to visit the sick. He went to see his bedridden, deeply pillowed mother almost every day after the office.

In the polite style of the times, neither you nor anyone else ever asked me why I took so keenly to philosophy. I have always been disposed to argument and quick enough on cue to be likely to prevail. You made it clear that, in principle, philosophical discussion was not to do with winning but with the common pursuit of truth, or true things, rather than The Truth, a dubious grail. My zeal was excited, as you may have guessed but were perhaps too courteous (unless it was embarrassed) to say, both by Freddie Ayer's idea that metaphysics, i.e. religion, was 'literal nonsense' (non/sense, as Derrida might have spliced it) and by the terse insolence with which he denounced the notion that there could be any validity in a priori proofs of, in particular, the existence of God.

Among the texts you recommended was C.L. Stevenson's *Persuasive Definitions*. His then quite bold thesis was that philosophers habitually procured results that were premeditated by loading the terms of their argument with implications that would yield seemingly logical results of an order that suited their books. Arguments that proved that

God existed were all of this order. In one of our supervisions, I summoned the nerve to illustrate Stevenson's observation by alluding to Macaulay's speech to the House of Commons in favour of the emancipation of the Jews. Macaulay's argument was that if you give a Jew a bad name, he is liable to be sly or snappy. The Jew had been persuasively defined, by Christian doctrine, as by Karl Marx, into the perfidious roles then said to be typical of his nature. My seemingly dispassionate passion was to dethrone a God who had proved either impotent or indifferent during what was not yet called the Holocaust or anything else in particular. You and Tony Becher listened politely. The topic was not pursued. Post-war Cambridge was, in many respects, a wilful reconstitution of what it had been before. Again, what we cannot be is part of what we are. The randy mouse says to the acquiescent elephant, 'Am I hurting you, darling?'

The first lustrum of the 1950s was a time of complacency for the British. The author of the myth of the finest hour was again at the helm, or at least on the bridge. The vindication of the patchwork society, jointed from crowned head to street-sweeper's tail, seemed beyond question. Butskellian economics made playing for a draw stand for tolerance, tolerance for magnanimity. The British forgave themselves their trespasses, especially when it came to Jews. Ernest Bevin had been quick to accuse the Jews of pushing to the front of the queue. No wonder the Foreign Office thought well of him: cockney prejudice was dignified as *raison d'état*. Bevin had already observed, not foolishly, that the deposition of the Kaiser after 1918 had been a mistake. The replacement of a traditional figurehead with a raving carnivore bore ugly fruit. Bevin's antisemitism was antique, not ideological: it excused the continued humiliation of Jews, but without any purpose other than to sustain Britain's privileged status. Why do I rehearse all this? Because it has some unprovable connection with the version of positivism that was taught at Cambridge and named for Oxford. The sequential connection between David Hume and the Vienna circle was no secret. That genial philosopher dismissed the clutter of metaphysics without schematic or polemical programme. The Vienna Circle, if never unanimous, was more purposeful and, as the uneasy Twenties turned into the nastier Thirties, confronted theories as specious as they were, very soon, bloodthirsty. The philosophical and ideological battles, metaphoric, then bloody, that centred on Vienna and Germany, were just the kind of thing which made the British pride themselves on their insularity. It was never hinted that Wittgenstein had been any kind of a Jew. I never heard Jews mentioned in any context in philosophical discussions, frivolous, descriptive or quasi-solemn. Did you, I wonder?

Brought home like holiday goodies, Freddie Ayer's 'principle of verification' did not long dodge the slings and arrows, tipped with *idées fixes*, of philosophical colleagues, not least those envious of his book's sales. Their unsmiling joke was that the principle itself was beyond proof as true or false, hence metaphysical. The criticism is formally unanswerable, but his text, so sweetly polemical, advocated a notion that, whatever its formal impropriety, has remained my familiar. It promised to purge the world, at an easy stroke, of that jumble of fanciful reptilian or domineering deities and ideologies that promised heaven, whether on earth or above, and delivered a whole range of hells. The promise could not be honoured, in theory or practice, but if it did little for (or against) ethics, it furnished an aesthetic which has sat with me for ever: whatever fictions occur to me, I am accompanied by a *daimonion* that requires something like plausibility when it comes to chat and action.

Fiction and verifiability stand strangely together, but whoever does not look and listen in order to furnish and garnish his work is never my kind of a writer. I remember, without shame, being on a panel, at the Cheltenham Festival, with David Grossman, soon after he had published a novel in which the hero was said to have escaped the Holocaust by diving into the Elbe and being transformed into a large salmon which then swam to the safety of the open sea. I asked, with polite ruthlessness I should not now repeat, whether he knew a lot of people who had got away by that means. Grossman's son was killed in the 1982 war when Israel invaded Lebanon.

Nothing has been more foreign to me, when it comes to literature, than so-called 'magic realism'. The future interests me less, much less, than what has been and is. How often is dialogue in science fiction anything but sloganeering? Doris Lessing's rockets to other worlds never took off, did they? Nothing has been a greater waste of time and money, so far as I am concerned, than Star Wars and its epigoni. Dare I say that the future of the planet is the least of my interests? Just because it is true, in the present moral climate, I should beware of saying it. And a little child shall lead them? Off you go then. For imagining philosophy as a mission, not a game, I have you to thank, although (I now realise, or at least suspect) that was not your view of it.

It is not very nice of me to think that, for all the gratitude I owe you for not a few favours, you were not quite the teacher to bring out the best in me, or to force it upon me. I have been tempted to imagine that Casimir Lewy, for specific instance, might have been more demanding, hence cudgelled me into relying less on turns of phrase and more on the grim meat of the subject, not least its continental congeries. Now I am not so sure. My friend Anthony Rudolf solicited Lewy with a view to switching to Moral Sciences and was told to go and read Descartes (in English) and Bishop Berkeley's *Principles of Human Knowledge* and then report whether he was, as Lewy never said, turned on. Had you said the same, I might well have backed off, as Anthony did, to his long regret. The problem was not with what you put on my reading list, which was admirably eclectic, but the fact, for which neither of us was to blame, that the current did not pass between us. Something that was never mentioned sealed Oxbridge philosophy in the 1950s in a kind of arrogant timidity. Sophistication sharpened the treatment of decidedly narrowed topics. What had happened on the continent was given little attention in Anglo-Saxon thinking. Lewy's instruction to Rudolf is proof enough that logic, never subject matter, was at the cold heart of insular philosophy. Wisdom's snakes were far from the only invisible beasts that were monstrously present.

You did your duty as a tutor but… what? Your devotion to Moral Sciences is not in question. Might it be that something in your past, provincial experience, made you flinch from bold application outside the calm haven of academic propriety? Freddie Ayer, pampered by the Citroen family wealth perhaps as well as by Etonian smartness, managed adroitly to bring the good news (as it then seemed) of logical positivism and render it into saleable, nicely phrased polemic. Never was heterodoxy more sweetly made over to deserve promotion on orthodox lines. I doubt if your ambition ever ran to professorial hopes. Your pen was carefully deployed, your sword sheathed: you placed a proper number of articles in the right places, but you were seldom if ever polemic, never prolific. My friend William Lyons, a Ryle expert, tells me, with no glee whatsoever, that your two published collections have not become canonic. You remained wary of self-revelation, even in the chaste form of going out on any brave sortie from accepted terms and topics. Bill's memory of you, at some philosophical *klatsch*, is of a man of forbidding coldness. Can it be that you always feared lest the heat you kept to yourself burst out of control?

I tried, back in the Sixties, to get you commissioned, by Tom Maschler at Jonathan Cape, to write a book, the first book in English it might then have been, about Wittgenstein;

you backed off, perhaps rightly. What did you know, or care, about the Vienna he had known before being Cantabulated? His mannerisms stood as camouflage to the unspeakable aspects, Jewish and homosexual, of his untailored person. Miss Anscombe and Peter Geach, who never wore socks, had become the guardians of W.'s flame. With the righteous insolence of the faithful, they purloined his corpse and gave it a Roman Catholic funeral and resting place. Was this the man, under the cross that marked the spot, who declared to Russell, late in the day, that he was not, as he had said, a quarter but three-quarters Jew?

It took a multitude of hands to wrestle him back to a plausible facsimile of the man who found merit in Otto Weininger; that precocious suicide proved, so Wittgenstein said, that there were important forms of falsehood. Guides too can be misguided: Wittgenstein toyed with emigration to the Soviet Union before becoming the emblematic genius of the logical positivism which, like so many things, he never fully embraced, professorial formality not least. How could any decent, provincial Englishman find the resource to unravel all the threads of a character so plaited with contradictions?

Ray Monk eventually did the job I had hoped you would, and very well too, up to a point. He was wise enough to concentrate on W.'s ideas and skate over the very thin ice of his psychological ambivalences to more reliable ground. There was a limit to what keen intelligence was prepared to treat: the topic of Semitic identity, whether 'natural' or presumed, which I was urgent and naif enough to hope that philosophy would put forever outside civilised attention. For all the good intentions of solemn accountants, the Jew and his bogeyman identity, inescapable or not, cannot be broached without some kind of literary, not merely academic, intuition.

Casimir Lewy's get-thee-behind-me Polish Jewish origins were never more clearly declared than in his cleaving to logic, a scalpel both clean and edgeless. Ryle's straight-faced rejection of the notion of interiority denounced, by implication, the Freudian rigmarole of psychological complexity. And yet, with whatever veridical validity, Freddie Ayer used to tell the story of asking Ryle, a man who looked as if he had never been young, whether he had had any sexual experience. Being a truth teller, Ryle said that he had not. Ayer asked him whether, had he had such an opportunity, his preference would have been for a male or a female. After thought, if one can dare to put it that way, Ryle said, with no confessional air, 'the former'.

Russell's displeasure with Ryle, for failing even to review Gellner's attack on linguistic philosophy, had his usual lordly clarity. If he disclaimed his title, it was in alignment with La Rochefoucauld's dictum that he who refuses praise asks to be praised twice. Through speaking up for Gellner, Russell was once again accused, as he had been nearly fifty years earlier, of being a troublemaker, an accusation to be proud of. For all his pugnacity, however, Russell never broached the dark side of what used to be called the Queen of Sciences, philosophy itself: why it has been so frequently a warrant for evil. Aristotle was perhaps the first illustrious figure to declare it virtuous to kill barbarians, a doctrine which leaked into Christianity when the time came for Crusades. Heidegger and Carl Schmitt, among many others, endorsed Nazism.

On just one occasion, the cosiness of the supervisions at which Tony Becher and I read you our dutiful essays, his written in trenchant ink, mine unprettily typed on my little Olivetti, was fractured by the presence of Norwood Russell Hanson. You must know how he came to sit in with us. I recall a brooding presence, bushy dark hair, seriousness that bore down, like an imminent storm, on dutiful repetitions of the going cant. Hanson had been a decorated U.S.A.A.F. fighter pilot in the war. He carried the weaponry of both philosophical insolence and bellicose manliness. As he listened with courteous impatience to our unadventurous preparation, I sensed boredom verging on contempt. He was just too polite to burst out with a salutary dismissal of our notion of getting anywhere by doubling on the spot.

I could wish that he had let go. His contribution to philosophy was akin to Stevenson's: he saw that the terms in which we declared what we saw were rarely as neutral or 'scientific' as complacency presumed. Where Austin put his faith in grammatical rectitude, Hanson saw the wilful arbitrariness of convention, the bias implicit in what passes for common sense. If I had had the nerve or the wit, I should have chased after him and solicited something close to correction. He was a threat when he should have been an inspiration. I played safe. Hanson's books confirmed his impatience with the going nostrum that made the way things looked pretty well the way they were and, without moral content, should be.

I funked what would have disrupted my vanity and, perhaps, offended you. Hanson had retained the pugnacity of the fighter pilot, power-diving on his target. He still liked to fly. Just over ten years later he went up on one of his regular solo flights. Habit must have made him lazy: he did not check whether his plane had been refuelled as usual. It had not; he ran out of fuel, crashed and was killed.

I do not at all doubt that you were a good teacher. Tony Becher's First in Finals was reference enough; Roger Scruton's work supplied the gilt. My 2.1 was, once again, probably my due, dammit. I had spent too much time writing a musical comedy and skits for the Footlights to have the range of apt and accurate reference to impress the examiners. It was probably all for the best. Tony's First led him into the academic enclave; after working at the Nuffield 'The Nuffers', he became Professor of Education at Sussex. It did no more for his melancholic disposition than did leaving his nice wife, Anne, for another woman. I remember the last time I saw you, buttoned and polished, at the last party Tony and Anne gave in Weech Road. We were as falsely easy with each other as ever.

And you, Renford, you too went as far as you could on the fixed rails of Cambridge life. My friend Paul Cartledge, now emeritus professor of Greek, has a happy memory of you conducting an auction of books selected by the classical faculty (to which you continued to adhere) at an annual party at which the merits of each selection was measured in the bids that you solicited with amusing impertinences. On home ground, you played a good game. Bill Lyons, now emeritus professor at Trinity College, Dublin, an expert on Ryle, remembers you, when he was a visiting junior academic, as supercilious.

I am not sure precisely when you first entered the race to be Master of St John's. You did not quite attract enough votes to gain the day. The feeling was that you were too young. Your day would come. There were rumours, I suspect true, that you took defeat, oh, philosophically, but also that you were tempted, without sin, into advisory talks with a millionaire called Robinson who was planning to found a new college. If you had respectable hopes of being Robinson's first Master, they were doused by the founder's wish that his foundation should specialise in science. The Robinson plot was neither furtive nor disloyal, but it may just have cast a fatal shadow on your second, futile, candidature for the mastery of St John's. You then knew that you would never achieve your long, not immodest, ambition. Some say you were bitter. Who can blame you? The curt J. that preceded Renford now seemed to stand for Jago, the overtaken front runner in C.P. Snow's *The Masters*, the only volume of his series *Strangers and Brothers* that anyone is ever likely to read again.

How we veer towards our end, or crash into it, rarely has much to do with what we deserve. I used to drive to Cambridge occasionally to have lunch with Guy Lee. He gave me generous counsel when translating Catullus and again, at length, when

I did my version of Petronius, which he applauded generously. No gossip, he indicated that you were not in prime form. He used to take you golfing quite regularly, I think. In the latish 1990s, he had to turn you physically on the tee to face in the right direction before you drove off.

Your death came suddenly to my ears. I am sure that I wrote to Moira. Why else did she invite me, perhaps with more politeness than enthusiasm, to come and see her when I was next in Cambridge? She was living in a flat in Portugal Place to which you had moved, I suspect, when your children left home and you found stairs difficult to manage. Bereavement gave Moira dignity and licensed candour. I suspect that my specific sympathy was not important to her. She had been cruelly used and needed to talk; an outsider could better be trusted than a local. Over tea, she told me how she had first realised that you were having some kind of a breakdown when you were due to read a paper on one of your favourite topics, the objective nature of moral judgments perhaps, and scrapped draft after draft. What had always come easily to you was now trapped in some mental deadlock. You suffered and sweated before managing to honour what would have been a petty obligation. At home, you were given to outbursts of rage. Your menu of regrets and reproaches grew louder, more ferocious, more accusing, more cruel. It was as if the repressed John burst out in rage against long confinement. Renford had spoken quietly for many years, bided his time; and it never came. Moira spoke quietly and with no hint of reproach: she suffered your suffering, even though it expressed itself with the malice which the mortally stricken so often reserve for those who have loved them. You told her that you hated her and had not had the life you really wanted. Hurting her was the only way, it seemed, that you stayed in touch with reality. Your condition accelerated to the point where she could no longer manage to take care of you, its devilish end.

I repeat all this only because it is true and because, in my eyes at least, it confirms you as a man buttoned into an identity assumed to suit your academic progress and, in particular, candidature for Master. Injustice breached your faith in the objective virtues you had been so determined to honour and you came apart at the seams. The objective value of being good proved no recipe for its due reward. It was no bad thing that you wanted, but you wanted it very badly. Had you known from the beginning that your chances were slim, the office unworthy of single-minded ambition, how much happier you might have been! No, I am not moralising; I am lamenting.

Moira was very touching that afternoon. Perhaps she sensed, though she never said, that even your loyalty to her, whether or not it amounted to fidelity, might have been an aspect of your determination to have no blemish on your private life, when it came to that longed for ascension. When she told me, in that quiet voice as we drank nice tea, that you had raged and, I think, struck her, was she aware that your fury was with the logic that had duped you into thinking that virtue would be rewarded? Might it be that the tantrums you turned on Moira had less to do with anything a loyal woman had failed to be than with her being the witness of the frustration of your sole lifelong ambition? Did you now wish that you had been the roaring boy whom scholarly custom aborted and that that tight mouth had come out with more than third-personal truths? You took such pains in public not to declare yourself. In the sorry end, the long abbreviated John in you burst out and shouted what you had never whispered, a tantrum of disappointment. Philosophy may have been a consolation for Boethius; it failed to serve you in that office. I'm truly sorry. F.

TO IRENE ROSE RAPHAEL.

Dear Irene,

When did I first call you Irene? I was certainly well over fifty. I heard Ron Mardigian, my Hollywood agent, calling his mother Alice and envied the easy way he did it. When I was small, I called you and Cedric (I never ever used his first name) Mummy and Daddy, in the style of nice American kids in the 1930s. The far side of World War Two seems both a very long and, with age, an increasingly shorter time ago. Life collapses into synopsis; chunks of the past melt into lacunae; names and faces become unglued. My memories of you (Ireen, never Ireen-y) fill a mental scrapbook, sharp at times, and as abruptly curtailed. The first is of living in St Louis, MO. Dad, as I called him all his life, had been promoted to a new job with Shell Oil. He had been working as a salesman in Chicago when he met you, a blind date, on snowy New Year's Eve 1929, at the Edgewater Beach hotel, a thirty-year-old very British Oxonian, one-time amateur world ballroom dancing champion, with a steady job with Shell Oil; unlikely chance companion for a nineteen-year-old beauty from Kansas City.

You were secretary to an architect in Chicago. The onset of the Great Depression ruined your father, Max Mauser, a man of charm, with the charmer's liability to be gulled. With little aptitude for business, he fancied himself an inventor of gadgets, the American artisan's art form. His good ideas – including a replaceable slot-on heel for worn shoes – were promptly filched. In the 1890s, he had travelled to America, by himself, steerage, from Bad Kreuznach at the age of fourteen, to seek out an uncle who had made it in the US. For all the warm smile and firm handshake, is it fair to say Max's shortened childhood never yielded to maturity? Whatever induced him to marry Fanny Rose, and vice versa, it was no lasting love match. By around the time you should have gone to college, the deli they had opened had gone bust, along with the marriage. You had to go out to work. You remembered all your life listening, in only child's anguish, to quarrels between Fanny and Max. Dreading the fate of Little Orphan Annie, you relied on your huddled helplessness to bring them together again before the next rupture. Max, then Fanny, would become more dependent on you (and Cedric) than you had ever been able to depend on them.

As soon as you had trained as a stenographer, you went to work in Chi. Dark and beautiful and, I suppose, in the jargon of the time, innocent, did you share an apartment with other girls? You had aunts and uncles in K.C. and St Louis, no family that I ever heard of in the Second City. You always talked happily of the rota of followers you had on the near North Side: Herman the rascal, Josh with the silver-papered walls in his bed-sit, Milton the bohemian who smuggled in that green-jacketed copy of Joyce's *Ulysses* when he came back from Paris with it (and without his virginity, could it be, to whichever sex he lost it?). He let you flaunt the Joyce while walking down State Street.

Was any of your suitors your lover in any but the nice sense? Your romance with Cedric disqualified them all; you were married exactly ninety years ago from the day I began this letter. He told you that if he ever discovered that you had been unfaithful, he would divorce you at once. He also declared, as honour required, his own previous loves (echoing Tolstoy, though I doubt if he knew it) and the child he had fathered on a Gentile, Maureen, who worked as a broker on the Baltic Exchange. She must have been quite a character. How many women were brokers in the early 1920s? I knew nothing of this until I was forty years old. I think Ellis, Cedric's father, must have paid her off. Although without any great income from Shell, Cedric was not in favour of your going out to work. Did he dread you having the independence that might come with a salary?

Clever girl cheated of a college education, pregnant before you had a career, you turned Art into a safe pursuit. My first memory of you, in St Louis, was by a concrete gradient with lock-up garages stepped along it. I was being left in some safe female hands before you went, with a ribbon-tied canvas roll of appropriate tools, to drive to a sculpture class. We still have the cast of a fine head you did of Cedric, another of Sarah, and one with your folded hands mounted on a block. Perhaps for fear of Dad's jealousy of the exotic company you might keep, you never became more than an able amateur. Hungrier for praise than for fame, you were satisfied by a teacher's approval, whether in St Louis or at the Putney, SW15, art school. How come your qualities never fired ambition to go further: dread of failure or of Cedric's distrust? How much did you love him? You once told me he was a very 'demanding' lover. Does that remark, uttered on a sullen day, suggest appetites that you never shared? Did marriage prove a harbour in which you were happy, never excited, to be anchored?

My other sharp memory of St Louis is of a visit to some friend of yours. She lived in a street with high-sided banks. Eight or nine steep stone steps climbed to the high sidewalk. Your friend's free-standing house had a Persian-style carpet in the living room. A little boy a year or so younger than me ran in, half-naked, from the back of the house, and pissed on the carpet in an insolent arc, belly out. Shocked and envious, I watched the uninterrupted splash. Did his mother's amused reaction make me suspect that he was more loved than I was?

What more durable specific against amnesia than self-pity? How much of what divided us, despite all the time we spent together in the US, came of my birth by Caesarean section?

Your gynaecologist was the father of Hemingway's third wife, the unintimidated Martha Gellhorn (she deliberately smashed his new Lincoln when he kept her waiting in a bar, quite a gal). Dr G. told you that the straight line that defined your pubic hair was evidence of femininity. I never saw you naked; you never gave me your breast. For some then current medical reason it was deemed 'unsafe'. How much did it affect us that we never had that physical intimacy?

You were also told by Dr Gellhorn that you would be unwise to have another child. Not yet twenty-one years old, were you deprived, or was it a relief to be spared another pregnancy? Both? Only children were no rarity during the depression. It seems sad you were denied multiple motherhood. You were always good with children; your grandchildren were devoted to you in a way in which, once we were locked in England, I failed to be, however proud I was – and was I ever! – of how you looked.

We left St Louis when I was three years old. I have no memory of where we lived. I can still see the floury air in Uncle Louis's bakery, the shameless rats in the wooden bins. I also see a rocker and a tall, flat-faced Philco radio in crutched aunt Lena's living room. Uncle Louis used to fall asleep listening to it. When Lena turned it off, he would open vexed eyes and say, 'I'm listening, I'm listening'. His fast driving on wet trolley tracks led to the accident that maimed her. My guess is he never forgave her.

Next, I see us driving, with all our portable belongings, up through Illinois and then across and down to New York, via Aurora; Fanny Mauser in back, outside in the rumble seat. Lucky it never rained. I was sideways in the narrow slot behind the stiff front seats. A Chevvy, was it? Dad would never stop for gas at any but a Shell station. We passed barely moving lines of unemployed men. I had no sense of any risk that C.M.R. might ever join them. I knew he was English, of course.

We were Americans, you and I. Even Cedric wore seersucker suits in summer. Except for catch, I do not remember playing childhood games with him. Later he tried to teach me golf, with small success. I never turned into any kind of a dancer either. I write and that's about it.

Apartments were easy to find in depressed N.Y.C. Our landlord at 30 W. 70th Street redecorated according to your pale green wishes. We had a nice second-floor apartment, with three bedrooms (one 'spare', but not for long). The dining room with flame-shaped pairs of electric lights bracketed on the wall. Under the carpet in the dining room was a bell that you could press with your foot to buzz for the help. I watched a silver-handled, polished coffin being carried, at a tilt, out of a steep brownstone on the other side of the street and into a stiff Packard, spare wheel in a metal holster ahead of the running board.

Pretty soon Fanny went back to K.C. Max took her place. Cedric went to the office in Rockefeller Center each day. Did he never resent your father's nightly presence? Finding no work in N.Y.C., Max spent his days walking the streets. Did he have dinner with you? I had a piece of cutlery he might have invented, but did not: it was called a 'pusher'. Did I love artichokes dipped in melted butter! When you needed to persuade me to eat my lunch, you recited the names of Cunard White Star liners we had sailed on, cabin class, when Daddy was entitled to three-yearly 'home leave'.

London never seemed anything like home to me. It needs no big guess that it gave small pleasure to you. My English grandmother Amelia Sophia was not welcoming. Her coloratura soprano sister, Minnie (who had sung for the Prince of Wales) had married, and divorced, money. Purple-haired, violet-eyed, she lived in Oakwood Court, a large, red-brick mansion block in what she would certainly have called Kensington. She had a plain daughter called Ivy, an amateur pianist we had to listen to. When Minnie told you Jews could never be 'ladies', you said, 'You seem like quite a lady to me'. 'I wasn't a lady', she boomed, 'until I became a Christian'. It must have been some relief to sail back to N.Y.C. Ivy's son, Jimmy Doll, flew thirty missions over Germany as observer in a Lancaster. He wore one wing on his tunic with an O at the base.

You had a succession of day-time helps in 30 W 70th, Irish and a colored woman called Fleggy. You and Cedric had many friends on the West Side. I had no sense of living in an enclave nor, since we did, of the hostility that kept Jews out of classy clubs and nice neighbourhoods. While Hitler ranted far away, I played with your friends' children in Central Park: Jimmy Scheuer, pretty little Mary-Jane Lehman with her freckled nose. I got given some heavy steel roller-skates; more threat than treat, they accused me, mutely, of clumsiness.

We used to go once a week in the Dodge to a square block of warehouse-market near the docks. A black guy would tote the long, double paper sacks in which a week's supplies were stowed in the trunk. What did you give him? A dime? A quarter? Depended, I guess. When we drove out to see the new buildings for the World's Fair, you had them roll off a dummy cover of the *New York Times* headlined: 'Freddy Raphael Visits World's Fair'. I still have it. You took me to day school at Ethical Culture. Its address on Central Park West told people that we were middle-class liberals, almost certainly Jews. Miss Henry thought me smart. We never went to synagogue, although there was one (Spanish/Portuguese) on the corner of our street. Cedric's boss, Kittinger known as Kitt, was a loud bully of Aryan provenance. Has anyone yet made it clear why that is such an enviable condition?

Having no brother or sister with whom to share naughty secrets, I was more watchful than boisterous. I sometimes went along when you spent time with your friends. Seymour

Wallis was the great joker. Remember him asking you all how they played strip poker in a nudist colony? The answer: 'Mit de tweezers'. I guess I was invisible. It has stayed with me, being present without belonging, but I did learn from Seymour that getting laughs was a good route to popularity.

Every plain Jewish girl wanted to be as smart as Dorothy Parker. Your beauty spared you the need to be a wisecracker: that white-toothed laugh and red smile were as good as snappy come-backs, not that you didn't work those sometimes. If none of your crowd could be called rich, all were well enough off to have cars and apartments. You might not have a cheque book, but you did have accounts at Saks, Lord and Taylor; also Bloomingdale's? You wore I Miller AA shoes. Cedric trusted you not to be extravagant, but not to have access to more cash than a modest allowance. 1930s wives might have a certain freedom, seldom freedom itself. Kay Thompson was a friend of yours; maybe you got to know her in St Louis, before she became a star. She wrote kids' books about a little girl called Eloise, an orphan, wasn't she, lived in the Ritz, a mouse cute enough never to be challenged?

I have a picture of you and me – three years old, in a wide white-collared sailor-suit – taken by a photographer friend of yours (not dad's) called Wollmer. Now and again you would leave me for the afternoon with Fleggy and go see him in his studio. Beautiful brunette in her early twenties, what did you do when you were with him? That Cedric was eleven years older than you, and from a quite different world, did not strike me as unusual. Everything that happened in America was usual, far as I knew.

Did you go on going to art classes when we were living at 30 W 70th? You certainly took me to the Museum of Modern Art. I saw my first movie there, a matinée of Abel Gance's Beethoven biopic. I can see the wild face, flopping hair, as he played but could not hear whatever fortissimo passage he had just composed. Harry Baur's leonine frustration promised his genius. Was there a thunderstorm at the same time? And a windmill somewhere? I was turned on by the image of creative frenzy. Imagine letting yourself go like that, hair all over the place! You decided the witch in Disney's *Snow White* was too frightening for me. We went to Radio City once. The chorus girls had some legs. *Two for the Road* opened there in 1967. I wish you coulda been there.

People in N.Y.C. found dad's Oxford accent attractive, didn't they? He made nothing of having been a world amateur dancing champion, but he never lost the quiet assurance of a man who had been the best in the world (it scarcely matters what at). We used to drive in and collect him from Rockefeller Center from time to time. Skaters glided on the ice rink next to the fancy plaza outside the silver rotating doors. Diego Rivera's wide, bold mural dominated the lobby. There was a concreted censored space where Karl Marx's face had briefly scowled at businessmen. The first-floor barber crowned Cedric with a rubber suction cup as a treatment for incipient baldness. I guess he was fresh out of snake oil.

You never jettisoned your American accent when you found yourself translated to London. Set to spend the rest of your life in an exile you swore you never resented, for the next seventy years you remained unmistakably American. When we arrived in Southampton on that third and final pre-war crossing, we had a brand new yellow 1938 Buick in the hold of the *Queen Mary* and a lot more luggage than we took on *Scythia* or *Britannic*. Dad was slated to return to New York after a year in London learning how to handle a complicated set of new ropes. He had been promised a much more important managerial job when he got back to Rockefeller Center; no Kitt.

You cannot have relished proximity to Cedric's mother. Possessive of her only son, prone to all the prejudices of the imperial and imperious British, Amelia Sophia held all foreigners suspect, pretty Americans not least. Docile as a good daughter-in-law was supposed to be, did you make much of an effort to endear yourself to the valetudinarian Amy? Youngest of the trio known, in Edwardian Eastbourne, as the beautiful Benson girls, she had decided to have a bad heart and be house-bound and pampered. Ellis worked for Raphael Tuck; the Raphael had nothing to do with us, it felt as if it did; so did the angel and the painter. Ellis had a chauffeur called Theobald. Happier at the office than at home, 'Can't stop' was his welcome exit line.

The emotional freeze between you and your mother-in-law served to curtail pious visits to Dorset House. Cedric, another only child, did not take sides; he endured, as he had Max's presence in 30 W 70th. He went almost nightly, after work, to visit his mother with grapes or flowers. Putney Heath was a long way from Dorset Square, a full sixpenny-worth on the 74 bus. On Sunday afternoons, I went with you and dad, in our Standard eight, EYR 332, enamelled Union Jack on the bonnet. Was the yellow drop-head Buick deemed too showy for green-fenced Highlands Heath SW15, where you took a first-floor apartment? I missed what I never saw.

When Amy heard where you were going to live in Putney, she said, 'I should call it Roehampton, if I were you'. I never saw the Buick, but I did dream about it. You would have looked good at the wheel, especially with the roof down. When you were well into your nineties, I stood near a London taxi driver as you set off, without elderly faltering, to drive back to Putney in the underpowered Morris you called 'my old lady'. His mouth puckered, chin tilted, with admiration.

I always sat in the back of EYR 332. The gear shift was stalky between the front seats. I remember a Wolseley police car, silver bell mounted on the front bumper, 'gonging' a motorist going more than 20 m.p.h. as you were driving through Hyde Park. One Sunday evening, after I had sat for four hours watching you all playing bridge (I learned the game, without having touched a card, during those involuntary sessions), I must have made some crack about your driving, or dad's. Cedric said, 'You had better remember you always come third in this family'.

On another occasion, he said, 'We love you, but we don't like you'. That married you to him against me. I am pretty sure that that remark too was made in the car which, at the outbreak of war, patriotism and petrol rationing required you to renounce. Cedric's tone was less wounding than supplying me with a kind of licence. When I got to know Stanley Donen, he said that I had the self-confidence typical of the only son of a Jewish mother. Did your glance in the mirror make a silent compact with me? Compact! Reminds me of the flat, round silver powder container, mirror in the lid, you always carried. You never had to pee: you powdered your nose.

I assumed you happy among other mothers who took their children to play, in a middle-class circle of plaid rugs, on Putney Heath. A local cricket team played in a wide clearing edged with silver birches. Quite soon, a sandbagged anti-aircraft battery would be installed where the big roller was parked. I watched the cricketers, as I had you and dad playing bridge, and absorbed the rules by osmosis. I did the same with the British accent which soon ousted American vowels. One pound sterling was worth more than four dollars.

Not long ago I read the memoirs of a man who, as a boy, survived three years in a concentration camp, at least in part because they came as no more of a surprise to him than any other aspect of early life. Adults were traumatised by abrupt falls from a more or less civilised routine into abject humiliation. Having suffered no very cruel experience, I was at no stage surprised by what followed our translation from New York to London. Whatever happened was what happened.

Nothing had to make sense; nor did it. I had a school cap to take off to ladies.

You had brought with you two brass-studded wardrobe trunks, of a style unknown to modern travellers: upended and opened, they revealed deep drawers on one side, hanging space, on flat wooden hangers, on the other. Labelled NOT WANTED ON VOYAGE, their compressed freight of clothing went straight into the hold. Your parents' bankruptcy made sure you kept just about everything, with mothballed care. You must have guessed that in due time whatever dresses, coats or shoes seemed obsolete were liable to have a second or third life. You never looked anything but stylish, wartime hair in a page-boy. Remember that Saks suit with the half-black, half-white scalloped buttons, worn with the Bloomingdale's silver-fox that bit its own tail? Knock-out company you were when we waited for a bus down the hill. Dad took taxis; you rarely. We waited for buses.

While we lived on Central Park West, I had had little idea of what was going on over the wide water. In Putney, I came to observe the old world's darkening horizon with the detached curiosity that I turned on its parlour-games. You spent more time with me in Putney than you had in N.Y.C. Marooned in suburbia, you took it well. You knitted complicated patterns that came with the hanks of wool you bought, several needles at the same time, a clicking solo with busy fingers, unchipped red nails.

In 1938, you took in an Austrian refugee who lived, I suppose, in the tight little spare room. Mitzi did cooking and housework. I was never left alone with her. The inhabitants of Highlands Heath were a whole lot less fun than New Yorkers. Careful to defer to local customs and conceits, you lacked company like Helen Walker, with whom you went on corresponding all her life, and Teddy Lehman, with her rare chuckle. Our Highlands Heath neighbour Adie Tutin was chatty and how, but no kindred spirit.

The Tutins' daughter Dorothy, Dottie for short, should have been my fond playmate. We knew each other as long as she lived. Years later, before she went to RADA, she took clarinet lessons from Roger Barsotti, conductor of the Metropolitan Police band. She and I played at a closeness that never led to kisses, even when heated by reading Noël Coward's *Private Lives* in your cream-covered Literary Guild edition while you were out celebrating VE-day. Dottie and I did smoke a secret cigarette or two. Many years later, Norman Rodway said, casually, that Dottie wasn't much when it came to acting. I felt quite hurt. I sent her a play of mine in the 1950s. I don't remember her acknowledging it. Twenty years later, when she was less in demand, I got her a small part in a radio play of mine. She never kissed me.

Adie had had a son, Eric, who had died when ten years old. John Tutin, doctor of engineering, had designed the revolutionary propellent screw of the Queen Mary. He never lost his swagger or his tendency to underlead aces when defending in contract bridge. Success unrepeated, he became an alcoholic. When he could no longer afford an office, he spent his days in the lounge (and bar?) of the Piccadilly Hotel. As he marched in, sporting black homburg, rolled umbrella, tall black coat, manly Eloise, who dared to challenge his right to be there? Didn't you wish you had had a pretty, eager-to-please daughter to be proud of like Dotty? Oh yes, you did too.

You took to London life without any complaint I ever heard. You had accounts at Barkers, Pontings, and Derry and Toms, in Kensington High St; Harrods in Knightsbridge. You had your hair done at Chez Maurice in Disraeli Road, Putney. Dad had always had a good lunch on Shell. He was liable to greet your best efforts with 'How nice! Just what I had for lunch'. Once you said, and more often thought, that his sense of humour made people cry, meaning he could be a little too dry to amuse you. With me, at midday, you relied on pot roast (my favourite) and 'Spanish rice', mince and rice seethed in a cast iron skillet that came with us from 30 W 70th street.

I learned to play Monopoly, with London place names, passing time with red-haired Martin Warburton. His father was a veteran of the First World War, his mother a retired chorus girl. He told me about the Tommy telling the story of how he was challenged by a French sentry: "'*Qui va là?*" says he. *Je*, says I, knowing the language'. We went to Knokke-le-Zoute for a fortnight in the summer of 1938. We saw a destroyer, British I think, patrolling offshore. I watched you and Cedric play boule at the casino. Having me along deprived you of access to the roulette tables.

My first English school was Leinster House, a red-brick Gothic day school on Putney Hill. Unlike at Ethical Culture, nobody was ever told to skedaddle on home. I was there long enough to win the form prize, a fat, illustrated volume of Nathaniel Hawthorne's *Tanglewood Tales*, an introduction to Greek myths I have been tangled with ever since. Hawthorne's versions were chaste and abstemious. His genius conveyed enough of their magic to kindle a long fuse. I had a schoolfellow also called Martin whose lapsed aitches led Cedric to warn me off his company, lest they prove infectious.

Were you more silent in London than you had been across the water? The English of those days aired prejudices like virtues. Your beauty and charm roused no suspicion, so far as I know, that you/we might be Jewish; it was bad enough to be a Yank. Cedric had chosen to live in south-west London. Reverting to being an Oxford man, he did not care, or need, to live in a Jewish enclave as we had in Central Park West. Landlords in wide tracts of upper east-side New York made no secret of denying leases to Jews. You were not interested in religion, but you sometimes came out with a Yiddish (or was it German?) expression: *schlemiel, heimeraus, schnook*. Out of loyalty to his father, Cedric joined the Liberal Jewish

Synagogue in St John's Wood. We never went to services. His old London friends, in Shell and from elsewhere, were mostly Gentiles or long assimilated. Guy Ramsey, unequivocal pro-Semite, said that Hitler had made people Jew-conscious. Cedric had done a bit of boxing. I never heard him shout, except 'Taxi!', upraised umbrella as prop, did you?

When war was declared, Shell asked him to stay in London to perform some specialised services. Eighteen at the end of the previous war, already in (officer's) uniform, he was too young to be called to the front. Now, about to be forty, he was too old for call-up; not for patriotism. Of course he would stay. We went to Wandsworth and crawled through a concrete building full of smoke; breathable air was close to the floor. If that was what was coming, it seemed quite fun.

You and dad discussed sending me back to America. With whom might I have been lodged? I hardly think I would have gone to Kansas City, even though Max and Fanny had been sufficiently reconciled to open another delicatessen. It did pretty well. Max had friends in the Prendergast gang that ran the city. They offered him a job inspecting grocery stores before they were given sanitary licences. It required no expert sniffing. If the owners paid the right bucks, they got clearance. Max declined to be even that harmless a kind of crook. He and Fanny had to pay dues to Prendergast by stocking a kind of soda pop nobody ever wanted to buy.

I have often imagined an alternative existence as a real-life nephew of Uncle Sam. I might have been just in time to be killed in Korea. Play it as it lays, right? As usual, people imagined that the second war with Germany would not last long. Shell promised that, soon as it was over, Cedric's plum job in N.Y.C. would still be ripe. When you talked about sending me back to the States while there was still time, did Cedric suggest you go too? You stayed; I stayed. Am I right in thinking that you had a continuing subscription to the

New Yorker? You may not have been nostalgic but 'Talk of the Town' supplied a regular dose of smart alecry which made me regard the Algonquin lunch table as a Parnassian rendezvous. One snippet was about a woman, burdened with Christmas shopping, who got into a crowded elevator and saw, in the corner, what she took to be the round button seat usually reserved for the attendant. She sank gratefully onto it only to discover… that it was a small boy wearing a brown beret. The story must have been told better than I have, or perhaps it belonged to an age of innocence. You and I laughed together, a lot; it seemed a lot like love.

When the first sirens wailed, only in practice, we went to stay with Teddy and Gladys Schlesinger at their double-fronted house in Sussex. It had an in and an out white wooden gate. Teddy had become a successful Harley Street surgeon. He must have become more deft with his scalpel than he had been, as a tiro, when he severed Cedric's urethra with a careless stroke. Dad was left forever scarred in such a way that he could pass water, as they used to say, only with increasing difficulty. He had the idea that Robinson's Lemon and Barley water made things easier. His mouth grew narrow with refusal to complain. When I called him brave, he said 'If you knew'.

The Schlesingers treated us like poor relations. They had boiled eggs at breakfast with silver-racked toast; we did not. Blonde Gladys, no beauty, could afford to be patronising (Cedric called her Glad Eyes). I have no memory of Teddy. I guess he was busy coining it with his scalpel. Their son John had an electric, quarter life-size Rolls Royce. He drove it around the grounds in a blue suit. One warm Sunday morning, 3 September 1939, we sat on the grass in the net-less, unmarked tennis court and listened to a brown portable radio. Neville Chamberlain's spent voice confessed that we were at war with Germany. Having done everything base to appease Hitler, the umbrella man now denounced him as evil. The declaration was uttered in a woeful, all but resigned tone. The company sighed and said little. Afterwards we went for a drive in EYR 332 and saw some more anti-aircraft guns.

Did you wonder what you were doing among these unbending people, about to be exposed to a war which, had we stayed in the US, would hardly have touched us? Not quite twenty-nine, too beautiful for our hostess, were you stirred by Europe's imminent catastrophe? The John Schlesinger in whose electric car I was not suffered to be so much as a passenger was not the same J.S. for whom I wrote *Darling* and whose father was also a medical man. I never saw him again.

Had we stayed in New York, would you ever have considered my going to boarding school? It was the common British means of educating middle-class children, without being encumbered by them when posted on imperial business. The Schlesingers lived near Copthorne, on Crawley Down, where there was an excellent prep school. A week or two after the declaration of war, you told me, as brightly as you could, that I was going to be a boarder. When sentence was pronounced, and understood, I cried and cried and hung onto the white bannisters of the Schlesinger house when the car was loaded with my trunk and suitcase. Did you want to weep yourself? Did I appeal to you to save me? Bet I did. That sudden operation, extruding me from that unfriendly house, was like a second Caesarean. Maybe you were not wholly horrified by the thought of my not being with you all day every day. Yes? No? Both?

My tears were an accusation. You were attending a petty execution that you could do nothing to stop and, I guess, wished was over. You loved and hated me, no rare condition, am I right? I wept. Did I feel betrayed? Severed. I was and was never again the same little boy who had stood with you in May 1937 and watched the silver cigar of the Hindenburg thread the blue sky above Central Park, heading for that fatal rupture as it moored in New Jersey (aka New Joisey). The radio commentator broke down as he described the sagging inferno.

I bet you and dad got into the car and drove away with much the same feelings that Beetle and I had when we left Paul, a year or more older than I had been, at Bedales thirty and a bit years later. Mrs Workman, the wide wife of the headmaster Skete Workman, treated me with brusque gentleness. She called me Raff-isle, as if I were some desert colony. You wrote me regular letters, on blue paper, in your confident, chatty hand. Cedric's were all dictated, usually confined to a single flimsy sheet; two had a businesslike paper clip. His secretary's invisible presence was a barrier to sentiment or spontaneity.

I had the luck, however tearful I was, to turn out to be 'good at school'. I began Latin quite soon and eased into the classical education in the last years of its dominion over the bourgeois curriculum. I was good at most subjects and keen to be better, a form of ostentatious invisibility. I discovered masturbation in those early terms at Copthorne School by rubbing myself anxiously against the bench as I tried to do the work, whatever it was, in time; my penis (not that I knew the word) Aladdin's secret lamp. We never talked about sex, you and I. Do you remember coming suddenly into my room when I was in my early teens, just as I had reached the point of no return? I am sure you knew what I was doing. You said nothing, backed out, wisely.

You adapted to London life during the Blitz with the borrowed patriotism that took you into the A.R.P. and then the W.V.S. I never heard you complain. Perhaps it was a good excuse for getting out of the house (as you called the flat). During the hols, I liked going to the air raid shelter at night and dreaded the All Clear. It put an end to listening to grown-up chat hyphenated by distant crumps and thumps. We took the *Sunday Express* and enjoyed Nat Gubbins's mockery of the

Germans ('*Dot voss ein bompf*'). It never occurred to me that you were half-German. Did it to you?

Just before France fell, Copthorne School was evacuated to Lee Bay, in North Devon, a six-hour steam, if all went well, from Waterloo. They put an extra engine on, back to front, to haul the train north from Exeter Central to Ilfracombe. Out and up there, I was about as far from you as England could set me. When the Blitz grew intense, it was decided that I should be safer if I stayed in Devon, as several other Copthorne boys did, during the holidays. There was a sandy beach, rock-pools with pale shrimps, sandcastles to construct and then watch as feelers from the incoming tide undermined them.

You came down once or twice, perhaps more, to alleviate my protracted summer solitude. Where did you stay? Did you count the days before you could get back to the loud city? I recall us having strawberries and Devonshire cream at a little outdoor café. If you were bored, you never showed it. Holiday time, you were free to take me out most days. The Workmans were polite, scarcely welcoming. Was a young American woman by herself close to an embarrassment? What did you do in the evenings wherever you stayed? I was glad to see you and, at the same time – there has been a lot of that in my life, and in yours? – I almost looked forward to what I dreaded: your return to London, reversion from Freddie to Raff-isle. Only in England, I would discover, was our name almost always mispronounced. I became wary of saying, then having to spell it. 'Like the painter' became habitual.

I noticed how men looked at you when we sat together. You showed no sign of being aware of them; I guess you were used to it. Cedric was the invisible third between and with us. I soon added Greek to Latin and grew further away from you and somewhat nearer him, the Greats man. When the Yanks started coming to England I was, yet again, both threatened by them – as if I might be held responsible for their pale gaiters, bold voices – and reminded of what I had been until a few years before. I remember one of them saying, outside the Lee Bay Hotel, as he unslung his pack and rifle, 'My fucking back!' It was as if, at first hearing, I knew the word from way back and why the G.I.s, many in their teens, laughed at the boldness. I got to know, but rarely use, all the usual obscenities, but I cannot remember who taught me them. I never heard dad say 'Fuck'. Did he ever even *think* it? He did say 'bugger' now and again. You used that word for the saline crumbs that accumulated in my nostrils, common usage in the US? Did the English ever speak of 'hang-nails'?

During the war, you and the Heaths and the Soulises had a Saturday night poker game, maximum rise six chips (pennies). You had several racks of different coloured chips and toted them to wherever that week's game was. When I was home from school I sat behind you and stayed unsurprised as you made your bets. Poker was added to the games I learned by watching, for hours, without ever playing. I borrowed all your (American) chips when Leslie Bricusse and I produced a musical at Cambridge based, very loosely, on the Monte Carlo rally. They all disappeared after the curtain had fallen on *Lady at the Wheel*. You never complained, but I know you were hurt by the loss. Those weekly poker games had stopped being played soon after VE-Day, but those chips were relics of old N.Y.C. I treasure two bone-handled kitchen knives that you probably bought for ten cents at Macy's, unless it was Gimbel's, in 1935. I value them more than any fancy cutlery. I once wrote a script for a guy called Roger Gimbel.

Your laugh was camouflage for whatever you did not have in common with the English. You looked to me pretty much as you had on Fifth Avenue; unsurprising, since you went on wearing your American wardrobe, when not in W.V.S. uniform, throughout the war. Rationing and shortage of choice made most women patriotically dowdy. You wore 'slacks' for the first time when on A.R.P. duty, and sported a snood for a while. When things got short, your larder was supplemented with big brown food packages sent by Fanny and some of your friends. We had all the Hershey bars we ever needed. Hershey never advertised because it never had to.

Were you a little bit relieved when the Japs, as they were always called, forced America into the war? The English had been proud of their solitary resistance to Hitler; they also sneered at F.D.R.'s yellow reluctance to send much more than his prayers. Churchill sucked up to him but was never going to be as persuasive as the raid on Pearl Harbour. When I was at home, after the Blitz had eased, I used to go with you to the Putney offices of the W.V.S. I sometimes had access to a typewriter and began the two-fingered exercise which I have never learned to improve. The W.V.S. organised a number of flag days. One time, you suggested I count the proceeds. The contents of several boxes were spilled onto a tray (can it have been plastic?), mostly heavy copper pennies and ha'pennies, some bearing Queen Victoria's rubbed profile. I looked at the brown spill and spread my hands, innocently, and said 'Vell…' I think you hated me at that moment. I doubt if anyone heard, or cared. You were mortified; then I was.

Among the packages from the US was one containing Leo Rosten's *The Education of Hyman Kaplan*. In the privacy of our new flat in Balliol House, Manor Fields, after you were bombed out of Highlands Heath, Hyman's mispronunciations and misunderstandings made us both laugh until we cried. I learned it was all right to be Jewish, as long as you kept it to yourself. Jewish jokes were fine when told by Jews; they were never funny when Gentiles, well-disposed as they might be, chose to tell stories like, 'When they said there was going to be a silver collection, the Jew fainted and the Scotsman carried him'. Notice who had the virile role? Sure I did.

As more and more Americans came to England, old friends rang the bell. Your kid cousin Irvin Weintraub was transformed into a pilot in the U.S.A.A.F. I have his picture, in officer's cap and uniform, on the desk in front of me. He gave me badges and wings and lieutenant's bars. Thanks to him and Milton and Buddy and Josh and who all else (not Herman), your larder bulged with booty from the PX. Irvin piloted a glider in the attack on Arnhem. We heard that he crash-landed perfectly. Before anyone could disembark the plane was surrounded by an S.S. platoon. There was no way not to surrender. The crew and troops were all in uniform and taking part in a legitimate operation. They were led away and murdered. I am not sure whether I was at home when you heard the news. I dread to think how I might have been jealous of the anguish his death caused. You bore the grief on your own. If Cedric ever alluded to it, I was not there to hear it.

As soon as the European war was over, you must have wondered when we would go back to the US. Shell kept their word; the big new job in N.Y.C. was still there. Did you talk about going back? Is it true that dad decided to stay in England because I had just won a scholarship to Charterhouse, having been cheated of one to Winchester, and you both thought that I should go ahead with my English classical education, nothing at all like Hyman Kaplan's? Or did his mother's health, which could always wane when it served her purposes, keep him in reach of Dorset House? I felt responsible; I also remembered coming third.

Can it be that you were happy to stay in London? You had friends in Manor Fields, but none were much fun that I could hear, until Caroline and Max Stewart came to live below us. Caroline and her accent were born in Baton Rouge, Louisiana. You and she, with her young grey hair, clinked midday whiskies with measured abandon. She kissed me once, when I was eighteen, as we were crossing the gardens on some festive night. She had stockings but no shoes on, for some reason. More shocked than excited, I was surprised how light she was, and available. Max was a drinker.

Max Mauser died in 1947. The following year, you and I sailed on the Queen Elizabeth to New York. How thrilled were you? I scarcely noticed. All the old crowd were still there. I had never seen so many motor cars as on Riverside Drive when Jack Walker took us for a tour of the booming, untouched city. We went on to Kansas City, via Chicago, on the Superchief. Dad came to New York to meet us on the way home. We had a few days in the big city. Mary-Jane Lehman was a pretty eighteen-year-old who liked kissing. We necked till three in the morning. Her mother came into the living room, to make sure we were home, she said. She seemed unsurprised and left us alone on the couch again. I did not dare do more than brush my hands against Mary-Jane's pretty breasts and listen to her shortened breath.

On the ship going home, I moped. You were annoyed and hinted that you too had left someone you missed. Was it the handsome, tall Reggie Monkhouse? He had been a major in the war. You stayed friends by mail with his wife Dixie, then his widow, until you were both a hundred years old. When I went back to Charterhouse, Mary-Jane wrote me some hot, scented letters. She was the best second best ever.

Dad's career with Shell was shunted into a siding when he (and you?) elected to stay in England. His kidneys troubled him, perhaps on account of that mismanaged operation years before. The stricture in his urethra tightened. He suffered humiliating pain and even more painful treatment when a catheter was inserted to widen the passage, which it did only for a short time. I was not a lot of comfort to him, nor company for you. My Cambridge scholarship opened a new life and I was too pleased with it, and myself, and a new girl-friend, to be anything but happy that Manor Fields ceased to be the centre of my London life. I hope I did my duty; not much more, I fear. You went, eventually, with Cedric to Norway where Dr Johannsen operated on him and removed the stricture. The two ends of the urethra sealed together naturally and, in time, for a time, took the dread out of every time that Cedric went – as we always said – to the bathroom.

You looked after him as a wife was supposed to do. You still smiled, you could still laugh, but what pleasure did you have? You were good at the *Times* crossword puzzle and used to call Guy Ramsey on Sundays to exchange intelligence on that day's puzzle. Dad played golf and bridge at Crockford's, where I played for two shillings a hundred. You went back to art school. When I met Beetle and brought her to meet you, you were not yet forty years old. You made her welcome, if not as welcome as dad, who was glad to learn she was a Paulina. I escaped solitude and was happy, very. I hardly noticed how you felt about things any more, and you noticed, didn't you? Even when Beetle and I were first married and came to stay for a night in Manor Fields, you had us sleep in separate rooms.

Dad made the best of his bad job at Shell; his salary scarcely rose; he was subordinate, as Press Officer, to Trevor Powell, the not very bright, spiteful Head of Public Relations. Dad brought shame home with him in annotated files which he then capped with his own annotations. You went on looking and enjoying your whisky, if little else. I never saw you the slightest bit drunk.

When I came home in the vacations from Cambridge, I could scarcely wait to get out of the door and on the 52 bus to see Beetle. My good success gave you both pleasure, especially in front of strangers. Beetle was amazed by the virulence of the 'discussions' as dad liked to call them which seemed to signal something like hatred between me and Cedric. It never troubled me. I knew that I was cleverer than he was. In the Sixties, my life soon became as glamorous as his had once been; richer too, after I won the Oscar. Beetle's life and mine expanded; we embellished the little place in Greece, bought a house in the Dordogne for the same amount that Willie Maugham paid for the Villa Mauresque. I was vain enough to subscribe to Durrant's cuttings service; thick brown envelopes brought almost daily proof of the silly attention the newspapers paid me, my books, my films. I was able to be generous to you and dad, a kind of apology, I guess. Whenever Beetle and I came to visit you in Manor Fields I instantly developed one of my migraines.

You went on being, or seeming to be, everything you should be, beautiful too: you helped teach Beetle to drive; you were great, in due time, with Paul and Sarah; no longer easy with me, nor I with you. When I gave you the manuscript of my second novel, *The Earlsdon Way*, in which suburban life was pilloried in the style of Sinclair Lewis's *Main Street*, you took Lesley Keggin to be based on yourself, although she was grey and British; Lesley's husband, Edward, did not in the least resemble Cedric. You handed back the folder and said, 'You'll do better'. I never cared to show you my work again, although I always gave you suitably inscribed copies. I did the right things but I did not have the right feelings. You too? Every time Cedric read, or looked at, a new novel of mine, he said, nicely, 'I hope you have yet to write your best book'. I have to hope he was right. My spells of fame made you proud to hear talk of me. I made up for whatever I had failed to be by giving you holidays and making a fat contribution to the purchase of a long lease on 12, Balliol House. Nobody ever liked anybody more for favours like that. When dad was watching me write the cheque, he asked me to round it up to the next thousand. I didn't.

Beetle was in hospital, having had her appendix out, when Fanny called to say that you had had a car accident. How long had she been living with you in Manor Fields?

For some reason, probably to do with the sense of having failed your parents when, in truth, they had failed you, you had persuaded her to leave Kansas City, where she was never short of canasta-playing company, and come to London, where she knew no one but you. Had the lease on her apartment lapsed? Anyway, over she came and into the spare room. Did Cedric mind? Part of his idea of being British was never complaining.

Fanny made great cookies, never forced her company on you both, was increasingly deaf and suspicious. Now she told us that the car you had been passengers in had had a serious collision. You were in back, badly bruised, but all right. The car was driven by the Brigadier, a colleague on the committee of the Royal Home and Hospital for Incurables. Cedric had thought it discourteous to put on the seat belt which was not yet a legal obligation. The talkative Brigadier drove across a STOP line. The car was hit by a truck. Dad was thrown through the windscreen into the roadway. He was unconscious and in hospital near Egham. The Brigadier was dead.

Dad was swollen and unrecognisable. He was now, as they like to say, stable. You were in shock. You kept telling me that you cared only that he survive, no matter in what condition. He did; but the accident was a caesura from which he recovered slowly, never entirely. He did not recover consciousness for three weeks. When he did he said he was going to teach one of his nurses Greek. Dad walked again, with effort, and was able to come home. You did your duty with something like love for a long while. Fanny Mauser thought you were doing more than any wife should have to do. If she had not been there to say so, maybe you would have continued until the end. Did she ever do as much for Max?

Luckily, Cedric's Shell pension increased with the cost of living. He worked at recovery with typical determination. He had had symptoms of Parkinson's Disease before; they now accelerated. When you resumed playing Saturday night bridge with the Piesses, he stuck his cards in a hair brush. He walked warily. Fanny's presence was no help. She thought he ought to go somewhere else to be looked after. Did it ever occur to her that she should? She was ninety-three when Dr Cooper told you that she needed an operation to correct the severe curvature of her neck. She fell out of her bed when a nurse failed to shutter it correctly. I am not sure if she broke any particular bones; the fall broke her; she never recovered. I came to the hospital where you were sitting with her. Every breath was a loud shudder. The rhythm of pain played on her unceasingly. Later you would say that she died without suffering. Poor Irene. Poor Fanny.

Poor Cedric, his old urinary misfortunes, which began when he trusted himself to his friend Teddy Schlesinger, grew more aggressive as his health waned. He was strong enough to survive but not to recover. After Fanny's death, you were, it seems, more encumbered by his needs than when you could share your feelings with her. I offered to pay for day and night nursing. You became set on dad's going to the R.H.H.I. I guess you had had enough, but I could hardly believe that you could bring yourself to ease him out of the flat which his years at Shell had paid for and deliver him to share a dreary room with a muttering, incoherent fellow-patient. He came home for weekends, to begin with at least. He said that Friday night was the happiest night of his week. He was no sooner back in Manor Fields than his time was soured by dread of the passing hours.

Too weak to protest, he was strong enough to wane for another nine years. We were living in France. I never felt guilty. Stee was going to the local school in Grives. I called every night. In the holidays, when we came back to England, we saw you with dutiful regularity. I went alone to the R.H.H.I. and did not find much to say to dad. We were back in France when his kidney and bladder infection became terminal. You sat with him day and night as he resisted death with laconic resignation. You called him 'Ceddy', you told me, as his mother had when he was a little boy.

Only children, all of us.

Much love, Freddie.

Dear Stanley,

The first movie of yours I remember seeing was *Deep in My Heart*, not, I suspect, among your favourites. On Sunday afternoons in 1955, under the bleak scrutiny of the Lord's Day Observance Society, movie houses could not open before mid-afternoon. London was dead pious. The company Beetle and I were in, Leslie Bricusse, John Morley (a cabaret singer) and others, selected the movie; we went along. Sigmund Romberg was played by José Ferrer; his namesake Mel (they had nothing else in common) had recently married Audrey Hepburn. Trapped, voluntarily, among people whose tastes were rarely mine, I seldom found musicals a pleasing placebo. *Singin' in the Rain* was an exception: Cyd Charisse, wow! Donald O'Connor in his ten minutes of one-take immortality, wow again. Sigmund Romberg? Get me out of here.

Carol Read's *Odd Man Out*, John Huston's *The Asphalt Jungle*, Jules Dassin's *Naked City*, all black and white, were my idea of classy movies. No one at Pinewood Studios, where Bricusse and I were enjoying £1,250-a-year contracts, was interested in anything but Norman Wisdom, hospital comedies ('What's the bleeding time?' asked the consultant surgeon, played by James Robertson Justice; 'Ten to four, sir', responded the student dreamer Dirk Bogarde, getting the longest laugh of his career) and steady-as-you-go glamorisations of British wartime exploits such as sinking the *Bismarck*: 'Model Shot', the script said. I remembered the actual sinking in 1943. Triumphant in public, Winston Churchill was privately sad about those thousand and more young men who went down with Hitler's pride.

Churchill has recently been targeted as a 'racist', a one-size-fits-all way of blackening (careful now) anyone who fails to subscribe to today's cant. Old style imperialist, stylish with it, Winston was among the last of those for whom chivalry had something to do with humane feelings for one's enemies; except for the socialist Aneurin Bevan, perhaps. When the member for Ebbw Vale was reported sick, Churchill did not resist saying 'Nothing trivial, I hope'. In 1955, Winston – back in 10 Downing Street – was himself suffering from nothing trivial, though the public was slow to learn of it.

Leslie and I wrote one movie for Rank and then I broke, amiably, with him and the idea of 'writing with' anyone else. Unable to afford England, Beetle and I went to live in good old Francisco Franco's 'E'paña'; the *Andaluz* peasants had a way of dumping their esses and swallowing their dees. We were in Fuengirola when the Generalissimo was scheduled to drive through the village on his way to Malaga. Official toadies whitewashed his name, several times, in large letters on the *Carretera*. With no TV, no movies, locals were apt to turn up for any show, even when it starred a dictator who denied their fishermen a concrete jetty because an earlier generation had resisted the fascist coup and burned down the village church.

In the *tranquilidad* of 1959, the only display of insolence came from the king of the gypsies, a slim old man in a long dark coat, soft black hat, flexing a shoulder-high bamboo cane with a manual stirrup. He came, all but dancing, on neatly laced feet, into the village from the direction in which *El Caudillo* was expected. As he came to the first FRANCO FRANCO on the roadway, he looked down, miming puzzlement, and skipped through and around the inscription. Can feet mock? You know they can. *Fuengirolistas* all but applauded each repetition of what the *Guardia Civil* chose not to challenge.

In overdue time, official black cars came swiftly, one after the other, along the road from Marbella. Each of the eight or more limousines had a driver in a peaked cap, a guard next to him, and a puff-chested moustachioed figure in the back who either was or could have been the Caudillo. No assassin could be sure which one to take a shot at. In a few seconds, they had all passed the unapplauding onlookers.

Years later, I published a story called *The Day Franco Came* in a small penniless magazine. Jonathan Dimbleby, who was producing a BBC series on the Spanish Civil War, was so impressed, he told me, that he had copies made and distributed to his expensive unit. How much would it have hurt to buy them a copy each? The impartial Corporation pulled his project when Mrs Thatcher became Britain's elected Caudillo.

Life can change fast when you hit your thirties, if you're very lucky. You were even luckier, and smarter, and didn't have to wait that long; I did: David Deutsch saw a play of mine on TV and commissioned a screenplay. The result, a couple of years later, was *Nothing But the Best*. No box office hit, the movie was applauded loudly in the press. Dilys Powell said nice things about me in the *Sunday Times*. Clive Donner, the director, who had suggested replacing me halfway through prepping the piece, claimed credit for my best ideas; most of them in my script before he was ever attached to the project. It was an early introduction to the way of all but a very few directors. Sweet guy Clive, he had a career to garnish. Truth to tell, you Stanley are the only director I ever met who delighted in the company of writers and never failed to sing – and, at belated Oscar time, dance – their praises.

Early in 1964, *Darling* was not yet shooting but the script was done, until it was done again; the budget was being put together; the word was out. I was a modestly hot property on Richard Gregson and Gareth Wigan's list. They had a new agency and rent to pay. Richard said that the next 'logical step' in my career was to work with a ranking Hollywood producer/director. He found me a plum job with veteran wisecracker

Norman Panama, seven hundred pounds a week for seventeen weeks: real money. *What Makes Tommy Run?* was set to star Kirk Douglas and Burt Lancaster.

Norman was one of many Hollywood emigrants who followed you to London. I turned up for work in his office, buoyed, just, by the prospect of a long run of riches. In the train from Colchester, I re-read the outline in which Kirk and Burt were US army generals, chests placarded with medals, competing for the same woman (yet to be cast) and for the same top job and so on and on. Just my kind of thing?

Norman sat me down, ordered coffee, and rolled a big trolleyed typewriter into place between us. We talked in general about the generals, Tommy and the other one. Norman said nothing in the least disagreeable. By the time he proposed that we break for lunch, at a kosher restaurant, I had appetite only for flight. The headache pile-driving my brain was scarcely alleviated by cold turkey and *lutkas*. Norman asked about my wife and told me about his: she fell down a lot.

Back in the office, my contributions became few. The typewriter never trundled. The current did not pass. Norman was understanding. The first day in a new relationship was always a strain. Why didn't I go on home? We could pick things up in the morning. Beetle had prepared my favourite supper. I couldn't eat. She said, 'Did you not like him?' 'He's all right; it's *it* I can't stomach. Seventeen weeks.' Beetle said, 'Call Richard. Tell him you don't want to do it.' 'Seven hundred pounds a week. He made a really good deal.' 'If he made one, bet you he can make another.' I called Richard. He was not sympathetic. He had given his word. If I wanted out, that was for me to handle. The post delivered irony: thanks to Peter Green, I had been elected a Fellow of the Royal Society of Literature, quite an honour back then.

I was in Norman's office promptly the next morning. There he was, smiling; there was the ready-to-roll typewriter, a sheet of white foolscap all set to lose its virginity. Norman said, 'Sit down'. As good as in front of a headmaster, I stood there. 'Listen, Norman…' 'Something wrong?' 'Probably. With me, I mean. I know very well that this is the end of me in the movies, but…' 'Why? What's happened?' 'I just can't do this. I don't know anything about these people and why they run. I don't think I ever will. I'm just… not that kind of a writer. You have every right to be sore, but…' 'Why should I be sore? Much better you tell me right away.' 'That's very nice of you, but…' Norman said, 'I'll tell you what'. 'And I don't blame you…' 'I was at a party last night and Stanley Donen was there. When I told him I was working with you, he said "How in heck did you manage that?" He loved your movie. So, how about I give him a call, tell him you're… available?' He picked up the phone. I resolved never to take another logical step as long as I lived.

Your offices were in Hamilton Place, near the eponymous bridge club in the ex-Rothschild mansion where I had spent more time than any muse could approve. I went up a narrow staircase lined, on the striped left wall, with your framed playbills, starting with *On the Town*: enough to impress and intimidate any mountebank. The office door was open. The first words I heard were, 'If I can't get the Duke of Marlborough, would the Duke of Westminster do?'

You were on the telephone to the exquisite Adelle, Lady Beatty until she married you, Frank Sinatra's lady before that. When he heard that she was planning to marry you, he sent her a telegram: NOT HIM. You are the only person who could have told me the story. Why Sinatra came to regard you with unwavering malice you never revealed. A woman? Had to be. Adelle? Who else?

You told me later how, not long after *Charade* had proved a big hit, you and Cary, in his mid-sixties already, were scheduled to appear on the platform in some charity do, in Boston, I think. A day or two before, Cary rang you up and said he was very sorry, but he had a favour to ask: would you please call in sick and, you know, not make it? You may not have been longing to go but you did insist on knowing what it was all about, unless you'd already guessed: Sinatra was the great attraction and he wasn't going to show up if you did. Cary was supposed to be your friend; but he was never quite the man he looked. Born Archibald Leach in Bristol, England, neither success nor charm ever quite covered the case. As you would never say and Horace almost did, *Nomina non animum mutant qui trans mare currunt*: they change their names, not their souls.

Peter Bogdanovich, champion butterfly collector when it came to colourful stories, told me how Cary was invited to some fancy charity occasion. The invitation threatened positively no admission for anyone who wasn't carrying a personal ticket. Wouldn't you know it, Cary was standing in front of the two heads-down ladies at the reception desk, before he realised his ticket was still on the mantelpiece at home. One of the ladies held out her hand, without looking up, and said 'Ticket'. Cary said, 'I'm terribly sorry but…' The lady said, 'You don't have a ticket, you can't come in'. Cary said, 'I'm Cary Grant'. The lady looked up for the first time. 'You don't look like Cary Grant.' Cary said, 'Nobody does'. His smile was his ticket.

You were seven years older than me; fame widened it to a generation. I guessed from how you had talked to her on the heavy old phone that the beautiful Adelle did not give you an easy time. She was your pride and, all but literally, your ulcer. You told me you took her to New York for your honeymoon, on the *Queen Elizabeth*. You had a first-class suite, of course, but when you went to reserve dinner on the super first-class terrace, the purser said that all the tables had been pre-booked. The only one or two left were held for those with a substantial investment in Cunard shares. When you told your bride, she said, 'Fix it'. You called and bought a chunk of shares right there and then and dined where she could be seen by smart heads that never failed to turn.

After lighting out from South Carolina, with your father's encouragement, you rose from being a sixteen-year-old Broadway chorus boy in *Pal Joey* (book by John O'Hara) to the producer/director whose calls were always returned, never in more of a hurry than the day I met you. *Charade*, with Audrey Hepburn and Cary Grant, had given you what you later called your only hit, i.e. chart-topping revenue-maker. You were tired of people telling you how much they loved *Singin' in the Rain* and *On the Town* and how unlucky you were not to get an Oscar for *Seven Brides for Seven Brothers*. When it came to awards, luck was almost always determined by studio fixers and the bloc of votes they as good as commanded.

You said how much you had liked *Nothing But the Best*. 'They all say it's the director, but I know it's the writer.' I recall only how easily we got along, and how soon. Eased out of my British vocal costume, I felt more American than I had for years. You wondered what we could do together; any ideas? A few weeks earlier, Beetle and I had been driving to the south of France in our new light blue Mercedes 280SE. As we flashed along the A6 and A7, which we had travelled quite a few times in less fancy motors, I said, 'Imagine if we overtook ourselves the way we were when we were hitch-hiking this same road'. And then I said, 'Might make a nice movie'. Beetle said, 'Make a great movie, if anyone ever...'

When we got back to London, I tried the idea on Jo Janni and John Schlesinger. They were too busy with the logistics for *Darling* to entertain a new project. When I told you what I had in mind, inter-cutting between a set of journeys at different times, but always driving on south, you said, 'Great idea. How do we do it?' I said, 'We don't. I do. I just came from trying to work with Norman Panama.' 'Sweet guy', you said, 'he just split up with Mel Frank after a long partnership. He had the idea Mel was holding him back. Mel's first solo movie was a smash. These things happen.' I thought about you and Gene Kelly. I didn't think about Betsy Blair. You said, 'Audrey, could she do it, your idea?' I thought about it, for a split second, then I said: 'She'd be wonderful'. You said, 'I'm all set to shoot a movie with Sophia, called *Arabesque*. Script could do with some work. I can pay you more than Norman was going to, a lot.' I said, 'I've done rewrites before. I don't want to do any more.' 'So how do we… you want to proceed, if…' I said, 'Ideally, you give me enough money to go and write the script and then, when I think it's good enough I'll let you see it.' You said, 'Last time I did that I never saw the guy again'. 'Up to you', I said, 'but I promise you you'll see me again.' You said, 'Who do I talk to?'

You had hired Stanley Price, a Cambridge friend of mine, never close, to work on *Arabesque*. However long afterwards, he told me how he hated working for you. You'd thought it sounded silly for two people to call each other Stanley, so you decided to call him Charlie for the duration. Stanley Price resented being, as they all say these days, disrespected. He worked for a different Stanley Donen than the one I knew and cherished for sixty years or so. How often do we know the same person that other people do? I cannot remember a sour word between us, you and me. You were the least pretentious big shot I ever met, but you did tell me how you hired a new secretary when eventually you went back to L.A. The first day she said, 'Do I call you Stanley or Stan?' You said, 'You call me Mr Donen'.

While you were settling with Gregson and Wigan on how to make me as happy as I needed to be, I was back putting one more coat of words, or set of buttons, on *Darling*. John, Jo and I used always to have lunch together. After I explained, on whatever day it was that our deal was closed, that I was going to have lunch with you, their can't-wait-to-hear-about-it reactions proved your legendary standing. The suited and peak-capped chauffeur I came to know as Hickey was polishing a ton of Rolls Royce in front of palatial Hyde Park Gardens. A pretty uniformed maid, with a seen-it-all smile, opened the door of the high-ceilinged apartment and showed me into a fine, long and wide living room overlooking the park.

You were in a dark suit; alone. The long living room had been abracadabraed by David Hicks. Long-throated oriental vases stood sentinel on shoulder-high, built-in white wooden pilasters either side of the Adam fireplace. Regency paperweights, colourful and all different, were glassed in a coffee-table in front of one of the dark blue couches waiting for a duke or two. Adelle wasn't in; but there she was. Maybe she was out with your small son Mark; maybe not. Whenever he was brought in to see you, he always said, 'Goodbye, daddy', assuming you were off to some location.

Did we have drinks before lunch? Memory doesn't serve them. We sat at a small round table, with a long-skirted undercloth; in the *avant*-dining-room. The pretty girl brought us whatever we ate. I took the elegant, floral china to be something rich and rare. You said, 'It's Haddon Hall. You just go to Goode's. They've got lots of it.' Conversation was easy, but fugitive; I am sure only that you said little about yourself.

Oh, but I do recall that you told me how, just before *Charade* began shooting in Paris, you went out to Orly with a chauffeur to meet Walter Matthau, who was playing a not very big part. He was, it looked, like Peter Sellers: too plain ever to be a movie star. It was the first time he had been out of the States. As you drove back into the city, he said, 'You know I should be playing the Cary Grant part, don't you?'. You laughed; Walter did not. No secret: he became a big, big star; never Cary Grant. Did Matthau ever kiss anybody on screen? His buddy-cum-straight man in a lot of movies was that slick performer Jack Lemmon who, for no reason I can specify, I could never stand to see or hear. *The Sunshine Boys*, Doc Simon's mixture as before, was pretty good though, wasn't it, if you liked boiled sweets?

After that first lunch, you played me the new disc of Elaine May and Mike Nichols, the one with the Dr Schweitzer sketch. Dr S. is quizzed to distraction by a tourist lady about his idea of the sacred nature of life. Did he include flies? It ended with Schweitzer saying 'If that woman comes back, kill her'. While we were having coffee, an American producer, whose name I'd best not recall, rang at the door and came on in. You were not markedly pleased to see him. He seemed in need of company. He told us a story about a producer, 'known to be a little fruity', who married a beautiful woman. The morning after their wedding night, he sneaked down to the kitchen and came up with a dream breakfast to surprise his bride. She looked at the prettiest tray anyone could ever hope to see and said, 'Aren't you just the sweetest man who ever lived? If only you could fuck.' After the producer had gone, you said, 'Guess what his trouble is'.

You asked me to outline each of the journeys my married couple had taken along the old A6 and A7. I rattled off fifteen typed pages, on flimsy yellow foolscap, and you sent them to Audrey, explaining the intercutting idea. She turned us down, despite your happy history together. She had just done a movie she feared was a little too like my idea: *Paris When It Sizzles*, written by George Axelrod. What worried her was less the similarity than the fact that it was a flop. You told her we were going ahead anyway.

Beetle and I and Paul and Sarah drove in our new pale blue Merc along the old *routes nationales*, between the plane trees Napoleon planted so that his men could march in the shade, and crossed into Italy at Ventimiglia. You had given us a new sound system and a stack of fat tapes that slotted into it. The Beatles were doing their yeah-yeah stuff as we drove through slow Genova (the stilted bypass wasn't built yet) and on down into Rome.

We rented an apartment in Vigna Clara. I bought a deck of *fiches* Bristol, and potted scene after scene of *Two for the Road*. Memory mothered the Muse, fancy fathered her. I spread the lined cards on the marble floor of our wide living room and made a game of patience jigsawing them into an order which seemed casual but made story-telling sense. Meanwhile, John and Jo were at last shooting *Darling*.

There was a protracted televised presidential election in Italy. The roster of candidates was repeated at each inconclusive ballot: Saragat, Leone, Aldo Moro, Giuseppe Saragat, Pietro Nenni, Leone Sergio, Cossiga Franceso, Nenni Pietro... all the old *gran'briganti*. Then the formula: '*Nessun candidato a ricevuto un maggioranza assoluta... La prossima votazione avra luogo domani alla stessa hora. La seduta e sospesa*'. Down came the gavel. I forget who won finally. Leone? Winston Churchill died and had a solemn, televised black-and-white funeral. I finished the script, went through it again, sought Beetle's imprimatur, mailed it to Hyde Park Gardens.

We drove up to Florence and stayed with the *Darling* crew in a hotel where the glass front doors slid open at our approach. We'd never seen that before. We were superfluous for a day or two and went back to Rome in time for Paul and Sarah to go to the Montessori school. Every morning the teacher said, '*Adesso facciamo la merenda*'. Sarah wanted to know what '*merenda*' meant. Paul said, 'snack time'. Italy was growing on us. We had sudden heavy spring snow. A man stood on the street corner looking up at the big flakes and said to me, '*Non e la neve di Roma*'. Branches broke under the weight in the Borghese gardens. It might not be Roman snow, but smart *donne* were soon skiing to the shops in the *Piazza medaglie d'oro*, maids trudging behind with baskets.

Beetle was already in bed late one evening when the telephone shrilled. I bet myself it was Jo Janni, wanting a line. It was you. You said, 'Freddie? I just finished reading it. It's going to be the best thing I ever did. I would have called you halfway through but I was afraid that would look silly.' You had a few details you wanted to talk about. Would we come back to London? You had room for us to stay. We all got in the car and headed for Calais. I rarely enjoy driving north; this was the exception. You showed us into a basement apartment under David Hicks's commissioned showroom. It belonged to Adelle's handsome grown-up son. His name began with A, I think. Many tailor-made suits rubbed shoulders in a long row in a built-in closet. Tall and handsome, he committed suicide in his twenties.

Hickey was outside, dusting the Rolls, if we wanted to go anywhere. As far as I was concerned, we were there. Willie Maugham had said that success never came as a surprise. You and I must have spent some time cutting this, clarifying that, rearranging a few things to avoid confusion; I recall only what fun it was to be working with a director with no apprehensions and a quick wit. Despite what Audrey had said, you were going to send her the complete script. How could she not like it?

Beetle and I returned to Rome on gossamer wings. Paul and Sarah resumed *facciendo la merenda*. Jo Janni called and asked me to do a little work on de script of *Darling*. I heard myself being a lot more trenchant than had been my previous not wholly servile practice. A short time afterwards, you called to say guess what: Audrey loved the script; she wanted us to come to Bergenstock to talk about it. If it wasn't too much trouble, would I go to a certain smart jewellery store in the Via Condotti and collect some things that Adelle had left there or chosen and bring them with me to Geneva? It required no overheated imagination to see myself being arrested as I left Italy or arrived in Switzerland. Can it be that what I collected was not precious stones but clever facsimiles? You told me that Adelle had a friend who was robbed of some expensive jewels and had decided it was too risky to sport the real things. Couldn't she just as well be mugged for fakes? Whatever they were, she got them.

You had hired a car with a driver to take us up and over the snow line. We stopped off and had creamy Swiss coffee and *croissants*. You were young again. Your bet had come off; my dream. Was it then that you told me the story about the producer and the writer who found themselves crawling across the desert, dying of thirst? They manage to haul themselves over the next bulging dune and see below them a circle of palm trees and – can it be? – the twinkling water of an oasis. With fresh energy they run and stumble down to their salvation. The writer gets there first and stoops to fill his cupped hands with water. The producer says, 'Wait a minute, wait a minute, we haven't pissed in it yet.' You promised me, and I believed you, that you wanted to make *Two for the Road* exactly as I wrote it. You kept your word.

Audrey and Mel's house could have been anybody's four-storey chalet. Audrey was as nice as she could be. Julie Christie never wanted to be a star; Audrey never began to be anything else. She said she wasn't going to say anything about the script because she didn't want to embarrass Frederic. We talked about how and when and who when it came to casting Mark to play opposite Audrey's Joanna. Audrey found me a pair of Mel's snow boots that almost fitted and we took a crunchy walk in deep, steep snow among ice-decked pine trees. We had just got back into the house when there was a creak on the stair and Audrey said, 'Here's Melchior!' Mel was polite but showed small interest in why we were there. Planning to produce and direct a movie about El Greco, he showed us a boxed deck of black-and-white photographs of various locations. It took little insight to guess that Audrey was living a facsimile of conjugal contentment. The closer you come to famous people the smaller they are liable to get, unless they're Orson Welles.

That reminds me of a story Peter Bogdanovich told me about Orson. Someone or other had invited him to lunch at *Ma Maison*, Wolfgang Puck's first fashionable, not his last overrated restaurant, on Melrose Avenue. The host arrived very late, full of believable apologies. Orson seemed quite mellow. The headwaiter came with menus and a straight face and took their orders. Orson declaimed his pitch and his host was lucky to get it. After coffee and cigars and who knows what else, the host called for the check. When it was presented, the recipient looked at it, looked at the waiter, looked again at the bill, looked at Orson, who was doing business with his cigar, and presented the usual credit card. The bill was for lunch for three. Orson had already eaten a complete meal before the latecomer arrived.

When we left Audrey's house, we were driven back down to Zurich to catch a plane to Geneva. As we had time to spare, you said 'Let's go buy some watches'. It was the first and last time I ever heard anyone propose the purchase of a plurality of watches. We went into a fancy lakeside store where the salesman put a black baized tray on the counter and paraded his gleaming stock. You invited me to choose. When I displayed British diffidence, you put two or three watches aside (one a pocket watch with a silver lid) and indicated to the guy to wrap them up. Was I a fancy whore? It didn't seem a cruel condition. For you, it was a small show of gratitude: we had Audrey's next movie; your bet had paid off. When you offered me a three-picture deal, ascending to eighty thousand bucks, Richard Gregson advised against taking it. Why limit ourselves? We could probably do a lot better in due time. Note the plural. Success always has a happy family; only failures walk alone.

By the time (on my three new watches) we got to the airport, fog was already dissolving the surrounding mountains.

In the departure lounge, all we could see through the wide windows was a milky swirl. Departing passengers were instantly absorbed. We heard the shrilling surge of departing planes, but saw nothing. I said, 'What do we do if a plane crashes and then they call our flight?' 'We go on out', you said, 'ever hear of two planes crashing in a row?'

I did, later; a local told us how a whole flight of new Tornados crashed one after another during the war taking off from Langham US airfield, right by our house in north Essex. Someone had misread the instruction booklet. There was a *New Yorker* cartoon of such a smoking scene. One boffin is saying to another, 'Back to the drawing board!' I once knew the whole part of Samson in *Samson Agonistes* and now it's pretty well all gone, aside from 'A little onward lend thy guiding hand'. More adhesive is another *New Yorker* cartoon I saw in Dorothy Tutin's parents' flat in Putney when I was fourteen: a flat-chested chorus girl is being told, 'Go see the wardrobe mistress after rehearsal'. Something like that. Funny? Not very. Unforgettable? I'm afraid so. Now Thurber's *Destinations* is more so. I've tripped on another of memory's stones: Dotty was very proud, when in Puffin Asquith's film of *The Importance of Being Earnest*, one shot of her was excised by the censor because her cleavage was deemed inflammatory.

You sent our script to Paul Newman. He passed. He said it was a director's movie. Maybe ten years later, I stood next to a small-size Paul Newman in the elevator at the Beverly Wilshire. Then I realised it was the only size he came in. I told you I wouldn't mind having Rock Hudson. I had no idea that he was known as Leroy or something equally minty. You wanted somebody fresh, and younger. After however long it was, you called with the news that we had Albert Finney. You seemed pleased. I wasn't sure I was. I wanted to make a Hollywood movie. Casting Albie made me feel as if I was back in the old country.

Beetle and I had had lunch with Finney, at John and Dudy Nimmo's flat, when he was still married to his first wife, Jane Wenham. Provincial, pleasant and cocky, he was at his best playing virile period drama at the National Theatre and as the roaring boy in the black-and-white *Saturday Night and Sunday Morning*. I remember him saying that Julie Christie was not very good with the chat. Was he? We'd soon find out.

You decided to do the whole thing in France, on the authentic locations that I had *Charade* to thank for making it possible. You called when you were in Nice to say that you were having trouble finding a boat. I said, 'What boat?' '*What boat?*' I had quite forgotten that sequence on the Channel steamer. Next case: where did I have the idea for a traffic signal that waved its arms up and down and flashed? I thought I'd seen them all over France. Turned out, when Jimmy Ware tracked it down, that there was just one to the script's specifications (Audrey mimicked its exercise to perfection). Who wants to be a film producer?

'Or director', Bill Goldman said to me, while I still had ambitions in that regard, when the three of us had dinner a few years later. You had a project with him, but it came to nothing. Who was better at his trade or more inventive within the limits of the biz? *Butch Cassidy and the Sundance Kid* was sweetly pitched between what everyone wanted and what nobody expected. Bill said that the great thing about movies was that they took three weeks to write and a week to polish (Willie Maugham had said the same about three-act plays). Insist on a twelve-week period for delivery of the first draft and you had time to write a novel before it came to rewrites. People in the biz could gauge how long it took to do most anything connected with technical detail. Writers were an unknown quantity; let's keep it that way, Bill said.

He had a lotta lotta of success. Welcome everywhere, he never looked like he was having a good time, not even when biting the studio that fed him. He and his brother James didn't talk to each other. Bill won two Oscars but he never got to stick either of them where he would have liked to. He told me how his friend, he thought, Bob Redford, was producing a new movie of theirs. Bill happened to be in the office and came on some pages he didn't recognise as his, and they weren't: Bob had hired another writer behind his back. Quite a few people seem embittered by success; none more than your friend Billy Wilder. Goldman's family history suggests that bitterness got in there first. You almost never talked about your parents. They ran a hardware store, didn't they? *A proposito*, you told me the neatest short story ever. The phone rang and your secretary said, 'Mrs Donen for you, Mr Donen.' You said, 'Darling!' A voice said, 'Stanley?' You said, 'Mother'.

The morning before shooting started on *Two for the Road*, Beetle and I drove down to Nice in our new grey Alfa Romeo 2800 convertible. In city traffic, its three carburettors were never in synch and it was liable to overheat; at a hundred and thirty miles an hour, it lapped up the motorway like smooth soup. We all met for dinner at the best restaurant in town. You were a king back on his throne, ten years younger for it. The only latecomer to table was one of the heads of wardrobe, Ken Scott. He came in, flustered, wearing white pants, yellow shirt, crimson velvet jacket. He apologised for being late; crossing the street, he told us, he had just escaped being run over by some crazy driver. 'Probably didn't see you, Ken', Albert said.

We stayed at the Negresco. Iced orange juice came in a tall silver-lidded decanter. Late one evening, after nostalgic *moules marinières* in a basement restaurant we used only just to be able to afford, down by the flower market, Beetle and I came up in the elevator and crossed Jackie Bisset coming out of your room. You had been rehearsing, she said. Your only instruction to her that I ever heard was 'Brush your hair, Jackie'.

In the scene in the little hotel where the girls' choir stopped for the night and wakes up to find that the party had been chickenpoxed, Albert had to come down a winding stair saying quite a few words, to find Jackie having breakfast all alone. 'Well, well, well…' Understandably pleased to find her alone, he asked a flirtatious question to which she was scripted to say 'Yes'. Action: he came down, talking, asked the question, and she said, 'No'. You cut and started again. Albert did his stuff with professional freshness and then Jackie said, 'No. I mean, yes'. You said 'Cut', again, nicely, again. Chris Challis, the cameraman, stretched a length of string between his hands and garotted the air. Jackie got the one-word speech right the third time, unless it was the fifth. Cue Audrey. Down she came, everything right first time, and the scene swam into the can without further problem. Jackie was undoubtedly and durably beautiful; she could be never be accused of charm. Audrey, twenty years older, outshone her without troubling to notice.

Several years later, you asked me to write the screenplay for an American version of a French movie with Yves Montand and Romy Schneider; A.N. Other the third point in the triangle. Beetle had the idea of calling it *Party of Three*. Your co-producer was Victor Drai, a Frenchman from Morocco; he owned the rights. Victor was living with Jackie Bisset. Once my script was approved for huddling over, Beetle and I flew to L.A., as we did regularly in those days. We were no sooner there than you and Victor had a terminal row; almost certainly about money and primacy. Your experiences with Gene, however sublime the results, had left you unhappy to be anything but your own boss.

I wondered how Victor had managed to land such a beautiful woman. You said, 'Nothing easier to get in this town than a young girl'. I thought of you and Elizabeth Taylor, when she was eighteen. You told her to find herself a voice coach.

Did she, ever? You were all set to marry her, maybe. Then she got an offer to shoot a movie in Europe, asked your advice; off she went. Imagine a man who gets rid of Elizabeth Taylor. Did you ever see a movie called *Trop belle pour toi?* We never met your first wife, Marion; Josh and Peter's mother. Everyone told us what a great woman she was. Today, the internet reports restaurateur Victor Drai to be worth $13,000,000. Think he's short of young girls?

Two for the Road was as close to a dream experience as I am likely to have while awake. Audrey and Albert worked happily together; happier still perhaps when not working, although I didn't know it at the time. As we were shooting somewhere in the Midi, I looked again at the scene in which Joanna/Audrey comes back to Mark/Albert after she has been off with the solemn, slow-speaking Georges Descrières. It was due to be shot in a day or two. I took it on myself to redo the scene and make it more logical. I guess I showed it to you but I remember only that I handed it to Audrey, special delivery, with all the confidence you and she had lent me.

A few minutes later, she came up to me and said, 'Freddie, I've never queried a single thing you wrote, but… I liked the original version much better'. I had the nerve to say, 'Believe me, Audrey, this makes much better sense'. She said, 'Will you come and read them both with me?' We went to her Winnebago and sat on the bed. She said, 'Which'll we do first?' I said, 'Whichever you like'. She picked up the original script and, short pause, began 'Hullo…' Maybe she got a little further, but not much, before I said, 'You're absolutely right'. Logic never helps a scene work. You know; she knew; I learned.

Beetle and I saw the rough-cut in a viewing theatre near the Lancaster Hotel where you put us up. It was the only hotel in Paris that promised linen sheets. I wasn't knocked out by Albert, but he did better than I had feared. He was a little heavy; Audrey was a dancer. Her nickname for Beetle was 'Legs'. Hank Mancini had yet to do his brilliant stuff, with Stefan Grapelli doing his, but the movie was already a present from the gods. You had the innocent idea of getting Leslie Bricusse to write the lyrics of a song to go over the titles. They were sweetly moony and Juney. I couldn't abide them. You left them off the actual movie, but the song was some kind of off-screen hit, I fear. How much good might it have done us, had I not minded having Leslie up there in the credits? He still figures in them in Wikipedia. You're right: as if it mattered. You once said to me, 'Some people compose on paper, some people compose at the piano, Leslie composes to the radio'.

In swinging London, you gave enough fancy dinner parties for Adelle to figure in the press as an A-list hostess with the mostest. Beetle and I were regular guests. One evening she was at a table with Charlie Clore and a rival property tycoon whose name eludes me. She asked you to keep it a secret, but she was again pregnant. You were so pleased for her that you immediately announced it to the applauding company. When the moment came for the ladies to leave the table, Adelle stood up and led the way. Beetle told Clore and the others at the table that she wasn't going. They seconded her sedate resolve with admiring smiles. Can it be that they liked her because they knew that her decision had nothing whatever to do with their money?

The banker son of 'Fruity' Metcalfe, the duke of Windsor's best man when others had deserted him, in what came to be known as Rat Week, was a regular at Adelle's table. No evident charmer, however loaded, it turned out that he was also an irregular in Adelle's bed. The only time I ever saw the Windsors was when I dined with the Guinzburgs (Tom's then wife was Rita Gam, on the nose name for a one-time movie actress) at some chic New York restaurant. The half-royal couple looked like wax works tactfully aged for the sake of verisimilitude, at the price of restricted facial mobility. My stamp-dealer great-uncle Godfrey gave me two full sheets of the now very rare stamps issued during Edward VIII's abbreviated reign. Damp got into the album and the stamps stuck inextricably, valuelessly together, just like the Windsors.

David Niven came to one of Adelle's dinner parties and sang for his supper with the practised spontaneity expected of him. No one who had not heard it before could have guessed how often he had amused all kinds of company with his story of how, when skiing, he absolutely had to have a high altitude pee. No sooner had he unbuttoned that he realised that he was literally freezing. He slalomed as fast as he knew how down to a warmer level, calling out '*cazzo gelato, cazzo gelato*'. You're right: it's how the star of self-mockery told them. Another set piece was about playing polo with Darryl Zanuck, a small man who liked to get above himself. What was the story exactly? Did David's mallet wind up in Darryl's pony's ass? Something like that.

David was with his second wife who has to have known, all the time, that she was understudying his true love. While playing sardines, his first wife opened what she thought was a closet door, hurried inside and plunged down steep cellar steps to her death. A story Niven didn't tell was of how, having been a professional soldier before he was an actor, he returned to England at the outbreak of war. Winston Churchill recognised him and said, 'Come back to fight for your country, Niven?' 'Yes, sir.' Winston said, 'I should... bloodywellthinkso'. Niven's humour was salted with mortal pain. He died, like that other generous clown Dudley Moore, of motor neurone disease. *Sunt lacrimae rerum*, Virgil said. There are tears in things. I'll say.

And laughter: I was in the apartment in Hyde Park Gardens when Audrey came to see you. She ran in and threw herself into my arms; a moment to treasure. Ten years later,

I sent her a script from my novel *Richard's Things*, about a woman who discovers that her husband, Richard, who has died suddenly on a business trip, was staying in a hotel with a Mrs who wasn't her. She confronts the mistress in a rage and finds that each of them miss the same but different man and…. so to bed. Audrey wrote back in her own claw, as Churchill would say, regretting that her fans would never accept her in a genuine same-sex relationship, although they had excused it when she played someone falsely accused of being in one. Lilian Hellman's *The Children's Hour* didn't have its cake but ate it all the same. You're quite right: Audrey didn't say that but that was the gist. Hellman was not very nice, they say, in all kinds of ways, but I bet it was you who told me about how she was in a restaurant when some successful, not very tall middle-aged producer came in with his second, token wife, a very tall good-looking blonde. Hellman said, 'Think he goes up on her?' Hellman's hell woman, Mary McCarthy, may have sported bluer stockings and trendier opinions, but was she ever a wit?

Deborah Kerr said yes to *Richard's Things* right away, but she was no longer bankable. Someone told me that she and Peter Viertel (son of Christopher Isherwood's Salka) were the most delightful foul-mouthed couple he had ever met. While cooking Beetle and me a delicious meal of roast lamb at their place in the South of France, Peter told me that someone had called to warn him that L.A. was being all but washed away by floods. Peter said, 'You're making my mouth water'.

In the end, Liv Ullmann took the money and then, *putain respectueuse*, didn't honour the script of *Richard's Things* she had promised she admired. Tony Harvey lacked the charm or the guile or the force to get her to drop the squeamishness. A few years ago I saw a French movie which depended, successfully, on two naked actresses *dans ses oeuvres*. Neither, it is said, were lesbians in real life; sometimes actors are better at faking it than being themselves, whatever that is. Not Burton and Rex Harrison in your *Staircase*, unfortunately. Beat whatever equal-sized drum you will, watching women embrace ain't the same as watching men, especially the middle-aged. Tony Harvey was one of those fortunate, unlucky people. He was the only man to win the New York critics' award, for *Lion in Winter*, and then not to go on and win an Oscar. When he hired a car at LAX, its engine went dead in the fast lane of the freeway and the car behind ran into and almost through it. The impact broke pretty well all the bones in his body. He was the editor on Stanley Kubrick's *Dr Strangelove*. Stanley never mentioned him. Katie Hepburn was his favourite aunt. She told him she would have loved to do *Richard's Things* if she'd been twenty years younger.

You guessed, early on, that *Two for the Road* was not going to be a big, big hit. Before it even opened, you offered to buy my 'points' (I had four) for a thousand pounds each. I never doubted you meant to do me a favour, but I hung onto my indeed worthless investment. Sentimental me.

Spring 1967 hangs like footage in a traditional cutting room, in vivid, discontinuous strips. I can see us, you and me, in Hyde Park Gardens and Warren Beatty coming in and throwing himself at your feet, saying 'Who do you have to fuck to get to work with you guys?' *Bonnie and Clyde* had just eclipsed us in the box office stakes. Warren is a curious character: Hollywood as Hollywood can get, superstag *de luxe*, with the grace always to seem to have been dropped by women of whom he had had enough, he had an appetite for the unusual. Master of self-advancement, famous for postponing decisive commitment to any project, there was a sliver of self-mockery in his electing to play Clyde Barrow who announces that he 'ain't no lover boy'. I don't know whether Warren and Faye were lovers; it just might be that it amused them, or him, not to be; then again, why deny themselves? Did you try to get him for *Two for the Road* before you settled for Albert? My guess is, he kept you waiting until you wouldn't wait.

Warren was still involved with Leslie Caron. He had detached her from Peter Hall after she had made an unwise decision to play the actress and went, like a meek wife, unless it was a miscalculated career move (or both, or both), to Stratford where Hall was king of the castle. He had no parts to promise her; she proved no patient pastoral princess. Marie Antoinette, *la pauvre*, used to play the milkmaid at Versailles; Leslie must have grown bored with English thespians who, I guess, never had the grace or the nerve to make passes at her. Enter Warren, who did not exit until Julie Christie won the Oscar, upon which he shed Leslie and took his hotter ticket for a long, long stay in a penthouse in the Beverly Wilshire. What did he and Julie talk about? There's an exercise for creative writers. I pass.

Tournent, tournent mes personnages. The strands of life are oddly entangled. I was at Cambridge with Peter Hall, though I cannot remember talking to him. I was never even auditioned for the Amateur Dramatic Club; vanity and dread of rejection were heads and tails in my silly coinage. One of what Charles Snow called 'the New Men', the post-war generation of thrusting outsiders, Peter – like Leslie Bricusse – came from no theatrical dynasty. His father was a station master in Suffolk. Neither handsome nor any rare actor, Peter took command of the Cambridge theatre and became as impregnable as any dispenser of favours is likely to be. We were both parents of kids at Bedales. His and Leslie's daughter Jenny and our son Paul became very close. Peter and I smiled and that was the only conspiracy we had.

Your race for success, from a start line deep in the sticks, was typical of a time when people never looked back if they could help it. South Carolina was no Old Country as far you were concerned. You did once mention that good ole boys used to use cattle-prods to quicken their black employees' cotton-picking hands. I never met a black person in your house (or anyone else's in Beverly Hills), but we did dine with you, at the same big table as Sidney Poitier and his wife, the beautiful Joanna Shimkus.

Did you ever voluntarily go to synagogue? *Moi non plus.* Being Jewish was a special way of being American, self-mockery implicit. For instance, what was Jewish foreplay? Two hours of pleading. You once met us in a new compact Cadillac you called 'my Jew-canoe'; you didn't paddle it for long. By that time Hickey must have died of the cancer you made sure he had the best possible treatment for. You came of a generation of those who chose to pitch away the past and set out, from however far back in the race, to be one hundred percent American. My father was once a passenger in the back seat of a Jaguar when a golf club suburbanite called Madge Dunnett, in the front seat, said, 'They call Jags the Jewish Rolls-Royce, don't they?' Then she looked round and said, 'Cedric, I didn't see you there'. My father was too Oxford to reply.

I was never more British than in the desire to be selected rather than a selector. Success in winning scholarships does more to encourage deference than spark insolence. You and Peter Hall and Leslie Bricusse and Tom Maschler, as mixed a bag as may be, were alike in not waiting for the examiner's summons before fashioning your own ladders and heading for the heights. I can imagine some deutero-Wittgenstein smiling at the allusion to self-promotion and the subsequent throwing aside of the ladder. Did I ever mention Wittgenstein in your presence? You bet I didn't. It has been my persistent pleasure to play several parts in my writing life. Honest deceit leads me never to commit myself wholly to any single camp. I reserve fidelity for Beetle. You once said to us, when things were not going happily for you, 'I always figured you two had it cracked'.

So did the characters in Henry James's *The Golden Bowl*, kinda, as if that fancy allusion could ever amuse you.

I regarded you, despite and because of your modesty and recurrent generosity, as a guardian being. If I never rated you as a totem of the quality of Michelangelo Antonioni, you were resident on the A-List. The Oscar was my last scholarship; it paid a lot of rent. Did you ever allude to it? Your silence had nothing to do with envy. I had won the lottery; good luck, not worth talking about. Movies were a business, not an art, at least until the smart asses *chez Les Cahiers du Cinéma* turned directors into *auteurs*, a presumption that never interested you a whole lot. The *auteur* theory implied the superiority of print authors; their unique credit was never in dispute. Your brilliance when it came to musicals put you in a class no fancy Frenchman ever broached. *Les Parapluies de Cherbourg*? Fold them up and put them away.

Stanley Kubrick's versatility never extended to more than a parody of song and dance in *A Clockwork Orange*. *Singin' in the Rain* just had to be in the pocket that he picked. When Peter Bogdanovich's vanity tripped him into writing and producing a musical, the result was *At Long Last Love*, so thudding a flop that someone said to Billy Wilder that you had to give Peter marks for courage. Billy said, 'Wrong: courage is *At Long Last Love* Two'. Billy hated Bogdanovich as Fred Allen used to hate, or pretend to hate, Jack Benny. Peter was once a film critic; did he make the career mistake of not raving over *Some Like It Hot*? I never laughed at it too much myself, though the last line – Tony Curtis's 'Nobody's perfect' – was a lulu.

Bogdanovich was a walking encyclopaedia of movie lore, fun to be with, but you could never like him. He was at the peak of a deserved run of success when he asked me to write the screenplay of *Daisy Miller*. Fortunately, it is one of Henry James's shorter stories. As I closed the thin book I wondered why he wanted to do it. He must, I thought, be wanting to do something bold and original. By the time he had promised to call me I had re-polished that *Four Times Two* skeleton I once sold you: I was as genuinely enthusiastic as any commission can make a man when I started telling Peter how Daisy could be the eternal American virgin visiting Italy. We could start with her in 1875 and have the story unwind, through a century, always without Daisy seeming to notice how styles and décor changed. How about that if you hadn't heard it before? Peter's transatlantic silence said it all. He wanted to do *Daisy Miller* pretty much exactly as it was, in period. Why? Because oracular Orson had said that Cybill Shepherd was born to play Daisy. After I had done a draft, Peter and Cybill came over to London and were given a suite at Claridge's. Peter and I worked in the living room while Cybill practised tap dancing in the tiled bathroom.

When she finally came out, all set to go shopping, she was quite a worldly and certainly beautiful Daisy, the kind that just might have been plucked a couple of times. Peter looked at her and said, 'What have you done to your face?' Cybill frowned. 'Your face', he said, 'you've done something...' 'I haven't done anything to it.' He looked as if he was wondering, in that case, who had. 'It's...' He indicated some kind of lopsidedness. I was an uneasy audience. Might this be for my benefit, the proof of who was the boss? Cybill never said anything much to me that I remember. I never went to the shooting, in Vevey, as H.J. specified, but she offered little evidence that she was born to play Daisy, or anyone else very much.

Don't think I don't remember your experience of working with Cybill. The producer of that TV series she did, way back, with Bruce Willis (*The Professionals*, was it?), asked you to come, as a favour, and stage a dance number in one of the episodes. You were more flattered than paid, but you went and did your inimitable stuff and then asked Cybill if she felt like giving it a go. 'Sure.' So, lights, camera, music and here comes our leading lady now. The Connaught bathroom girl went through the moves you had plotted and then you cut. 'Good for me', she said. You said, 'Take a short break, OK? And then we'll do it again.' She said, 'Do we have to?' 'Excuse me?' 'I thought that was pretty good. This is for TV, you know.' You may have said, or you may just have thought, that Fred Astaire did take after take until he and you were satisfied he couldn't do better. If he couldn't, who could?

Daisy Miller made to play safe where there is no safety. Bogdanovich fell from critical grace and never climbed back up again. No one much seemed inclined to give him a hand. He had been a movie critic before he did that eleven-day wonder that isn't listed among his credits any more. Maybe too many people remembered what he had said about them. Bad notices sure lodge in the mind. Harold Pinter went literally a long way out of his way to attend some festival where he had a chance to jump on Carl Foreman. John Russell Taylor roasted *Two for the Road* when it opened in London. A couple of years later, we were in Peru at the same he was. I should gladly have nudged him over the cliff at Macchu Picchu if we had happened to coincide there. What local magistrate would ever divine a personal motive? I'd do the same today to a direct descendant of William Ewart Gladstone whom I have not seen in more than seventy years. I reserve a special category of malice for critics who have given our children bad reviews.

Your alpha movies are superbly free-standing, despite the credit that you shared with Gene. Why did you do things like *Deep in My Heart*? Can it be you dreaded falling back into self-doubt if you were not working? It wasn't just the money, it was the pick-you-up. Stanley Donen was his best self when he took command. 'Gotta dance' was very much you. I was never any good at it. My father was amateur tango champion of the world back in the early Twenties. He and Phyllis Haylor never rehearsed; they danced, his hand on the tiller.

Cedric rarely mentioned what I am sure he never forgot. My mother and Phyllis Haylor became friends in very late life. Phyll was living with a lady novelist who lived in the same block of flats as Irene. *Tournent, tournent* keeps coming round.

You did your stuff in the Broadway chorus, but you didn't long need other people to get you moving. Stanley Kubrick declared some kind of envy when he told me that he didn't want dialogue I wrote for him to sound like anything I'd do for you. After *Barry Lyndon* was slated in the US, as if to prove how unpatriotic S.K. had been by transplanting himself to England, you met us in Westwood wearing a pin proclaiming admiration for the other Stanley's movie. This at a time when your own *Lucky Lady* had been anything but fortunate with critics or public. That was classy, in a way S.K. was never known to be. You had been particularly pleased when Alfred Hitchcock called to congratulate you on *Two for the Road*. What really impressed him, he said, was that it was all done on location: no 'travelling matt'. Just what you wanted to hear?

How many people remember who John Simon was, unless he still is? He took the occasion, when reviewing *Lucky Lady*, to say of Liza that she was so incurably lacking in charm or beauty that she should never appear on the screen unless she had her legs wrapped tightly around her face. Simon's inoperable Hungarian accent rendered his fancy malice just a little Shavian, even on the page. Did he have any idea of the dynastic bindweed that had Liza cast in your movie? Legend tells me, unless you did yourself, how you had been having an affair with Judy Garland, when she was still married to Vincente Minelli. Vincente, no manifest pugilist, all but burst into your office, in whatever studio, Metro probably, and challenged you to a fight. He may even have come round the desk at you. You kept saying, 'Don't be silly, Vincente, you don't want to fight anybody'. 'Yes, I do, I want to fight you.' How it ended, I don't know, but not with black eyes.

Vincente came to see me in Langham, Essex, in the days when studios paid the fares for their favourites. Leslie Bricusse had it written into his deals that he be given a bunch of round-trip, first-class tickets from Malta (whence Evie originated) to L.A.; in truth they were cashable pocket money. A very pleasant lady producer came all the way to the Dordogne, on somebody's ticket, to get me to write a script for Mick Jagger and Arnold Schwarzenegger. She came; she went. Vincente wanted me to write a movie for Liza based on an Italian novel about the Marchesa Marchati, who ate only white lunches. He was supposed to bring a cheque with him from the producer. When he failed to produce it, I left him to sweat in a country hotel near our house until it arrived.

It finally did and I sprang him from solitary, He came to our house, not markedly resentful, though he did prefer tumblers of neat gin to anything solid we had to offer. Yes, I did the script but it wasn't to his taste. I'm more than a little ashamed of how I treated him. Vincente had his moments (*The Bad and the Beautiful* merits a remake, thanks to Kirk and Gloria Grahame), but he seems to have invited humiliation. An early number of *Cahiers du Cinéma* nominated him an *auteur*, but he was so lacking in wit (and Losey-like self-importance) in the interview he came to do with them that they recycled his badge. I heard that when he was shooting some movie, he wanted to have peacocks paraded on the set. They kept making unscripted moves, so he had their claws stapled to the floor. Terrible? What ranking director wouldn't do the same?

Is Bosley Crowther a pundit who excites anyone with nostalgic admiration? Unlike Judith Crist, who raved about *Two for the Road* in the *Herald-Tribune*, he gave us a sour notice in the crucially influential *New York Times*. It was not the first, or last, time that he did you down. You told me how you happened to go into a bar on 42nd Street and he called out,

'Hey Stanley'. You said, 'Hullo' in a tone to ice the Hudson. He came over, frowning, 'Stanley? It's Bosley. Bosley Crowther'. 'I know.' 'Is something wrong?' You said: 'Bosley, do you ever read the things you say about my movies in the paper?' Bosley said, 'Stanley, I'm one of your biggest fans. I think of myself as your friend. That's why I only want to see the very best you can do.' You said, 'Bosley, don't be my friend. Just say nice things about my movies in the paper.'

I went with Tom Guinzburg, my publisher at Viking, to see *Two for the Road* at the Radio City Music Hall, rather too cavernous for a movie that depended on intimacy. Audrey's pictures always opened there. The laughs came, but they were dispersed under the high ceiling. Dick Zanuck told me he went to see the picture three times in Westwood and each time the audience stood and applauded at the end. Darryl would sooner have had silent, seated money. The studio never lobbied for Oscars, even for Audrey. She was actually nominated for something else, in which she played a blind girl: *Wait Until Dark*. Fox had a big, big investment in *Dr Doolittle*. Leslie Bricusse got an Oscar for one of the songs: *I Talk to the Animals*. Why not?

May 1967, you and I flew up to Boston for a gathering, sponsored by Fox, of College editors from all over the US. Some PR guy – Sam Rosenberg was it? – thought we could give the kids the impression that Fox was on their side. May 1967, the Vietnam War was increasingly unpopular. The young men who might have to fight in it were especially principled when it came to Lyndon Johnson's foreign policy, as few Americans, except for Gore Vidal, had been in the case of Guatemala, for instance, a decade earlier.

I don't remember you talking too much about Gore, but I'll bet you told me the story of how he wrote a script, maybe of *Myra Breckinridge*, that the producer was not too happy with. After they'd spatted for a while, the producer suggested getting some actors in to do a reading. A covey of unemployed thesps convened in Mulholland Drive. The script was read with audibly decreasing enthusiasm. The actors took their $200 and went their way. Gore said, 'That was a truly terrible experience'. The producer heaved the statutory sigh of relief. 'So what do you think we should do?' Gore said: 'Get some other actors' (emphasis on '– [-ors]').

In my *Sunday Times* review of *Myra Breckinridge*, I wrote, 'Gore Vidal announced recently that the novel is dead. Now he has sent Myra B. to the funeral'. Gore told my friend Brian Glanville, with a maximum of syllables 'Frederic Raphael is too clever by one quarter'. That counted for a pretty good notice, I thought, from that particular mouth. I did a radio broadcast about the ancient world with Gore while I was in N.Y.C. I suspect I was a little grand with him when it came to the detail, but his reading of the Persian Wars was as smart as it was counter to scholarly routine. Mandarin pomposity was a form of camp that worked for him. His abiding defect was that his novels were closer to essays; never short of intelligence but without a single tune, so to speak, that you closed the book singing. His characters were targets whose bulls he shafted.

As for women, he was forever getting his own back against the mother to whom he never spoke after some climactic spat. Was she ashamed of his being gay? Success was his revenge. His affection was vested in his grandfather the senator from Oklahoma, for whom, when young, he acted as *amanuensis;* not a lot of those to be found where the corn was as high as an elephant's eye. Insiders' outsider, Gore's bravest novel attacked US banana-republicanism in good king Ike's golden reign. Bill Buckley jr. dumped him with a below the belt charge of faggotry. Gore was always proving that you didn't need to have been to a fancy college to turn into a smart-ass.

Cut back to wherever it was that the college editors had had their expenses paid to come and heckle their olders and no-betters. You and I sat on the platform along with Dick Zanuck, Irvin Kershner, who had just directed *A Fine Madness*, no great hit. He would become rich, a little later, directing one of those *Star Wars* episodes that helped to ruin the movies except for perpetual pigeons, nodding again and again at indistinguishable crumbs.

Sam Rosenberg, Fox vice-president of PR, had prepared a speech of welcome for Darryl, who was late in showing up. He had been witless enough to invite Bosley Crowther to share the platform with the defendants. This did not dispose any of us to sing or dance. Rosenberg was busking as best he could when Darryl bustled in, short and brisk as an aging prodigy could be. Rosenberg handed him a typewritten pre-cooked speech and sat down to mop his face. Darryl started reading. We were, he announced, honoured to have so many of America's college editors to come and talk to Twentieth Century Fox. We had, he went on, with waning volume and enthusiasm, come to learn and listen to what the young had to teach us about a changing world. Pretty soon, Darryl stopped, crumpled the yellow pages, dropped the ball on the floor, and said 'Who wrote this shit?' Sam Rosenberg's face was a Niagara of distress. Where else was he going to make a quarter of a million a year?

Darryl resumed with tart spontaneity. Twentieth Century Fox was not some mammoth monster; it was a set of people, like those on the platform, who worked their asses off making the best movies they could that they hoped people would like. Their jobs depended on being steady on the tight rope. Pretty soon, the kids were invited to say their piece. The Beatles and the Rolling Stones had filled them with entitlement. One took it upon himself to tell us that we had to build a bridge between Twentieth Century Fox and the young people of America before it was too late for whatever it would otherwise be too late for. Kersh took licence from Darryl. 'You don't get no fuckin' bridge', he said, 'we swam; you swim.' I took the occasion to have a not-smart-enough-to-remember swipe at Bosley and we all went and had some kind of a buffet lunch. Some young guy came up to you and said, in a tone that didn't bode well, 'About your movie, Mr Donen…' You said, 'Beat it'. He said, 'I liked it. A lot.' 'Well, you little toady, aren't you?' It's about the only time I ever heard you snap.

Dick and Darryl and David Brown were as loyal to us as if we had had a smash hit. You and they were reckless enough to endorse my idea of a four-part movie covering a single century-long romance. It began with a silent movie, progressed to a golden age musical, then into in a thriller and ended with science fiction, without the lovers ever recognising the passing of the years and the change of styles. The sci-fi episode opened with a car on the motorway, the passengers in the back seat are asleep; the passenger in the front seat is asleep and then we pan across to the driver and… you guessed it: he's asleep too.

The future world was literally divided: there were high barriers between the haves, with their caged mobility and their luxurious living, and the kept-outs, relegated to the overgrown, fly-blown past. My super-civilised couple crash the barrier into what they find to be an untended Garden of Eden, complete with serpent. You warned me that the four-part format was bound to lead to endless rewrites: as soon as one section looked really good, at least one of the others would not.

The project never got far enough to stall. As Hollywood's finances foundered, it was said that grass was growing in the streets in L.A. I made my first trip there, with Jo Janni, in 1969, when you were still in England. Dick and David liked my new script, *Guilt*, and were confident I could direct it. By the time Jo and I were back in London, Dick and David had been fired by Dick's father and that was the end of my dream of being a big-time director.

You and I had not seen each other for some time. When you called, you told me how miserable you were, how your marriage to Adelle was a pain, without sex and with every prospect of a divorce. My reaction was both sympathetic and, I confess, close to disappointment. I had taken you, gratefully, for a father figure, able to deal with the world with magisterial assurance. Pretty soon, you were threatened with an expensive, possibly ruinous divorce suit. I had a telephone call from someone in Quintin Hogg's chambers, eager for evidence of your sexual promiscuity. I put the phone down. Others, it seemed, did not. Adelle was as pitiless as she had been beautiful. The situation was saved by an unlikely witness. Hickey had not only polished the Roller, he had also been at the disposal of Adelle. Her vanity discounted the possibility of a mere driver disclosing the destinations to which she bid him take her when you were otherwise, or otherwhere, engaged. Hickey's loyalty impelled him to offer you dates and details of Adelle's horizontal afternoons. Quintin Hogg, who had, in his role as senior statesmen, denounced the loose women and randy minister who threatened to disgrace the Tory party, must have advised Adelle to turn reasonable. Your pride was not quite your fall, but it was badly bruised.

The settlement left you with the means to buy a fine house in Montpelier Square. Nothing of David Hicks's décor was transferred to your new address. It was furnished, from sofa to crockery, in the shining fashion of the early 1970s. The sitting room table was white plastic and all but covered with a collection of contemporary petty artefacts, none worth a single one of those regency paperweights (whatever happened to them?). No sign of Haddon Hall. I remember having tea with Dudley Moore and his latest pretty woman, a starlet called Susan. Adelle had been replaced by the bright, francophone, grown-up Barbara. You weren't so much happy as relieved.

I was busy being busy busy: I did a script of *Byron*, for MGM, which Schlesinger backed away from when *Far* (as we collapsed its title) was a flop in the US and he switched his attention to what became *Midnight Cowboy*. Neither Jo Janni nor I could summon any enthusiasm for it. As well as the Wick, Beetle and I now had a small house in Seymour Walk. Stephen was born there in 1967, a celebration of new life in our marriage. In 1969, Beetle saw an advertisement for a house in the Dordogne, with white shutters. Lagardelle cost us £19,000, the same amount as Willie Maugham had paid for the Villa Mauresque back whenever. The place needed work, but the purchase scarcely dented our bank balance. I should have been happy, but I was only rich. Just in time: the movies went into their slump soon after my fat double deal was made with Fox.

When they moved to another studio, I did another script for Dick Zanuck and David Brown, *The Day of the Fox*, about Sir Walter Ralegh, more in inventive thanks for *Two for the Road* than with confidence that it would be made. The uniformed *facteur* came up to Lagardelle from the village with a telegram (we had no telephone). Dick and David thought (on two pages of text) that my script was the best thing they had ever read and they were going to find the best director in the world to make it.

Are you smiling? You have every right to. I never heard another word. When I next saw the always charming David Brown, in Hollywood in 1974, I asked him casually about *The Day of the Fox*. 'What a great script that was!' he said. 'I'll never know how you made something so good out of the book we were stupid enough to buy for a lotta lotta money'. I said, 'So…?' David said, 'Freddie, I'll tell you. They all said, "Who the fuck is Sir Walter Ralegh?"' 'No answer to that', I said, an Eric Morecombe catchphrase David was unlikely ever to have heard.

I wanted to go back to writing novels. The Sixties had made me rich enough to grow a fresh conscience. I set off on the high road with a long novel about the Greek civil war which had ended in 1949. The Colonels had recently mounted their *coup d'état*. *Like Men Betrayed* contained no mention of the word Greece or Greek, just as 'Jew' was never used in *Lindmann*. Such are the conceits which win never fame nor fortune but allow the invention of another small world, free of petty accuracies of the kind that now pepper, but rarely salt, historical novels. I was glad to be responsible to no one but myself (and the Happy Few), though I was wise enough, in this at least, not to say so out loud. Mark Rydell came in to direct *Roses, Roses...*. We worked together at the studio for quite a while in the hot summer. When the air conditioning went on the blink, I asked what we should do. Mark said, 'Send for the *goyim*, that's what they're for'. A story I should never repeat? You know what: nuts to it all. Rydell got as far as choosing locations and then broke with Fox over the budget.

It has to have been right around then that you bought the movie rights to Kingsley Amis's novel *I Want It Now* and, with deference to a supposedly brilliant guy, commissioned him to write the script. You never allowed for that mixture of greed, laziness and anti-American conceit to be found in any number of Englishmen whose final idea of cleverness was ripping off foreigners, Yanks especially, who, by definition, deserved it. However many weeks later, Kingsley turned in what you soon realised was nothing but the book retyped in screenplay format. Did you suspect he'd rented someone to do the drudgery? I should not be surprised if jewing a Jew gave Kingsley a sense of righteousness. When he deigned to come and see you and talk about what needed to be done to render the thing feasible, he soon became impatient. As fancy intellectuals often do when asked to do the professional job they'd been happy to take the money to do, Kingsley took the line that you had to understand that he was an artist (not a claim he was liable to make in English company). 'I'll tell you what else you are', you told him: 'a thief.'

A few years later, you called me in France and told me how you had been in the South of France, for some festival or other, and ran into Lew Grade, who had been a hoofer, as you had, in your youth. Lew had made plenty of money in television and the theatre but he had realised only late in life how much more fun it was to make movies; the bigger the gamble, the bigger the kick, possibly. You and he did a literal duet on some fancy dance floor and were sudden buddies. When he asked you to direct a project called *Saturn Three*, which he had in preparation, you didn't think it was for you, but you undertook to produce it.

You had taken to directing, in your early twenties, as easily, naturally, as you had to dance. As a result, you never bought into the mystique of *auteur*-ship. Directing had been a job in old Hollywood, never a fine art. Any number of directors supplied footage which was often then delivered to editors over whom they had little or no control. Only a huge hit gave men (back then Ida Lupino was the only female director I heard of) the right to final cut, or something close to it. When Lew said to find a director, you didn't think it was a big deal. John Barry is now billed on Wiki as 'the man with the Midas touch'. He won all kinds of awards for the music for any number of hits. When he told you how he had always wanted to direct as well as compose, you – as Leslie Bricusse used to say – welcomed him aboard. You had Kirk and Sarah Fawcett (whom your handsome, ambitious son Josh was dating around that time) and Harvey Keitel, whom you saluted as 'General von Keitel'. As for the script, you were pretty proud to tell me that young Martin Amis was on the case. He had made quite a prodigious name for himself with his outrageous, 'street' novels. As so often in the biz, buying people at the top of the market was a way, executives kept hoping, of buying their luck as well. Two or three weeks after you told me how pleased you were, you called me at Lagardelle again.

'Freddie, you're talking to a drowning man'.

I said, 'Water's come up pretty fast, hasn't it?'

You said, 'You have to help me. Martin Amis has turned in a script that isn't any use to me at all. Will you take a look at it and maybe…'

'Stanley, I'm in the middle of writing a novel.'

'You still do that? Lew Grade's got lotsa money. Give me a week. Two weeks. Give me two weeks.'

I said, 'Stanley, I don't know how people talk in space. It's not my kind of thing one bit.'

Remember what you said? 'They talk just like people on earth but they wear helmets a lot. Two weeks is all I'm asking.'

Mixed motives are a recipe for the writer's life. I wanted to be your salvation because I liked you more than anyone else in the biz. I also knew damn well that you were over a barrel with lotsa money in it. I said, 'Two weeks, Stanley, no more truly.'

'Who do I talk to?'

'Jane Annakin at the Morris office.'

As soon as I put the phone down, I called Jane and asked her to ask for $25,000 a week. Business is business. You called back two minutes later, before she did. 'That's all fixed.' Forgive me, but I snapped my finger silently: if I'd been the kind of man I never was, I should have asked for fifty grand a week. You told me it wasn't your money.

In those days, there was no fax, no form of instant photographic transmission. You said, 'When can you start?'

'Not before I have the script.'

'The driver's on his way. He should be there in around eleven hours.'

He was too. He handed me the script, refused so much as a cup of tea and set off on the road home. How often have you known a bad, bad script that could be redeemed by plastic surgery? I did what I could but have no memory what it was, except for one thing. When Harvey, the bad guy, arrived on Saturn Three he was greeted, under their oxygenated dome, by Kirk and *la* Fawcett and their pet dog. Harvey, under whatever name he was space-travelling, gave the cute little thing a scratch behind the ears just as he was saying, 'How soon do we get to eat him?'

Shooting began when it had to begin and almost immediately there was another crisis, one that I could do nothing to ease: John Barry had watched all kinds of directors doing their stuff on classy movies and it must have seemed to him that saying 'action' and 'cut' required no rare competence. But as soon as he was all by himself in command of what was still, I fear, not the sort of script that directed itself, he froze. A day or two later, he resigned his command. You were left to pick up the pieces. You did the best you could but *Deep in My Heart* was way way better.

I never worked with Harvey Keitel, but I like him and his work, especially for Marty Scorsese. He was not the kind of star that fitted smoothly into the setting of the Claridge's. One evening, when he came home from the studio in the usual limo and pouring rain, there were so many cars at the door that the driver had to pull up in the middle of Brook Street. One of the top-hatted flunkeys came through the puddles with a prompt umbrella. When he reached Harvey's car, he bent down and saw who the passenger was. He folded the umbrella and skipped back under shelter.

I had made it a non-negotiable aspect of our deal that my name not figure on the credits. Martin Amis had been sufficiently applauded by his in-group to presume that he was a person of consequence. Like his dad, he took your money but no responsibility. I suspect, keenly, that he told the usual journos that I had blighted his handiwork. If only such things really mattered, what an idyllic life we would have to be living.

At some point, when I was not looking, you joined Carl Foreman and who all else in returning to California. As so often, the biz reorganised itself; the studios recovered their vanity and found some new bankers. When he had directed only *Duel*, Steven Spielberg flirted with *Roses, Roses...* which honoured the second of my good old days contract with Fox. He sat modestly next to me on Laddy's office couch and made some bright suggestions and then went off and worked on something called *Jaws*. He was driving a green Mercedes 280SL in tribute to *Two for the Road*.

You must have been very busy, because the next director my producer Robert Shapiro tried *Roses, Roses....* on was Bob Altman, who was enthusiastic until he wasn't. Playing the maverick, Altman acted the genius who did not share the prevailing taste and form; at the same time, he proved a pretty fancy operator, as Kubrick did. *Nashville* was classy evidence, despite its overdose of the Chaplin lady. Bob not only directed *The Player*, for David Brown, he was one. *M*A*S*H* was the masterpiece that gave him the last of many laughs. I had all his phone numbers, but that was it.

Steven Spielberg was still driving that green Merc when you came back to California. Thanks not least to Hickey, you had escaped Adelle with ample means to buy yourself, and Yvette, your new wife, a prime piece of secluded real estate at 300, Canyon Drive, Bel Air. At some point, you had brought Yvette with you down to the Wick. In her late twenties, she was so pretty and so young that you wondered, quietly, to Beetle how long she would want to be with a man twenty years older than she was. You kinda knew what you were getting into, but you couldn't wait.

The first time Beetle and I came out to stay in L.A. we rented Yvette's modest, delightful single-storey place up, up, up at the top of Oak Pass. Every day we drove past Leslie

Bricusse's fancy pad, white statue in front, in whatever-it-was Drive at ground level. Yvette's hill-topping one-storey house had a caravan, on bricks, in the garden just below it, where her brother and his wife Ampara were living. You loved the way she cared for her family. Two fine, slim, golden retrievers patrolled the grounds and kept it clear of rabbits and coyotes. Their grand, springy appearance was at odds with the hollow parody of a bark with which they greeted approaching strangers. Yvette had had their vocal cords severed to avoid their disturbing the peace. Vincente Minelli would have done the same, I'm sure.

She told me how pleased you always were when I was around. While we were in L.A., I played tennis a few times with a coach called Walker. When I mentioned Yvette, he said, 'Oh I know Yvette'. It is no great secret, just as it was never any sort of scandal, that Yvette had had a long relationship with 'Kerk' Kerkorian before she met you. You certainly did everything you could to make her happy. How long did you keep that red brick house above Malibu beach? I remember being there just one time, for lunch, when our son Stephen was seven years old. Spielberg's green Merc had still not been replaced and was parked in the drive as we waited for lunch until Yvette came back from the hairdressers.

She arrived hot and beautiful. The beach was at the bottom of a zigzag brick pathway. When she heard that Stee was keen to have a swim, Yvette said 'Let's go'. She took him by the hand and they ran down to the beach hut where, I guess, she must have changed. A minute later, they ran together into the sea. She dived in, to encourage him, no doubt. After a thorough dunk, they came back up the bricks, Yvette's new hair turbaned in a towel. Beetle's look at me as good as said, 'Who goes to have her hair done and then goes straight down and plunges into the ocean?'

That house, with its dream view of the Pacific from the huge double bed, furnished throughout with flawless impersonality, perhaps by my agent Ron Mardigian's interior decorator wife Merle, might as well have been a mirage. It was fugitive proof of how happy you and Yvette were. We never went there again and I have no idea when you sold it, well, I am sure. Marriage with a much younger woman served your pride and reminded you of mortality. The big office in Stone Canyon, with that secretary who called you Mr Donen, became half filled with exercise machinery, on which you worked for two or three hours a day, as if to pedal away the years. The other half was soon filled with an early computer, cumbrous as Elizabeth Taylor's luggage. It could crank out scripts faster than the slickest hack could compose them.

I was in California to talk to Alan Pakula about an original screenplay I had written called, provisionally, *Hullo, Angel!* It was based on the neat idea of a man who happens by chance, in some kind of airline snarl up, to find himself seated next to a very good-looking woman with whom, very soon, he is embarks on an improbably flirty conversation. It turns out – had you guessed? – that he is her ex, she his. And then? They talk, agree how wise they both were to admit their mistake and make new lives with new people. Neither of them has any business in the place this particular flight is going to, so they will head in different directions as soon as they land in wherever the hell they're headed. They can afford the honesty they never managed when they were living in that tight apartment, with the one-legged guy upstairs who was never short of pussy, on Albany Street, Brooklyn. Then – did you guess again? – there is a crisis; no, not engine failure but an elderly patient (in first class) who has what the usual doctor who happens to be on board diagnoses as a potentially lethal heart attack.

The plane has to land at the nearest airport, with a less than full-length runway, and offload the impatient patient. Sure you can smile; I hope you do. Because, yes, the pilot hits the ground hard and – 'bang, if not bingo' (as my script said, I'm afraid) – one of the tyres on the undercarriage burns out and explodes. It's OK, kinda, because no one is hurt. But? The airport does not usually handle big jets. A spare tyre is going to have to be flown in as soon as possible, which will not be in a minute or two.

Ben and Caroline, our couple, are used to having things their way. So? Ben and his credit cards go to the Avis desk and ask to rent a car they can dump when they get back to the twentieth century, or better. They are closing the deal when the man who was promising to die on the airplane comes up and asks if they can give him a lift to wherever they are going and he can get another flight. In his present condition, although it seems the local doctor can't find anything very wrong with him, he doesn't dare drive himself. Ben and Caroline look at each other like the frustrated lovers they truly are not and make faces they have made before, when they were. They set off in the big Ford with the old guy in back with the one biggish bag he has with him. Luckily enough, they all have only hand luggage.

Cut to: they are out on the highway from who knows where the hell to Topeka or somewhere Kansan like it. The old guy asks more questions than he chooses to answer in an accent that owes something to some old country, probably Italy. They stop for a quick hamburger and drive on. Caro and Ben smile together; the presence of the old guy makes them closer, damn him. You've guessed it: the hamburger seems to have disagreed with him. Back on the highway, the symptoms he had on the plane start to recur. Caro is suspicious of the old man's ability to be sick, then well enough to travel, then… But Ben has little choice but to pull in. The old guy takes some deep breaths, then he says he has something in his bag he needs, so they wait while he unzips it, takes a deep breath, and comes up with… a gun.

This had to be in the days when people didn't have their luggage x-rayed. The gun shakes slightly but not too much. What does he want? Money? 'Money!' He laughs huskily, shakes his head. 'What?' 'The car.' 'The car?' 'Get out, the two of you, and walk away slowly.' Ben says, 'And then what do we do in the middle of where-the-hell?' 'Not my problem.' Ben looks at Caro. What does she expect him to do? He takes her and, as he pushes her to the ground, he puts one foot forward, pivots and kicks the old guy right in the mouth. The gun goes off as he crashes against the car and then down on the ground. Ben jumps on him. There is no resistance. You're right again: seems he really has had a heart attack this time. He's dead. They have to laugh and Caro has to kiss Ben. Of all the people the old guy messed with, it had to be a professional stunt man! Should we establish this in the plane? They laugh and then they stop laughing. The guy has actually shot himself as well as whatever else has happened to him. Dead as can be.

Caro says, 'Now what?' Ben says, 'You're the writer'. (She co-writes a quite classy TV sit com – establish earlier, as Pakula's notes would be sure to say). 'So you tell me now what?' 'Might be a help if we knew who the hell the old guy is. Was.' Caro unzips the old man's fat reddish leather bag. Under a flimsy camouflage of clothing and stuff, it is bulging with dollar bills, mostly of high denomination. There is an envelope fat with several passports, from different countries, with different names, all with the old man's somewhat younger photograph. 'Señor Felipe Verdugo, Signor Ettore Conti, Signor Federico Janni, Mr Gareth…'

Ben says, 'Good news or bad news?'

'Try both.'

'How much money do you think…?'

'Too much to come out of his piggy bank, that's for sure.'

Ben says, 'How about we leave him in the bushes, we take the money, and hit the road? Nothing to connect him with us.

No sense in calling the cops because…'

'That would cost us however the hell much he's got in here.'

'And then some, betcha. Why'd he… need to get them to put the plane down in Hicksville? You're the writer on the show.'

Caro says: 'How about because of whoever's waiting for him in Topeka? And who will any minute now be coming looking for him.'

They get in the car and… what do you think of it so far? I was with David Brown in some meeting and I had got a lot less far than I have here when he said, 'Freddie, as your agent I advise you not to say another word before you make the deal'. In truth, that dated coinage, I went a lot further in the script I gave Pakula when we first got to L.A. He was editing *Klute*, so he didn't get back to me for several days. The welcome party he and Hannah gave for us was quite a classy affair, designed to make us feel appreciated as well as impressed. There was a twenty-million-dollar table, with a lot of sparkling old widows, right on down to two-a-penny millionaires.

Alan had become a big success since the days we knew him in London when he was dating Judy Scott-Fox, my large, aristocratic William Morris agent. Alan had a strange personality, blowing warm and cold, binary red-head, from one meeting to the next. He wrote with equal facility, but a different slope, with either hand. He dumped Judy, gently, when he became a successful director and married Hannah, mother of somebody else's children and a serious historian. He was always neatly groomed and dressed like the slightly dated Yaley we was. When I went to see him to talk about the movie, he led me past the main house to a tall rectangular one-storey building. Copies of the Yale magazine were fanned on the wide desk. There was the usual make-yourself-at-homeliness and a dais at the far end with a tall, closed, double-doored mahogany cabinet on it. 'Alan', I said, 'you've built yourself a synagogue.'

There are all kinds of people in the biz, a good many of them no better than they do not bother to pretend, but not a few, scoundrels as they might be, such as David Begelman, were fun to be with. Careful: so was Hermann Göring for the parents of a Cambridge friend of mine. Begelman was an embezzling scoundrel but was he ever dull? I remember when you and I went to see him in his new offices overlooking the exclusive Los Angeles country club's golf course. David said he particularly enjoyed watching the *goyim* surreptitiously kicking their balls into a better lie. Better lies were a speciality of his: you told me that when he was a top agent and someone suggested that you be approached to direct a picture he had a client in mind for, David said, 'Stanley Donen? Haven't you heard? He's in an institution.' You bore him no ill will: business is business. Did anyone ever have an enjoyable evening with Alan Pakula or Norman Jewison? Alan Ladd junior became head of Fox, was it because he said so little that he seemed wise? Willard Huyck told us about a dinner at La Scala with Laddy as host at which he and Gloria might as well have not been there. At the end of the evening, out on the sidewalk on little Santa Monica, Laddy held out his hand. Willard shook it and said, 'How do you do?'

Alan and I had parted, as they used to say, brass rags and there was no reconciliation. He spared me days of earnest tedium of the kind that probably would have made Norman Panama seem like Bob Hope. Alan went on to make *All the President's Men*. I remember only that he had a top shot from under the dome of the Library of Congress, looking down from where no one could possibly be on Redford and Hoffman doing research. Such a shot – need I tell you? – serves only to rupture the narrative and draw attention to the director. Oh, I also remember a scene in an underground car park. How many of those have you seen? Poor Alan, he missed the Oscar three times. His ultimate bad luck came when he was driving on the Long Island Freeway, I think it was, and a truck in front of him picked up an iron bar that was lying in the road and kicked it right through the windshield that Alan was behind. He was killed, we have to hope, instantly.

I cannot remember a single evening with you, even when things were not going well for you, when there was not a lot of laughter. Whenever we called you, after arriving in L.A., and you said, 'You're here!', that always seemed like the real reason we'd come. You were very busy with this and that, with Larry Gelbart and who all else. I am not sure I ever met Gelbart. I remember about him only an anecdote you told me. When he was asked if it was true that Sony was making a deal to buy Paramount, he said 'All that's left to do is cross the tees and slant the eyes'. No line for today's woke world.

Your musical version of *The Little Prince* should have brought back your Metro days, but something I didn't ask about seems to have gone wrong. During the accompanying wrangles, someone advised you to take immediate action. 'So I immediately did nothing', you told me. I wanted things to be good between you and Yvette, but we never saw much of her when we were in town. Your relationship needed a hit and *Lucky Lady*, broken-backed from the script on, brought nothing but an expensive flop. I never put on a better performance than the night we with you and watched it. The press was pitiless. The *L.A. Times* reported Gloria Katz (aka Mrs Huyck) as saying that you had ruined their script. You called and asked her if she had been misreported. She said, 'As a matter of fact, not'. You said, 'Oh Gloria'.

You seem to have borne the Huycks no ill will; more surprisingly, nor did they you. When what you dreaded more than any flop happened and Yvette said she didn't want to be married any more, Willard and Gloria kept you regular company and helped you out of the deepest depths of depression. Losing Yvette was bad, but having everyone know it has to have been worse; worst of all was the speed with which she married Howard Ruby, who had become multi-multi building sets of identical apartment houses all across the country.

Billy and Audrey Wilder were your other saviours. Beetle and I came less frequently to L.A. I had plenty of things to do, including a new ten-part TV series for Granada. We did fly in, on Mike Medavoy's ticket, in 1990 and were on our way to pick up a car when I heard, 'Freddie?' It was your now grown-up son Mark. He assumed we had come to L.A. for the same reason he had: you were getting married again. As soon as Mark (studying for a PhD) told you we were around, you asked me to be one of the best men.

Over dinner in some latest place to go, down in Santa Monica I think, you told us the story how you and Yvette, very good friends again, had been out shopping in La Ventura boulevard, right by the New York Pizzeria we all used to go to a lot, and went into a boutique where Yvette went to try a few things on. You and the young salesgirl – 'Pam' on a pin on her breast – started talking and she was as nice as you could imagine. Yvette took her time and you found that Pamela was studying to be whatever it was. Yvette came back and bought whatever she wanted, and a few more things probably, and you both thanked Pam and went on out.

You told Yvette what a nice kid Pam seemed and Yvette said that she had really liked you. 'Think so?' 'Sure so', Yvette said, 'trust a woman' (there's a title for you). A step further and Yvette said, 'Go back and ask her to go out with you'. You maybe hesitated, but what the hell? You went back and asked her, a little like the young guy you no longer were, whether maybe she would come to a movie with you. She was quick, very, to say yes.

You had a couple of dates during which two or three people at least recognised you and called out 'Hullo, Stanley!'

Several such hullos later, Pam said, 'Are you famous or something?' You found it endearing that she had gone out with you without any idea of who you were. Granted that you made no big deal out of all the things you had done, how likely a story is that? Yvette was very pleased for you when you told her, 'Imagine: that girl I met in the store with you that day says she wants to marry you!' Yvette said that she and Howard would stage the ceremony in their well-fenced mansion and then some on Mulholland Drive or wherever the hell it was. And staged it sure was. Beetle and I arrived in suitable costumes and passed through a cordon of suitable unsmiling men with bulging armpits. Money like Mr Ruby's did not come without hostages to fortune.

We passed through the rich house and into a huge, sunny room with rows of neat, rented non-denominational chairs. White, pew-end flowers spiralled up to the ceiling. I was lined up with the five other best men, Peter Stone, Billy Wilder, Willard Huyck and that little guy whose name I don't remember who made millions producing TV programmes like the one in which old or otherwise incompetent candidates played golf or tennis or raced around a track (I only ever heard about it) and made gasping fools of themselves for prizes that excited them to bust a gut. He was also rumoured to be a CIA hit-man, wasn't he, like that English actor in *Arabesque* who made tax-free money as a killer for British Intelligence? The world, my masters…

After the ceremony, with Pam in what looked like a wrap-around, fancily-pierced doyley, we all went out onto the wide terrace overlooking a sunken ornamental garden. A dozen tables were laid for lunch under wide awnings. Beetle and I were at the first on the right writers' table where the best laughs were likely to be found. No one made any kind of fun of what Michael Frayn might have called 'Gatsby Day', the name he applied, with small grace, when 'thanking' Beetle, for inviting him to a modest lunch party we once gave at the Wick. Trust an English smartass to eat first, bite afterwards and never ask you back.

Back to the Ruby terrace, heads up we saw a small plane trailing a sign GOOD LUCK PAM AND STANLEY. It was a gift from the killer best man whose name I can't retrieve from memory's trash can. There must have been speeches, but I cannot recall who made them. Did Pam have any of her friends or family present? I doubt if you were keen to be to them as you had been to Yvette's entourage. The occasion was more production than a ceremony. We all wanted to be happy for you; few failed to see the occasion as a sumptuous apology for the way you had been deleted from Yvette's CV.

When she came over and talked to us, Peter Stone was surprised that the grounds seemed not to contain a tennis court. Yvette pointed to the mini-ornamental garden below where we'd been eating. 'Used to be one right there. Could be again, I guess.' I said, 'Not easy to get to the net'. I attributed the remark to Peter Stone; it sounded more like him than like me. It's always wise to put wisecracks in other people's mouths, especially if you mean to repeat them. As Cicero said, when vaunting himself, ''twere better another had said it'.

The big party dissolved in the late afternoon. None of us wished you anything but the best of luck; who doubted that you'd need it? The more the people at our table talked, quietly, about your romance with Pam, the more it seemed to resemble one of those old staple movies in which the young girl has no idea that the man she happens to find attractive is in reality a millionaire in some kind of disguise. It smacked of too good to be true that Yvette just happened to want to go into that particular store where Pam had taken a temporary job. Could there be any doubt that the chance encounter was not altogether fortuitous? There was kindness in the calculation. Your loneliness had been painful to observe, although you bore it with public dignity. What you had dreaded back at the Wick, more than ten years before, scarcely came as a surprise. If *Blame It on Rio*, or the movies that preceded it, including the clever *Double Bill*, had been the hit that Larry Gelbart's script seemed to promise, who knows whether Yvette would have broken away? She was an honest woman in her way. If she had never broken with Kerkorian, she was careful not to embarrass you. There was something almost thoughtful in her choice of Howard Ruby as a last resort. He was no sort of Hollywood celebrity nor was he a charmer. She could not be accused of any cruel betrayal by doing literally what you had always called, when selecting a shot on the set, 'going with the money'. You meant keeping the camera's eye on the star; she observed the literal meaning. Howard had made so great a fortune that he had no need of another, but you know as well as anyone that the appetite for another hit is never quenched by a smash. His next idea, or the next one someone sold him, was a nationwide investment in a system for developing photographs at supermarkets. Patrons could leave their reels of film on the way in and collect prints on the way out. It's difficult to make this sound like a gold-mining operation in the present world of instant electronic imagery, but it has to have seemed a good idea at the time. Howard Ruby lost a lot of money on it, but he still had a whole lot left.

After that sumptuous wedding brunch, the company dispersed for a few hours before the A-list met again for dinner in a private room at Chasen's. The reunion of your loyal, close friends chimed with what a script of yours called 'Hollywood Ending'. Chasen's on N. Canon Drive had been the in place all the way back to the 1930s, long before Wolfgang Puck made Spago the place to find Swifty Lazar opening and closing deals on that red telephone of his. How many of us did you ask that night? Fewer than twenty. Walter Matthau and his blanched wife had not been at the Ruby mansion. She was said to rise late and then take most of the day applying the mask of white make-up which, in her view, rejuvenated her appearance or concealed whatever blemish no one was ever going to see if she could help it. The atmosphere was altogether less formal. The speeches, from I can't remember who, were not quite racy but they broke into a familiar trot. Looking back, I see Pam, at once the star and an extra in company she did not know, playing her part with brave modesty. We ate and drank well. When the speeches were done, Walter Matthau leaned down from near the top of the table and said, 'What are you going to do when the money runs out, Stanley?' Who else could have got away with saying it, let alone have raised a laugh? The evening ended, in a sort of rueful cheer, alleviated by Dudley Moore improvising at the piano with the generosity typical of him. I don't remember what he played but there was something in his manner that capped a day of ostentatious make-believe with what came across as genuine affection and celebration of the human comedy.

Who but you and Pam can ever say whether you were happy together for a while? You had had several wives and who knows how many affairs. Which had made you happy or for how long is nobody's business but yours. If none of them made you as happy as you had hoped, might it be that no one ever could? You and any number of people craved happiness and hits with the same insatiable, maybe impossible, appetite. Pam, to put it plainly, furnished your last attempt to stay as young as you wanted to feel. Am I wrong to suspect that your wives and lovers were more like dance partners than social or erotic companions, unless the dance was all of that and more. Arm-candy is the cant phrase, but for a dancer, as you were and my father was, the beauty on your arm empowered, as nothing else could, a sense of defeating time that no other activity ever quite did?. The command of a woman on the dance floor was not a matter of power but of a literal conspiracy against mortality, hers, yours, whoever you both were in so-called reality. Sentimental me? Probably, but wasn't there always a sort of wishful innocence in all your sophistication? Beetle and I went back to Europe and never saw Pam again.

Hollywood had indeed ended for you. Pretty soon you sold whatever was left to sell in the way of real estate and moved to New York, right back where you started from, in the biz at least. New York was not exactly right back where you started from, but near as dammit. Walter Matthau was not alone in guessing that you and Pam wouldn't last together all that long. The marriage ended but, as no one had predicted, you stayed friends; perhaps you were both relieved. You had no lack of company in N.Y.C. Beetle and I had dinner with you and Peter Stone, who had some kind of a hit on Broadway. He was large without ever having been big; good company too, without ever seeming to be anybody in particular.

You never directed another movie, but you did do a neat piece of late work for television. I don't know what happened to Pam, but a year or two after we last saw you in the US you took up with Elaine May. She had not been short of screenwriting work but, like John Barry (who died soon afterwards), as a director she had met what Jimmy Clark's wife, Malou, called her 'up and comings', when directing *Ishtar*, with Warren and Dustin, one of the all-time disasters. The movie was shot on location in Morocco, I think. The word was that they had all been encouraged to have a good time and spend lots of money because the studio had a blocked account in Marrakesh and couldn't extract a penny. That didn't mean they weren't hoping for a hit, not the one they took. Jim Clark edited *Charade* as well as *Darling* and I took us to be friends within the biz's meaning of the word. He and Malou came to see us when we were living in Oak Pass, and then again to lunch in Lagardelle. It turned out, when he wrote a book about his successes, he didn't like me very much. I sensed it the day I first met him. I did all I could, not much, I confess, to help him get a film to direct and I never said a sour word about him, nor anything much. He and Malou asked us to dinner some time in the eighties. On the day we were due to go, he called and said the party was off. He sounded stressed and I feared that he had suffered some domestic misfortune. My offer of help embarrassed him. He couldn't get off the line fast enough. I swear to God I have no idea what his trouble was. It hasn't kept me awake.

You stayed with Elaine, she with you, for as much time as there was left. Funny that you played that record of her and Mike Nichols' that first time I came to see you when you were living in David Hicks's fancy set. New York suited you fine. You and Elaine had an office where you wrote screenplays. I never heard that any of them got made, but it was a kind of exercise, probably a whole lot more fun than running and running on the spot at 300, Stone Canyon. You always sounded cheerful when I called, rarely because you'd seen a movie you liked. The last time you called was in 2012. You had been invited to Paris by some Film Institute; you wanted us to come from Lagardelle to see you and the faithful Elaine. I sighed quietly: quick there-and-back trips had become more arduous than they used to be. You said that whoever they were would be happy to give us a suite at the Hôtel Lutétia. That wasn't why I said we'd come.

On the eve of your staged interview, in front of a large audience, we all drank champagne in our suite. You said that we were there because we loved each other. We clinked glasses and had to smile at what we knew and didn't say. The Lutétia had been Gestapo headquarters during the Occupation. After your gig, we had dinner with several people in a restaurant no better than showbiz people usually manage to pick. Elaine's daughter sat next to me. She looked older than her mother who must have had have had the surgical equivalent of a rewrite or two. She has to have been the smartest, most modest and funniest of all the women in your life.

There was something gallant and generous in everything you did. We did too love each other. I wouldn't say as much of anyone else I ever met in the biz, though I liked quite a few. All we have to show, professionally, for fifty years of friendship is *Two for the Road*. I wish there'd been more, but it's enough for me. Not long ago, a critic on some paper in New York state wrote that he had only recently seen our movie. From now on, he said, his life would be divided between before and after seeing *Two for the Road*. Print that one?

Love, Freddie.

Darling Dizzy,

I heard you before I saw you. I was cooking green beans
for Paul and me while Beetle was in labour upstairs in The
Old Mill House, East Bergholt, once the home of John
Constable's father. In 1960 it was no part of male conjugal
duties or pleasures to be present at a birth. Beetle, whose
determination, you will confirm, is rarely baulked, insisted
on having you at home. The midwife, Nurse Bray, panicked
halfway through. Dr MacBride came swiftly and, with
unalarmed competence, undid whatever was impeding your
arrival. Not long afterwards that first cry promised that all
was well. I led Paul up the twist of black box stairs from the
kitchen to where Beetle was holding you. Nurse Bray handed
me a tied and sealed little brown paper parcel and asked me to
bury it. I had small idea of what the afterbirth consisted. As
I interred it beside the asparagus patch, I had a furtive feeling
that I was secreting some part of you in the East Anglian earth
of what Constable heard a peasant call 'Old England'.

You were conceived in Franco's Spain. The little pierless
seaside village of Fuengirola, in Andalusia, was one of the
cheapest places in Europe to live in. We could not afford to
live in London while I wrote my next novel, *A Wild Surmise*,
and the one after, *The Trouble with England*. Then the chance
to write plays for the sudden greedy market of commercial TV
provided the supplement that allowed us to return to England,
and rent that cottage in Bergholt, for your arrival. We had
bought a scooter for Paul to be given him on your birth
day. 'Got a sister, got a cooter' was the two-year old's happy
reaction. You and he were close as could be, until Bedales.

Spain had been a liberation. After not quite a year in Bergholt, where I once made seven not out for the village team, we loaded our possessions and a pregnant-although-she-denied-it Irish nanny called Nuala into our new grey Standard Ensign and set off again for Fuengirola. Paul once said, when not more than five, 'The same thing isn't the same thing the second time', an observation true of our upgraded return to Franco's '*E-paña*' as our *cociñera y todo*, toothless Salvadora, always-in-black widow with four daughters, called it. Franco was driven through Fuengirola that summer, in one of a fleet of long black cars, all containing a small moustached, black-suited figure who might have been the Caudillo. The place had been decorated in his honour but his cortège never slowed over the whitewashed VIVA FRANCO printed on the *Carretera*. Salvadora said, '*Con mis ojos le he visto*' [with my own eyes I saw him], but which one was him, who knows? Fuengirola had no pier because it had resisted the fascists over twenty years earlier. I wrote a story called *The Day Franco Came*.

We set off at the end of an uneasy summer to drive back to England. You were always a delight; not yet the beauty you became. You had neither Paul's long, dark eyelashes and black eyes nor his demanding temper. When we stopped at Sainte-Maxime, for a rendezvous with Stella Richman of Atv, my Maecenas, I had a surprise call from London. Film producer David Deutsch had seen one of the plays I had written for Stella and wanted me to rewrite it as a movie. We turned our wheels onto the yellow brick road.

Having stayed in London long enough only to meet David, close the deal, buy a blue Standard station-wagon, we set off again, for Rome. A furred Contessa, chauffeured in a Fiat 1100, rented us a neat ground floor flat, on Monte Mario, 2719, and we were happy, without TV. In the mornings I let the tight little island have it, nicely, as I wrote

Nothing But the Best. Every afternoon, without fail (did it never rain that winter?), we drove to a museum, a cathedral or a classical site up and down and around Rome. You lay on the floor of the Sistine chapel and I told you the story of Michelangelo's labour of genius for the unpitying Pope Julius II. Rome was inexhaustible, never dull, unlike the classical education that furnished my irreverent commentary. I always tried to tell you and Paul more than you needed to know.

Might you remember the so-called *Happily Married Couple* on the Etruscan sarcophagus in the Villa Giulia opposite where Paul and I played football on Sunday mornings? Their pose was conventional, but fancy read them as sated smilers joined at the clay hip and thigh. One such Sunday, while we were kicking about in the Parioli gardens, a snappily-suited Roman came back, perhaps from visiting his mother, put one of his calfskin gloves on the roof of his big Fiat before unlocking the door, and then drove off, dandy glove still there. You came to be amused by play with convention and its deregulation, in life as in art. Who else ever thought to do a drawing of the Minotaur as a calf at Pasiphae's breast? Someone made off with that seven-feet wide, horizontal charcoal cartoon, designed to go over the door of a show in Islington.

On other Sundays, we drove out to Tivoli and had Hadrian's villa and its sprawl of unpatrolled grounds to ourselves. I can hear Paul saying, 'Come on, Wairah, let's go' and you would fly after him in your blue jeans-material skirt. You might remember the stone crocodile at the edge of the pool, a sorry memorial to Hadrian's lover Antinous, who lost his boyish charm as his beard grew ineffaceable. Did he jump or was he pushed into the Nile, crocodile sacrifice? Grief and/or guilt drove the peripatetic emperor (all those arches and that long Scottish wall testify to quasi-ubiquity) to his Tivoli retreat. He never much liked Rome, I told you, nor did the Romans applaud his Greek tastes.

When I had posted my script, and David Deutsch was scouting for a director, we loaded our stuff in the Vanguard and drove past Gaius Marius' and Cicero's birthplace, Samnite Arpinum, to Naples and then across to Brindisi, where we caught the ferry. We landed, in a hurry for Hellas, at Igoumenitsa in northern Epirus, where Byron saw a patriotic Greek arm hanging like a road sign and went on to dine with Mohammed Ali, the local Turkish tyrant. He told B. how much he loved English sailors.

Rome had been a feast; Greece was a revelation. I wish you had found time to make something of the mountainous site of very ancient Dodona. We drove up, passing shepherds tented under orange sheepskins, to the sacred grove of oak trees where credulous postulants once hung tributes and rustic requests to Zeus. Priests who never washed their feet interpreted the responsive shivering of the leaves. Dodona was the oldest oracle, too out-of-the-way not to be outshone by better-placed Delphi.

We went there too, before heading into Athens. I am quick to fiction, slow to falsehood, but I did lead Thalia Taga, a travel agent, to believe that Dilys Powell was a personal friend. Actually, she had been recommended in an article by the *Sunday Times* Hellenophile film critic. Where should we go? Sandy Skyros? Thasos? Where? As we were having coffee and tall glasses of water in Thalia's office, just off Syntagma, while you and Paul sucked on sticky *loukoumadia*, she had a phone call from Artemis Denaxas. He had been Minister of Marine for ten days, unless it was ten minutes, in some fleeting government and was saluted as such ever after.

Thalia told him of our desire to find some sandy island to settle on for a while. Samos? Spetsai? Thalia answered a few questions, with nodding glances at us, and then said that the Minister would like us to go to Ios, a depopulated Cycladic island which, it seemed, he more or less owned. He was keen for English people to discover it before the Germans and promised we would be looked after once we got there. 'This is a sign for you', Thalia said.

At noon the next day, in Piraeus, we boarded *Despina*, an old Dover-Calais ferry re-christened for the Aegean run to Syros and most stations to Santorini. Our luggage included the folding wooden cot that Harry Gordon had made for you in Fuengirola. We were up on deck when a sudden ship's siren shrilled in our ears; and then again. You burst into terrified tears. After explanation, you said, 'No more hoo-der!' Yes, yes, such scraps are made for the wind, but such scraps go to freckle life's montage once you learn where to stick them, right? The *Despina* rode the Aegean like the creaking veteran she was. Did you see the group of two army officers and a bearded priest, in his black sack and tall hat, talking together by the rail? Future events in Greece have given the trio a sinister back-light. You and I did not take the heaving sea well, ever. Remember that *aliscafo* bumpbumppump crossing from Naples to Capri when they were shooting *Darling?*

Fourteeen hours later, at three in the morning, a red light was seen blinking in the black. As a sailor called 'Ios, Ios', *Despina* swung to port and into the dark sack of the harbour. The anchor rattled; cigarettes glowed towards us as ferrymen came to meet the boat, its passengers, sheep and goats and cargo. Ios sported no deep dock in 1962. We had to go down a rope ladder to reaching arms. Beetle, one-time ribboned Paulina the gymnast, carried you. Paul and I followed. A lame garter-sleeved porter promised to bring our bags and your folded bed. I heard '*Dthen piradze*' [don't worry], for the first, never the last time. Had we expected Artemis Denaxas to have arranged for some Hermes to be watching for us? None announced himself. Donkeys queued like taxis on the concrete dock. Experienced hands loaded them with local passengers' luggage. Left alone, the only *xenoi* on the emptied dock, my classical Greek, in a salad with phrase-book modern, was enough to find us beds in the dockside hotel above the cafe that carried the name of Denaxas. It had nothing I ever discovered to do with *ho plousios* [the rich man] who had lured us there.

The next day was Beetle's birthday. She was beautiful but scarcely radiant, marooned with two small children in the small middle of nowhere. What next? A Romanian presented himself and said he would find us a place to live. Large and jaundiced and not my first choice for a best friend, he was as good as his word (as that nice Miss Pearce had not been). He can't have got much out of making the deal for Nikos's whitewashed cottage of three rooms. With an outside, sack-covered hole for a loo and a well for fresh water, it would cost three pounds a week. The metal double bedstead in one room had a plank base, a straw-filled mattress. The centre room, where we rigged the cot for you, had a single deckchair for luxury (shades of Wittgenstein's rooms in Whewell's Court) and a bed for Pab. There was a gas ring on a stone shelf in the tight kitchen. Lame Giorgos Galatsios brought us all our luggage charged on a single donkey, Phreeni, saddled with a wooden rack. Yorgo was quick to give you a ride. Your passion for donkeys was born.

Outside our rented *spiti* (from the Latin *hospitium*) was a long concrete table under a grapevine, buds just splitting into green. I had started a novel in Rome, but Ios graced me with fresh inspiration. Nikos's old father, in Turkish trousers, brought goat's milk in a tin can feathered with hairy traces of caprine authenticity. The old man watched as my keys chattered. He had never seen a typewriter before. I worked at *Lindmann* without hesitation under an umbrella-turned-sunshade suspended on the wires for the nascent vines. At the far end of the table, you and Paul spent the mornings with bucket and plastic spade, making sandcastles on the wide white wall. Paucity of means mothered invention. You never interrupted me once.

Flora came down from the village to sweep the place and bring us dishes from the *phourno*, weekend *pastitsou*, baked pasta in a wide dish, enough for two days. The Romans and Venetians left verbal as well as visible traces. After the dockside apron of concrete, there were no paved roads on Ios, no cars or buses to use them. Donkeys did all the portage, as George Steiner would say, or at least write. Years later, now years ago, he challenged you to draw him. You never warmed to him and feared it couldn't be done, and then did it; there he is on our wall, his quizzical vanity, no sad arm in the frame. In the Ios afternoons, we walked on a tumble of shards of volcanic rock twenty metres to the beach. Your quick, confident, long middle finger sketched a donkey, saddled and stirrupped, on the easy sand. And another.

Ios seemed stocked with the past. We would pass the butcher's assistant (I suspect his lover) with a live lamb scarfed around his neck, in unconscious imitation of that sixth-century statue, its legs clasped in his fist. One day, lame Yorgo came to the cottage leading Phreeni and proposed to take you and Paul on a ride into the interior. Parents might have hesitated in the modern world, but in Arcadia it did not occur to us to be suspicious. Off you all went and Beetle and I had a rare hour or two alone. Perhaps I lumbered her with fresh pages of *Lindmann*, my literary far-from-a-donkey. My work is my work, my self is charged with sentiments I shall never submit to public scrutiny; well, only a fraction, as here. In the late afternoon, it struck us that we had committed the two most precious people in our lives to the care of a gap-toothed Yorgo in a cloth cap whose last name we did not yet know. Filled with belated apprehension, I walked along the valley, past the site of what had not yet been discovered of the antique city, calling, then shouting your names. What had we done?

After however many minutes and seconds, a call came echoing back off the hillsides '*Pepeeko*', not some vernacular password, but a Cycladic 'Beetle'. So, home you came happy and not ill-used, eager for the next time, and a donkey of your own. Meanwhile you constructed one out of a duffel-bag with a pillow on top and sat side-saddle, as Yorgo and the others did, and kicked your heels into the slow luggage with a mimicked cry of Yorgo's that sounded like 'Whoops, a-na!'

The Greek Easter brought Artemis Denaxas and his wife to the house on a low, private hill behind the Ios harbour. Denaxas's Anglophilia was proclaimed by flat cap, blue blazer with gold buttons, walking stick and an Alsatian dog called Dick. '*Ela dtho, Deek*', was a frequent call. We were invited to lunch one Sunday and went with ready appetites. You and Pab were playing happily on the little low-walled terrace outside the open front door while we guzzled. Suddenly Kiria Denaxas said, '*Echei paee!*' [She's gone]. You had climbed onto the low wall and… fallen over the other side, a six-feet drop. We rushed out and looked with dread over the wall.

You were sitting in the only thick bush on the baked, rocky surface. No wonder the Greeks came to build more temples to *Tyche*, luck, than anything else, until the cult of J. Christ and his force of quasi-spiritual imperialists came along. I'm reminded of a story about your daughter Becky on one of the occasions Stee took her to Queen's Club where he was playing tennis. Four-year-old Becks was sitting on the ground when the secretary came along. He squatted down nicely beside her and said, 'Hullo, I'm Christian'. Becky said, 'Hullo, I'm Jewish'. Less than twenty years later she was awarded a First in the History of Art at the Courtauld; Annie is in her second year at the Royal College of Art; the beautiful Bindle – you always had faith in her – paints and teaches in Berlin.

I still cannot say why fidelity to Jewishness, never Judaism, has seemed so important to me, and us, in various way, unless because desertion would be cowardice. Before we took the ferry at Brindisi, the town that might have been named for kissing Italy goodbye, I had had the idea that we would go on from Greece to Israel. It was curiosity, though, not piety, that drew me, not strongly once chance landed us on Ios, 'that place' you came to call it. Paul spent some time in Israel, picking pineapples to no marked spiritual advantage. Funny, it had never occurred to me to a be *Jewish* writer; nor to you to be a Jewish artist, but your work and mine would boast a Semitic streak.

A ferry from Santorini back to Piraeus anchored twice a week in the bay before us. Yorgo came to tell us if any *xenoi* came ashore, as if we were certain to know him (rarely her). You dreaded the day when we no longer ate *koukia* [broad beans] with our many fried eggs and occasional slices of calves' liver, kept for us in the *chorio* by that nice butcher. You and Pab were our passports to friendly faces. You wanted nothing more than to stay on Ios forever.

I asked Yorgo if there was any chance of buying and restoring one of the many dilapidated cottages left behind by emigrant islanders. '*Pos gar ouk*' an old Hellene would have said, contracted by a modern to '*pos...*', implying possible. So he and I, sometime you too, on Phreeni, walked up and down the island, looking at one possibility after another. Even the best of them, so Yorgo first told us, was no more than a few hundred pounds. Just as well; I had little left until we returned to London and I could collect my next tranche of Wardour Street tin. Every time our interest was kindled, the price of the property, ruin or not, went up; and up again. The days in paradise coming to an end, was frustration to be our only memento?

The last morning that Flora came to Niko's cottage, I explained our disappointment. She smiled an archaic smile. 'I have a *spitaki* I can sell you'. '*Pou einai?*' '*Sto Milopota*'. Milopota bay was on the far side of the central peak which was stepped with the flat-roofed mostly whitewashed houses of *to chorio*, the village, built up there to give the Ios men high time to be ready to repel boarders should piratic predators be spotted. A row of steep-roofed Venetian houses proved that not a few had landed. Tethered donkeys nodded and nodded and never quite agreed.

Flora led me down a solid ladder of uneven stones to a great arc of sand, a small *taverna* at each end, no buildings between. We were like two Fridays on Crusoe's unblemished beach. We climbed up and up over sidelong stone walls to a low cottage, with a lapsed roof of dry bamboo, sitting above the terraces, olive and fig trees, bristling cactus between them with their 'figs of India' like spiked green hand-grenades at the ends of their paddles.

We had to breach a screen of cobwebs to get into the *spiti*, much like Niko's in which we had spent the last six weeks but cumbered with rustic junk. The place had, as the estate agents say, 'possibilities', but what sane man would choose to be bothered with it? '*Poso thelete?*' I said. How much did she want. Flora had a drunken husband and two children she wanted to send to a good school on Santorini. '*Dtheka chiliades*'. Ten thousand drachmae translated into a hundred and fifty pounds. Done!

I shook hands with Flora and we went down through the scrub to the earth road and back towards the beach, past a long fat, desiccated trapezoid field. Flora said, 'You can have that too, if you want;. '*Poso?*' '*To idthio.*' The same. What would we ever do with a beachside field? Done again. We went straight to the *eirenodthekes*, justice of the peace, and the paperwork was drawn up, in manuscript, for both properties, and signed in time for us to board the boat to Piraeus the next noon. Your tears were not staunched by the promise that we would now certainly return to what was at that moment our only address: Ios, Cyclades, Greece.

By the time we returned, two years later, our fortunes had changed. I had been ready to be a struggling novelist; I was suddenly a successful screenwriter. *Nothing But the Best* was made; *Darling* had been green-lit. We had already bought The Wick, a Georgian farmhouse, in Langham, not far from Bergholt, and we were on the lookout for a London 'pad', as Clive Donner would call it in between claiming credit for all the ideas that were in my *Nothing But the Best* script before he set eyes on it. Later, you had a charming and beautiful friend, much prized, with many prizes, I mean. You dropped her after she imitated the slatted shutters in a set of your paintings. Even J.M.W. Turner was quite a plagiarist. No one could say that of you, or me, I trust.

Yorgo Galatsios had promised to clean out the cottage on Milopota. We filled the old khaki duffel bag with Athenian provisions and there, eventually, we were, lording it over that shimmering scimitar of sand which served as your drawing block. We still have film, taken with Tom Maschler's sixteen-millimetre camera, of you finger-sketching on a damp skirt of beach, with instant sureness, another donkey with a sagging belly under a stirrupped saddle. Art then life: we bought Kapa for your fourth birthday that summer, a neat-hipped donkey with a natural white 'k' on its muzzle. With a cloth cap on your head, a switch in your hands, 'whoopsa-na' on your lips, when was there a happier little girl?

Two years later, I had just won the Oscar when Tom Maschler steered the yacht he had hired with Elizabeth Jane Howard and Kingsley Amis into Milopota Bay. If not young, Elizabeth was still a beauty. They came up to the *spiti* for drinks and then suffered us to take them to the *taverna* owned by Giorgos Drakos's brother. On the way Elizabeth spread her legs and pissed on our field, like a man.

Kingsley was hungover, I think, and no more than picked at an omelette. Later he wrote an article for the *Observer* about

Greek food. You fell asleep during our chat. I had to carry you, by no means a baby, along the soft sand and up to the house. It was the last time I toted you like that. Tom and Kingsley proposed to take us out to supper the next night, but they sailed away like flying Dutchmen. Years later, Elizabeth, when not young at all, took a fancy to Nick and lured him away at weekends for creative writing sessions while you looked after the girls. Later, she spoiled an Ios holiday of yours by complaining about everything. Old beauties demand tribute people once hurried to give them; Michael Ayrton had been one. You and Michael and I once sat and drew Belvès from the opposite hill. You were fifteen. He said with congratulatory gloom, 'I expect she'll be better than I am'. He died later that year.

You grew to be a rare beauty, prizewinning painter and draughtsman. Stanley Donen said you could have been a movie star. You loved many men; many more loved you. You and Paul were photographed together and appeared along the side of London buses for a season or two. More people had time for you than you for them. I said to you one morning, when you called in the tearful middle of an amorous crisis, 'Sarah, whatever happens, we work in the morning and weep in the afternoon'. You honoured my words. When you were in agony from those recurrent migraines, you still produced immaculate stuff, never tolerating anything but the best you could do.

Among the best moments in my life began with you knocking on my never-locked door at Lagardelle and saying, 'Got time for a chit-chat?' You and I were never so alike as in our sense that painting and writing drew their force from much the same current, with nobody else's fingers in it. Oh yes, I do remember times in the Wick when you woke early and I came in to try and hush you. You would take one look and say, 'I don't want you, I want Beetle'. And got her, of course. Spoilt? Loved.

Sometimes frightened, you were always fearless. You jumped off the top board at the Ocho Rios Hilton when you were eight years old and landed smack, SMACK, on your belly. And then went back and did it again, right. I once told you the story of Charlie Lederer, smart and handsome screenwriting habitué of William Randolph Hearst's Xanadu, when he was in India on some diplomatic wartime mission. His snooty British hostess had a priceless jade collection in a tall cabinet. She told Charlie Lederer how much nicer Delhi had been before the influx of outsiders, including Jews. 'Don't you like Jews?' 'I don't think anyone likes Jews, do they?' 'Got a reason?' She shrugged. Lederer reached up to the crest at the summit of the showcase and brought the whole collection smashing onto the marble. 'Now you've got a reason.'

Years later, in 1982, Beetle, you and I went to an academy screening of the Paul Newman film *The Verdict*. It was long, not to say draggy. We were nearly two hours into it when a trendy young couple, in fringed leather gear, came chattily into the screening room, sat behind us and kept up a mocking commentary of what was left of the movie. When the lights went up, you picked up the half a glass of orange juice you had brought in, turned and threw the contents all over the chatty pair. Drops of juice rolled to the tips of their fringes and became pendant. They just sat there. You turned to me and said, 'Charlie Lederer'. You had the instant nerve I have never had. We left the couple, speechless, where they were, dripping.

You were invited, when first famous, to do a portrait of the retiring Master of Jesus College, Cambridge. You were never keen on commissions but did go to see the man who clearly thought well of himself. When you had chatted for a while, he asked how you wanted to proceed. You said, 'The best thing would be if I started by making sketch'. 'To see whether you can get a likeness?' said the Master, from high-up. You said, 'So you can see what you look like'. He came down; but I suspect you never got as far even as the sketch. You did one of George Steiner, who was sure you would never catch him. You were not markedly pleased with the result, but there he is, haughty and winsome, guarded and unmasked, the very image of what Isaiah Berlin said: 'a *genuine* phoney'. George was not disposed to buy it. Gary Sobers was delighted with the portrait of him that you did for the M.C.C. Long Room. You were the first person ever to take him for a ride on a London bus; and the last?

Oh my darling Dizz.

INDEX

Gomme) 18, 390-1
Goodden, Robert 340
Goodman, Arnold (Baron) 146-7
Gordon, Charlotte 46, 216, 221-2
Gordon, Harry 46, 218, 220-2, 501
Gore-Lloyd, David 74, 402
Göring, Hermann 47, 106, 232, 487
Gosse, Edmund 316
Gottlieb, Bob 14
Gould, Gordon 15
Grade, Lew 61, 478-9, 498
Grahame, Gloria 151, 470
Grant, Cary 167, 445-7, 449
Grapelli, Stefan 460
Gray, John 232
Gray, M. Harrison 171
Green, Peter 43, 92, 103, 261, 264, 268, 278, 444
Greene, Graham 12, 17, 21, 34, 62, 134, 138, 199, 245-8, 311, 318
Greene, Grahame 56
Greenstreet, Sydney 135
Greenwood, Joan 28
Gregson, Richard 29
Griffith, Melanie 85
Grossman, David 406
Guerra, Tonino 372, 383, 386
Guinness, Alec 135, 196, 389, 392
Guinzburg, Thomas 460, 471
Haigh, Ken 94
Hall, Peter 12, 77, 187, 272-3, 464-5
Halton, Kathleen 98, 374, 378
Hamilton, Guy 21
Hamilton, Ian (poet and editor) 43

Hamilton, Ian (publisher) 43
Hamilton, Julie 15, 20, 27
Hampshire, Stuart 394
Hampton, Christopher 127, 148
Hanson, Norwood Russell 409-10
Harlan, Veit 130, 372
Harris, Bernard 182
Harris, Julie 76
Harris, Richard 49
Harrison, Rex 28, 97, 463
Harvey, Anthony 383
Harvey, Larry 352, 365
Harvey, Tony 462-3
Haxton, Gerald 320, 324
Hayden, Sterling 135, 165
Hayes, Michael 271
Haylor, Phyllis 468-9
Head, Stanley 181-2
Hearst, William Randolph 509
Hecht, Paul 216
Hellman, Lilian 462
Hemingway, Ernest 96, 100, 118, 220, 316, 393
Hendren, Patsy 392
Hepburn, Audrey 97, 149, 441, 447-8, 450, 452-4, 456, 458-62, 471
Herlihy, James Leo 80
Herr, Michael 155
Hewison, Robert 348
Heywood, Anne 62
Hicks, David 449, 452, 475, 495
Higgins, Claire 188
Hill, Lucienne 23
Himmler, Heinrich 228
Hitchcock, Alfred 337-8, 469
Hoare, Dermot 17
Hobson, Harold 93, 332, 343
Hobson, Valerie 335
Hoffenberg, Mason 134
Hoffman, Dustin 81-3, 487,

494

Peter, John 34-5, 125, 342, 348-9
Philby, Kim 336
Phillips, John 20
Picasso, Pablo 40, 53, 285, 288, 297
Pinter, Harold 51-3, 93-4, 341, 468
Piron, Hans and Juliana 217-10, 223
Poitier, Sidney 465
Polanski, Roman 79, 136
Pollack, Sydney 75, 135, 166
Porter, Cole 14
Porter, Eric 221
Potter, Larry 214-223
Powell, Dilys 443, 500
Prebble, John 182
Preminger, Otto 141
Price, Stanley 209, 448
Priestley, Jack 78, 140, 318-9
Prior, Jim 263
Profumo, John 335
Proust, Marcel 36, 100, 128, 199, 266, 318, 335, 370
Quashie-Idun, Johnny 215
Raeburn, Chrissy 71
Raine, Craig 188
Ramsey, Celia (née Celia Dale) 204
Ramsey, Guy 126, 169-84, 199, 211, 265, 327, 396, 427, 436
Raphael, Cedric 63-4, 71, 171, 173-4, 178, 181, 242, 329, 414-6, 418-23, 426-8, 430-1, 434, 436-9, 465, 469
Raphael, Enid 199
Raphael, Irene Rose 246, 414-40
Raphael, Paul 41, 45, 50, 126, 136, 189, 211-12, 215, 222, 259-60, 339, 343, 369, 430, 437, 450-2, 464, 497, 500-3, 505, 508
Raphael, Sarah Natasha 44, 45, 50, 93, 99, 122, 129, 130, 189, 194, 222, 289, 296, 343, 347, 369, 416, 437, 450-2, 497-510
Raphael, Stephen 57, 206, 343, 346, 348, 476, 482
Raphael, Sylvia Betty (Beetle) 11, 14, 17-18, 20-1, 24-8, 30-1, 33, 41-6, 48, 50-2, 54, 57, 59, 61,63, 72, 75-79, 92, 95, 97, 110, 112, 114-16, 119-20, 126, 129-30, 144, 184, 186-7, 189, 191, 194, 197-8, 201-7, 211, 215-6, 219, 221-2, 243, 251-3, 258, 268, 280 291-2, 294-5, 306-7, 311-14, 330, 334, 337, 339-40, 342-3, 346-7, 354, 361, 364-6, 368-72, 383, 385, 400, 430, 436-7, 441-2, 444, 447, 450-2, 456-60, 462, 465, 476, 481-2, 482, 489-90, 494, 497, 501-4, 508-9
Rattigan, Terence 89
Raven, John 265
Raven, Simon 261-3, 310, 336, 344
Rawicz, Piotr 111,158
Read, Piers Paul 391
Rebatet, Lucien 105
Redford, Robert 75, 457, 487
Rees-Mogg, William 263
Reese, Terence 171-3, 175-7
Reisz, Karel 40, 52
Reisz, Matthew 40
Reiter, Charlie 45-6
Rennie, James 304